Women Under the Law

Women Under the Law
The False Promise of Human Rights

Aileen McColgan

LONGMAN

Pearson Education Limited
Edinburgh Gate
Harlow
Essex CM20 2JE
United Kingdom
and Associated Companies throughout the world.

Visit us on the World Wide Web at:
http://www.pearsoned-ema.com

First published 2000

ISBN 0–582–29451–7 PPR

British Library Cataloguing-in-Publication Data

A catalogue record for this book is available from the British Library

Typeset by 35 in 10/12pt New Baskerville
Produced by Addison Wesley Longman Singapore (Pte) Ltd.,
Printed in Singapore

Contents

To baby Rionach, for her patience during my proof-reading.

Preface

The Human Rights Act 1998 will be implemented in full on 2 October 2000. From that date, British subjects who take the view that their rights have been violated will, insofar as those rights are protected under the European Convention on Human Rights, be able to seek redress in the British Courts. British judges will not be empowered to strike down primary legislation. But, as Lord Borrie put it during the Bill's Second Reading debate:

> 'the political reality will be that, while historically the courts have sought to carry out the will of Parliament, in the field of human rights Parliament will carry out the will of the courts.' (HL Debs 3 November 1997, col 1275)

The premise of this book is that this shift of power should be a matter of concern to all of those concerned with equality issues and, in particular, with the law as it impacts on women. Experience of entrenched rights elsewhere has shown their tendency to operate in the interests of the powerful, while leaving the powerless unprotected from the might of the private sector. To the extent that women are characterised by a relative lack of economic and social power, and are rendered vulnerable by their reproductive role, they have much to fear and, perhaps, little to gain from incorporation.

My thanks are owed, as ever, to Professor Keith Ewing for this unfailing generosity and support. Thanks also to Professor Conor Gearty, for his comments on an earlier draft, to Penney Lewis, for her help with chapters 4 and 5, and to the London School of Economics for its marvellous library. All errors are, of course, my own.

Aileen McColgan
London, May 1999

Table of Cases

European Court of Justice

European Court of Human Rights

Ireland, Republic of

United Kingdom

United States

Table of Legislation

European Union

Germany

Irish Republic

New Zealand

United Kingdom

United States

Table of Treaties and Conventions

Chapter 1

Entrenching 'Human Rights'

Introduction

On 9 November 1998 the Human Rights Act, which incorporates elements of the European Convention on Human Rights into UK law, received Royal Assent. The implementation of the Act will be completed on 2 October 2000.[1] Its provisions, and those of the Convention, are discussed in more detail in Chapters 2 and 10 below. Here it is sufficient to say that the Act's explicit aim is to 'bring home' to UK subjects the rights guaranteed by the Convention by permitting their enforcement at the national, as well as the international, level.[2] This, in turn, entails a transfer of some power from the legislature to the judiciary. Although the judicial role is more circumscribed than in other 'rights'-based jurisdictions such as Canada and the US (see, in particular, Chapter 2), British judges will nevertheless be empowered to interpret existing legislation in accordance with the incorporated rights, to strike down secondary legislation inconsistent with those rights and to issue 'declarations of incompatibility' in respect of primary legislation. The legislature will not be obliged to remedy primary legislation in the face of a declaration of incompatibility, but it has been accepted by all concerned that failure to take remedial action is likely to be very rare (see further below and Chapter 2).

The aim of this book is to challenge the view held by most people of a liberal bent, as well as by many who would consider themselves radical, that 'rights' are, in general, a 'good thing'. The challenge rests on the particular nature of 'entrenched' or 'constitutional' rights, such as those introduced into UK law by the Human Rights Act 1998, and upon the

---

[1] 18 May 1999, col 293 (written answer).
[2] See further Chapter 2 below.

distinction between them and statutory 'rights' the benefits of which are not, in principle, questioned. The book aims to illustrate the perils of entrenched rights by examining their impact upon women, but the dangers are by no means unique to them. For 'women' could be substituted any group of relatively disadvantaged people, the degree and type of danger posed by such rights varying with the nature of the disadvantage.

The characterisation of women as 'relatively disadvantaged' will be defended below, and some introduction to the dangers associated with entrenched rights will be attempted. First, however, it is important to explain the differences between 'entrenched' or 'constitutional' rights on the one hand, and statutory rights on the other. The latter have made very significant contributions to the position of women and of others. Not only have the Sex Discrimination Act 1975 and the Race Relations Act 1976 provided protection against sex and race discrimination respectively, but employment-related statutory rights (whether the right not to be unfairly dismissed, to time-off for ante-natal care, trade union duties, etc, or to a minimum wage under the Wages Councils system) have served the interests of workers. The protections afforded by the Sex Discrimination and Race Relations Acts, in common with those of the Employment Rights Act 1995 and the Trade Union and Labour Relations (Consolidation) Act 1992, are flawed and, particularly in the case of the 1992 Act, sometimes outweighed by the advantages accorded to employers by the restraints on trade union action. Further, the interpretation by the courts of many of the statutory rights accorded to workers has been such as to restrict their scope considerably. But the strength of statutory rights such as those provided by the employment legislation is that they are specific, can be appropriately tailored to meet particular needs, and can be revised to the extent that judicial interpretation subverts or undermines their purpose. Whether they are adequate in practice is largely a matter of political will.

'Entrenched' or 'constitutional' rights are, by contrast, usually characterised by a level of abstraction not common to statutory rights (the 'right to life', for example, or to 'freedom of speech, or of the press; or the right of the people peaceably to assemble'[3], the right to 'due process of law'[4] or to 'equal[ity] before and under the law and . . . to the equal protection and equal benefit of the law'[5]). This abstraction, which renders them of general application, also means that this application turns very significantly upon their interpretation. Their interpretation, in turn, is ultimately a matter for the judiciary. The degree of judicial power varies with the nature of entrenchment, which varies from the US model, at

---

[3] First Amendment to the US Constitution.
[4] Fifth and Fourteenth Amendments to the US Constitution.
[5] Canadian Charter of Rights, s 15.

one extreme (in which the Constitution, with its Bill of Rights, stands as the supreme law by virtue of which judges can strike down any legislative measure); to the New Zealand model (in which the Bill of Rights may be used as an interpretative document alone). The Irish and German constitutions are drawn along the lines of the US model, the Supreme Courts of those countries being empowered to strike down legislation regarded as inconsistent with entrenched rights. Between these extremes lies the Canadian model, that country's Charter of Rights permitting Parliament to 'Charter-proof' legislation by means of a 'notwithstanding' clause, in which case any inconsistency between it and the rights entrenched by the Charter will not result in its being struck down. Beside Canada, though closer to the New Zealand than the US paradigm, lies the model of entrenchment adopted in the UK by the Human Rights Act.

It might be argued that the rights incorporated into UK law by the Human Rights Act should not properly be regarded as 'entrenched', giving rise as they do to no judicial power of override. This view has, it is true, been suggested by Labour pronouncements as to the compatibility of the Human Rights Act approach with the sovereignty of Parliament. The White Paper which preceded the Act declared that:

> In enacting legislation, Parliament is making decisions about important matters of public policy. The authority to make those decisions derives from a democratic mandate . . . To make provision in the Bill for the courts to set aside Acts of Parliament would confer on the judiciary a general power over the decisions of Parliament which under our present constitutional arrangements they do not possess, and would be likely on occasions to draw the judiciary into serious conflict with Parliament. There is no evidence to suggest that they desire this power, nor that the public wish them to have it. Certainly, this Government has no mandate for any such change.[6]

It is true that a declaration of incompatibility gives rise to no automatic process of repeal or amendment. But, as eager as the executive has been to stress the sovereignty-friendly nature of the 1998 Act, it has been equally keen to emphasise that a declaration of incompatibility 'will almost certainly prompt the Government and Parliament to change the law'.[7] Indeed, such was the eagerness of the Labour Government to grease the progress of such changes that the 'fast track' procedure initially proposed (and modified only after a back-bench rebellion) would have conferred upon Ministers the power to make such 'incidental, supplemental, consequential and transitional provision as the person making it considers appropriate' as a result of a declaration of incompatibility.[8] Parliamentary

---

[6] See *Rights Brought Home: The Human Rights Bill* (London: HMSO, 1997, CM 3782), para 2.10 (available on the world wide web at the HMSO site – http://www.official-documents.co.uk).

[7] *Ibid.*

[8] See HC Debs 24 June, cols 1124–1143 and, for comment, K Ewing, 'The Human Rights Act and Parliamentary Democracy' (1999) 62 *Modern Law Review*, forthcoming.

approval for such orders could, in some cases, be secured *ex post facto*. Section 10 now provides that primary legislation may be amended by Ministerial order only where the Minister 'considers that there are compelling reasons for proceeding under this section', and that only those amendments 'as he considers necessary to remove the incompatibility' may be made by Ministerial order.

In theory, the Human Rights Act does not give judges the degree of power associated with more traditional forms of 'entrenched' or 'constitutional' rights, these rights generally being characterised by their overriding quality as well as by the degree of generality with which they are expressed. In practice, however, it will almost certainly be the case that any declaration of incompatibility will, almost automatically, result in the repeal or amendment of the offending legislation. This was accepted by the Government in the White Paper and by its spokespersons on numerous subsequent occasions,[9] and the position summed up approvingly by Lord Borrie during the Second Reading debate in the House of Lords:

> while no court may strike down legislation on the ground that it infringes the convention, the High Court may make a declaration to that effect, after which Ministers are expected to . . . amend the legislation so that it conforms to the convention. If that works as seems to be intended by the Bill, the political reality will be that, while historically the courts have sought to carry out the will of Parliament, in the field of human rights Parliament will carry out the will of the courts.[10]

Certainly, whereas in the US politicians appear perfectly content to enact laws which they know will be regarded as unconstitutional by the courts (see, in particular, Chapter 4 below); in Canada, where the legislature has the ultimate say, provincial and federal governments alike have been 'exceedingly reluctant'[11] to enact legislation bearing the 'notwithstanding' clause. Quebec's government did enact such legislation as a matter of course between 1982 and 1985, and on several occasions thereafter.[12] But this action was motivated precisely by that provincial government's determination to display its lack of satisfaction with the Charter, it alone

---

[9] *Rights Brought Home: The Human Rights Bill*, note 6 above, para 2.10 states that 'A declaration that legislation is incompatible with the Convention rights will not of itself have the effect of changing the law, which will continue to apply. But it will almost certainly prompt the Government and Parliament to change the law.' Jack Straw, Secretary of State for the Home Office, reiterated this view in the House of Commons on 16 Feb 1998 (HC Debs, col 772) and, again, on 21 October 1998 (HC Debs, col 1301) when he stated that a declaration of incompatibility was bound to result in a change to the law '[i]n the overwhelming majority of cases, regardless of which party was in government'.

[10] HL Debs 3 November 1997, col 1275, citing the Government's own White Paper as support. Cf Jack Straw's statement, during the Third Reading (HC Debs, 21 October 1998, col 1358), that: 'One of the Bill's many strengths is that it promotes human rights while maintaining the sovereignty of Parliament and the separation of powers which underpins our constitutional arrangements.'

[11] P Hogg, *Constitutional Law of Canada* (2nd ed, Ontario: Carswell, 1992), p 898.

[12] *Ibid*, p 893.

of Canada's provinces never having given assent to the Constitution Act 1982 of which the Charter forms part. Outside Quebec the clause has almost never been used in the 16 years since the Charter's implementation. Even in cases where the federal legislature has enacted provisions in an attempt to avert what were seen as unacceptable repercussions of judicial Charter-based decisions (as in the post-*Daviault*, post-*Seaboyer* and post-*O'Connor* legislation discussed in Chapter 9 below[13]), it has done so without incorporating any 'notwithstanding' clause despite real doubts about the ability of said legislation to withstand Charter-based challenges.

According to Peter Hogg, this 'exceeding[] reluctan[ce]' 'stems partly from a principled commitment to the Charter ... and partly from the political resistance that could be expected from opposition parties, the press, the organized bar and civil liberties groups'.[14] It is possible that a similar approach would be taken by the British Government, which is unlikely to wish to be seen to contravene the 'basic human rights' embraced by the Human Rights Act. The UK model may well, like that adopted in Canada, avoid 'draw[ing] the judiciary into serious conflict with Parliament'. But while, as Hogg points out in relation to Canada, the retention of the 'last word' with politicians avoids the 'court-bashing and the court-packing that is a staple of federal politics in the United States'[15], the deference which is likely to be shown to the decisions of the courts may well render judicial control over the incorporated rights almost absolute in practice, if not in theory. Thus, in answer to 'the fear that judges might be drawn into politics' we have only the statements of the Chief Justice, Lord Bingham, that judges would 'strive to decide ... cases which have political, sometimes even party-political, implications ... on a firm basis of legal principle'.[16]

Entrenched rights: potential problems

The likely approach of the UK judiciary to the rights incorporated by the Human Rights Act 1998 is considered further in Chapter 10, the political hue of that judiciary having been discussed in Chapter 2. Here it is useful to introduce some of the potential difficulties associated with

---

[13] Respectively, [1994] 3 SCR 63; [1991] 2 SCR 577; [1995] 4 SCR 411.
[14] Hogg, note 11 above, p 898.
[15] *Ibid*, p 900.
[16] HL Debs 3 November 1997, col 808. Robert Maclennan MP's Third Reading comments (HC Debs 21 October 1998, col 1364) that 'I anticipate that, as [judges] have inspired confidence that they would use the power judiciously, they will feel less reluctant to take the greater responsibility of deciding that Parliament has gone beyond the accepted view of people, as expressed in a written constitution. I do not consider that an embarrassing prospect; indeed, I think that many would regard it as highly desirable', can only be regarded as chilling.

entrenched rights, whether those rights take a legally 'weak' or 'strong' form.

One of the most obvious issues which arises is resource-related: to the extent that entrenched rights must be enforced through the courts, only those who can afford legal action can benefit from them. This point is particularly germane in the UK in light of the Lord Chancellor's proposals to withdraw legal aid almost entirely from civil cases. The 'public interest fund' promised, as an afterthought, will not be on a scale such as that which would be required effectively to safeguards the 'rights' of all but the few wealthy enough to provide their own funding. And while contingency fees are intended to cover the bulk of civil cases, the very small sums involved in Human Rights Act cases will render them unsuitable for such arrangements.[17]

The issue of funding is considered further in Chapter 10, it having been raised here only in order to point to one of the difficulties likely to become apparent after the implementation of the Human Rights Act. One might argue, of course, that the lack of legal aid does not leave the impoverished in any worse a situation after incorporation than they were before. But this overlooks the facts that their position will decline *relative* to that of those whose rights are enforceable through the courts and, in particular, that the advantaged may use their 'rights' further to damage the position of the disadvantaged. This latter possibility is aggravated by the decision of the Labour Government, contrary to the position taken by the party under the late John Smith MP, to extend the benefits of entrenchment to legal as well as human, persons (this having the effect, for example, that tobacco companies will be able to sue over their 'free-speech' (advertising) 'rights', that corporations will be able to utilise 'rights' to challenge government efforts to ameliorate disadvantage). Such companies will not, however, themselves be subject to the obligations imposed by the 1998 Act, entrenched rights being binding, in general, only upon the State (though see Chapters 2 and 10 for discussion of the possibility of a degree of 'horizontal' enforceability).

The various threats which are posed by entrenched rights are explored in Chapters 4–9, from which a number of themes arise. These themes are then considered in Chapter 10 in the context of the rights actually entrenched by the Human Rights Act, together with their interpretation by the European Convention organs. The focus is, as was mentioned above, on the impact of entrenched rights upon women. Given the current

---

[17] On the one hand, such claims will be new and, therefore, their chances of success very uncertain. On the other hand, they will frequently not be such as to give rise to substantial money claims, and those which do will be subject to the provision in s 8(4) that 'In determining – (a) whether to award damages, or (b) the amount of an award, the court must take into account the principles applied by the European Court of Human Rights in relation to the award of compensation under Article 41 of the Convention' – see further Chapter 2.

widespread view that women now have the 'upper hand', this focus perhaps requires some justification.

Women and disadvantage

Much concern has been expressed recently about the extent to which girls are surpassing boys in terms of educational achievement, about men's declining dominance of the labour market, their reduced importance as family breadwinners and their increasing confusion in the face of sexually provocative and aggressive women who expose them to conflicting messages before crying 'rape' and running off, cloaked in anonymity, to the courts. These concerns, it is true, are expressed more often as anxieties about men's decline, rather than women's relative advance. But the message is clear – women are 'having it all' while men are losing out in terms of education, work, and family life.

The reality is far removed from the common perception. Girls do exceed boys in terms of school performance, and women have taken an increasing share of the labour market. But, save for the fortunate few, women work in jobs which are underpaid in comparison with those done by men. Sex discrimination, both deliberate and systemic, is widespread, and contributes in large part to the low earnings level of women relative to men (see further Chapter 6). Women experience sexual harassment to an extent absolutely foreign to the majority of men. They are overlooked for promotion, subject to glass ceilings, penalised for pregnancy and motherhood. They are denied work-related benefits (from pensions to company cars to health insurance) available to men. To the extent that girls are leaving school with better qualifications than those of their peers, this edge may help to offset, to some extent, the impact of entrenched labour market discrimination. But, whereas men have always been permitted to benefit from their 'aggression' and 'drive', as well as from their perceived lack of interest in assuming primary caring roles, there is a growing pressure for women to be denied the advantage of their greater levels of youthful application.

The lack of fit which exists between perception and reality in the sphere of work applies also to the 'private' relations between men and women. Far from having gained the upper hand in their domestic relations, many women find themselves shouldering the same household tasks and childcare responsibilities as they have always shouldered while being responsible, in addition, for contributing a significant part of the household income. Many women are subject to terrifying violence from their partners and ex-partners. Every day, women are beaten, kicked, scalded, cut, strangulated, suffocated, raped and burnt by the men they live with, and by men they have tried to escape. The British Medical Association recently estimated that one in four women has been victim to domestic violence. Every week in the UK, two are murdered. The response of the police and (on the rare occasion when the matter goes that far) the courts to this 'domestic violence' is absolutely inadequate. Coupled with the practical difficulties of 'disappearing' (which is, in effect, what women have to do to avoid the escalation of violence which generally accompanies attempts to leave), police and judicial ineptitude condemns thousands upon thousands of women to live in the most abject conditions – imprisoned in their own homes, frequently watching their male and female children begin to act out the roles, respectively, of abuser and abused. Yet the comparatively few women who finally kill in order to protect themselves and their children are frequently dealt with by the courts more harshly than abusive men who kill 'nagging' or allegedly 'unfaithful' wives.[18]

Every day women are raped, usually by men they know (whether as husbands or acquaintances), less commonly by strangers. Such is the current backlash that those rapes falling within the former category are generally termed 'date rapes', largely condoned by the system and trivialised by the press. The few women who find themselves in court find themselves raped once again by a system which, although granting them 'anonymity' from those who do not know them sufficiently to identify them from circumstance and reported detail, publicly scrutinises their sexual morality, abortion, contraceptive, psychiatric and counselling history and their taste in underwear. Conviction rates are low (10 per cent of reported rapes in 1995) and falling, while the pressure builds for the 'protections' afforded to rape complainants to be extended to the accused (the 'real' victims of rape, indicative as every failure to convict apparently is of a false and malicious allegation).[19]

Finally, the control women have over their reproductive capacity is under increasing threat. At present, women in Great Britain (but not those in Northern Ireland) may terminate unwanted pregnancies if they can obtain the approval of two doctors and either find themselves fortunate enough to be in an area with reasonable NHS abortion provision or to be in a position to pay for one privately. The legality of abortion does not appear to be under immediate threat (though for the possible implications of the Human Rights Act 1998, see Chapter 10 below). Demands are occasionally heard for the decision to be subject to veto by the would-be

---

[18] See, for example, Sue Lees' article, *Scotland on Sunday*, 13 July 1997, highlighting the cases of David Swinburne, freed after stabbing his wife to death on being told she wished to leave him; Roy Greech, given a two-year suspended sentence and told by the judge that he was a 'good man' after he killed his unfaithful wife by stabbing her 23 times; Joseph McGrail, who kicked his alcoholic wife to death and was freed by Mr Justice Popplewell, apparently on the grounds that his victim 'would have tried the patience of a saint'. These cases, in none of which the women had posed a threat to their killers, can be contrasted with the judicial treatment of Zoorah Shah, Sara Thornton, Emma Humphreys, Kiranjit Ahluwalia, Janet Gardner and others (all discussed in Chapter 8 below).

[19] Discussed in detail in Chapter 9 below.

father (even, bizarrely, by the would-be siblings[20]), but the political will does not exist in the UK radically to change the current position. When it comes to pregnancies which are intended to be carried to term, the position is less clear. In the US, though not yet here, women have been prosecuted and detained because of conduct perceived to threaten their 'unborn children'. This has not, so far, extended to the 'protection' of the 'unconceived', but has resulted in orders being made in respect of foetuses of as little as three months' gestation (at which stage abortion is clearly and without exception, in the case of adult women, lawful).

This early-stage intervention has not yet been seen in the UK. But what has occurred here, as in the US, is increased forcible intervention by the medical profession towards the end of pregnancy. There have been a number of UK decisions (further discussed in Chapter 5 below) which have declared that competent women's wishes may not be overridden, regardless of the outcome for the foetus. But these cases' apparent lack of impact on medical practice points to a growing perception of the foetus as a 'second patient' (perhaps even the primary patient, as in most cases the woman's life is not in any danger) and the pregnant woman as a potentially malevolent vessel in which that patient resides. The implications of this for women's autonomy are chilling, not least because of the developments in foetal surgery discussed further in Chapter 5.

Conclusion

Women do not have the upper hand. They are not the only or the most disadvantaged group. Nor are all women equally disadvantaged or, indeed, all women disadvantaged by comparison to all men. But women, as a group, are disadvantaged by comparison to men as a group, just as ethnic minority Britons are disadvantaged, as a group, by comparison with those who are white. The nature of women's group disadvantage is not the same as that of ethnic minority Britons, and those who occupy more than one disadvantaged group (black or Asian women, for example, poor and/ or disabled women) are subject to multiple disadvantage.

The issues which will form the focus of Chapters 4–9 are of particular concern to women, though not all of them will be of especial concern to all women and not all issues of concern to women in general, much less to those women who are subject to multiple disadvantage, are considered (no detailed consideration is given, for example, to areas of family law such as divorce, custody or maintenance). Women's life experiences are broken down into three major categories: women as reproducers (Chapters 4 and 5), women as workers (Chapters 6 and 7), and women

---

[20] R Stein, *The Family in Question* (London: Demos, 1998).

as the victims of violence (Chapters 8 and 9). Within these categories, the impact of entrenched rights upon women is considered. The major focus is on Canada and the US, though a number of other jurisdictions are considered.

In considering the experiences of women within these categories, it is possible to draw some conclusions as to how human rights 'bite' on women. In addition, Chapters 4–9 highlight a number of more general problems associated with entrenched rights. The issues raised in Chapters 4–9 are then considered, in Chapter 10, in the context of the UK and the particular rights entrenched by the Human Rights Act 1998. The aim is to draw some conclusions about how the incorporation, albeit partial (see further Chapter 2), of the European Convention on Human Rights will affect women's lives and, more generally, how it will impact on those who belong to relatively disadvantaged groups.

Chapter 2

'Bringing Rights Home'

Introduction

The incorporation into British law of the European Convention on Human Rights represents a victory for organisations such as Liberty which (in its previous incarnation as the NCCL) has pressed for incorporation since 1977.[1] Many previous attempts had been made to incorporate the provisions into domestic law, but none had passed the Commons. While organisations such as Liberty were, for a substantial time, voices calling in the wilderness, the thrust towards incorporation has steadily gained force over recent years, the bulk of the judiciary as well as two of the three major political parties numbering amongst its more recent proponents.[2]

The Labour Party first embraced the idea of incorporation in 1993, replacing its previous expressions of hostility[3] with support, at party conference which, in addition, backed the creation of a human rights commission and a 'home grown' Bill of Rights. In December 1996, by which stage Tony Blair had replaced the late John Smith as party leader, the Labour Party's consultation paper, *Bringing Rights Home*, was silent as to the second stage. And by the time the White Paper, *Rights Brought Home*, was published in October 1997, the commitment to a Human Rights Commission had also been abandoned.

The rationale behind both the 1996 consultation paper and the 1997 White Paper was the fairly modest proposal that British subjects should be enabled to enforce their Convention rights in the domestic sphere,

---

[1] More accurately partial incorporation, see K Ewing, 'The Human Rights Act and Parliamentary Democracy' (1999) *Modern Law Review*, forthcoming.

[2] See W Wade, 'The United Kingdom's Bill of Rights', in Beatson *et al*, *Constitutional Reform in the UK: Practice and Principles* (Oxford: Hart, 1998), where Wade notes (pp 61–62) that the late Lord Taylor CJ, Bingham LJ and Lord Woolf MR had all expressed their support for incorporation prior to the Government's taking action.

[3] See Ewing, note 1 above, in particular his discussion of the Labour Party document, *The Charter of Rights*.

rather than being obliged to bring their cases to the European Court of Human Rights. The White Paper declared that the old system was 'no longer adequate' in view of the 'importance which [the Government] attaches to the maintenance of basic human rights in this country' and the sheer volume of cases in which the UK had been found in breach of the Convention.[4] According to the White Paper: 'It is plainly unsatisfactory that someone should be a victim of a breach of the Convention standards by the State yet cannot bring any case at all in the British courts, simply because British law does not recognise the right in the same terms as one contained in the Convention'. The White Paper drew attention to the delays (around five years) and cost (averaging £30,000) of enforcement at the European level, as well as the benefits of having the Convention rights 'brought much more fully into the jurisprudence of the [UK] courts . . . their interpretation . . . far more subtly and powerfully woven into our law'.

The Human Rights Act 1998 requires that all legislation be interpreted, as far as possible, so as to be consistent with the Convention.[5] If consistent interpretation is not possible, the higher courts (High Court and above in England) may declare secondary legislation invalid 'unless the terms of the parent statute make this impossible', but in respect of primary legislation may only make a 'declaration of incompatibility' which, in the view of the White Paper, 'will almost certainly prompt the Government and Parliament to change the law'.[6] To this end a 'fast-track' procedure is established whereby Parliament (or, in the event that there are 'compelling reasons', Ministers) may, but will not be required to, amend the legislation accordingly.[7]

In respect of each new piece of legislation, the Human Rights Act 1998 requires that the Minister responsible make a declaration as to its compatibility with the incorporated Convention or, if this is not possible, that 'the government nevertheless wishes . . . to proceed with the Bill'.[8] This, in the view of the White Paper: 'will ensure that all Ministers,

---

[4] 50 (25 since 1990), giving Britain a violation record worse only than that of Italy.

[5] The courts 'must have regard to', but are not bound to follow, the jurisprudence of the European Court of Human Rights, Commission opinions and decisions, and decisions of the Council of Ministers (s 2).

[6] See *Rights Brought Home: The Human Rights Bill* (London: HMSO, 1997, CM 3782), para 2.10; see also Secretary of State for the Home Office, HC Debs 16 February 1998, col 772.

[7] Human Rights Act 1998, s 10. As a result of what has been described by Ewing, note 1 above, as 'perhaps the most significant parliamentary victory of this particular Bill', primary legislation is required to amend or repeal primary legislation save where 'compelling reasons' require faster action, in which case Ministerial amendments are permitted to the extent only that they are necessary to remove the incompatibility. The Bill as originally drafted conferred Ministerial power to deal with such 'incidental, supplemental, consequential and transitional provision as the person making it considers appropriate' as a result of a declaration of incompatibility (see HC Debs 24 June, cols 1124–1143). See HC Debs 21 October 1998, cols 1325–1334, for an unsuccessful attempt to restrict the scope of these 'compelling reasons'.

[8] Human Rights Act 1998, s 19(1)(b).

their departments and officials are fully seized of the gravity of the Convention's obligations in respect of human rights'.[9]

The Act makes it unlawful 'for a public authority to act in a way which is incompatible with a Convention right', unless bound so to do by primary legislation.[10] 'Public authority' is defined to include courts and tribunals as well as 'any person certain of whose functions are functions of a public nature', though such a person will not act as a 'public authority' in relation to acts which are 'private'. The Act further excludes from 'public authority' 'either House of Parliament or a person exercising functions in connection with proceedings in Parliament',[11] and defines 'act' so as include a failure to act, but not 'a failure to introduce in, or lay before, Parliament a proposal for legislation', or to 'make any primary legislation or remedial order'.

The Human Rights Act 1998 may be relied upon both as a sword and as a shield, in legal action taken under the Act or otherwise, but only by a person who 'is (or would be) a victim of' an act rendered unlawful by that legislation. This restriction of standing echoes that in the Convention itself and applies also in cases where the legal action taken consists of judicial review, in respect of which more generous rules usually apply.[12]

The Act provides that a court 'may grant such relief or remedy, or make such order, within its jurisdiction as it considers just and appropriate' where an unlawful act is established under the Act, but restricts awards of damages to cases in which 'the court is satisfied that the award is necessary to afford just satisfaction to the person in whose favour it is made' and, in particular, states that 'the court must take into account the principles applied by the European Court of Human Rights in relation to the award of compensation under Article 41 of the Convention' in determining whether and, if so in what amount, damages should be awarded.[13] This will have the effect that any compensation will be limited, in practice, to between around £5,000 and £15,000.

The Human Rights Bill – parliamentary progress

The importance of the Human Rights Bill should not be underestimated. Conor Gearty has remarked that 'the United Kingdom's system of laws will experience a dramatic and radical reorganisation. The Bill's extraordinary breadth, its new approach to statutory interpretation, and the depth

---

[9] The White Paper also recommended the establishment of a new Parliamentary Committee on human rights, though this is a matter for Parliament.

[10] Human Rights Act 1998, s 6.

[11] It does include the House of Lords acting in its judicial capacity.

[12] Supreme Court Act 1981, s 31(3) and RSC Order 53, r 5, require only that an applicant have 'sufficient interest' in the matter to which the application relates – this has been interpreted to permit applications by interest groups where they are in the public interest.

[13] Human Rights Act 1998, s 8.

of its apparently intended impact on the common law, make it unlikely that many areas of domestic law will escape scrutiny . . . It is unlikely that there has ever been an Act of Parliament which has . . . had anything like the extraordinary effect that this Bill is certain to precipitate'.[14]

Much of the attention which has been focused on the Human Rights Bill has concerned its status as an interpretative document, rather than as one which permits the judicial override of primary legislation. Rabinder Singh categorised as 'remarkable', given the British doctrine of implied repeal, the subordination of the incorporated Convention to past, as well as future, legislation.[15] In this, the model chosen for incorporation of the Convention owes more to the New Zealand Bill of Rights Act 1990 than to either the US or Canada, in both of which jurisdictions judges are empowered to strike down any legislation on the grounds of its incompatibility with, respectively, the Constitution and Canada's Charter of Rights.

Under the title 'Fudging British Rights' the American *Economist* condemned the Government's 'timid plan' to incorporate the European Convention on Human Rights as 'a missed opportunity'. Citing the failure to give power to the judiciary to overrule primary legislation, even in line with the Canadian model (under which Parliament can re-enact offending legislation 'notwithstanding' the breach), the *Economist* described the Government's reluctance to interfere with Britain's 'constitutional tradition, which has stood for centuries on the rock of parliamentary sovereignty' as 'peculiar coming from a government which is supposedly so committed to modernising Britain's constitution'.[16]

The relatively weak model of incorporation was justified by the Government, both in its White Paper and in parliamentary statements, on democratic grounds:

> In enacting legislation, Parliament is making decisions about important matters of public policy. The authority to make those decisions derives from a democratic mandate . . . To make provision in the Bill for the courts to set aside Acts of Parliament would confer on the judiciary a general power over the decisions of Parliament which under our present constitutional arrangements they do not possess, and would be likely on occasions to draw the judiciary into serious conflict with Parliament. There is no evidence to suggest that they desire this power, nor that the public wish them to have it. Certainly, this Government has no mandate for any such change.[17]

Much of the debate in the House of Lords was concerned with the application of the Convention to religious bodies, and a number of

---

[14] C Gearty, 'The Human Rights Act 1998 and the Role of the Strasbourg Organs: Some Preliminary Reflections', in G Anderson (ed), *Rights and Democracy in Canada and the UK* (London: Blackstone, 1999, forthcoming).

[15] *The Lawyer*, 30 September 1997.

[16] 25 October 1997.

[17] *Rights Brought Home: The Human Rights Bill*, note 6 above. See also statement by Secretary of State for the Home Office, HC Debs 16 February 1997, col 772.

amendments were secured in this regard. This issue will not be considered. More important, in the context of this book, were the criticisms relating to the Bill's approach to standing and to remedies, and its failure to establish a Human Rights Commission. The restriction of enforcement measures to 'victims' has been noted above. Lord Lester's proposed amendment[18] would have permitted an applicant to apply 'for judicial review provided that the court considers that he has a sufficient interest in the matter to which the application relates'.[19] He argued that the test adopted in the Bill was inappropriate in the context of judicial review, in respect of which the domestic courts permitted applicants who had 'a sufficient interest in the matter to which the application relates'.

The amendment was supported *inter alia* by Lords Ackner and Slynn who warned that the narrow approach would create gaps in human rights protection and complications in judicial review cases involving human rights points, in respect of which two different tests of standing would apply.[20] But the Lord Chancellor, Lord Irvine, insisted that '[b]ringing rights home means exactly what it says – to mirror the approach taken by the Strasbourg court in interpreting convention rights'.[21] The approach taken by the government in this respect underlines its apparent perception of the Human Rights Bill, not as a comprehensive attempt to entrench human rights in the UK, but as a limited measure designed solely to apply the Convention rights in the British courts. Having said this, Lord Lester drew attention to the deliberate exclusion by the Government of procedural rules of the European Court of Human Rights permitting third party interventions by bodies such as Justice, Amnesty International, etc. This being the case, it could be argued that the Convention rights as incorporated do not receive the same measure of protection as they do under the Convention itself.

Further evidence of the intentionally limited nature of the 'human rights' venture can be seen in the Act's approach to remedies, the Lord Chancellor refusing to accept an amendment permitting larger damages than those generally awarded by the Court on the grounds that people should, so far as is possible, 'receive the same remedies from our domestic courts . . . as they would receive if the case went to Strasbourg'.[22]

The restriction of damages to those generally awarded by the European Court of Human Rights was not the only criticism made in both

---

[18]   HL Debs 5 February 1998, col 747.
[19]   *Ibid*, cols 747–807. Amendment was also attempted in the House of Commons, see HC Debs 24 June 1997, cols 1058–1091.
[20]   HL Debs 5 February 1998, cols 808–809. It was also a matter of debates in the Commons.
[21]   F Klug *et al*, *Rights Brought Home: A briefing on the Human Rights Bill with Amendments* (London: The Constitution Unit School of Public Policy, UCL, 1998), p 7 point out that: 'in the same case the court will have to refuse to hear a public interest body raising a point about fundamental human rights, when it will hear the same body on less fundamental issues'.
[22]   HL Debs 29 January 1998, cols 386–388.

Lords and Commons of the Human Right Bill's approach to remedies. A number of amendments were proposed to deal with the Bill's failure to incorporate Article 13 of the Convention which provides the right to 'an effective remedy before a national authority' in respect of violations of the Convention.[23] The Lord Chancellor insisted that clause 8 'gives effect ... to Article 13 by establishing a scheme under which convention rights can be raised before our domestic courts' and was sufficient to that end, and that the express incorporation of Article 13 'might lead [the courts] to fashion remedies other than the Clause 8 remedies, which we regard as sufficient and clear'.[24] Further, according to Lord Irvine, the courts should have regard to Article 13 whether or not it was incorporated, given that clause 2(1) provides that: 'A court or tribunal determining a question which has arisen under this Act in connection with a Convention right must take into ... account any ... judgment, decision, declaration or advisory opinion of the European Court of Human Rights'.[25] A similar approach was taken by Home Secretary Jack Straw in the Commons.

Another criticism made of the Bill in the House of Lords related to its failure to establish a Human Rights Commission (or at least a Commissioner). Liberty had identified such a Commission as having a vital role in promoting compliance with human rights and investigating alleged violations. But an amendment put forward by Lord Lester was defeated on a vote,[26] the Government's resistance to the Commission being defended largely on the grounds of difficulties which might arise between it and the Equal Opportunities Commission and the Commission for Racial Equality, as well as the newly proposed Disability Rights Commission.[27] Lord Lester, by contrast, argued that a very significant role of his proposed Commissioner would be precisely to sort out 'the mess of anti-discrimination legislation which has now become a patchwork of bits and pieces with different enforcement mechanisms'.[28] His amendment was supported by fellow Liberal Democrat, Baroness Williams of Crosby, who cited an Institute of Public Policy Research report which criticised the lack of such a body as 'a major weakness in the current institutional ... arrangements for the protection of human rights in the United Kingdom'.[29]

Among the points raised in the Commons was that of Edward Leigh MP, who decried the Government's failure to define 'public authority', a

---

[23] See HL Debs 18 November 1997, cols 467–468; HL Debs 29 January 1998, cols 381–388; HC Debs 20 May, cols 975–986.

[24] HL Debs 18 November 1997, col 475.

[25] *Ibid*, col 476 and HC Debs 20 May 1998, cols 981–982.

[26] HL Debs 5 February 1998, cols 820–821.

[27] HL Debs 3 November 1997, col 1233. The Government may establish a Commission at some future stage.

[28] HL Debs 5 February 1998, col 822.

[29] *Ibid*, cols 823–827.

failure which he suggested was borne out of embarrassment: 'While a huge organisation such as the Murdoch newspaper empire may be considered a private body, a small local parish church will be considered a public body because it conducts marriages, and will therefore be liable to be sued'.[30] The liability of religious bodies under the Act will, in fact, be very limited. But the point is well made that the incorporated rights, being enforceable only against 'public authorities' however defined, do not provide direct recourse against 'private' organisations which may, nevertheless, exercise enormous control over individuals, unless those 'private' organisations carry out 'functions of a public nature', in which case they will be bound in respect of those functions. It is the case that Convention rights have been held to have some horizontal effect (see discussion below). But the extent to which these rights are effective against 'private' bodies is certainly more limited than is the case against the State. This is an issue to which we shall return frequently throughout this book.

Kevin McNamara MP's criticisms focused in part on the inadequacy of the Convention's prohibitions on discrimination (this issue is further discussed below). He also criticised the Human Rights Bill on the ground that it 'deals with individual rights, and does not deal with community, cultural, ethnic and language rights'.[31] Mr McNamara's criticisms dealt specifically with Northern Ireland but, as he himself recognised, the reasoning behind them is of much wider application:

> Discrimination is only part of the problem . . . Social need should be properly targeted, which may require affirmative action programmes. . . . We should establish principles that would enable full equality to be achieved and would give people the ability fully to participate in decision making. . . . Those ideas go beyond the concept of human rights in the Bill.[32]

This, too, is an issue to which we shall return. Turning to the substantive content of the rights to be incorporated, Humfrey Malins MP complained that: 'the language of the articles [of the European Convention on Human Rights] . . . is language for another time'.[33] Also of concern to Mr Malins was his fear that the Convention would 'be used an enormous number of times in claims to stop deportation'.[34] Mr John Bercow MP, too, found the content of some of the Convention Articles 'profoundly flawed and unsatisfactory'. He pointed out the qualifications imposed by the Convention on many of the rights guaranteed: '[a]lthough the convention is full of good intentions, it is replete with contradictions and ambiguity'.

---

[30] HC Debs 16 February 1998, col 794. See also HC Debs 17 June 1998, cols 399–435.
[31] HC Debs 16 February 1998, col 803.
[32] *Ibid*, col 804.
[33] *Ibid*, cols 812–813.
[34] *Ibid*, cols 813–814.

European Convention on Human Rights

Before considering further the potential shortcomings of the rights guaranteed under the Convention, it is useful briefly to outline them. Section 1 of the Human Rights Act 1998 provides that 'the Convention rights' to which the Act's other provisions refer 'means the rights and fundamental freedoms set out in . . . Articles 2 to 12 and 14 of the Convention [and] Articles 1 to 3 of the First Protocol . . . as read with Articles 16 to 18 of the Convention'.[35] Article 2 guarantees the right to life; Article 3 and 4 the rights, respectively, to be free from torture and inhuman or degrading treatment or punishment and from slavery and forced labour; Articles 5 and 6 respectively the rights to liberty and security of the person and to a fair trial; Article 7 the right to be free from retrospective criminal laws; Articles 8, 9 and 10 the rights, respectively, to respect for private and family life, home and correspondence, to freedom of thought, conscience, religion, and to freedom of expression. Article 11 provides the right to freedom of peaceful assembly and association; Article 12 the right to marry and found a family and Article 14 the right to be free from discrimination in the exercise of these rights and freedoms. Articles 15–18 deal with derogations from and restrictions on the rights guaranteed.[36] The First Protocol, one of the few to which the UK is a signatory protects the rights to peaceful enjoyment of processions (Article 1), to education (Article 2) and to free elections (Article 3).[37] The Sixth Protocol, incorporated only after a back-bench Labour revolt, extends the right to life to prohibit the death penalty.[38]

In addition to the shortcomings of Article 14 highlighted by Kevin McNamara (above) and John Bercow,[39] flaws in the Convention include its lack of any right to information from public bodies; its failure (save where the right to family life – restrictively interpreted – is implicated) to cover deportation issues;[40] and the generous qualifications to the rights set out both in Articles 16–18. Further qualifications are inherent in the right-bestowing Articles themselves. Thus, for example, the 'right to respect for private and family life' permits *inter alia* 'interference by a public authority . . . [where] necessary in a democratic society in the interests

---

[35] Those Articles are to have effect for the purposes of the Act subject to the subsections of s 2 which deal with religious organisations and to any designated derogation or reservation (as to which see ss 14 and 15).

[36] Article 15, which is not incorporated, concerns derogations '[i]n time of war or other public emergency threatening the life of the nation'.

[37] See *Rights Brought Home: The Human Rights Bill*, note 6 above, para 4.5.

[38] HC Debs 20 May 1998, cols 987–1012.

[39] To which one could add Article 14's failure to provide any protection from discrimination on grounds of disability or sexual orientation.

[40] See Liberty, *Bringing Rights Home: Response to Labour's plans to incorporate the European Convention on Human Rights into UK Law* (1997), on http://users.ox.ac.uk/~liberty/echrbrh.html.

of national security, public safety or the economic well-being of the country [or] . . . for the protection of . . . morals' and the rights to freedom of expression, assembly and association may be restricted by law where 'necessary in a democratic society', *inter alia* 'in the interests of national security or public safety' and 'for the protection of health or morals'. These qualifications are hugely significant to the utility of entrenched rights – the devil truly is in the detail. And the detail of many Convention rights leaves a lot to be desired.

In pointing out these qualifications there is no suggestion that 'rights' can generally be other than qualified, a point pursued throughout this book. Rather, attention is drawn to the qualifications incorporated within the European Convention, and thus in the Human Rights Bill, in order to show how wide some of those qualifications are and to point out that the Bill, in common with all other rights-granting statutes, is subject to issues of interpretation. Even in respect of those rights which are not expressly qualified in the Convention (eg the right in Article 3 not to be 'subjected to torture or to inhuman or degrading treatment or punishment') interpretation is required as to the meaning and scope of those rights (in this respect, the meaning of 'torture', 'inhuman', 'degrading', 'treatment' and 'punishment').[41]

Entrenching rights

This point opens up the wider issues concerning the advisability of entrenching 'human rights'. On the face of it, any challenge to such entrenchment appears reactionary: even the *Economist*, a magazine not known for left-leaning views, decried the fact that Britain was 'one of the few established democracies where even basic civil liberties, such as the freedoms of speech and assembly or the right to a fair trial, do not enjoy special legal protection' and criticised the Government 'which, in its zeal to fight crime and to have its way on a variety of other issues, has already betrayed some impatience with the very idea of basic rights'.[42] But the effect of entrenching rights is to assign to the judiciary control over them, whether that control is absolute (as in the US, where the judiciary have the last say over rights, subject to the possibility of constitutional amendment), limited (as in Canada) or (as in the UK), largely a matter of politics. As has been made clear above, the UK courts will have no power to strike down primary legislation. In this, their formal role is weaker than that of

---

[41] This is very well illustrated by *Tyrer v UK* (1978) 2 **EHRR** 1.

[42] *Economist*, 25 October 1997, quoting Prime Minister Tony Blair: 'A decent society is not based on rights. It is based on duty. Our duty to each other.'

courts in the US and Canada. But as Lord Borrie pointed out in the House of Lords' Second Reading debate (citing the Government's own White Paper as support[43]):

> while no court may strike down legislation on the ground that it infringes the convention, the High Court may make a declaration to that effect, after which Ministers are expected to . . . amend the legislation so that it conforms to the convention. If that works as seems to be intended by the Bill, the political reality will be that, while historically the courts have sought to carry out the will of Parliament, in the field of human rights Parliament will carry out the will of the courts.[44]

In addition, the power of the courts to interpret primary and other legislation so as to accord with the judicial view of the rights accorded by the Human Rights Act will be wide. Robert Maclennan MP suggested that the model adopted for incorporation was 'deferential to the sensitivities of the judiciary about being given an overriding constitutional power'.[45] But, whereas in the US politicians appear perfectly content to enact laws which they know will be regarded as unconstitutional by the courts (see, in particular, the comment in Chapter 4 below), it has already been noted in Chapter 1 above that Canadian politicians have not made use of the 'notwithstanding' clause in order to circumvent judicial rulings. In theory, the adoption in the UK of the 'weak' model of incorporation retains decision-making power over 'important matters of public policy' in the hands of elected politicians and, as the White Paper suggested, avoids: 'confer[ring] on the judiciary a general power over the decisions of Parliament'. Just as in Canada, politicians remain free to incorporate 'notwithstanding' clauses, so here they will remain free to amend legislation the judicial interpretation of which displeases them, and not to act on declarations of incompatibility, at least until any ensuing unfavourable decision from the Strasbourg Court. In practice, however, 'the political reality will be that . . . in the field of human rights Parliament will carry out the will of the courts'.[46]

The transfer of power to the judiciary was a matter for much comment from Conservative MPs during the Bill's passage through the Commons,[47] but did not appear to be a matter of concern for the present Government, the Parliamentary Under-Secretary of State for the Home Department

---

[43] HL Debs 3 November 1997, col 1275. Gearty, note 14 above, points out that Ministerial failure to amend might itself be subject to judicial review.

[44] HL Debs 3 November 1997, col 1275.

[45] HC Debs 16 February 1998, col 807.

[46] Lord Borrie, HL Debs 3 November 1997, col 1275, citing the Government's own White Paper as support. Cf Jack Straw's statement, during the Third Reading (HC Debs 21 October 1998, col 1358), that: 'One of the Bill's many strengths is that it promotes human rights while maintaining the sovereignty of Parliament and the separation of powers which underpin our constitutional arrangements.'

[47] See, for example, HC Debs 16 February 1998, cols 811–814 and HC Debs 3 June 1998, cols 426–464.

(Mike O'Brien MP) concluding the debate on the Second Reading in the Commons by paraphrasing Lord Denning to the effect that: 'we have to trust someone, so why not trust the judges' and declaring his confidence in the judicial ability to 'distinguish law from their own socio-political theories'.[48] This flippancy is perhaps surprising in view of the enormous importance that this issue is accorded in those legal systems having entrenched rights.[49] But the Under-Secretary was not alone in appearing contented to accord British judges a much greater role in the human rights arena than had previously been the case. In the White Paper preceding the Human Rights Act, and in addresses of Lord Irvine to the Lords and the Prime Minister to the Council of Europe, the Government rejoiced in the opportunity for 'a distinctively British contribution' from UK judges to the development of European human rights jurisprudence.[50]

The wrongs of 'rights'

The entrenchment of rights may well serve to curb the excesses of government. But it also has the potential to operate against progressive forces. In 1997, for example, Ireland's Supreme Court struck down legislation which required employers to make reasonable accommodation for disabled workers on the grounds that it violated employers' constitutionally protected property rights (see further Chapter 7 below). And more widely known is the history of the US Supreme Court, particularly in the period between the mid-1880s and 1937. In this, the 'heyday of substantive due process', right-wing courts employed the guarantees provided by the Fourteenth Amendment's right to procedural due process[51] to thwart remedial social legislation. Liberty of contract, including liberty in the context of 'personal employment, by which labor and other services are exchanged for money', was elevated to an entrenched constitutional right. And, whereas in the non-economic field, the Supreme Court tended to presume the constitutional validity of legislation unless the reverse could be demonstrated, the opposite held true in the economic field, and in labour law in particular. The court accepted, in theory, that freedom of contract was not absolute, but by 1905 (in *Lochner v State of New York*) was

---

[48] HC Debs 16 February 1998, cols 856–858, internal citations omitted.

[49] Albeit that, in general, those systems accord more power to the judiciary by giving them a *de jure* final say even where, as in Canada, this is subject in theory to veto by Ministers using the notwithstanding clause.

[50] See also the discussion in Ewing, note 1 above, of the extraordinarily pro-judicial approach taken by P Mandelson and R Liddle in *The Blair Revolution: Can Labour Deliver?* (London: Faber & Faber, 1996).

[51] Section 1 of the Fourteenth Amendment declares that 'No State shall . . . deprive any person of life, liberty, or property, without due process of law; nor deny to any person within its jurisdiction the equal protection of the laws.'

placing the onus upon legislators to establish the constitutional validity of legislation such as that restricting hours of employment.[52] In doing so, as Oliver Wendel Holmes (dissenting) pointed out, the court was relying upon a particular economic doctrine to override the clear expression of the legislative will.[53]

The Supreme Court continued to scrutinise labour legislation for compliance with its particular *laissez-faire* conception of substantive due process[54] until the Depression era when Franklin Roosevelt, confronted with judicial intransigence in the face of his efforts to implement the 'New Deal' legislation, threatened to add a further six of his own appointments to the nine-strong Supreme Court. Prior to this point the Supreme Court had, in 1908, struck down federal legislation banning 'yellow dog' contracts (whereby employees promised not to become union members)[55] on the grounds that the restriction of freedom of contract was 'an invasion of the personal liberty, as well as of the right of property' guaranteed by the Constitution – employees were as free to quit as employers were to dismiss them 'and any legislation that disturbs that equality is an arbitrary interference with the liberty of contract which no government can legally justify in a free land'.

Seven years later, in *Coppage v State of Kansas*,[56] the Supreme Court applied *Adair* to find unconstitutional, for breach of due process, a state prohibition on 'yellow dog' contracts. The argument that 'employees, as a rule, are not financially able to be as independent in making contracts for the sale of their labor as are employers in making a contract of purchase thereof' was met with the assertion that 'it is from the nature of things impossible to uphold freedom of contract and the right of private property without at the same time recognizing as legitimate those inequalities of fortune that are the necessary result of the exercise of those rights . . . the 14th Amendment . . . recognizes "liberty" and "property" as coexistent human rights, and debars the states from any unwarranted interference with either'.

In *Truax v Corrigan*[57] the Supreme Court struck down legislation legalising all peaceful strikes, picketing and boycotts in the absence of any independent torts (and, in particular, precluding the judicial enjoining thereof). According to Chief Justice Taft, for the Supreme Court, the behaviour of the employees in this case, although not violent, was an unlawful attack upon the property rights of their employers, the protection of which rights the employer was entitled to under the Due Process

---

[52] *Lochner v New York* 198 US 45 (1905). Cf, prior to the change of tack, *Holden v Hardy* 169 US 366 (1898).
[53] *Lochner v New York, ibid,* at 75–76.
[54] *Muller v State of Oregon* 208 US 412 (1908), *Adkins v Children's Hospital* 261 US 525 (1923).
[55] *Adair v US* 208 US 161 (1908).
[56] 236 US 1 (1915).
[57] 257 US 312 (1921).

and Equal Protection Clauses of the Fourteenth Amendment (referred to below). On 'Black Monday' 1935 the Supreme Court emasculated the progressive labour provisions of the National Industrial Recovery Act 1933, the centrepiece of President Roosevelt's 'New Deal' strategy for national recovery from Depression.[58] A series of similar decisions followed, including *Morehead v Tipalo* (in which New York's minimum wage law was struck down), which was afterwards castigated as 'among the most unpopular ever rendered by the Supreme Court'.[59] In 1937, confronted with Roosevelt's landslide re-election and his threat to pack the Supreme Court, that court upheld Washington legislation setting a minimum wage for women and children and, subsequently, the National Labour Relations (Wagner) Act 1935, on the basis of which US industrial relations are organised to this day.[60] It was not until 1952 that this acceptance was extended, albeit in restricted terms, to what was regarded as general minimum wage legislation.[61]

The Supreme Court retreated from enforcing substantive due process in the economic sphere in the face of Roosevelt's threat and the deep unpopularity of some of its more reactionary decisions. Ironically, when this doctrine resurfaced, it did so in the context of struggle towards social and sexual, rather than economic, liberalism. As such, it tends to be a doctrine beloved of those on the left. But although the concept of substantive due process was utilised, in the late 1960s, to strike down restrictions on inter-racial marriage, on the use of contraception and on abortion,[62] (the efficacy of these decisions is considered further in Chapter 4 below) it is important to recall its roots in the determination of judges to defeat social legislation designed to protect the working poor from the worst excesses of capitalism.

According to Peter Hogg, 'the *Lochner* era cast its shadow over Canada as well'[63] and it was in response to the US Supreme Court's development of 'substantive due process' in the economic arena that the Charter omitted reference to property and to contracts and replaced the concept of 'due process' with the 'principles of fundamental justice', which principles were entrenched in provisions dealing solely with non-economic 'legal rights'. This course of action did not, in the end, prevent Canada's Supreme Court from embracing a doctrine of substantive due process, although this has been restricted to the criminal justice field (see Chapter 8 below).[64]

---

[58] *Schechter Poultry Corporation v United States* 295 US 495 (1935).
[59] *Morehead v Tipalo* 298 US 587 (1938). See J Grossman, 'Fair Labor Standards Act of 1938: Maximum Struggle for a Minimum Wage', *Monthly Labor Review*, June 1978.
[60] *West Coast Hotel Company v Parrish* 300 US 379 (1937); *NLRB v Jones & Laughlin Steel Corp* 331 US 416 (1947).
[61] *Day-Brite Lighting Inc v Missouri* 342 US 421 (1952).
[62] *Loving v State of Virginia* 388 US 1 (1967); *Griswold v State of Connecticut* 381 US 479 (1965); *Roe v Wade* 410 US 113 (1973).
[63] P Hogg, *Constitutional Law of Canada* (2nd ed, Ontario: Carswell, 1992), p 1028.
[64] *Ibid*, p 1033.

Bearing in mind these examples, it is important to note that Article 1 of the First Protocol, which is among those provisions incorporated by the Human Rights Act 1998, states that: '[e]very natural or legal person is entitled to the peaceful enjoyment of his possessions' and that '[n]o one shall be deprived of his possessions except in the public interest and subject to the conditions provided for by law and by the general principles of international law'. Article 1 does go on to provide that it does not 'in any way impair the right of a State to enforce such laws as it deems necessary to control the use of property in accordance with the general interest or to secure the payment of taxes or other contributions or penalties'. How the 'general interest' is interpreted is a matter for the judiciary, guided by the jurisprudence of the European Convention organs. But those who would put their faith in British judges should bear in mind decisions such as *Bromley London Borough Council v Greater London Council*, in which the House of Lords struck down the GLC's subsidised transport policy (which policy had been part of the Labour Party's manifesto commitment upon which it had won control of that body). Their Lordships preferred the interests of the ratepayers to those of transport users on the basis of dubious statutory construction and, in so doing, gave short shrift to the democratic choice of the electorate (most of whom would have been transport users as well as ratepayers). Lord Denning, in the Court of Appeal, displayed an extraordinary lack of regard for the democratic process when he declared that '[w]hen [a] party gets into power, it should consider any [manifesto] proposal or promise afresh, on its merits, without any feeling of being obliged to honour it or being committed to it'.[65] The decision was greeted with general incredulity.

Keith Ewing has pointed out that incorporation of the European Convention on Human Rights recently took place in Sweden at the behest of the political right 'which saw [it] as a restraint on social democracy' – in particular, as a chance to 'protect . . . certain liberal icons (such as private property) and to restrain certain social democratic institutions (such as strong trade unions)'.[66] Entrenched rights are generally individualistic in their nature, consisting as they do of 'political' rights to be free from state interference, rather than 'economic and social' rights to be provided for by the State. Even where the rights which are guaranteed deal with collective, rather than with individual, issues (such as the right to freedom of association), their judicial interpretation tends to render them into individual rights. In the US, for example, the right to withdraw one's labour, as an incident of the Thirteenth Amendment's right against involuntary servitude, does not apply to collective action (see Chapter 6 below). And in Canada the Supreme Court regards freedom of association

[65] [1982] 1 All ER 129, at 134, CA. The decision of the House of Lords is at [1982] 1 All ER 152.

[66] K Ewing, 'Human Rights, Social Democracy and Constitutional Reform', in C Gearty and A Tomkins (eds), *Understanding Human Rights* (London: Mansell, 1996), pp 41–42.

as an individual, rather than a collective, right – this has the effect that
the Charter's guarantee of freedom of association 'does not protect an
activity solely on the ground that the activity is a foundational or essential
purpose of an association'.[67]

The law appears hostile to those rights which need, of their essence, to
be exercised in conjunction with others. And even in the sphere of individual rights, the history of the US Supreme Court should indicate room
for concern. That court chose, in 1856, to deny black Americans their
constitutional rights by dint of defining them as non-citizens.[68] The Fourteenth Amendment was passed to preclude this approach, whereupon
the Supreme Court embraced the 'separate but equal' doctrine to permit
the practice of apartheid.[69] Not until 1954 in *Brown v Board of Education*[70]
was this approach abandoned.

These examples are put forward simply to illustrate the point that
constitutionally entrenched rights are subject to interpretation in their
application and that the judiciary, as those primarily responsible for
interpreting these rights, may do so in ways neither intended nor foreseen
by the drafters of those rights. There is no suggestion that the present day
judiciary, either in the US or here, would permit slavery or adopt a 'separate but equal' approach to race discrimination. But who is to say what the
British House of Lords might carve from the provisions of the European
Convention, whether the right to enjoyment of property protected in the
First Protocol or the right to life enshrined in Article 2? Just as the British
courts may interpret the right to property as inconsistent with some forms
of employment regulation, so, too, might they interpret Article 2's right to
life to demand greater restrictions on abortion than currently apply in
Great Britain. These and other issues are discussed in Chapter 10 below.

Judging judges

The uncertainties of judicial interpretation are inescapable in any system
of law. Generally, the problems arising can be dealt with by legislation.
To the extent that the unelected and usually unaccountable judiciary apply
the law otherwise than in accordance with the intention of its drafters,
legislators can amend the law in order to make its meaning unambiguous (or relatively so). Throughout the first eight decades of the 20th
century, successive governments could, and did, act so as to neutralise
the effects of judicial hostility towards trade unions by providing expanded

---

[67] *Re Public Service Employee Relations Act* [1987] 1 SCR 313, *per* McIntyre J, *PIPSC v Northwest
Territories* [1990] 2 SCR 367, *per* Justice Sopinka.
[68] *Dred Scott v Sandford* 60 US 393 (1856).
[69] *Plessy v Ferguson* 163 US 537 (1896).
[70] 347 US 483 (1954), at 494.

immunities to the ever-increasing range of industrial torts created by the courts. By contrast, where entrenched rights are concerned, the judiciary may, as is the case in the US, effectively have the last word.

It should be stressed once again at this point that the power given to the judiciary by the Human Rights Act 1998 does not, in theory, permit judges to override the Parliamentary will. Judges may not strike down primary legislation and, even in the case of secondary legislation, the effect of any judicial action can be counteracted by subsequent legislative measures. But the interpretative obligations placed upon the judiciary by the Human Rights Act 1998, together with the likely political impact of any declarations of incompatibility, serves radically to increase in practical terms the power of the judiciary *vis-à-vis* that of Parliament. This, in turn, renders even more significant the identity and attitudes of the judges charged with implementing the legislation.

The British system of judicial appointment and promotion has frequently been criticised, not least for its closed and secretive nature. Save in the case of the most junior appointments which have, since 1994, been advertised and in respect of which appointments panels have been involved, candidates for appointment 'emerge' from secret soundings taken by the Lord Chancellor (in Scotland, the Lord Advocate) from senior members of the judiciary. Unsurprisingly, this system has resulted in a high degree of homogeneity at the bench. The senior judiciary consist almost entirely of upper-middle class white men (of 96 High Court judges all are white and all but seven male, the Court of Appeal and House of Lords are exclusively white and all but entirely male,[71] and some 80 per cent of senior judges have been privately educated[72]). Of even greater concern, this homogeneity extends, for the most part, to political hue. In 1987 Tony Blair, then a young barrister, criticised the 'inherent conservatism' of British judges.[73] More recently, Austin Mitchell MP described judges' politics as 'rang[ing] from right, to extreme right, to lunatic right'[74] (although the last Conservative Lord Chancellor, Lord Mackay, did make some very liberal appointments during his office).[75]

Judicial politics (whether with a small or a capital 'P') clearly influence decision-making. The Public Law Project, in its analysis of judicial review cases during the 1990s, found 'a huge disparity in the divisional court over how willing judges were to let cases go forward against the government'.[76] The proportion of cases which individual judges allowed to proceed varied between 20 per cent and 80 per cent. As a spokesperson for the project

---

[71] *Guardian*, 24 February 1998.
[72] *The Times*, 27 May 1997.
[73] (1997) 126 *New Statesman* 22, 21 November.
[74] Press Association *Newsfile*, 1 April 1998. See, more generally, J Griffith, *The Politics of the Judiciary* (5th ed, London: Fontana, 1997).
[75] *New Statesman*, note 73 above.
[76] *Ibid.*

stated in 1997, '[t]here is no reason to suppose that this will not be true for ECHR cases'. In the aftermath of the *Spycatcher* case, Tony Blair stated that to enact a Bill of Rights which entrusted 'inherently conservative' judges with the protection of civil liberties would be 'bizarre'.[77] More recently, Lord Irvine conceded that, in applying the Human Rights Act, judges would sometimes be required to give 'a decision on the morality of the conduct, and not simply its compliance with the bare letter of the law'. The manner in which judges reconciled the provisions of the Act with legislation restricting the rights protected by it would, in Lord Irvine's words, reflect their 'moral sensitivity'. As the *Guardian* pointed out, 'moral sensitivity' amounts to 'political attitudes' by another name.[78] And Beverley McLachlin, now a Justice of Canada's Supreme Court, herself pointed out (prior to her appointment) that the judicial weighing of protected rights 'against the collective interest of the State . . . is essentially a judgement of a political rather than judicial nature'.[79]

Given the influence of judicial politics on decision-making, the implementation of the Human Rights Act 1998 renders even more imperative the reform of judicial appointments. In 1992, Derry Irvine QC wrote in the *Guardian* that the judiciary must be made more representative, that the arrangements governing judicial appointments were 'outdated, secretive and elitist'[80] and called for the establishment of a Ministry of Justice and an independent judicial appointments commission. The Labour Party Policy Handbook for election candidates in 1997 stated that: '[t]he selection of judges is too important to be conducted in the secrecy of the Lord Chancellor's Department . . . Labour will replace the current system of secretive patronage with a judicial appointments and training commission, independent of the Lord Chancellor's Department . . .'[81]

Shortly after the Labour Government had assumed office in 1997 and Derry (now Lord) Irvine had assumed the Lord Chancellor's mantle, his department began work on proposals for an appointments commission for High Court positions, this to consist in part of lay members.[82] Senior judges were extremely critical of the proposal, the Judges' Council claiming that it would 'introduce politics into the process' and the late Lord Taylor, then Lord Chief Justice, claimed in 1996 that he could not 'imagine anything more horrific'. Lord Saville, a senior Court of Appeal judge, who added his voice to those warning of 'politicisation', claimed that the existing system worked well.[83]

---

[77] *Ibid.*
[78] *Guardian*, 18 December 1997.
[79] B McLachlin, 'The Charter of Rights and Freedoms: A Judicial Perspective' (1988–89) *University of British Columbia Law Review* 579, at 583–584.
[80] *Guardian*, 2 April 1998. See also D Bean, *Law Reform for All* (London: Blackstone Press, 1996) in which Lord Irvine proposed the appointment of non-lawyers to the House of Lords.
[81] Quoted in *Guardian*, 25 February 1998.
[82] *The Times*, 27 May 1997.
[83] *Ibid.*

The idea that a system which seeks to produce some variety on the bench is any more 'political' than one which produces fairly homogeneous conservatism is, of course, open to challenge. But in October 1997 Lord Irvine announced that the commission would not be established, although appointments to the High Court would be advertised (the first such advertisement appeared in February 1998).[84] Not only did Lord Irvine reserve the right to appoint those who did not apply, but he went on the offensive against those who criticised the closed nature of the existing system, rejecting the term 'secret soundings' for his preferred 'information gathering exercises',[85] and appearing to locate the responsibility for the composition of the judiciary in the reluctance of women and ethnic minority candidates to come forward.[86] 'Don't be shy! Apply!' was his rallying call to the Association of Women Barristers in February 1998.[87]

The British system leaves much to be desired. But it is difficult to determine what might best be put in its place to appoint those who, as enforcers of entrenched rights, have the power to trump democratically elected politicians (whether *de jure*, as in the US or *de facto*, as in Canada and the UK). Certainly, the approach adopted in the US (and which William Hague, in his first major speech as Conservative leader, suggested as a model for reform[88]) is, if anything, even less desirable than that currently in place in Britain. In the US, all lower federal judicial appointments are ultimately in the hands of the President. As far as the Supreme Court is concerned, the President nominates a candidate upon whom the Senate votes. Some nominations have always been more contentious than others. In 1987, for example, President Reagan's nomination of Robert Bork was defeated by the Democratic Senate after 12 days of nationally televised hearings.[89] And three years later, President Bush's nomination of Clarence Thomas provoked similar outrage, the Senate hearings with their sexual harassment allegations and counter-allegations gripping the US for months, although in this case the nomination succeeded.

---

[84] Press Association *Newsfile*, 9 October 1997, *Guardian*, 24 February 1998. The Lord Chancellor, however, reserved the right to appoint those not applying.

[85] 29 November 1998, speech to the Minority Lawyers' Conference. The text is at http://www.open.gov.uk/lcd/speeches/1997/speechfr.htm. According to the *Guardian*, 25 February 1998: 'Lord Irvine . . . worries that allowing an independent commission would inevitably lead to politics being introduced into the selection of judges'.

[86] The Labour Party's *volte face* was presaged by the effusive remarks of Mandelson and Liddle, note 50 above, to the effect that 'even the most prejudiced class warrior' had been convinced of judicial 'independence and integrity' by virtue of their recent record (see further Ewing, note 1 above).

[87] 11 February 1998. The text is at http://www.open.gov.uk/lcd/speeches/1998/1998fr.htm. Lord Irvine has not shown the same commitment to open competition in his own appointments, being the subject of race and sex discrimination claims after the private appointment of a special adviser – see *Guardian*, 26 February 1998 and 18 December 1997.

[88] *The Times*, 25 February 1998.

[89] See *Newsday*, 14 January 1988. For the aftermath of this, see *Boston Globe*, 10 July 1994.

Politics and the law

If the process of judging, particularly at the level of constitutional application, were truly a non-political one, one would have to assume that
controversies such as those in the US surrounding the nominations of
Bork and Thomas concerned the intellectual qualities of the judges concerned. This was not the case. While the Judiciary Committee of the
Senate refused to endorse the nomination of Clarence Thomas, perhaps
in part because of reservations about his qualifications and experience,[90]
the real concern about his appointment to the Supreme Court, as with
the appointment of Robert Bork before him, was political.

Thomas, like Bork, had been selected by a Republican President
determined to reverse the liberalising tendency of the Supreme Court by
reversing decisions on affirmative action, school prayer and, not least,
abortion. Reagan's appointments of Justices O'Connor, Scalia and
Kennedy having repositioned a bench previously liberal on the abortion
issue, it appeared that the replacement of Thurgood Marshall's successor
to the Supreme Court would either retain the majority in favour of *Roe v
Wade*[91] or result in the overruling of that case.[92] President Bush was determined to have *Roe v Wade* overruled and in his selection of judicial candidates, whether at the lowest level or that of the Supreme Court justices,
he made it his project to appoint only those who took an anti-abortion
stance. It was the President's pursuit of the overturn of *Roe v Wade* which
was largely responsible for the fact that, in January 1992, more than one
in six federal judges' positions was waiting to be filled.[93]

In the face of the manoeuvrings which typically surround the appointment of US Supreme Court judges, any claim that the application of
entrenched rights is a non-political project is unsustainable. One might
argue that the US process, whereby Presidential nominations are subject
to public confirmations, injects some kind of accountability into the appointment of judges. But any such accountability is *ex ante*, rather than *ex post
facto*. A judge can be rejected by the Senate on the ground that, when in
office, he is likely to reach particular decisions (this was what happened
to the aspiring Justice Bork) but he or she cannot, on the basis of his or
her decision-making in office, be removed.

To the extent (if at all) that the application of law is non-political (or,
at any rate, not party-political), security of judicial tenure is appropriate:
great importance is laid in many systems on an independent judiciary.
But the interpretation of typically vague and non-absolute 'constitutional'
rights is inherently political. And if judges are to be appointed on the

---

[90] *National Law Journal*, 30 September 1991, 'Still Searching for the Real Clarence Thomas'.
[91] 410 US 113 (1973).
[92] The decisions of Justices O'Connor and Kennedy in fact rendered the appointment less
crucial – see Chapter 4 below.
[93] *Los Angeles Times*, 25 January 1992.

basis of their politics, and are appointed to perform a political role, one could argue that they should be accountable politically for the decisions that they have made, as well as those that they are deemed likely to make. Without this, entrusting the enforcement of rights to the judiciary serves to inject a time lag into the democratic process by allowing previous incumbents of the appointing body to exert a political influence after they themselves have been replaced. The Republican administrations of Presidents Reagan and Bush may have been rejected by the electorate, but Justices Scalia, Kennedy, O'Connor and Thomas still exert their influence on the Supreme Court. Had it not been for the unanticipated moderation of Justice Souter (Justice Brennan's Bush-appointed replacement), and the determination of Justice Blackmun to hang on to his seat, well into his eighties, until the election of Democratic President Bill Clinton, the Supreme Court today would be a staunchly right-wing body.

To deny that entrenched rights perform any protective role is, of course, to exaggerate. The right to abortion in the US is in danger because it is not clearly granted by the Constitution but, rather, depends upon a particular juristic interpretation for its very existence (see Chapter 4 below). Equally, nowhere does the Constitution expressly stipulate that disadvantaged US citizens be assisted by means of affirmative action (see Chapter 7 below). If such 'rights' were expressly stipulated, all the judicial creativity in the world might find it difficult (though not impossible[94]) to deny them.

The problem is not with those issues in the collective mind of the legislators at the time when the legislation intended to entrench rights is drafted – in the US, for example, the Third Amendment's right not to have 'soldiers in time of peace . . . quartered in any house, without the consent of the Owner' is so specific that it has resulted in not one Supreme Court decision in the two centuries since its ratification.[95] But no Bill or Charter of Rights ever seeks to enumerate all the detailed entitlements it grants: rather, such documents rely on broad statements concerning rights to 'privacy', to 'free speech', perhaps to 'security of the person'. It is inevitably the case that these broad rights must be interpreted in order to determine whether they cover particular situations in dispute, and how, in case of conflict, they may coexist. But it is at this point that the political nature of the venture becomes clear.

Whether the debate concerns the question whether 'citizen' includes women and blacks as well as white men, whether it relates to the scope of the discrimination prohibition in the US Constitution, the answer will relate as much to a judge's view of the world and of contemporary mores

---

[94] See discussion of the approach to the US Fourteenth Amendment above.
[95] Save for the curious case of *Engblom v Carey* 677 F 2d 957 (2d Cir, 1982), 724 F 2d 28 (2d Cir, 1983), there has been no judicial explication of this Amendment at all.

as it will to his or her grasp of legal principle. To claim, as defeated Supreme Court candidate Robert Bork did, that the US Constitution should bear only the meaning that its original framers intended, is to adopt as political a stance as one who states, as did the European Court of Human Rights in *Tyrer v UK*,[96] that the European Convention is a 'a living instrument . . . which . . . must be interpreted in the light of present-day conditions'.

Robert Bork's view, if followed, would to this day, deny the full protection of the US Constitution to women, and thus explicitly entrench discrimination into the very heart of the US system. The only defence of such a stance is that it has, at least, the merit of relative certainty (although those who adjudicate constitutional rights will still have to determine what the original framers meant), while the latter approach makes the content of entrenched rights a matter of intense speculation. No one could have foreseen that the US Supreme Court would, in *Roe v Wade*,[97] find a right to abortion in the Due Process Clause of the Fourteenth Amendment. Welcome as that right may be to the women who rely upon it, it was certainly never the intention of those who drafted the Fourteenth Amendment in 1868 that it be applied to this end.

One might, of course, argue (with Lord Denning and Mike O'Brien MP) that, if rights must be interpreted and weighed, the judiciary is as good a body as any to which to entrust the task. After all, it could be claimed, elected politicians are self-serving, always with an eye to re-election, too ready to sacrifice the unpopular cause for the sake of tabloid approval. And it is true that, faced with a government which acted in a manner of which one disapproved, it would be comforting if one were able to categorise such action as 'illegal', 'unconstitutional', and therefore at least potentially remediable, rather than as merely 'wrong'. But this argument cannot be sustained in any democratic system: if the nature of the judging process is itself political and if judges are to be given the power (whether as a matter of strict law or political reality) to 'trump' the legislature, then in order that democracy be preserved the judges must themselves be accountable to the electorate. To achieve real, rather than partial accountability (the latter being practised in the US), judges must be directly elected or, perhaps in order to ensure that they have some knowledge of law (however bare), appointed by an organ of the state, and be removable by a similar process. Yet, if this pattern is to be followed, the question must be asked whether it would not be preferable to dispense with the judges altogether and leave the matter up to the politicians they would, under the proposed system, represent. At least such a course of action would be immune from allegations of dissimulation on the part of government.

---

[96] (1978) 2 EHRR 1.
[97] Note 91 above.

Women and rights

This chapter simply outlines the provisions of the Human Rights Act 1998 and points to a number of the issues which the Act raises, both in particular by virtue of the rights embraced by it (ie those set out in the European Convention on Human Rights) and the model it has chosen for incorporation of those rights; and in general in the very fact of entrenching 'rights' by whatever model. The most significant problem identified thus far relates to judicial interpretation of rights: to the extent that any system of rights depends upon the courts for their application, the scope and weight of those rights is in the hands of the judiciary. It is for this reason that the core of the book (Chapters 3–9) considers how the judiciary, largely in Canada and the US, have interpreted and applied constitutionally protected rights in a number of spheres.

This book does not deal generally with the utility of rights. Its aim is rather narrower: to consider how constitutionally entrenched and judicially applied rights have benefited or disadvantaged women. In so doing, the main focus of the book will be on Canada and the US, although reference will be made at various points to the experience elsewhere. The utility of comparing the US and Canadian 'rights' models to that in the UK can be challenged on the grounds that the judicial power is greater in those systems then here, British judges being denied any power to strike down primary legislation.[98] (New Zealand's model of rights is closer to the UK system but has been in operation for too brief a period for any real lessons to be learnt from it.) But it has been suggested above that this distinction may prove to be more important at the level of theory than practice, and that the very ability of the British legislature to have the 'final word' may render it, in common with its Canadian counterpart, rather more than less deferential to judicial pronouncements.

Canada and the US are chosen for primary scrutiny because their constitutional rights, in common with those to be entrenched in the UK, are broadly liberal (by contrast with South Africa, for example, whose recent Constitution also embraces social and economic rights), because they share the UK's common law system while having entrenched rights and because, in addition, they stand as examples of opposite ends of the spectrum in the relative age of their entrenching provisions (in the US, broadly the late 18th century with those provisions of most concern to us having been embraced largely in the late 19th century: in Canada, 1982). This has had an impact in the particular rights entrenched – Canada's attempt to avoid the *Lochner* era, for example, by excluding property guarantees from its Charter of Rights, and the approach taken by the Charter to

---

[98] Much less to do so in a way which (as in the US) is immune to legislative override save in the event of constitutional amendment.

discrimination. In addition, the attitude of Canada's senior judiciary is rather different to that which has prevailed in the US.

In contrast with the rigorously individualistic approach taken to rights both by the US Constitution (many of whose guaranteed rights provide for no express qualification) and the Supreme Court (in particular, in relation to affirmative action – see Chapter 7 below – and pornography as 'free speech'[99]), Canada's Supreme Court has recognised that: '[i]n interpreting and applying the Charter . . . the courts must be cautious to ensure that it does not simply become an instrument of better situated individuals to roll back legislation which has as its object the improvement of the condition of less advantaged persons'[100] and that 'freedom has often required the intervention and protection of government against private action'.[101]

In making this latter statement, Madam Justice Wilson consciously distinguished the attitudes of Canadians 'towards government and its role' from that of 'our US neighbours'. In its approach to individual rights, Canada's judiciary is at one with the Charter which, again by contrast with that in the US, provides express authority for the restriction of the rights guaranteed by it. Not only does s 1 provide that '[t]he Canadian Charter of Rights and Freedoms guarantees the rights and freedoms set out in it subject only to such reasonable limits prescribed by law as can be demonstrably justified in a free and democratic society', but s 33 permits Parliament to pass legislation inconsistent with the Charter where an express declaration to this effect is made. As mentioned above, this provision is not, as a rule, actually used (Quebec aside). But its existence is a recognition that, on occasion, government can prefer the collective over the individual. This recognition is afforded only indirectly by the US Constitution, the Supreme Court permitting the restriction of constitutional rights according to varying degrees of judicially imposed scrutiny. Aspects of the US Constitution and Canada's Charter of Rights – in particular, those relevant to discrimination – are considered in more detail in Chapter 3 below.

---

[99] The US Supreme Court permits the regulation of 'obscene' material, by virtue of defining it as 'non-speech' but, by contrast with the Supreme Court in Canada, any attempt to regulate 'pornography' – defined in terms of its attitude towards women – would fall foul of the First Amendment. For the definition of 'obscenity', see *Jacobells v State of Ohio* 378 US 184 (1964), at 197. Cf the approach of Canada's Supreme Court in *Butler* [1992] 1 SCR 452.

[100] *Edwards Books and Art Ltd et al v R* [1986] 2 SCR 713, at 779, *per* Dickson CJ, cited by R Elliott, 'The Supreme Court's Rethinking of the Charter's Fundamental Questions (Or Why the Charter Keeps Getting More Interesting)', in P Bryden *et al* (eds), *Protecting Rights and Freedoms: Essays on the Charter's Place in Canada's Political, Legal and Intellectual Life* (Toronto: University of Toronto Press, 1994), p 136.

[101] Justice Wilson, dissenting, in *McKinney v University of Guelph* [1990] 3 SCR 229, at 356 cited in Elliott, *ibid*, p 137.

Chapter 3

Discrimination and the US and Canadian Constitution Provisions

Introduction

Much of the substance of this book is devoted to the impact of entrenched rights upon women in the US and in Canada. As mentioned in Chapter 1 above, not all areas of women's lives will be considered, the emphasis being on reproduction, work and violence. Nor will the law as it relates to women in these contexts be considered in any detail in its broader terms. The concern of this book is not with whether, and to what extent, the legal systems examined respect women's reproductive autonomy, secure their equality in the workplace and protect them from violence. Rather, the question it addresses is relevant to the impact in these areas of constitutional rights. The distinction between these and statutory/common law rights has been considered in Chapter 1, and the relative approaches of the US and Canadian systems to entrenched rights were indicated very broadly in Chapter 2. Here it is useful to consider in more detail the approaches of the relative constitutions and courts to discrimination in particular.

The US Constitution and discrimination

A number of general points can be made about the US Constitution. As it was originally drafted, the Constitution contained no prohibition on discrimination and, in particular, was not intended to confer any rights upon women.[1] The right to equal treatment, such as it is, is contained in the Equal Protection Clause of the Fourteenth Amendment, s 1 of which states that 'nor shall any State . . . deny to any person within its jurisdiction

---

[1] See letters of Abagail and John Adams in E Cary and K Peratis, *Woman and the Law* (Stokie, Illinois: National Textbook Company, 1978) pp 1–2.

the equal protection of the laws'. The Amendment was passed to ameliorate the decision in the *Dred Scott* case[2] and applies only to state, rather than to federal action. The Supreme Court has, however, interpreted the Fifth Amendment's federally binding guarantee of 'due process' to incorporate the same protection from discrimination as is found in the Fourteenth Amendment's Equal Protection Clause.

For the first 100 years after the passage of the Fourteenth Amendment, its Equal Protection Clause was not applied to prohibit discrimination against women. The clause was originally intended solely to apply to black American men, its initial draft containing the first express restriction of US constitutional rights to 'male' persons.[3] The sex-specific wording of the Amendment was altered, but the general view that it applied only to benefit black men was affirmed in 1873 by the US Supreme Court in the *Slaughterhouse Cases* in which the court declared that the provision was 'so clearly a provision for that race and that emergency, that a strong case would be necessary for its application to any other . . . [w]e doubt very much whether any action of a State not directed by way of discrimination against the negroes as a class, or on account of their race, will ever be held to come within [its] purview'.[4]

Early challenges to sex discrimination were greeted with Supreme Court decisions which recognised 'the wide differences in the respective spheres and destinies of man and woman' and regarded as the 'paramount destiny and mission of a woman', the 'fulfill[ment of] the noble and benign offices of wife and mother'.[5] But whatever the intent behind the Fourteenth Amendment, its Equal Protection Clause began to be interpreted as extending beyond discrimination based on race to regulate, more generally, governmental classifications between people. But the standard of regulation is not uniform: the Supreme Court applies 'strict scrutiny' classifications based on race, which will be unconstitutional unless 'necessary' or 'narrowly tailored' to promote a 'compelling interest' of government. By contrast, most classifications will be acceptable if they pass a much more relaxed standard of review: that is, if they are not totally irrational or utterly arbitrary.

As recently as 1961, the Supreme Court, under the pioneering influence of Chief Justice Warren, rejected a challenge to legislation dealing with jury service, stating that the legislature was permitted to recognise the 'special responsibilities' borne by women by relieving them of this civic obligation.[6] By contrast with the Supreme Court's later, formal,

---

[2] *Dred Scott v Sandford* 60 US 393 (1856) – see Chapter 2, note 68 and accompanying text.
[3] Cary and Peratis, note 1 above, pp 19–20.
[4] 83 US 394 (1873), at 410.
[5] *Bradwell v State of Illinois* 83 US 130 (1872), *per* Justice Miller. The early approach of the UK courts to cases brought under the Equal Pay Act 1970 and the Sex Discrimination Act 1975 was not dissimilar – see *Peake v Automotive Products Ltd* [1978] QB 233 and, more recently, *Clymo v Wandsworth London Borough Council* [1989] IRLR 241.
[6] *Hoyt v State of Florida* 368 US 57 (1961), at 62.

approach to discrimination, contextualisation was regarded as appropriate in a case in which a woman, rather than a man, challenged discrimination (here the challenge was made by a woman convicted, by an all-male jury, of the murder of her husband). But by 1971 the Supreme Court had struck down legislation which favoured men over women in the administration of estates.[7] And, while a relaxed standard of review appears to have been applied in this case and some confusion ensued about the appropriate level of scrutiny,[8] by 1976 the 'intermediate standard' had been firmly established in *Craig v Boren*.[9]

Under the intermediate standard of review, the Supreme Court first examines the statutory or administrative scheme under challenge to determine if its purpose or objective is permissible and important. Secondly, it ascertains how well the classification serves the end, and whether a less discriminatory one would serve the same purpose without substantial loss to the government. Where the sex-based classification is seen to rest on stereotype, such classification will not pass even relaxed scrutiny.[10] Where the classification had some basis in fact, intermediate scrutiny requires evidence of the existence of that fact and its close relationship to the condition for which sex is taken as a proxy.

Perhaps the most significant limitation on the Equal Protection Clause lies in almost complete non-application to indirect discrimination.[11] An intention to discriminate requires, not merely that the body imposing the rule knew of its disparate impact, but also that the decision-maker 'selected or reaffirmed a particular course of conduct at least in part "because of", not merely "in spite of", its adverse effects upon an identifiable group'.[12] Even if an intention to discriminate was one of the reasons behind the imposition of a disparately impacting practice, a violation of the Fourteenth Amendment will not be made out if the rule would have been imposed even in the absence of this motive.[13] Finally, one strand of Supreme Court decisions requires that, when evaluating the evidence to ascertain whether discriminatory intent has been established, each piece of evidence must be considered separately and discriminatory intent may be found only if this can be done on the basis of one or more factors *viewed in isolation*.[14]

If the Supreme Court had been motivated by the desire to make it as difficult as possible for applicants to prove discrimination under the Equal

---

[7] *Reed v Reed* 404 US 71 (1971).
[8] *Frontiero v Richardson* 411 US 677 (1973).
[9] 429 US 190 (1976).
[10] *Stanton v Stanton* 421 US 7 (1975) and 429 US 501 (1977); *Orr v Orr* 440 US 268 (1979); *Parham v Hughes* 441 US 347 (1979); *Kirchberg v Feenstra* 450 US 455 (1981).
[11] *Washington v Davies* 426 US 229 (1976).
[12] *Massachusetts Personnel Administrator v Feeney* 442 US 256 (1979).
[13] *Village of Arlington Heights v Metropolitan Housing Development Corp* 429 US 252 (1977).
[14] *City of Mobile v Bolden* 446 US 55 (1980), cf *Rogers v Lodge* 458 US 613 (1982).

Protection Clause, it could not have done much better. And problems of proof aside, the interpretation of the Equal Protection Clause as applying to direct discrimination alone permits the disadvantages women suffer *as women* to go unchecked. (As Catherine MacKinnon has put it 'applied to women [this approach] means if men don't need it, women don't get it'.[15]) Equality only exists at the most formal level and the law will be satisfied as long as like is treated alike. But to the extent that men and women are not 'like', the concept of formal equality has little to say about the disadvantages which women may suffer as a result of being judged by a yardstick designed for men.

The approach taken by the Supreme Court to discrimination has had the effect of restricting significantly the extent to which the Equal Protection Clause can be relied upon to improve the position of women in those matters dealt with in Chapters 4–9 of this book, women frequently being thrown back on the Due Process Clauses of the Fifth and Fourteenth Amendments instead. This in turn creates problems because of the rather suspect status of substantive due process rights. The right to abortion, for example, was found by the Supreme Court in *Roe v Wade*[16] in the right to privacy which was, in turn, found in the 'penumbras' of rights found elsewhere in the constitution and applied through the general equal protection and due process clauses. As welcome as that right might be to women, its provenance is dubious – one house of cards built atop another. Had the Supreme Court's approach to the Equal Protection Clause been wider it might, instead, have regarded the prohibition on abortion as a restriction bearing exclusively upon women, this restriction then requiring justification under the Equal Protection Clause. To the extent that the sex discrimination can be justified in line with the intermediate standard of review, this justification might have been found. But had a strict scrutiny approach been adopted by the Supreme Court in sex discrimination, restrictions on abortion would perhaps have been struck down under the Equal Protection Clause, this footing being somewhat easier to defend than the substantive due process approach.

Canada's Charter: learning from the past

Turning next to Canada's approach to discrimination, the Charter of Rights was drafted specifically in order to avoid a number of difficulties which had arisen in the US, as well as those which had become apparent

---

[15] Cited in K Mahoney, 'Charter Equality: The First Twelve Years', paper presented to the Warwick Legal Research Institute Rights and Democracy in Canada and the UK Conference, 17 May 1997, p 13.

[16] 410 US 113 (1973).

in the judicial application of Canada's 1960 Bill of Rights. The Charter, which was enacted as part of the Canada Act 1982, contains a clear commitment to sex equality, s 15 providing that 'Every individual is equal before and under the law and has the right to the equal protection and equal benefit of the law without discrimination and, in particular, without discrimination based on race, national or ethnic origin, colour, religion, sex, age or mental or physical disability'. Section 15(2) goes on to permit some types of affirmative action, and s 28 declares that 'Notwithstanding anything in this Charter, the rights and freedoms referred to in it are guaranteed equally to male and female persons'.[17]

Sections 15 and 28 of the Charter were drafted in an attempt to force a purposive approach upon the judiciary, Canada having experienced the judicial mangling of the equality guarantee provided by the Bill of Rights, s 1(b) of which recognised 'the right of the individual to equality before the law and the protection of the law'. The Bill of Rights was not entrenched but provided (s 2) that '[e]very law of Canada shall, unless it is expressly declared by an Act of the Parliament of Canada that it shall operate notwithstanding the *Canadian Bill of Rights*, be so construed and applied as not to abrogate, abridge or infringe . . . of any of the rights or freedoms herein recognized and declared'.

The approach taken by Canada's judges to the Bill of Rights should be regarded as compulsory reading for all those inclined to place blind faith in the judiciary. The Supreme Court generally embraced the 'frozen concept theory' of rights whereby that which was acceptable prior to the Bill of Rights 1960 remained acceptable within the concepts set out by it.[18] Not only was this approach inconsistent with the general principle of implied repeal (whereby, to the extent that legislation is inconsistent with subsequent legislation, the former is regarded as impliedly overruled), but the Bill of Rights itself (s 5) provided that the Bill applied to all laws then in force as well as to those subsequently enacted. Further, the Supreme Court, with one exception,[19] refused to strike down legislation which was inconsistent with the provisions of the 1962 Act on the grounds that the Bill of Rights was merely an interpretative document, and/or that it could not be used to strike down legislation passed under the British North American Act[20] (as all federal legislation was). Finally, until 1975 the Supreme Court generally interpreted s 1(b) of the Bill to require only that citizens be treated equally *before* the law in the Diceyan sense that those to whom the law applied had to be treated equally, without regard to the substantive content of the law[21] and, even when it eventually

---

[17] Sex alone, of all the prohibited grounds of discrimination, is protected by s 28 from the legislative override otherwise permitted to government by s 33.

[18] *Robertson and Rosetanni v R* [1963] SCR 651; *Gonzales* (1962) 37 WWR 257, BC; *Smythe v R* [1971] SCR 680; *Miller & Cockriell v R* [1977] 2 SCR 680.

[19] *Drybones* [1970] SCR 282.

[20] Now the Constitution Act 1982. See *Attorney General v Lavell* [1974] SCR 1349.

[21] *Attorney General v Lavell, ibid.*; but see *Burnshine* [1975] 1 SCR 693.

resiled from this view, the Supreme Court adopted a purely formal approach to equality.

Under the Diceyan notion of equality, as it was interpreted by the Supreme Court, legislation which stripped aboriginal women, but not men, of their status when they married out and which imposed particular legal handicaps on those classified as 'Indians' was upheld.[22] Section 1(b) was no more than a guarantee of equality in the *procedural administration* of the law, and was satisfied where all aboriginal women are treated equally under a law relating to aboriginal women, and where all aboriginal people are treated equally under a law relating only to aboriginal people, regardless of any disparity between the treatment of aboriginal women, or aboriginal people generally, and that accorded to others under different laws.[23] This approach was in flagrant contradiction of the egalitarian notion of equality embraced by the Universal Declaration of Human Rights, which document Canada helped to prepare, and even the requirement for procedural equality was further limited by the Supreme Court in 1976 in the first *Morgentaler* case,[24] in which it ruled unanimously that the Bill of Rights did not require *efficiency* in the administration of legislation. That challenge concerned Canada's abortion legislation, which permitted terminations only where a hospital committee certified its opinion that the pregnancy was likely to endanger the woman's life or health. Hospitals were not obliged to establish such committees, and committees were not obliged to issue certificates even where the woman's life or health was endangered, so women's access to abortion depended on the whim of their local hospital.

In 1975 the Supreme Court moved away from the Diceyan approach to equality but, in scrutinising legislation which discriminated against individuals on one of the grounds enumerated in s 1(b), asked simply whether federal legislation had been adopted to achieve a legitimate federal end and imposed no requirement of proportionality between the end sought or means adopted and the degree of infringement inflicted.[25] Under this test it continued to uphold legislation which discriminated against aboriginal people.[26] And even with the abandonment of the Diceyan approach to equality, the Supreme Court's formal approach resulted in its unanimous decision, in *Bliss v Attorney General of Canada*,[27] that pregnancy-based

---

[22] *Attorney General v Lavell, ibid.* Cf *Drybones* [1970] SCR 282; *Attorney General v Canard* [1976] 1 SCR 170.

[23] See D Gibson, *The Law of the Charter: Equality Rights* (Toronto: Carswell, 1990) pp 33–35 for criticism of this interpretation of Dicey's concept of equality.

[24] *Morgentaler v R* [1976] 1 SCR 616.

[25] Or a ground analogous thereto: *Burnshine*, note 21 above; *Attorney General v Canard*, note 22 above; *Solosky* (1980) 105 DLR (3rd) 745, SC; *MacKay* [1980] 2 SCR 370. See also *Prata* [1976] 1 SCR 376.

[26] *Attorney General v Canard*, note 22 above. This approach has been retained since the adoption of the Charter and despite dissents in *MacKay v R* (1980) 114 DLR (3d) 393 and *R v Beauregard* (1986) 30 DLR (4th) 200.

[27] [1979] 1 SCR 183.

discrimination did not amount to sex discrimination under s 1(b) because not all women become pregnant. The court further held that Bliss,
who was denied access to unemployment benefit because she was pregnant, and to pregnancy benefits because she did not meet the qualifying
period imposed by legislation, had not, because she was merely denied
benefits rather than being 'penalised', been denied equality *before* the law.

Canada: the Charter and equality rights

It was in part as a response to the decision in *Bliss* that s 15 of the
Charter of Rights incorporated no fewer than four aspects of equality:
'equality before *and under* the law', 'equal protection *and equal benefit*' of
the law.[28] The 'equal benefit' provision was designed to prevent a repetition of the reasoning in *Bliss*, the guarantee of equality 'under' the law
to preclude a reversion to the Diceyan approach. Neither s 15 nor s 28
imposes an absolute prohibition on discrimination, whether on the
grounds of sex or another listed or analogous characteristic. Section 1
renders the rights guaranteed 'subject . . . to such reasonable limits prescribed by law as can be demonstrably justified in a free and democratic
society'. Nevertheless, when comparing the record of the US and Canadian
Supreme Courts on the interpretation of the equality guarantees set out
in their countries' respective constitutions, it is useful to bear in mind
that Canada's judiciary operate on the basis of much clearer equality
provisions than those provided by the US Constitution. In turn, the wording chosen for s 15's equality guarantee depended on Canada's 'conceptions of the capacities and responsibilities of government. [As Canadians,
w]e are not burdened with visions of the equality that Lincoln sought.
Minimum standards of welfare – welfare payments, subsidized housing,
unemployment insurance, public health insurance, legal aid – are expectations which distinguish us from American society'.[29]

Turning to the application of the Charter of Rights by Canada's
Supreme Court, a preliminary point concerns the purposive approach which,
from the earliest decisions, the Supreme Court took to the provisions of

---

[28] L Smith, 'Have Equality Rights Made Any Difference?', in P Bryden *et al* (eds), *Protecting
Rights and Freedoms: Essays on the Charter's Place in Canada's Political, Legal and Intellectual
Life* (Toronto: University of Toronto Press, 1994), p 66, note 32, author's emphasis. See
also G Brodsky and S Day, *Canadian Charter Equality Rights for Women: One Step Forward or
Two Steps Back?* (Ontario: Canadian Advisory Council on the Status of Women, 1989),
pp 14–15. This was recognised by the Supreme Court in *Andrews v Law Society of British
Columbia* [1989] 1 SCR 143, Justice McIntyre refusing to take into account case law
under the Bill of Rights in the application of the Charter.

[29] A Bayefsky, 'Defining Equality Rights', in M Eberts and A Bayefsky (eds), *Equality Rights
and the Canadian Charter of Rights and Freedoms* (Toronto: Carswell, 1985).

the Charter (see *R v Big M Drug Mart*).[30] Early commentators on the Charter pointed out that this approach boded very well for those who would use it to challenge sex discrimination, the Charter's purposes including 'the fulfilment of Canada's international human rights obligations and the amelioration of group disadvantage' and the continuation of 'the twentieth century trend of increasing human rights protections for disadvantaged groups'.[31] Supreme Court decisions on the scope of s 15 were delayed by the three-year moratorium placed on that section, which did not come into effect until 1985 but, despite *Big M Drug Mart*, the approach initially taken by the lower courts caused a great deal of concern amongst feminists. Certainly, it was widely anticipated that the Supreme Court 'would likely follow the American view that adverse-impact or unintended results are excluded from the definition of discrimination for the purposes of constitutional law and that the similarly situated test of equality would be accepted'.[32]

In 1987, Judy Fudge lamented that neither 'academic exhortation' nor 'repeated litigation' had had much impact in fostering a 'radical new stance to equality rights' on the part of the courts, and remarked that 'commentators who initially hailed the *Charter* as an unqualified victory are now having second thoughts regarding its efficacy in the struggle to end the oppression of historically disadvantaged groups, women included'.[33] And in 1989, after three years of equality litigation under s 15 of the Charter, Gwen Brodsky and Shelagh Day, of the Canadian Advisory Council on the Status of Women, expressed their concern over the formal model of equality at that point adopted by the lower courts: 'if section 15 is reduced to a guarantee of formal equality, women would probably be better served if judges systematically rejected *all* sex equality claims . . . formal equality theory . . . enables men to argue that pregnancy benefits and other special programs for women should be struck down'.[34] Unless the Supreme Court embraced a substantive model of equality, the writers concluded, 'the entrenchment of equality rights may go down in history not as one step forward for women, but as two steps back'.[35]

At that time the lower courts had relied upon s 15 to strike down regulations banning male prison guards from strip-searching women

---

[30] [1985] 1 SCR 295.

[31] Brodsky and Day, note 28 above.

[32] Mahoney, note 15 above, p 10 citing W Tamapolsky, 'The Equality Rights', in W Tamapolsky and G Beaudoin (eds), *The Canadian Charter of Rights and Freedoms: Commentary* (1982) p 442.

[33] 'The Charter and Feminist Struggles' (1987) 25(3) *Osgoode Hall Law Journal* 485, at 487.

[34] Brodsky and Day, note 28 above, p 38.

[35] *Ibid*, p 198. At this stage the Supreme Court had ignored the intervention of the Women's Legal Education and Action Fund (LEAF) in *Canadian Newspapers Co v Canada (Attorney General)* [1988] 2 SCR 122 (see Chapter 9 below), which they decided without reference to equality arguments relating to the complainants.

prisoners and a law which provided benefits for single mothers[36] (in each case on the ground that men were not treated equally). But in 1989 the Supreme Court, in *Andrews v Law Society of British Columbia*, handed down its first s 15 decision.[37] In it, that court expressly adopted a substantive, rather than a formal, model of discrimination. Dealing with a challenge to legislation which made Canadian citizenship a prerequisite for legal practice, Justice McIntyre stated for the court that the distinctions forbidden by s 15 are those which involve prejudice or disadvantage (Justice Wilson going so far as to state that: 's 15 is designed to protect those groups who suffer social, political and legal disadvantage in our society'). Justice McIntyre went on to define discrimination to include its indirect form: 'discrimination may be described as a distinction, whether intentional or not . . . which has the effect of imposing burdens, obligations, or disadvantages on [an] . . . individual or group not imposed on others, or which withholds or limits access to opportunities, benefits, and advantages available to other[s]', and further, stated that '[t]o approach the ideal of full equality before and under the law, the main consideration must be the impact of the law on the individual or the group concerned'.

The decision in *Andrews* was seen as a huge victory for those who concerned themselves with the amelioration of disadvantage, the intervention of the Women's Legal Education and Action Fund having been broadly accepted by the Supreme Court.[38] Not only did that court require that the impact of legislation, rather than its form, be considered, but it also sought to move beyond the sterile search for 'similarly situated' individuals that has bedevilled so much discrimination jurisprudence in the UK and the US.[39] Recognising that 'the concept of equality is a comparative one, the condition of which may only be attained or discerned by comparison with the condition of others in the social and political setting in which the question arises', the court went on to insist that 'every difference in treatment between individuals under the law will not necessarily result in inequality and . . . identical treatment may frequently produce serious inequality'.[40]

In order to fall within s 15, the Supreme Court requires that the complainant 'show not only that he or she is not receiving equal treatment before and under the law or that the law has a differential impact on him or her in the protection or benefit accorded by the law but, in

---

[36] *Phillips v Social Assistance Board (NS)* (1986) 73 NSR (2d) (NSTD), (1986) 34 DLR (4th) 633.

[37] Note 28 above.

[38] See S Razack, *Canadian Feminism and the Law: The Women's LEAF and the Pursuit of Equality* (Toronto: Second Story Press, 1991), pp 104–105.

[39] See also *McKinney v University of Guelph* [1990] 3 SCR 229.

[40] The similarly situated test was rejected because 'it uncritically accepted the distinction drawn by the questioned statute and then proceeded to rely on that same categorisation in order to justify the distinction drawn'. Nevertheless, some comparison was needed as 'discrimination cannot be identified in a vacuum'.

addition, must show that the legislative impact of the law is discriminatory'.[41] This requires an examination of 'the larger context [in order] that a court can determine whether differential treatment results in inequality or whether, contrariwise, it would be identical treatment which would in the particular context result in inequality or foster disadvantage. A finding that there is discrimination will, in most but in perhaps not all cases, necessarily entail a search for disadvantage that exists apart from and independent of the particular legal classification being challenged'.[42]

Not every distinction drawn on the grounds of sex or another personal characteristic protected under s 15(1) breaches that section,[43] because not every such distinction amounts to 'discrimination'. In *Conway v Canada (Attorney General)*,[44] for example, the Supreme Court rejected a challenge by male prisoners to a practice whereby, although female prisoners were not subject to close surveillance or 'frisk' searches carried out by male prison guards, male prisoners were subject to surveillance and search by women guards. Justice La Forest declared, for the unanimous court, that 'the historical trend of violence perpetrated by men against women is not matched by a comparable trend pursuant to which men are the victims and women the aggressors . . . the effect of cross-gender searching is different and more threatening for women than for men. The different treatment to which the appellant objects thus may not be discrimination at all'. In reaching this conclusion the Supreme Court met Brodsky and Day's criticism of the lower court's decision in *Weatherall* (which dealt with similar facts): the demand for 'formal equality . . . ignored completely the reality that unwanted touching by men is a central element of women's inequality in the world and a systemic practice by which they are oppressed and terrorized'.[45]

The decision in *Conway* did not mark the outer boundaries of the Supreme Court's contextual approach to 'discrimination'. In *Eaton v Brant County Board*[46] the court interpreted the purpose of s 15 not only as the elimination of discrimination 'by the attribution of untrue characteristics based on stereotypical attitudes relating to immutable characteristics such

---

[41] *Law Society of British Columbia*, note 28 above. See also *R v Turpin* [1989] 1 SCR 1296; *McKinney v University of Guelph*, note 39 above; *Symes v Canada* [1993] 4 SCR 695; *Miron v Trudel* [1995] 2 SCR 418; *Eaton v Brant County Board* [1997] 1 SCR 241; *Egan v Canada* [1995] 2 SCR 513.

[42] *Turpin, ibid.*

[43] Or grounds analogous thereto.

[44] [1993] 2 SCR 872.

[45] Brodsky and Day, note 28 above, p 79. The decision in *Weatherall et al v Attorney General of Canada et al* (1987) 59 CR (3d) 247, FCTD, is discussed in Brodsky and Day. In the US, the non-discrimination guarantee is regarded as requiring that male prison guards perform the full range of duties in female prisons. The unhappy results of this are documented in *The Human Rights Watch Global Report on Women's Human Rights* (New York: Human Rights Watch, 1995), Chapter 3.

[46] Note 41 above.

as race or sex', but also as the demand for 'the accommodation of difference' which, as the court had pointed out previously in *Andrews v Law Society of British Columbia*,[47] 'is the true essence of equality'.

The full force of the Supreme Court's 'indirect discrimination' test was seen in *Eldridge v British Columbia*,[48] a challenge mounted by deaf applicants to the province's Medical and Health Care Services Act. The Act, which provided free medical treatment, did not provide free translation facilities for deaf people to make use of this treatment. The appellants challenged the Act on the grounds that, in order to benefit from the province's free medical care, they had themselves to meet the cost of translators. The Supreme Court accepted that the application of the legislation violated s 15 because its effect was to 'deny . . . the equal protection or benefit of the law . . . To argue that governments should be entitled to provide benefits to the general population without ensuring that disadvantaged members of society have the resources to take full advantage of those benefits bespeaks a thin and impoverished vision of s 15(1)'.

The analysis set out above should not be taken to mean that there have not been problems with the Canadian Supreme Court's approach to s 15. Not only can one criticise the failure of the majority in *Symes v Canada*[49] to accept women's greater vulnerability to child care costs, and in *Thibaudeau v Canada*[50] to recognise the issue as one of sex discrimination (see Chapter 6 below for discussion of these cases), but there has been increasing tension within the Supreme Court about the meaning of 'discrimination' under s 15. This surfaced most particularly in *Miron v Trudel*[51] and in *Egan v Canada*,[52] which decisions were released concurrently in 1995. In each of these cases four Supreme Court judges (on each occasion joined by a fifth as to result, although not reasoning) took the view that distinctions drawn on grounds protected under s 15 (or analogous thereto) did not constitute 'discrimination' where the grounds were 'relevant' to the object of the legislation.

The approach taken by the plurality in the 1995 decisions was perilously close to the 'similarly situated' test rejected by Canada's Supreme Court in *Andrews*.[53] Just as the latter test accepts the premises of legislators as to who should be regarded as 'similarly situated', thereby failing to challenge the very basis of classification, so the 'relevance' test accepts the premises of legislators as to appropriate ends, and defines as 'not discrimination' the distinctions drawn in order to achieve those ends. In doing so, it requires no more than the 'rational basis' approach applied

---

[47] Note 28 above. See also *Symes v Canada*, note 39 above, discussed below.
[48] [1997] 3 SCR 624.
[49] Note 39 above.
[50] [1995] 2 SCR 627.
[51] Note 48 above.
[52] [1995] 2 SCR 513.
[53] Note 28 above.

(though not in the context of sex discrimination) to the Equal Protection Clause by the US Supreme Court, and would certainly permit more discrimination that that allowed under the 'intermediate scrutiny' of the US Supreme Court.[54] That this interpretation should be adopted in the context of a Charter which, by dint of s 28, regards sex discrimination at least as seriously as it does race discrimination is indeed to be regretted.

The impetus behind judicial retrenchment from *Andrews* appears to have been, as Justice Gonthier put it in *Miron*, the belief that s 15 was never intended to 'become a tool for the wholesale subjection to judicial scrutiny of variegated legislative choices in no way infringing on values fundamental to a free and democratic society'.[55] It was this belief, too, which impelled Madam Justice L'Heureux-Dubé's rethinking of *Andrews* in the *Thibaudeau*, *Miron* and *Egan* cases. Her approach, however, was radical rather than conservative and turned on whether the distinction drawn by legislation was 'capable of either promoting or perpetuating the view that the individual adversely affected by the distinction is less capable, or less worthy of recognition or value as a human being or as a member of Canadian society, equally deserving of concern, respect and consideration'. None of the other justices acknowledged Madam Justice L'Heureux-Dubé's approach either in *Egan* or in the other cases in which she expressed it.

The problems highlighted with the definition of 'discrimination' are not insignificant, and the Supreme Court has yet to determine (if it ever will) a united approach to the application of s 15.[56] What can be said, however, is that, at least in relation to distinctions drawn on the basis of sex, Canada's Supreme Court does not suffer from the unduly formalistic approach which has beset the US Supreme Court. The 'relevancy' test adopted by four Supreme Court justices in the cases of *Egan* and *Miron* is capable of having a profoundly conservative impact on s 15. But this test is unlikely to be embraced by any of the other justices in place at the time of the decisions and, Justice La Forest (who with Justice Gonthier put forward the 'relevancy' test) having resigned from the Supreme Court in September 1997, it may be that Gonthier J will become more, rather than less, isolated in his application of it. Certainly, the degree of scope it permits legislatures to disadvantage the already disadvantaged is out of keeping with the context in which the increasingly deferential approach was developed (ie post *Oakes* (see below), in relation to legislation intended to assist the disadvantaged) and out of character with the tone

---

[54] Mahoney, note 15 above, pp 32–34, citing R Hawkes and R Martin, 'Democracy, Judging and Bertha Wilson' (1995) 41 *McGill Law Journal* 1, suggests that the shift in approach was a response to the increasing criticism of judicial intervention.

[55] Citing Justice La Forest in *Andrews v Law Society of British Columbia*, note 28 above.

[56] Mahoney, note 15 above, suggests that the shift, although not yet followed by a majority of the Supreme Court, was having an impact in the lower courts.

of decisions such as *Eldridge* above, in which Justice La Forest himself delivered the court's unanimous decision.

Canada: qualifying rights

The next issue which must be considered, in the Canadian context, relates to the role of s 1 of the Charter of Rights. In the US, as mentioned above, constitutional rights may be restricted to the extent that these restrictions pass varying degrees of judicial scrutiny. Canada's Charter expressly permits guaranteed rights to be subject to such 'reasonable limits prescribed by law as can be demonstrably justified in a free and democratic society', this provision containing, as was pointed out by early commentators, 'three of the most open-ended concepts in any language'.[57]

In *R v Oakes*,[58] the Supreme Court set out the analytical framework to be applied under s 1 in assessing whether the limits imposed by the State on the rights and freedoms set out in the Charter were 'reasonable'. The Supreme Court ruled that s 1 required that the objective in pursuit of which entrenched rights were limited was of 'sufficient importance to warrant overriding a constitutionally protected right or freedom' and that the party invoking s 1 shows that the means chosen to achieve the objective are 'reasonable and demonstrably justified'. This latter requirement involved the application of a proportionality test which would be satisfied only if 'the measures adopted . . . [were] carefully designed to achieve the objective in question', and were not 'arbitrary, unfair or based on irrational considerations'; that 'the means, even if rationally connected to the objective in the first sense . . . impair as little as possible the right or freedom in question'; and that 'there . . . [was] a proportionality between the effects of the measures and the objective which has been identified as of sufficient importance'.

According to the Supreme Court in *Oakes*, the standard imposed under the first limb of the test would be high 'in order to ensure that objectives which are trivial or discordant with the principles integral to a free and democratic society do not gain s 1 protection. At a minimum, an objective must relate to concerns which are pressing and substantial in a free and democratic society.' And, as far as the third element of the proportionality test was concerned, '[t]he more severe the deleterious effects of a measure, the more important the objective must be if the measure is to be reasonable and demonstrably justified'.[59] Where the measure

---

[57] A Lajoie and H Quillinan, 'The Supreme Court Judges' Views of the Role of the Courts in the Application of the Charter', in Bryden *et al* (eds), note 28 above, p 95.
[58] [1986] 1 SCR 103.
[59] *Ibid.*

chosen, although rationally related to the achievement of an objective acceptable under the first limb of the test, would result only in partial achievement of it, the third limb of the proportionality test would measure 'the underlying objective of a measure and the salutary effects that actually result from its implementation' against 'the deleterious effects the measure has on fundamental rights and freedoms'.[60]

In *Oakes* the Supreme Court stated that the nature of the proportionality test under s 1 would vary with the circumstances. It appeared, subsequently, that that decision was a high water mark for the Supreme Court's interventionist approach and, although the court has retained the analytical framework of *Oakes*, it has become more accepting of government action. In *Edwards Books and Art Ltd et al v R*,[61] for example, it drew a distinction between cases in which the legislature 'mediates between the competing claims of different groups in the community', and those in which 'government is best characterized as the singular antagonist of the individual whose right has been infringed'.[62] Although, in the latter case, the courts should require that the government had chosen the ' "least drastic means" for achieving the purpose'(citing *Irwin Toy v Quebec*[63]), where competing claims were concerned, it was enough that government:

> has made a reasonable assessment as to where the line [between those claims] is most properly drawn, especially if that assessment involves weighing conflicting scientific evidence and allocating scarce resources on this basis, it is not for the court to second-guess. Democratic institutions are meant to let us all share in the responsibility for these difficult choices . . . as courts review the results of the legislature's deliberations, particularly with respect to the protection of vulnerable groups, they must be mindful of the legislature's representative function.[64]

In *Slaight Communications Inc v Davidson*,[65] the Supreme Court declared that Canada's international human rights obligations should be taken into account in the application of s 1, objectives which were reflective of internationally recognised human rights properly being regarded as having a high degree of importance.[66] The Supreme Court relied upon Canada's ratification of the International Covenant on Economic, Social and Cultural Rights, and its commitment to protect the right to work, in upholding a reinstatement order under Canada's Labour Code against challenge by the employer:

---

[60] *Dagenais v Canadian Broadcasting Corporation* [1994] 3 SCR 835.
[61] [1986] 2 SCR 713.
[62] *Ibid.*
[63] [1989] 1 SCR 927; *McKinney v University of Guelph*, note 39 above; *Stoffman v Vancouver General Hospital* [1990] 3 SCR 483; *Laba* [1994] 3 SCR 965.
[64] *Edwards Books and Art Ltd et al v R*, note 61 above, at 779.
[65] [1989] 1 SCR 1038.
[66] See also *Ross v New Brunswick School District No 15* [1996] 1 SCR 825.

It cannot be over-emphasized that the order was a legislatively sanctioned attempt to remedy the unequal balance of power that normally exists between an employer and employee. Thus, in a general sense, this case falls within a class of cases in which the governmental objective is that of protection of a particularly vulnerable group, or members thereof . . . the courts must be cautious to ensure that (the Charter) does not simply become an instrument of better situated individuals to roll back legislation which has as its object the improvement of the condition of less advantaged persons.[67]

The approach taken by the Supreme Court to s 1 has been explicitly contextual, to the extent that it has been accused of citing *Oakes* 'as a formalistic foundation to embed fundamental judicial principles . . . [in an] attempt to avoid the appearance that they are involved in undemocratic decisions on the fundamental norms and values of a society that has a representative form of government'.[68] More positively, the Supreme Court has emphasised that s 1 should not be conceived of as a 'rigid and technical provision',[69] that '[i]t is important not to lose sight of factual circumstances in undertaking a s.1 analysis, for these shape a court's view of both the right or freedom at stake and the limit proposed by the state',[70] that 'Parliament . . . need not always choose the absolutely least intrusive means to attain its objectives but must come within a range of means which impair Charter rights as little as is reasonable possible',[71] that 'the *Oakes* test must be applied flexibly, having regard to the factual and social context of each case [although] . . . [c]ontext . . . cannot be carried to the extreme of treating the challenged law as a unique socio-economic phenomenon, of which Parliament is deemed the best judge'.[72]

The contextual approach, which tends to manifest itself in a generous degree of judicial deference to the legislature, has become increasingly marked over time as the Supreme Court 'has rethought its position on . . . the conception of the state and the proper scope of judicial review'[73] and, to a lesser extent, on the conception of freedom. As Robin Elliott points out, the justices of the Supreme Court had shared 'strictly negative' 'conceptions of the state and of freedom' in *Oakes* and were 'distinctly unimpressed with claims that the court should exercise caution in its

---

[67] *Slaight Communications Inc v Davidson*, note 65 above, at 105 (internal citations omitted). For the evolving approach of the Supreme Court to s 1, see R Elliott, 'The Supreme Court's Rethinking of the Charter's Fundamental Questions (Or Why the Charter Keeps Getting More Interesting)', in P Bryden *et al* (eds), note 28 above, p 146.

[68] E Mendes, 'The Crucible of the Charter: Judicial Principles v Judicial Deference in the Context of Section 1', in G Beaudoin and E Mendes (eds) *The Canadian Charter of Rights and Freedoms* (3rd ed, Ottawa: Carswell, 1996), p 332.

[69] *R v Keegstra* [1990] 3 SCR 697.

[70] *Ibid.* See also *Harvey v New Brunswick* [1996] 2 SCR 842.

[71] *Swain* [1991] 1 SCR 933.

[72] *RJR-MacDonald v Canada* [1995] 3 SCR 199. See also *Eldridge v British Columbia*, note 48 above.

[73] See Elliott, note 67 above.

checking function under the Charter'. Chief Justice Dickson stated in *Hunter v Southam*[74] that the Charter 'is intended to constrain governmental action inconsistent with [individual] rights and freedoms; it is not itself an authorization for governmental action' and, in *Big M Drug Mart*,[75] that '[f]reedom can primarily be characterized by the absence of coercion or constraint'.[76] In *R v Morgentaler (No 2)*,[77] Madam Justice Wilson had characterised rights as fences around individuals wherein they can be free from the State. But in 1986, the decision in *Edwards Books* had already indicated the seeds of a more positive approach to the State.[78]

In *R v Keegstra*,[79] in which the Supreme Court upheld the restriction of racist propaganda, Justice Dickson, for the majority, stated that 'self-autonomy stems in large part from one's ability to articulate and nurture an identity derived from membership in a cultural or religious group'.[80] The judgment recognised that s 15 could be utilised, not only to strike down law which conflicted with the equality guarantee, but also to support laws which impacted on other rights protected under the Charter (there to determine the appropriate limits of freedom of expression).[81] And finally, in *McKinney v University of Guelph*,[82] Madam Justice Wilson (who was generally regarded as the most strongly interventionist of judges[83]) declared 'untenable' the proposition that 'freedom is co-extensive with the absence of government', and stated that 'freedom has often required the intervention and protection of government against private action'.[84] While this approach does not extend to requiring positive action on the part of the State (see below), it does permit the courts to take into account Charter rights in upholding laws which impinge on other rights.[85]

Canada: State action

However positive the approach of Canada's Supreme Court to the application of s 15 of the Charter of Rights, much of the potential benefit of the Charter has been restricted by the narrow interpretation the Supreme

---

[74] [1984] 2 SCR 145.
[75] *Big M Drug Mart Ltd* [1985] 1 SCR 295.
[76] Elliott, note 67 above, p 134.
[77] [1988] 1 SCR 30.
[78] *Edwards Books and Art Ltd et al v R*, note 61 above. See also P Monahan, 'The Charter Then and Now', in Bryden *et al* (eds), note 28 above, p 112.
[79] Note 69 above.
[80] *Keegstra*, ibid.
[81] See Mahoney, note 15 above, p 24. Cf the approach to records in sexual assault cases, for which see Chapter 9 below.
[82] Note 63 above.
[83] See Lajoie and Quillinan, note 57 above.
[84] Note 63, at 356.
[85] Mahoney, note 15 above, p 24.

Court has adopted to the Charter's scope. In common with most constitutional rights (see Chapter 10 for discussion of the European Convention on Human Rights), the Charter does not bind private individuals but has effect only against 'government'.[86] The Canadian Supreme Court has taken a very narrow approach to 'government' within s 32. The fact that a body is 'engaged in activities where the provision of services that are subject to the legislative jurisdiction of either the federal or provincial governments'[87] is insufficient to render it subject to the provisions of the Charter.[88]

Where the body whose action is challenged under the Charter is accepted by the courts to constitute part of 'government' properly so-called,[89] the Charter will apply to its 'private' or 'commercial' arrangements: 'governments should not be permitted to evade their *Charter* responsibilities by implementing policy through the vehicle of private arrangements'.[90] But where, as is more commonly the case, the fact that a body carries out some 'inherently governmental actions' is not sufficient to render that body 'part of the fabric of government', the Charter will apply to it, as in *Eldridge* above, only in so far as it acts 'in furtherance of [the] specific governmental programme or policy'. Notwithstanding the Supreme Court's claim that it was adopting a wide view of the Charter's application in *Eldridge*, its approach in that case and in *McKinney* permits governments to avoid Charter obligations in respect of 'private' or 'commercial' activities by contracting out governmental functions to private sector bodies which are not, then, bound by the Charter in relation to their 'private' or 'commercial' activities.

However unfortunate the limitations on the scope of the Charter already discussed, they pale into insignificance in comparison with the limitation imposed by the Supreme Court in the now infamous *Dolphin Delivery* decision in 1986, in which the court ruled that the common law was not vulnerable to review under the Charter.[91] The Charter applies to the common law, whether in public or private litigation, only to the extent that the common law is the basis of governmental action which is claimed to infringe a Charter right.[92] According to Ontario's Court of Appeal in *Domm*[93]: 'the Charter is not designed to constrain judicial conduct in the

---

[86] Section 32(1).
[87] *McKinney v University of Guelph,* note 39 above.
[88] See *McKinney, ibid*; *Stoffman v Vancouver General Hospital,* note 63 above.
[89] This having been accepted to extend to Crown agencies established to implement government policy, to Canada's post office, to some statutory bodies, to law societies, municipal governments and government appointed adjudicators – see *Douglas Faculty Association v Douglas College* [1990] 3 SCR 570; *Chyz v Appraisal Institute of Canada* (1984) 13 CRR 3; *Klein and Dvorak v Law Society of Upper Canada* (1985) 16 DLR (4th) 489; *McCutcheon v City of Toronto et al* (1983) 147 DLR (3d) 193.
[90] Justice La Forest in *Eldridge v British Columbia,* note 48 above, citing his own judgment in *Lavigne v Ontario Public Service Employees Union* [1991] 2 SCR 211.
[91] *RWDSU v Dolphin Delivery Ltd* [1986] 2 SCR 573.
[92] See also *Tremblay v Daigle* [1989] 2 SCR 530; *Hill v Church of Scientology of Toronto* [1995] 2 SCR 1130. Cf the approach of the US Supreme Court in *Shelley v Kraemer* 334 US 1 (1948).
[93] [1996] OJ No 4300, Ont CA. See also Madam Justice L'Heureux-Dubé, dissenting, in *Dagenais v Canadian Broadcasting Corporation,* note 60 above.

same way it restrains legislative activity . . . compliance with the Charter cannot be seen as a mandatory condition precedent to the exercise of judicial authority in the same way as it is in respect of legislative activity'.

The court order at issue in *Dolphin Delivery* consisted of an injunction against secondary action, such action being prohibited by the common law. In 1991 David Beatty described the decision as 'the most criticized judgment the Supreme Court has issued on the *Charter*', and condemned it on the ground that:

> it turns the entire organization of our system of government, and the place of the Constitution, on its head. In putting the judge-made rules . . . beyond the reach of the *Charter* whenever they regulate the behaviour of two or more individuals or groups, the Court disregarded the principle of constitutional supremacy enshrined in section 52 of the *Charter* [and] elevated its own rules to a position above and beyond the Constitution itself. It reversed the hierarchy that logically exists between constitutions and ordinary, subordinate law and, in so doing, licensed the judges . . . to exercise their legal authority free of any constitutional constraints.[94]

But the Supreme Court has gone even further in recent years to isolate portions of the law from Charter review. In *Young v Young*,[95] Madam Justice L'Heureux-Dubé, with Justices La Forest and Gonthier, reached their decision in a custody dispute on the basis that, the 'best interests of the child' test adopted by the Divorce Act itself being constitutional, 'the order of the trial judge is not subject to the *Charter*'. Of the other four justices who took part in the decision, only Justice Sopinka expressly found that the Charter was applicable to judicial orders granted under the Divorce Act. According to Madam Justice L'Heureux-Dubé:

> the state['s] role in custody and access decisions does not transform the essentially private character of parent–child exchanges into activity which should be subject to *Charter* scrutiny. The principles enunciated in *Dolphin Delivery* [apply] as custody and access matters are essentially private in nature and there exists no state action to be impugned.[96]

Positive rights?

The approach to discrimination under the Canadian Charter of Rights could scarcely be more different than that which applies under the

---

[94] 'Labouring outside the Charter' (1991) 29(4) *Osgoode Hall Law Journal* 841, at 843. Cf P Hogg, *Constitutional Law of Canada* (2nd ed, Ontario: Carswell, 1992), p 844. See also G Anderson, 'Filling the "Charter Gap"?: Human Rights Codes in the Private Sector' (1995) 33(4) *Osgoode Hall Law Journal* 749, at 762.

[95] [1993] 4 SCR 3.

[96] *Ibid*, at 90–1. This is not to say that the Charter has no impact upon the common law – see *Power v Moss* (1986) 61 Nfld & PEIR 5; *R v Robinson* [1996] 1 SCR 683; *Cloutier v Langlois* [1990] 1 SCR 158; *Dagenais v Canadian Broadcasting Corporation*, note 60 above.

Fourteenth Amendment of the US Constitution. These differences can be seen not only in the provisions themselves, but also in their application by the judiciary. Disparities in approach can be seen, further, in the final, very significant, restriction on the rights guaranteed under both the US Constitution and Canada's Charter of Rights – that is, their generally negative nature. This nature is connected in part with their 'bite' only upon the State, rather than private individuals – the courts will not interpret the rights so as to protect against their infringement by private individuals, there bring no obligation on the courts positively to promote these rights, as distinct from protecting them from government-implicated interference. But the character of rights as 'negative' goes well beyond this, shielding even government itself from the obligation positively to protect them.

The US Supreme Court has been more ready to protect constitutional rights against private interference, albeit in limited situations, than Canada's courts. According to Lawrence Tribe, in the US 'common law is state action – that is . . . the state "acts" when its courts create and enforce common law rules'.[97] Thus, in *American Federation of Labor v Swing*,[98] the US Supreme Court ruled that a common law injunction against secondary picketing violated the free speech guarantees of the First Amendment. The US courts have, more generally, been willing to apply the Constitution to action 'under color of law' – that is, which has been permitted by law, whether or not it is required.[99] This is not to say that every action permitted by law is subject to challenge under the US Constitution. But where the disputed action involves 'the exercise of some right or privilege created by the State or by a rule of conduct imposed by it or by a person for whom it is responsible, and . . . the party charged with the deprivation . . . may fairly be said to be a state actor, either because he is a state official, because he has acted together with or has obtained significant aid from state officials, or because his conduct is otherwise chargeable to the State', the constitutional protections will apply.[100]

To this extent, but this only, the US courts afford to those rights a measure of positive protection. On the other hand, the US courts are steely in their refusal to impose positive obligations upon the State. The Supreme Court has, on occasion, ruled that access to government benefits cannot be conditioned upon the sacrifice of constitutional rights.[101] But the application of what has been called the 'unconstitutional

---

[97]   L Tribe, *American Constitutional Law* (2nd ed, 1988), p 1711 cited by Hogg, note 94 above, p 846.
[98]   312 US 321 (1941).
[99]   *American Federation of Labor v Swing, ibid.*; note 92 above.
[100]   *Lugar v Edmondson Oil Co* 457 US 922 (1982); *Jackson v Metropolitan Edison Co* 419 US 345 (1974); *Lebron v National Railroad Passenger Corporation* (Case no 93–1525, 1995).
[101]   *Speiser v Randall* 357 US 513 (1958); *Sherbert v Verner* 374 US 398 (1963); *Shapiro v Thompson* 394 US 618 (1969). See also *Graham v Richardson* 403 US 365 (1971), in which the denial of benefits to aliens was held unconstitutional.

conditions' doctrine has never been consistent, John Hand arguing that, in this context, the Supreme Court 'reaches its decision based purely or primarily on the particular facts and retrospectively tailors its opinion to comport with this first conclusion'.[102] Those cases in which Hand found that the doctrine was particularly unlikely to be applied involved indigent plaintiffs (in particular, women seeking abortions) and Native Americans, even when the latter challenged religious restrictions generally struck down in respect of other categories of plaintiff.[103]

Turning to cases particularly relevant to the subject matter of this book, the 1970 decision of the Supreme Court in *Dandridge v Williams*[104] is of particular interest. In it, the Supreme Court upheld 'family cap' legislation imposing an absolute limit upon welfare payments, regardless of family size. The plaintiffs argued that the legislation infringed the Equal Protection Clause by penalising large families who were denied the level of support accepted as necessary on the State's own calculations. The court dismissed the argument, stating that no 'invidious' or 'suspect' classification had been adopted by the State and that the legislation was acceptable to relaxed scrutiny, being rationally related to the State's interest in encouraging employment. According to the Supreme Court:

> [i]n the area of economics and social welfare, a state does not violate the Equal Protection Clause merely because the classifications made by its laws are imperfect. If the classification has some rational basis, it does not offend the Constitution simply because the classification is not made with mathematical nicety or because in practice it results in some inequality.[105]

It need hardly be pointed out that the impact of legislation such as that upheld in *Dandridge* is to deter the exercise of any right to procreate.[106] The Supreme Court itself recognised the huge differences between the 'regulation of business and industry', in respect of which the 'rational basis' test had been established, and 'the administration of public welfare [which], by contrast, involves the most basic economic needs of impoverished human beings'. Nevertheless, it refused to apply a heightened standard of review, one majority failing even to address the impact of the welfare restrictions upon fundamental rights. Justice Marshall, dissenting, protested that the restrictions impacted on 'the stuff that sustains . . . children's lives'. However inconsistent the decision of the Supreme

---

[102] J Hand, 'Buying Fertility: The Constitutionality of Welfare Bonuses' (1993) 46 *Vanderbilt Law Review* 715, at 737.

[103] *Ibid*, at 738. The former subgroup never won, and 69% of indigents lost. By contrast, 'deadbeat fathers' had a high chance of success.

[104] 397 US 471 (1970).

[105] *Ibid*, at 485, internal citations omitted.

[106] The right to procreate was recognised in *Skinner v State of Oklahoma* 316 US 535 (1942), see Chapters 4 and 5 below. Family caps also serve to punish children for the 'sins' of their mothers, contrary to the minority reasoning in *King v Smith* 392 US 309 (1968). See also *US Department of Agriculture v Moreno* 413 US 528 (1973).

Court in *Dandridge* with those in *Speiser v Randall, Sherbert v Verner* and *Shapiro v Thompson*,[107] the *Dandridge* approach has been applied in relation to abortion funding, the state being at liberty to fund the child-bearing option while refusing to provide funds for terminations. These cases, and their application in the abortion context, are discussed further in Chapters 4 and 5 below.

The extent to which the State is free practically to restrict or deny rights to the poor by making access to benefit conditional upon their sacrifice is unclear, although the trend away from the 'unconstitutional conditions' doctrine, at least in this area, is apparent in a series of decisions reached between 1986 and 1988, in all of which cases the Supreme Court permitted government to coerce families into particular living arrangements in order to qualify for welfare payments.[108] While the Supreme Court accepted that there was a constitutionally protected right to freedom of family living arrangements; in each of these cases the majority judgments relied upon the claim that the welfare rules did not 'directly and substantially' interfere with the right of welfare recipients to live as they choose and that, therefore, no heightened scrutiny was appropriate.

Leaving aside those cases in which the State conditions benefits on sacrifice of a constitutional right, it is clear that the US Constitution does not require the State to fund the exercise of rights, even where funding 'may be necessary to secure life . . . interests of which the government itself may not deprive the individual'. The relevant law is set out in the Supreme Court's decision in *DeShaney v Winnebago County*,[109] in which that court rejected a claim made by a child against the social services department which had failed to protect him from his father.[110] The department had been notified about the beatings to which the child was subjected, and which eventually resulted in brain damage which left him profoundly retarded but, although they did take some steps, they did not remove him from his father's custody. It was claimed on behalf of the child that the department had deprived him of his liberty interest in bodily integrity, in violation of the Due Process Clause of the Fourteenth Amendment, by failing to protect him. The Supreme Court ruled that:

> the Due Process Clause . . . imposes no duty on the State to provide members of the general public with adequate protective services. The Clause

---

[107] All cited at, note 101 above.

[108] *Lyng v Castillo* 477 US 635 (1986); *Bowen v Gilliard* 483 US 587 (1987) and *Lyng v Automobile Workers* 485 US 360 (1988). The distinction between 'penalties' and 'non-subsidies' drawn in *Dandridge v Williams*, note 104 above, and *Rust v Sullivan* 500 US 173 (1991) appears to have originated in *Maher v Roe* 432 US 464 (1977) – see further Chapter 4 below.

[109] 489 US 189 (1989).

[110] See also *MLB v SL J* (Case no 95–853, 1996) and the line of authorities therein distinguishing access to court being made dependent on a fee which a person cannot meet. The same approach is taken in criminal appeals: *Mayer v Chicago* 404 US 189 (1971); *Griffin v State of Illinois* 351 US 12 (1956); and in some civil proceedings: *Boddie v State of Connecticut* 401 US 371 (1971).

is phrased as a limitation on the State's power to act, not as a guarantee of certain minimal levels of safety and security; while it forbids the State itself to deprive individuals of life, liberty, and property without due process of law, its language cannot fairly be read to impose an affirmative obligation on the State to ensure that those interests do not come to harm through other means.[111]

The decision in *DeShaney* was made in relation to the Constitution's Due Process Clause. But the denial of positive effect is a general one.[112] As the American Civil Liberties Union (ACLU) has pointed out, the non-application of constitutionally entrenched rights to corporations which 'dwarf state and local governments'[113] together with (in the US) the very limited nature of employment regulation, has left employers free to violate the civil liberties of their employees. Among the many examples of such violations is the fact that at least two million Americans are subject each year to psychological recruitment tests which include intimate questions such as those relating to candidates' sex lives.

The approach taken by the Canadian Supreme Court is somewhat different to that of its US counterpart. On the one hand, the application of the Charter only to the 'State', narrowly defined, is a cardinal rule (even the courts being exempted, for the most part, from its strictures). On the other hand, that court has been much more prepared than the US Supreme Court to impose positive obligations on government itself to act (see, for example, *Eldridge* above). If the obligation on the State to take positive action were sufficiently strong, the non-application of constitutional rights against private individuals would be rendered largely meaningless, as the State would be required to safeguard such rights by legislation. Indeed, it has been argued in the Canadian context that the existence of human rights legislation both federally and in each province renders irrelevant the non-application of the Charter's equality provisions against private bodies (all these codes prohibiting *inter alia* sex discrimination).[114] But it has been pointed out that Canada's various human rights codes fall short of filling the 'Charter gap':

> the more closely one examines the *Charter* and human rights regimes, the more they appear to have in common . . . they are both individual comparator-

---

[111] *DeShaney v Winnebago County*, note 109 above at 195, internal citations omitted.

[112] See also the decision of the US District Court in *Brzonkala v Virginia Polytechnic Institute and State University* 935 F Supp 779 (1996) on the limitations on the power, as distinct from the obligation, of government to legislate on the basis of the Equal Protection Clause (a constitutional basis being required for federal legislation). Although the decision was overturned – 132 F 3d 949 (1997) – the later decision did not rely on the Equal Protection Clause.

[113] ACLU, *Workplace Rights: Wrongful Discharge*, available at http://www.aclu.org/issues/worker/legkit6.html. See, more generally, http://www.aclu.org.

[114] Labour law being regulated at the provincial level save in the case of a relatively limited number of 'federal' employees. For discussion of these statutes, see A Aggarwal, *Sex Discrimination: Employment Law and Practices* (Toronto: Butterworths, 1994), Chapter 1 and *passim*.

based systems enforcing liberal rights . . . the institutional structure of the human rights codes prevents an effective challenge to established patterns of inequality . . . the doctrinal framework within which both regimes operate is committed to removing certain private issues from regulation in the name of equality.[115]

Returning to the issue of the extent to which the Canadian Charter of Rights imposes positive obligations upon government, even prior to the decision in *Eldridge* there had been suggestions from the Supreme Court that 'a government may be required to take positive steps to ensure the equality of people or groups who come within the scope of s 15' (*Haig v Canada Chief Electoral Officer*[116]). But this has never been taken to require more than that, 'once the state does provide a benefit, it [must] do so in a non-discriminatory manner', even if that requires positive action from government in the form of extension of benefits previously denied, and possibly that 'in taking this sort of positive action, the government should not be the source of further inequality'.[117]

In *Haig*, in the context of the right to freedom of expression, Madam Justice L'Heureux-Dubé stated that 'genuine autonomy presupposes the legislature's active intervention if necessary . . . in order to make a fundamental freedom meaningful . . . positive government action might be required'. And in *Vriend v Alberta*,[118] the Supreme Court ruled that the failure of Alberta's Human Rights Code to enumerate sexual orientation amongst its prohibited grounds of discrimination amounted to a breach of the Charter: 'the fact that it is the underinclusiveness of the [legislation] which is at issue does not alter the fact that it is the legislative act which is the subject of *Charter* scrutiny in this case'.[119]

In *Vriend* Lamer CJ, for the majority, stated that it was 'unnecessary to consider whether a government could properly be subjected to a challenge under s 15 . . . for failing to act at all', noting that this possibility had been left open by Madam Justice L'Heureux-Dubé for the majority in *Haig*, by Chief Justice Dickson in *Reference re PSERA (Alberta)*[120] and by Justice La Forest for the Supreme Court in *Eldridge*. But despite occasional tantalising hints it seems likely that, if pressed, the Supreme Court would follow the ruling made in 1997 by Ontario's Divisional Court in *Ferrell v Attorney General of Ontario*:[121]

---

[115] Anderson, note 94 above, at 777.
[116] [1993] 2 SCR 995.
[117] *Eldridge v British Columbia*, note 48 above, para 73, *per* Justice La Forest citing *Tétreault-Gadoury v Canada* [1991] 2 SCR 22; *Haig v Canada* [1993] 2 SCR 995; *Native Women's Association of Canada v Canada* [1994] 3 SCR 627; and *Miron v Trudel*, note 41 above.
[118] [1998] 1 SCR 493.
[119] *Ibid*, at para. 55. The Supreme Court read it in by a majority on the assumption that the legislature would have enacted the statute including this provision, rather than not enacted the statute at all.
[120] [1987] 1 SCR 995.
[121] 149 DLR (4th) 335. The Court of Appeal's decision is at 168 DLR (4th) 1.

The application of the Charter must be confined to government action as opposed to inaction . . . we must take care to distinguish between effects which are wholly caused, or are contributed to, by an impugned provision, and those societal circumstances which exist independently of such a provision. The overwhelming weight of authority negates the existence of any duty under the Charter to legislate. There is nothing in s 15, either explicit or implicit, or elsewhere in the Charter for that matter, which can be pointed to as imposing such an obligation.[122]

Conclusion

This chapter has provided an introduction to the approaches taken under the US Constitution and Canada's Charter of Rights to equality and discrimination (in particular, sex discrimination). It has also outlined some of the most important general issues which arise in the application of 'constitutional' rights to those areas which form the subject matter of Chapters 4–9. These issues are not those which every scholar would flag as the most potentially problematic. But in terms of the application of constitutional rights to women as reproducers, as workers and as the victims of violence they are among the most significant. This will become apparent in the discussion in the following chapters.

---

[122] *Ibid*, citing Justice Iacobucci in *Symes v Canada*, note 41 above (internal citations omitted) and (US) *Board of Education of Kiryas Joel Village School v Grunet* (1994) 124 US 2481. See also the unanimous decision in *R v S (S)* [1992] 2 SCR 254, in which the Supreme Court ruled that the non-exercise of discretion by the Attorney General (there to establish alternative programmes for young offenders) could not be reviewed under s 15 of the Charter.

Chapter 4

Reproducing Women

Introduction

In order to consider the extent to which constitutionally entrenched rights may function to women's benefit, it is useful to cover the issue of abortion in the US in the wake of the Supreme Court's 1973 decision in *Roe v Wade*.[1] In that case the Supreme Court ruled that the Fourteenth Amendment to the US Constitution protected women's 'right to choose'. This right was not express in the Amendment but was carved by the Supreme Court out of the right to privacy which was, in turn, located in its Due Process Clause. The right was qualified by the legitimate interests of the State in protecting 'both the pregnant woman's health and the potentiality of human life'. But because the right to privacy was fundamental, government interference with it was subject to strict judicial scrutiny: such interference would be unconstitutional except where necessary to serve a compelling and legitimate government interest.[2]

According to the Supreme Court, a woman's interest in privacy waned, and the interests of the State became more compelling, as the pregnancy progressed. Applying the 'strict scrutiny' approach, the court adopted a three-stage test. Justice Blackmun, for the majority, declared that the woman's right to privacy was paramount during the first trimester, decisions regarding termination being left to the medical judgment of her doctor; that the State's interest in the woman's health permitted the regulation of the abortion procedure 'in ways that are reasonably related to maternal health' after that trimester and that, once the foetus was viable, the State's 'interest in the potentiality of human life' permitted it to 'regulate, and even proscribe, abortion except where necessary, in appropriate medical judgment, for the preservation of the life or health of the mother'.

[1] 410 US 113 (1973).
[2] See *Skinner v State of Oklahoma* 316 US 535 (1942).

The decision mandated a very liberal abortion regime – termination on request for the first three months of pregnancy followed, until month seven or eight (depending upon when and how viability was established) with only those restrictions imposed in the interests of the woman's health, rather than those of the foetus. Not until the foetus was capable of being born alive were abortion restrictions based upon that prospective life permitted, and even these were subject to overriding concern with the health, as well as the life, of the woman. Having said this, it should be noted that the 'right to choose' did not rest with the woman herself, in which case at least early termination would necessarily be lawful. Rather, the right was to be exercised in conjunction with the woman's doctor, with the effect that terminations by persons other than doctors remained unlawful even after *Roe*.[3]

Women in the US have a constitutionally protected right to abortion (albeit one which requires that the termination be performed by a doctor) which goes far beyond any legal rights of women in Great Britain (abortion remaining largely unlawful in Northern Ireland). In theory, British women have no 'right' to abortion – the Abortion Act 1967 requiring that two doctors agree that the foetus has a substantial risk of serious abnormalities, that the pregnancy poses the risk of 'grave permanent injury to the physical or mental health of the pregnant woman', or that continuation of the pregnancy would involve risk, 'greater than if the pregnancy were terminated', either to the life of the pregnant woman or 'of injury to the physical or mental health of the pregnant woman or any existing children of her family' (his latter is the so-called 'social clause').[4] In Britain, by contrast with the position in the US, abortion is only available on medical grounds, albeit grounds that are generously drawn.[5] Here, again by contrast with the position in the US, abortions are permitted after viability (here fixed at 24 weeks) only in cases of foetal handicap or where the woman risks death or 'grave permanent injury'.

It would appear that women's right to choose is more protected in the US than it is in Britain. But closer examination reveals that this may not in fact be true. In practice, the 'social clause' permitting abortion in Great Britain is fairly widely interpreted and the difficulties that women experience in securing pre-viability abortions generally relate to NHS funding rather than absolute availability. This is not to downplay those very real difficulties regarding practical access to abortion (not least for Northern Irish women who must, like their Southern sisters, travel to Britain or elsewhere for abortions). Nor is it to deny that reproductive freedoms are threatened in the UK. There are occasional outcries such as those

---

[3] *State of Connecticut v Menillo* 423 US 9 (1975). See R Rotunda, '*Roe*'s Defenders Should Question Whom it Protects', *National Law Journal*, 25 January 1993.
[4] Abortion Act 1967, s 1(1)(a).
[5] In the US there are no restrictions on the reasons behind the abortion until viability.

over the selective abortion of one of twins in summer 1996 and the launch of 'lunchhour abortions' by the Marie Stopes organisation in summer 1997; and periodic attempts to restrict access to abortion.[6] But wholesale politicisation of the issue has not occurred despite attempts by Scottish Cardinal Winning and the Pro-Life Alliance to make abortion into a polling issue in the May 1997 election.[7] And those cases in which access to abortion is challenged (such as *Kelly v Kelly*,[8] discussed in Chapter 10 below) more often lead to calls for relaxation, than for restriction, of the laws governing the procedure.

In the US, by contrast, abortion ranks as among the most divisive of political issues. Recent polls suggest that the majority in favour of legal abortion has dropped from around two-thirds of those polled in the early 1990s to only 56 per cent in 1997, and up to 42 per cent of the electorate would place their vote on the basis of the candidates' attitudes to abortion.[9]

In 1996, at the federal level alone, abortion figured highly in the Presidential election with the defeated Republican candidate Bob Dole and his party declaring themselves in favour of a constitutional ban; Republicans unsuccessfully attempted to eliminate state funding for abortions save where the woman's life was at risk and, during federal moves to ban the dilation and extraction abortion procedure (see below), 27 million postcards were distributed by Christian churches in an attempt to influence the outcome. Nor was 1996 atypical, or activities at the federal level unrepresentative of what was going on in the states: during the Bush and Reagan Presidencies, the Federal Congress had about nine abortion-related votes every year and in 1995 and 1996, by which stage both Houses were under Republican control, 53 votes took place; in 1990, almost 400 abortion Bills were debated in 41 US state legislatures and most US states have passed one or more restrictions on abortion in the past two years.[10] These restrictions, which include the imposition of waiting periods and parental consent requirements, are discussed below.

Opposition to abortion in the US is such that it was not until 1993 that the US lifted an import ban on RU 486 (mifepristone), a drug which permits medical abortions and could do much to undermine the effectiveness of the anti-abortion activists in the US. Although the pill is relatively widely available in Europe, the strength of the US anti-abortion lobby

---

[6] Attempts to restrict abortion were unsuccessful until the reduction of the time limit in respect of 'social clause' abortions from 28 to 24 weeks by the Human Fertilisation and Embryology Act 1990. Even this was in the context of a generally liberalising Act which was widely seen as a massive defeat for the anti-abortion movement – see I Kennedy and A Grubb, *Medical Law: Text with Materials* (London: Butterworths, 1994), p 867.

[7] Prospective Alliance MPs gained only 0.8% of the vote in those seats which they contested.

[8] 1997 SLT 896, 1997 SCLR 749.

[9] *Agence France Press*, 22 January 1997. Cf *Reuters Financial Service*, 14 May 1992, which reported that 71% were in favour of keeping abortion legal – surveys at the time more typically suggested a two-thirds majority in favour of the right to choose.

[10] The *Christian Science Monitor*, 30 April 1997; *The Reuter Library Report*, 11 September 1991.

in the US deterred its manufacturer from testing it for Food and Drug Administration (FDA) approval. Not until the Population Council, a charitable organisation, put itself forward as a sponsor of clinical trials involving 2,100 women in the US could trials begin, which they did in late 1994.[11]

Hostility extends beyond abortion to contraception. The 'morning after' pill, available in the UK since the 1980s but regarded by many anti-abortion activists as an abortifacient, was not approved by the US FDA until 1997, Presidents Bush and Reagan having blocked its testing prior to this. Even then, the fear of product boycotts meant that no drug company came forward to sell or market it.[12] It is estimated that ready availability of such a drug could prevent up to 1.7 million unplanned pregnancies per year in the US, and half that number (ie two-thirds of the total) number of annual abortions. In 1996, Republicans tried, unsuccessfully, to end state funding of family planning (the National Abortion Federation estimated that this would increase the number of abortions carried out annually in the US from around 1.5 million to over 2 million). More than half the states are currently considering, or have already passed, parental rights legislation which would, among other things, permit parents to veto sex education in schools and to prevent their children from receiving advice on contraception and sexually transmitted disease – this in a country which has the highest abortion rate of any western democracy and among the highest rate of teenage pregnancy, where teenagers undergo almost a quarter of all abortions and where fewer than half the states require sex education in schools.[13] Research and development of new contraceptive measures 'has virtually ground to a halt' as a result of pressure from the right.[14]

The strength of public feeling against abortion in the US might be taken to indicate that American women's continued access to the procedure is indicative of the benefits of constitutional entrenchment. Certainly the federal courts, including the Supreme Court, have struck down a number of the cruder attempts made by individual states to restrict access to abortion. South Carolina laws detailing physical specifications for abortion clinics, mandating medically unnecessary tests on women

[11] *Reuters*, 18 September 1996; K Houppert, 'The Politics of Birth Control: How Prolife Forces Strangle Research', *Village Voice*, 1 October 1996.

[12] Houppert, *ibid.* The medication is, in fact, available in the US, given that it consists simply of specific doses of particular readily available contraceptive pills. But drugs companies' fear of product liability lawsuits, consumer boycotts and harassment by anti-abortion groups have prevented them labelling their contraceptive pills as suitable for this purpose despite FDA encouragement to do so. Many US doctors do not tell their patients of the potential use of contraceptive pills for emergency purposes and, according to an article in *Time* magazine (vol 149(17), 28 April 1997), some pharmacists refuse to honour prescriptions of contraceptive pills made out for this purpose.

[13] J Hadley, *Abortion: Between Freedom and Necessity* (London: Virago, 1996). The statistics are from the Alan Guttmacher Institute and the National Abortion and Reproductive Rights Action League (NARAL) (respectively, http://www.agi-usa.org and http://www.naral.org).

[14] Houppert, note 11 above.

seeking abortions and granting state officials unrestricted access to the files of women who have had abortions have been enjoined by the federal courts, as have Michigan laws regulating where abortion clinics can be established; Utah and Louisiana laws prohibiting abortions almost entirely; laws passed in Minnesota, Ohio and South Carolina which tightly restricted late-term abortions and in Minnesota, Tennessee and Massachusetts which imposed rigorous parental notification or consent requirements for abortions on minors. Further, a number of state constitutions have been interpreted as applying greater protections to women seeking abortions than those provided by the Federal Constitution.[15]

For all of this, American women's access to abortion cannot be regarded as secure. Barely a year goes by without the Supreme Court hearing yet another challenge to its decision in *Roe v Wade*; individual states are increasingly passing restrictive abortion laws; and in both 1996 and 1997 the Federal Government attempted to impose the first nationwide restriction on abortion procedures by banning the 'dilation and extraction' method – the so-called 'partial birth abortion'. The ban was twice vetoed by President Clinton despite the intervention of the Vatican which described his 1996 veto as bordering on 'infanticide'.[16] Efforts continue to implement the ban at federal level.

A woman's 'right to choose'

Roe v Wade has operated so as to retain an element of freedom of choice for women in the US. But there is much that the decision failed to secure. The Supreme Court restricted states' powers to prohibit abortion but, as the decision was subsequently interpreted, it imposed no positive right to affordable, accessible, termination of pregnancy by requiring that states or the Federal Government provide funding for the procedure, or even permit abortions to be carried out at facilities contributed to,

[15] These include California, Connecticut, Idaho, Illinois, Massachusetts, Minnesota, Montana, New Jersey, New Mexico, Oregon, Vermont and West Virginia – see American Civil Liberties Union (ACLU) press reports, available on the world wide web at http://www.aclu.org. See also the Supreme Court decisons in *Hodgson v State of Minnesota* 497 US 417 (1990) and *Bellotti v Baird* (II) 443 US 622 (1979).

[16] *Agence France Presse*, 19 April 1996. Bizarrely, according to *Newsday*, 9 June 1997, President Clinton endorsed Tom Daschle's anti-abortion legislation intended to head off the partial birth ban Bill. Daschle's Bill would outlaw all post-viability abortions unless pregnancy threatens the woman's life or 'risk(s) grievous injury to her physical health' because of 'a severely debilitating disease or impairment *specifically caused* [my emphasis] by the pregnancy'. *Newsday* called Clinton's endorsement 'downright amazing' – not least because of its disregard for 'psychological health'. The Bill was defeated at which point Daschle supported the partial birth ban, while admitting its unconstitutionality, in order to help 'accelerate the legislative process to allow the earliest review of the law by the Supreme Court'. See HC Debs 4 December 1996, cols 1041–1044, for an unsuccessful attempt by Elizabeth Peacock MP to ban the procedure in England and Wales.

however indirectly, by the public purse.[17] Latterly, *Roe v Wade* has also proved to be consistent with many procedural restrictions imposed by states whose intentions were to frustrate access to abortions.

The practical provision of abortion has always turned upon the will of federal and state governments. Those in the US who have very low incomes (8.5 million women of child-bearing age in 1997) rely on Medicaid for their health care and upon clinics funded by Title X of the Public Health Service Act for their family planning, as well as for other basic health care services. Medicaid funds only such treatment as is 'medically necessary', yet in 1977 the Hyde amendment withdrew Medicaid funding for abortions, a position which has been maintained since, subject to exceptions covering abortions necessary to save the woman's life and, from time to time, for pregnancies resulting from rape or incest. One of the more bizarre results of such Medicaid restrictions was seen in March 1997, when the state of Nebraska charged with welfare fraud a young woman who applied for a funded abortion on the grounds that she had been raped, having become pregnant in an incident after which she had come home 'in tears, with a torn shirt and jeans', and called a rape crisis line. The charge, which carried a sentence of up to 12 months' imprisonment, was filed because she had not reported the alleged rape to the police.[18]

Just as federal governments have restricted access to abortion under the Medicaid scheme, so, too, they have excluded abortion from the scope of Title X funding. Since the inception of Title X clinics in 1970, the use of these federal funds for the purposes of abortion has been prohibited. In 1988 a 'gag rule' was applied to prohibit them from counselling, advising or providing information about abortion, and from referring women for abortion services even when such information was specifically requested (in such a case the doctor should instruct the woman that 'abortion is not an appropriate method of birth control'). The rule was upheld in 1991 by the Supreme Court in *Rust v Sullivan*,[19] even to the extent that it forbade health care professionals from informing women that abortion was a legal option, and remained in place until 1993. The Republican Party's 'Contract with America' called, in 1994, for the gag to be reimposed.

Restrictions upon the funding of abortions have not been confined only to the non-availability of federal health care funds. Under the Reagan administration, federal employees' health insurance schemes were prohibited from funding abortions save in cases of rape or incest or where the woman's life was at stake, and federal prisons from providing abortions for prisoners in their custody. These restrictions were removed in 1993 by President Clinton but reinstated by an anti-choice Congress in

---

[17] *Maher v Roe* 432 US 464 (1977); *Harris v McRae* 448 US 297 (1980); *Williams v Zbaraz* 448 US 358 (1980), *Webster v Reproductive Health Services* 492 US 490 (1989).

[18] ACLU *News*, 7 August 1997, see note 15 above. The case was eventually dropped after five months.

[19] 500 US 173 (1991).

1995. And even when women have been prepared to finance their own abortions, many have been prevented from so doing. Since 1979, US military personnel stationed overseas have been prohibited from having abortions, even if self-financed, in military hospitals save where their lives are in danger. The ban was removed as far as self-financed abortions were concerned in 1993, but reinstated in 1995 subject to further exceptions covering pregnancies resulting from rape and incest.

Federal restrictions are not the only hurdles faced by women seeking access to abortions. Even under *Roe v Wade*, state legislatures remained free to prohibit the use of public personnel or facilities to perform abortions; to require that minors notify parents about or receive consent from parents for any abortion (as long as some provision was made for notifying or seeking consent from a judge – the so-called 'judicial bypass' – where parental notification or consent was not appropriate); and to impose procedural burdens upon doctors performing abortions as well as, as we saw above, denying funding for most abortions.[20] And to the extent that *Roe v Wade* restricted states' freedom of action, the Supreme Court's subsequent retreat in *Planned Parenthood of Southeastern Pennsylvania v Casey*,[21] in which the 'strict scrutiny' standard applied in *Roe v Wade* to interference with pregnant women's freedom of choice was replaced with a requirement that restrictions not 'unduly burden' the exercise of that freedom, opened the way for increasingly onerous constraints on women seeking abortions.

Retreat from *Roe v Wade*

In *Roe v Wade* the Supreme Court ruled that restrictions on the freedom to choose could be justified only in accordance with the State's 'compelling interests', whether in protecting the woman's health or the potential life of the foetus, and then only after the first trimester and viability respectively. Nineteen years later, in *Casey*, and despite its express reaffirmation of *Roe*'s 'essential holding' (although this was by a bare majority), the Supreme Court rejected *Roe*'s 'rigid' trimester approach and asserted that the State had 'legitimate interests *from the outset* of the pregnancy in protecting the health of the woman and the life of the foetus that may become a child' (my emphasis). The State's 'interest in potential life

---

[20] See *Webster v Reproductive Health Services*, note 17 above; *Bellotti v Baird* 428 US 132 (1976); *Planned Parenthood Association v Ashcroft* 462 US 476 (1983); *Hodgson v Minnesota* 497 US 417 (1990); *State of Ohio v Akron Center for Reproductive Health* 497 US 502 (1990); *Simopoulos v State of Virginia* 462 US 506 (1983); *Planned Parenthood of Missouri v Danforth* 428 US 52 (1976); *Beal v Doe* 432 US 438 (1977); *Poelker v Doe* 432 US 519 (1977); *Harris v McRae*, note 17 above and *Maher v Roe*, note 17 above.

[21] Case no 93–150, 1994.

throughout pregnancy' permitted it to take measures to regulate abortion from the outset, as long as the measures did not impose an 'undue burden' on the woman's exercise of her right to choose.

The 'undue burden' approach had appeared as early as 1976, with the decision of the Supreme Court in *Planned Parenthood of Missouri v Danforth*,[22] and had been used by the court in the *Bellotti v Baird* decisions (1976 and 1979) and in *Maher v Roe* (1977).[23] But in these cases, the attitude of the Supreme Court towards express restrictions upon abortion, as distinct from the refusal to fund, was rigorous. The legislation upheld in *Danforth* imposed requirements which were so modest that, according to Justice Blackmun for the majority, they were not properly characterised as restrictions on abortion, which restrictions he stated could not be imposed in the first trimester at all, and could be imposed after this point but pre-viability only where 'reasonably related to maternal health'. And while the first *Bellotti* decision upheld some restrictions on access to abortion for minors, and four of the eight justices who struck down the parental consent legislation in the second case relied on the 'undue burden' approach to do so, these judges expressly stated that the constitutional rights of minors to abortion 'cannot be equated with those of adults', a conclusion they justified on the basis of 'the peculiar vulnerability of children; their inability to make critical decisions in an informed, mature manner; and the importance of the guiding role of parents in the upbringing of their children'.[24]

The major shortcoming of the early post-*Roe* decisions related to state funding of abortion, the Supreme Court refusing to accept that the refusal to fund imposed any restriction upon the right to abortion. In *Harris v McRae*,[25] for example, the Supreme Court held that: '[t]he Hyde Amendment places *no governmental obstacle* in the path of a woman who chooses to terminate her pregnancy, but rather, by means of unequal subsidization of abortion and other medical services, encourages alternative activity deemed in the public interest' (my emphasis).[26] This matter is discussed in more general terms in Chapter 3 above. But prior to 1992, and whatever the terminology employed, the Supreme Court did not permit pre-viability restrictions on abortion, save in respect of minors and excepting those reasonably related to the woman's health.[27] In *Casey*,[28] by contrast,

---

[22] Note 20 above.
[23] Note 17 above.
[24] *Ibid*, at 633 *per* Justice Powell. But see Justice O'Connor's dissent in *Akron v Akron Center for Reproductive Health* 462 US 416 (1983) and *Thornburgh v American College of Obstetricians and Gynecologists* 476 US 747 (1986), together with the decision in *Webster v Reproductive Health Services*, note 20 above.
[25] Note 17 above.
[26] *Ibid*, at 315. See also *Maher v Roe*, note 17 above and *Beal v Doe* 432 US 438 (1977).
[27] *Akron v Akron Center for Reproductive Health*, note 24 above; *Planned Parenthood Association v Ashcroft*, note 20 above.
[28] Case no 93–150, 1994.

the Supreme Court accepted that the State had an interest in the foetus throughout the pregnancy and permitted substantial restrictions, not limited to cost-based or other practical hurdles, on women's right to abortion.[29] The effect of *Roe*'s 'reaffirmation' in *Casey* was that the Supreme Court accepted, as constitutional, interventions in abortion that it had previously rejected as inconsistent with *Roe*.[30]

The willingness of the Supreme Court to permit the restriction of fundamental rights as it did in *Casey* is not unique to abortion, the court having permitted restrictions on, as distinct from complete denials of, other fundamental rights where those restrictions were reasonably related to important and legitimate government ends. In *Burdick v Takushi*,[31] for example, a majority of the Supreme Court upheld a statute which prohibited last-minute nominations of political candidates.[32] In *Burdick*, the interest of the State in 'avoid[ing] the possibility of unrestrained factionalism at the general election' was regarded by the majority as outweighing the plaintiff's 'limited interest in waiting until the eleventh hour to choose his preferred candidate'.[33] And in *Roe* itself, post-first trimester restrictions on abortion which were intended to protect women's health were required only to be 'reasonably related' to that end. But the imposition of the 'undue burden' test by the plurality in *Casey* is different in kind from the *dicta* in *Roe* and the decision in *Burdick*. The interests at stake in these latter cases – government protection of women's health and government interest in ordered, fair and honest elections respectively – were not directly in conflict with the rights (to abortion and vote) upon which they required restrictions to be imposed. In *Casey*, by contrast, the Supreme Court set against each other the inevitably conflicting right of women to terminate unwanted pregnancies, and interest of government *throughout pregnancy* in protecting foetal life.

How is a court to determine whether an abortion restriction, imposed in the interests of protecting foetal life, imposes too great a burden on

---

[29] This against Justice Brennan's dissenting protest that *Roe* 'and its progeny established that the pregnant woman has a right to be free from state interference with her choice to have an abortion – a right which, at least prior to the end of the first trimester, *absolutely prohibits* any governmental regulation of that highly personal decision'. Justice Brennan took the view that the limitation (and not solely the denial) of fundamental rights was subject to strict scrutiny, a position in support of which he cited *inter alia* the decisions of the Supreme Court in *Shapiro v Thompson* 394 US 618 (1969); *Sherbert v Verner* 374 US 398 (1963); *Griswold v State of Connecticut* 381 US 479 (1965), and *Eisenstadt v Baird* 405 US 438 (1972).

[30] See *Thornburgh v American College of Obstetricians and Gynecologists*, note 24 above; *Planned Parenthood of Missouri v Danforth*, note 20 above.

[31] 504 US 428 (1992).

[32] Citing *Norman v Reed* 502 US 279 1992 and *Anderson v Celebrezze* 460 US 780 1983. Cf Justice Brennan's approach in *Planned Parenthood of Southeastern Pennsylvania v Casey*, Case no 93–150, 1994.

[33] A minority including Justice Blackmun dissented on the basis that the legislation imposed a 'significant burden . . . on the right of voters . . . to vote for the candidates of their choice'.

a woman's right to choose? The answer, it would appear, may be that restrictions will be invalidated only where they wholly deny, perhaps for reasons unrelated to cost, the right to terminate a pregnancy. In *Casey*, Justice O'Connor stated that an undue burden would be imposed by legislation which 'has the purpose or effect of placing a substantial obstacle in the path of a woman seeking an abortion of a nonviable fetus'. But although the Supreme Court did strike down a spousal notification requirement because it could impose a total ban on abortions for a group of women, however small;[34] the plurality in *Casey* accepted statutory provisions imposing rigorous administrative requirements, including anti-abortion counselling, a mandatory waiting period, public filing of abortion information and a parental consent requirement in respect of minors, on abortion providers. It would appear that, in order to amount to an 'undue burden', the obstacles imposed in the way of women seeking abortions must be very substantial indeed.

The threat to abortion

The Pennsylvania abortion statute which was implemented subsequent to *Casey* was, at that time (1994) the most restrictive in the US. But since the 1994 Supreme Court ruling, many more states have enacted restrictive legislation. In 1995, four states enacted laws requiring mandatory waiting periods for abortions and 22 states introduced similar legislation. By 1996, over 60 per cent of states had implemented 'informed consent' laws.[35] In 1996, 220 pieces of anti-abortion legislation were filed and nine states enacted 14 anti-abortion provisions[36] (this marked a significant increase in the enactment of anti-choice legislation over previous years) and in 1997, almost one in four US states enforced at least three types of restriction upon abortions and just under half of all states enforced at least two. These restrictions typically consisted of requirements for parental consent or notification for minors, mandatory waiting periods and/or 'informed consent' prior to abortions, prohibitions on late abortions, bans on state and health insurance funding for abortions and restrictions on the provision of abortion by public employees or in public facilities.[37] More recently still, many states have attempted to restrict the type of procedure which may be used in order to perform abortions.[38] And at the

---

[34] Less than 1% of those seeking abortions, given the exceptions provided by the legislation.

[35] Information obtained from NARAL (http://www.naral.org).

[36] According to NARAL, above, 220 anti-choice Bills were introduced in 37 states during the 1996 legislative session and 'proposals to restrict abortion passed at least one legislative body in 20 states'.

[37] See NARAL, *Who Decides? A State-by-State Review of Abortion and Reproductive Rights* (see http://www.naral.org).

[38] See, for example, *Orlando Sentinel*, 29 April 1997; *New York Times*, 6 May 1997.

federal level, the decision in *Casey* was followed by a new 'incrementalist approach' by the opponents of abortion, 'steadily curbing access to the procedure here, defunding it there . . . their objective is the same as always: make the procedure difficult to obtain, prohibitively expensive for poor women and physically risky for physicians and woman alike'.[39]

The potential of funding prohibitions and 'gag rules' to deny women abortions is obvious. But requirements for 'informed consent' (sometimes known as 'Women's Right to Know' rules[40]) mislead women by, for example, requiring that women be informed of the availability of 'medical assistance for ante- and post-natal care and childbirth (but not of the fact that they may not be eligible for it) and be informed that the father of any child is liable to assist in its support (not that assistance is awarded to less than a quarter of never-married women, and then only after court action, and that only half of these woman receive it in full[41]). Nor do they require that women on welfare be informed about the common 'family caps', discussed in Chapter 5 below. Further, the 'informed consent' typically required by such legislation amounts, in fact, to persistence in the face of sustained efforts to dissuade women from terminating their pregnancies. And mandatory waiting periods increase the cost of abortions for the many women who have to travel some distance to obtain the service, and also function to deprive women of privacy and subject them to harassment. The National Abortion and Reproductive Rights Action League (NARAL) reports that the 24-hour waiting period imposed in Mississippi was used by anti-abortion activists to trace women, telephone and visit their homes to harass them and contact 'husband[s], boyfriend[s], parent[s], clergy, or anyone else they think might be able to interfere'.[42]

In some circumstances the imposition of mandatory waiting periods amounts to the spousal notification prohibited by the Supreme Court in *Casey*. Equally problematic is the impact of mandatory waiting periods upon the timing of abortions. In 1996, for example, NARAL reported a 17 per cent rise in the number of women from Mississippi having abortions after the first trimester when that state imposed a waiting period.[43] Abortions are more complex to carry out after the first trimester, present more of a risk to women's health, are more costly and are provided by far fewer clinics and hospitals – in Tennessee, for example, such abortions are not available anywhere and only 48 per cent of abortion providers nationwide will perform the procedure after the 13th week.[44]

---

[39] NARAL press release, 10 July 1995.
[40] See *Wisconsin State Journal*, 11 August 1995.
[41] National Abortion Federation (NAF), *Informed Consent for Abortion*, available at http://www.prochoice.org.
[42] NARAL Factsheet, Mandatory Waiting Periods and the Freedom to Choose (see http://www.naral.org).
[43] *Ibid.*
[44] S Henshaw and J Van Vort, 'Abortion Services in the US 1991 & 1992' (1994) 26 *Family Planning Perspectives* 100.

The impact of mandatory waiting periods is most severe in those areas where abortion provision is most restricted – a woman who has to travel some distance to an abortion provider which performs the procedure on only two days each week, for example, could easily be delayed several weeks between first visit and abortion by her inability to remain near the provider for several days at a time or to make the journey on the next day or days on which the procedure is available. In 1995, 84 per cent of US counties did not have a single abortion provider, and women in some parts of the US had to travel as many as 700 miles to undergo abortions.[45] This situation was in part the result of the targeting of rural clinics by anti-abortion activists on the basis that their closure would have maximum effect on abortion access.

Late terminations do not result solely from the increasingly common mandatory waiting periods. They are also caused by restrictions on abortion funding. According to the American Medical Association, low-income women in the US typically have abortions two to three weeks later in pregnancy than do higher-income women.[46] Another study suggested that about half the abortions which took place after 16 weeks' gestation had been delayed by financial considerations.[47] And in 1984, 44 per cent of low-income women who had abortions paid for them with money which they had to divert from food, rent and utilities.[48] Given that many women having abortions already have one or more children, the restrictions imposed on abortion funding impact on these children too.

Mandatory waiting periods and restrictions on public funding of abortions are not the only legal requirements which obstruct women's access to the service. Equally problematic is the now common requirement, in respect of abortions on minors, for parental consent or notice (which, in the case of adolescents, amounts to much the same thing[49]). At first blush the involvement of parents in such major decisions may seem appropriate and, even in the absence of any legislative requirement, the majority of US minors who have abortions do inform at least one parent.[50] (Indeed, if such an obligation is to be imposed in respect of abortion, one might

---

[45] NARAL, Mandatory Waiting Periods and the Freedom to Choose, note 42 above.
[46] Council on Scientific Affairs, American Medical Association, 'Induced Termination of Pregnancy Before and After *Roe v Wade*' (1992) 268 *Journal of the American Medical Association* 3231, at 3238. See also S Henshaw and L Wallisch, 'The Medicaid Cutoff and Abortion Services for the Poor' (1984) 16(4) *Family Planning Perspectives* 170.
[47] A Torres and J Forrest, 'Why Do Women Have Abortions?' (1988) 20 *Family Planning Perspectives* 169.
[48] Alan Guttmacher Institute, cited by ACLU Factsheet, Access Denied: The Scarcity of Public Funding for Abortion (see http://www.aclu.org).
[49] Justice Blackmun pointed this out in his dissent in *Ohio v Akron Center for Reproductive Health*, note 20 above.
[50] ACLU Factsheet, Parental Involvement Laws (see http://www.aclu.org), citing S Henshaw and K Kost, 'Parental Involvment in Minors' Abortion Decisions' (1992) 5 *Family Planning Perspectives* 199.

ask whether it should not also be imposed on youngsters who wish to put their children up for adoption.) But, according to the American Civil Liberties Union (ACLU), many of those who do not choose to involve their parents in abortion decisions 'come from families where such an announcement would only exacerbate an already volatile or dysfunctional family situation'. The ACLU cite evidence that 14 per cent of minors having abortions believed that they would be subject to physical abuse if they informed their parents, 11 per cent that violence would take place between their parents and others that a parent's drug or alcohol problem would be exacerbated.[51]

Most statutes do provide for judicial bypass (indeed, the constitutionality of those which do not is in doubt[52]). But such a bypass frequently requires a court appearance by the applicant, with all its attendant anxieties and the possibility, whether real or imagined, that confidentiality will not be preserved. The Supreme Court has upheld legislation in which 'confidentiality', rather than anonymity, was promised but which made no provision to secure confidentiality, other than declaring that the records involved were not 'public records' and pointing to state law which criminalised the disclosure by 'any state employee [of] . . . documents not designated as public records'.[53] By contrast, as Justice Blackmun pointed out in his dissent, the same state required that the anonymity of juveniles adjudicated as delinquent or unruly be protected by means of their records being sealed and later erased.

The Supreme Court was unmoved by 'the *mere possibility* of unauthorized, illegal disclosure by state employees' (my emphasis) of information relating to abortions sought by minors. Justice Blackmun, dissenting, pointed out that, 'A minor, whose very purpose in going through a judicial-bypass proceeding is to avoid notifying a hostile or abusive parent, would be most alarmed at signing her name and the name of her parent on the complaint form. Generalized statements concerning the confidentiality of records would be of small comfort, even if she were aware of them.'

The shortage of abortion providers has been mentioned above.[54] By the early 1990s, only one in ten hospital residency programmes required doctors training as obstetricians/gynaecologists to learn how to perform even the simplest of abortions and 7 per cent instructed in post-

---

[51] ACLU Factsheet, Parental Involvement Laws above.
[52] There is some dispute where notification rather than consent is required.
[53] *Ohio v Akron Center for Reproductive Health*, note 20 above.
[54] The Alan Guttmacher Institute in 1995 and NARAL in 1997, see note 13 above reported a decline in the number of abortion providers. According to the *International Herald Tribune*, 23 January 1995, more than 500 hospitals and clinics stopped providing abortions between the early 1980s and 1995 and access to abortion had declined particularly in small communities in the South and Midwest. See also *The Times*, 26 November 1992 – between 1982 and 1988 the number of abortion clinics declined by 11%. In rural areas, however, the number of clinics halved in that time.

first trimester abortions.[55] (Efforts made in 1996 to insist that abortion training be included in obstetrician/gynaecologists training programmes save where the individual or institution had a moral or religious objection to the procedure were thwarted by the Federal Government which voted to continue federal funding of such programmes without abortion training.) Eighty-four per cent of obstetricians/gynaecologists believe in the right to choose. But fewer than one-third actually provide abortions. The number of doctors prepared to perform the procedure is expected to decline further as a result of the ever more burdensome requirements being imposed upon providers by many states whose aim is to hinder or prevent access to the procedure. In addition to the rules requiring 'informed consent', parental notification or consent and mandatory waiting periods before abortions may be informed, rigorous and inflexible requirements relating to record-keeping and reporting, mandatory ultrasound dating of foetuses and even to the size of corridors and provision of air conditioning equipment are increasingly being targeted at abortion providers.[56]

One of the most recent US abortion controversies, and one which seems likely to continue, concerns the D & X procedure which is carried out in a very small number of late abortions (it is commonly reported that only two doctors in the whole of the US perform abortions in the third term, and abortions after 24 weeks constitute 0.01 per cent of the total[57]). The details of this operation are gruesome, involving as it does the delivery of all but the head of the foetus into the birth canal, whereupon suction is used to extract the contents of the skull which is collapsed for easier removal. But the procedure is extremely rare, when carried out it is frequently used to abort anencephalic foetuses (those in which no brain has developed) or others which have no chance of survival even if carried to full term, and carries considerably less risk to the woman than the more commonly used (and scarcely less gruesome) methods of D & E (in which the foetus is removed piece by piece from the womb) or induced labour with all its attendant horrors.[58] Despite this, opponents of abortion have used the D & X procedure to galvanise public opinion on the abortion issue and have enlisted a number of otherwise pro-choice individuals against the use of this particular abortion procedure. Many states have legislated so as to prohibit the use of D & X and the struggle for a federal ban continues, at present hanging only on President Clinton's use of his power of veto.

One of the difficulties with the D & X ban as it is typically drawn up is its use of the emotive 'partial birth abortion' terminology. The 1997

---

[55] *The Times*, 26 November 1992.
[56] ACLU Factsheet, Burdensome Clinic Regulations (see http://www.aclu.org).
[57] NAF figures, see http://www.prochoice.org.
[58] Patricia Schneider (President of the National Organisation for Women), evidence to the Judicial Subcommittee on the Partial Birth Ban (12 July 1995).

federal legislation, for example, would have criminalised any abortion where the doctor 'partially vaginally delivers a living foetus before killing the foetus [alternatively 'the infant'] and completing the delivery'[59]. Such a prohibition could extend to D & E abortions, which comprise 90 per cent of those carried out after the first trimester, and also to intervention in an induction which goes wrong (this procedure accounts for the other 10 per cent). The American College of Obstetricians and Gynecologists opposed the federal prohibition on the grounds that it was difficult to know what was banned under the federal Bill: 'the descriptions are vague and do not delineate a specific procedure recognized in the medical literature'. And Patricia Schneider, of the National Organisation for Women, said of a previous, similar attempt at legislation: '[t]his Bill is so vague and broad and void of legitimate medical terminology that, to paraphrase one of our witnesses . . . it is legislatively mandated malpractice'.[60]

This vagueness must have, and would appear to have been intended to have, what was described by the Supreme Court in *Colautti v Franklin*[61] (*per* Justice Blackmun) as a 'chilling effect on the exercise of constitutional rights'. In addition, the ban which it was sought to impose at federal level, in common with those generally embraced at state level, contained no exception where the procedure posed less risk to the health of the woman than alternative methods of abortion, or where the foetus was incapable of survival even if carried to term.[62] Further, as Patricia Schneider pointed out in relation to the first federal legislative ban attempted, although doctors could perform the procedure in order to save the woman's life, this was by way of an affirmative defence to a criminal charge with the effect that 'the doctor is still arrested and must stand trial'. The Bill was, in Schneider's view 'but one part of a concerted, multistep effort to effectively deprive women of their constitutional rights and access to abortion'.[63]

Constitutional shortcomings

It may well be the case that the right to abortion, however limited by *Casey* will defeat such legislative efforts. Ohio's D & X ban was enjoined

---

[59] Under the federal definition, a partial delivery would take place when the doctor 'deliberately and intentionally delivers into the vagina a living fetus, *or a substantial portion thereof* [my emphasis] for the purpose of performing a procedure the physician knows will kill the fetus'.

[60] See note 58 above.

[61] 439 US 379 (1979).

[62] Whether because of impairment or viability. According to Kate Michelman of NARAL (*The Dallas Morning News*, 12 July 1997), only about 600 third trimester abortions are carried out annually in the US.

[63] See note 58 above.

in 1996 because the imprecision with which its prohibition was expressed 'does not provide physicians with fair warning as to what conduct is permitted, and as to what conduct will expose them to criminal and civil liability' and, although the method was safer in some circumstances than any of the alternatives, the ban applied save where the alternative 'poses a significantly greater risk of the death of the pregnant woman or a serious risk of the substantial and irreversible impairment of a major bodily function'. The D & X ban therefore amounted to an 'undue burden' within *Casey* as that case, in common with *Roe v Wade*, made the State's interest in the potential life of the foetus subordinate to considerations of the woman's health.[64] And, as of March 1998, 'partial birth abortion' bans had been struck down in all 12 states in which they had been challenged, and the Supreme Court had refused to hear an appeal against one of these decisions.[65]

President Clinton's replacement of the anti-abortion Justice White with the 'moderate' Madam Justice Ginsberg[66] shifts the balance in the Supreme Court slightly towards a more liberal attitude to abortion. Although Justice Blackmun has been replaced with 'moderate' Justice Breyer, leaving Justice Stevens the only (generally) liberal member of the court, the current line-up consists of three right-wing judges (Chief Justice Rehnquist, Justices Scalia and Thomas, all of whom would see *Roe v Wade* overturned), one liberal, and five 'moderates' (at least on the abortion issue – Justices Kennedy, O'Connor and Souter together with Clinton's appointments): this line-up is unlikely to mandate state funding of abortion on request; it is also unlikely to permit the banning of a method which might be safer than the alternatives. But this situation is unstable: the election of a Republican President, together with the death or retirement of a couple of moderate judges, or of the sole remaining liberal, could render the 'right' to abortion very vulnerable indeed. It was perhaps in part because of his recognition of the slender thread by which the right to abortion hung under President Bush that Justice Blackmun remained on the Supreme Court for as long as he did: in *Casey*, the 83-year-old judge remarked that he could not 'remain on this Court forever, and when I do step down, the confirmation process for my successor well may focus on the issue before us today'.

---

[64] *Women's Medical Professional Corp v Voinovich*, Case no C-3-95-414, 1996.
[65] ACLU Press Release, March 1998, see http://www.aclu.org. In *Thornburgh v American College of Obstetricians and Gynecologists*, note 24 above, the Supreme Court overruled legislation requiring that that doctors performing post-viability abortions must use the 'degree of care' required to preserve the life and health of any unborn child intended to be born and to use the method of abortion most likely to preserve the life of the fetus, even at some risk to a woman's health. The same decision is likely in respect of any federal ban imposed in the future, particularly as the wording favoured prohibits the procedure save where the woman's life is at stake.
[66] Madam Justice Ginsberg actually founded the ACLU's reproductive freedom project but, since her appointment to the Supreme Court, has been considerably less radical.

Some of the legal difficulties experienced by those who would favour women's right to control their reproductive destinies could be attributed, in the US, to the absence of an explicit constitutional provision relating to abortion. But even if the right to abortion were to be so entrenched, the history of abortion access in the US illustrates the disparity between formal legal right, on the one hand, and practical, enforceable, useful right on the other. Even under the pre-*Casey* approach, many women in the US did not, as a matter of fact, have access to safe, legal abortions. Federal and state restrictions upon abortion funding were upheld in a succession of cases in which the majority of the Supreme Court judges stated that *Roe* had given women a freedom *from* particular restrictions which states might otherwise place upon abortions, as distinct from an 'affirmative right' *to* an abortion. Yet, as Justice Brennan protested in *Maher v Roe*,[67] the practice of funding childbirth, but refusing to fund abortions, for women on Medicaid 'clearly operates so as to coerce indigent pregnant women to bear children they would not otherwise choose to have, and just as clearly, this coercion can only operate on the poor, who are uniquely the victims of this form of financial pressure'.[68]

Despite the continued dissent of Justices Brennan, Marshall and Blackmun, the majority of Supreme Court judges in the subsequently decided *Harris*,[69] *Webster v Reproductive Health Services*[70] and *Rust v Sullivan*[71] ruled that the right recognised in *Roe* did not entitle women to Medicaid funding even of medically necessary abortions (other medically necessary treatment being funded under the programme), to have abortions carried out in publicly funded facilities or by publicly funded personnel, or to have access even to information about, or referrals for, abortion through family planning programmes funded by the State.[72]

All of these prohibitions stood despite the court's recognition that they served, in practice, to deny poor women access to abortions. As noted in Chapter 3 above, 'Due Process Clauses generally confer no affirmative right to government aid, even where such aid may be necessary to secure life, liberty or property interests of which the government itself may not deprive the individual.'[73] To the extent that a state decision to fund health care generally, or reproductive health care in particular, did give rise to any obligations on the part of the State, these obligations related only to equal protection, there being no fundamental positive right to abortion.

The women disadvantaged by the State's refusal to fund abortion were poor, but the category of 'the poor' is accorded no special protection

---

[67] Note 17 above.
[68] *Ibid*, at 483.
[69] Note 17 above.
[70] Note 17 above.
[71] Note 19 above.
[72] See also note 18 above.
[73] Chief Justice Rehnquist in *Webster v Reproductive Health Services*, note 17 above, citing *DeShaney v Winnebago Co Dept of Social Services* 489 US 189, at 196 (1989).

under the US Constitution and discrimination against them was subject only to relaxed scrutiny (see further Chapter 3 above). The State fulfilled its obligations simply by ensuring that the programmes pursued were 'rationally related' to a 'legitimate governmental interest' – typically in these cases the Government's interest in promoting 'normal' childbirth over abortion (as in *Maher*). This test is not difficult to satisfy in the context of abortion. As Justice Marshall pointed out in his dissent from the majority decision in *Harris*, to uphold the Hyde Amendment's refusal to fund even medically necessary abortions for financially needy women, the Government interest pursued in that case could not be one in 'normal childbirth', since the Hyde Amendment refused funding even 'where the foetus will die shortly after birth, or in which the mother's life will be shortened or her health otherwise gravely impaired by the birth'.

Justice Stewart declared, for the majority in *Harris*, that the situation was analogous to that of private education: the fact that 'government may not . . . prevent parents from sending their child to a private school' did not impose upon it 'an affirmative Constitutional obligation to ensure that all persons have the financial resources to . . . send their children to private schools'. He went on to state that the interpretation of the right to abortion in positive terms 'would require Congress to subsidize the medically necessary abortion of an indigent woman even if Congress had not enacted a Medicaid program to subsidize other medically necessary services'. The minority, on the other hand, claimed that the pregnant woman's 'right to be free from state interference with her choice to have an abortion' required that the State 'refrain from wielding its enormous power and influence in a manner that might burden the pregnant woman's freedom to choose whether to have an abortion' – in this case, by subsidizing the costs of ante-natal care and childbirth, but not of abortion, for the indigent woman.

The State's refusal to fund abortion in an otherwise comprehensive medical scheme can be distinguished from a refusal to fund private schools. While a government policy of regulating those schools for which it provides funding is rational as a means to ensure the appropriate use of those funds, government refusal to fund medically necessary abortions, while funding all other medically necessary procedures, is rational only as a means of dissuading women from exercising their constitutionally protected right to terminate their pregnancies. As John Hand points out in relation to the Supreme Court's decision in *Rust v Sullivan* (see below): 'the government could offer welfare only to Republicans or Catholics since the others are no worse off than if government offered no benefit and since the government has no duty to subsidize rights'.[74]

---

[74] J Hand, 'Buying Fertility: the Constitutionality of Welfare Bonuses' (1993) 46 *Vanderbilt Law Review* 715, at 732.

The policy of refusing to pay for abortions cannot be justified on the grounds of cost, as the costs of ante-natal care and childbirth are far in excess of those associated with terminations. And even if the State's interest in the potential life of the foetus is recognised (even if, contrary to *Roe v Wade*, this interest is treated as compelling from the beginning of pregnancy), it is clear from *Roe v Wade* and from the subsequent decisions in *Webster* and in *Casey* that that State interest is subordinate to considerations of the woman's health even after fetal viability.[75] Thus no legitimate State interest is advanced by the refusal to fund medically necessary abortions and the refusal to fund such terminations, while funding all other necessary medical care, amounts, as Justice(s) Brennan and Blackmun pointed out in *Harris*, to a practice of conditioning receipt of a government benefit (here free health care) on the sacrifice of a constitutional right (here the right to choose a termination).[76]

The application of such a condition has, other than in the context of abortion, generally been held unconstitutional (see Chapter 3 above). Nor can the possibility of choosing to terminate a pregnancy be carved off from all other medically necessary care with the effect that the pregnant woman can be seen to qualify for all medically necessary care *except for* abortion[77] – abortion may be indicated (though not essential to save life) as part of the treatment for a medical condition such as cervical cancer, diabetes, epilepsy or tuberculosis. To deny an abortion in these circumstances may be to deny a woman what would, absent the abortion ban, be considered best medical treatment. Nevertheless, the Supreme Court has been adamant in its refusal to protect any positive right to abortion, going so far in *Webster* as to uphold legislation which prohibited any but life-saving abortions being carried out in 'any physical asset owned, leased, or controlled by [the] state or any agency or political subdivisions thereof', a definition which, as Justice Blackmun pointed out for the minority, would operate so as to prohibit abortions being carried out at the private clinic which, in 1985, had carried out 97 per cent of the post-16 week abortions for the entire state.

---

[75] See Justice Marshall in *Harris v McRae*, note 17 above.

[76] Justice Brennan cited *Sherbert v Verner*, note 29 above and *Speiser v Randall* 357 US 513 (1958); *Frost & Frost Trucking Co v Railroad Commission* 271 US 583 (1926); *Elfbrandt v Russell* 384 US 11 (1966); *Goldberg v Kelly* 397 US 254 (1970); *US Department of Agriculture v Moreno* 413 US 528 (1973); *Southeastern Promotions Ltd v Conrad* 420 US 546 (1975). Cf *Shapiro v Thompson*, note 29 above; *Memorial Hospital v Maricopa County* 415 US 250 (1974).

[77] Even if it could, Justice Brennan pointed out in *Harris v McRae*, note 17 above, that 'it is no answer to assert that no "penalty" is being imposed [on the exercise of a constitutional right] because the State is only refusing to pay for the specific costs of a protected activity rather than withholding other Medicaid benefits to which the recipient would be entitled or taking some other action more readily characterized as punitive. Surely the Government could not provide free transportation to the polling booths only for those citizens who vote for Democratic candidates, even though the failure to provide the same benefit to Republicans represents simply a refusal to subsidize certain protected conduct . . . and does not involve the denial of any other governmental benefits' (internal citations omitted).

Just as poverty rendered illusory the 'right to choose' for many women in the US, the activities of those opposed to abortion rendered illusory any hope of speedy, confidential access to the procedure. The anti-abortion protesters' tactics of identifying, tracing and harassing women seeking abortions was mentioned above.[78] In addition, anti-abortionists have restricted access to abortions by reducing the pool of those prepared to carry out the procedure. Abortion providers have, since they were first established, been subject to harassment and physical violence, and an unsuccessful attempt was made on the life of Mr Justice Blackmun himself after the decision in *Roe*.

Incidents of kidnapping, death threats, bombing and bomb threats, arson, invasion, vandalism, picketing and hate mail and phone calls have been recorded since at least 1977, but the level of harassment has increased over the years and levels of physical violence have remained high since the early 1990s. Between 1992 and 1994, five abortion providers were murdered and a further seven shot and wounded. In 1998, a further three murders occurred.[79] These deaths were just the tip of the iceberg – in 1995, 50 per cent and in 1996, 30 per cent of abortion clinics were the targets of violence, death threats, fires or harassment and, between 1977 and 1996, almost 2,000 violent attacks on abortion providers were reported (31 of these attacks involved bombings, and almost 150, arson).[80] In one week in January 1997 alone, attacks included the bombing of clinics in Washington, Atlanta and Oklahoma (six bombs exploded in all in 1997, the highest number in any single year since 1984).[81] Many clinics have been subjected to repeated arson and/or bomb attacks and, in addition to serious violence such as that outlined above and cases of kidnapping, assault, death threats and stalking, incidents of hate mail and phone calls, bomb threats and picketing ran at between 1,800 and 4,500 per annum between 1992 and 1996.[82] The impact of the physical violence and harassment directed at abortion providers has been to reduce the number of those willing to carry out abortions to the present levels, mentioned above.[83] The problem is particularly acute in rural areas, where much of the protest has been directed and the closure of clinics has the greatest impact. In addition, the experience of battling through anti-abortion protesters, being pushed and jostled, shouted at and besieged, renders the already difficult experience of abortion substantially more traumatic.[84]

---

[78] See note 42 above and accompanying text.
[79] NAF figures, 1 October 1998, available at http://www.prochoice.org/violence/98vd.html. To the two murders there reported has been added that of a New York abortion provider on 23 October 1998.
[80] *Irish Times*, 23 January 1997; Arkansas *Democrat Gazette*, 30 January 1998.
[81] *Ibid*.
[82] Statistics collated by the NAF, see note 41 above.
[83] *International Herald Tribune*, 23 January 1995; *Agence France Presse*, 22 January 1997.
[84] This was recognised by the Supreme Court in *Madsen et al v Women's Health Center*, Case no 93–880, 1994.

The US Constitution poses a real threat to legislative or other attempts to protect fundamental liberties by restricting the activities of anti-abortion activists. The Freedom of Access to Clinics Act 1994, passed in order to protect clinic workers and patients from physical and other abuse by anti-abortion activists has, for the most part, been upheld by the courts.[85] But constitutional arguments have been successfully employed by anti-abortion activists to thwart attempts to protect clinics and their patients from the most outrageous levels of harassment, abuse and physical assault.

In *Schenck v Pro-Choice Network*[86] the Supreme Court restricted an injunction imposed on anti-choice activists who had persisted in physically violent and intimidatory behaviour towards the workers and patients of abortion clinics. The protestors had not merely blockaded the clinics, but had entered them and jostled, grabbed, pushed, shoved and yelled at the women attending them. The Supreme Court accepted that the police had not been able successfully to deal with the protesters, in part because of the reluctance of patients to make their identity public and the protestors' harassment of police officers and those who testified or 'invoked the legal process' against them.[87] The protestors had persistently violated a previous restraining order, and it was only in the wake of this that the order appealed to the Supreme Court had been issued. The injunction, which permitted protesters to 'picket, carry signs, pray, sing or chant in full view of people going into the clinics', was struck down in part by the Supreme Court as a violation of the demonstrators' First Amendment rights to freedom of speech.

The reluctance of the Supreme Court to interfere with anti-abortionists' rights to speak might be contrasted with the attitude of the same court in *Rust v Sullivan*. Whereas, in *Schenck*, an injunction aimed at protecting women seeking abortions and those providing them from a real threat of violence was seen as an impermissible infringement of anti-abortionists' freedom of expression, a rule aimed, in *Rust*, at deterring poor women's exercise of their constitutional 'right to choose' by prohibiting their medical advisers from discussing the issue of abortion was not regarded as an impermissible interference with those advisers' freedom of expression.

In considering the constitutionality of the 'gag rule' imposed upon those working in Title X-funded clinics, the Supreme Court in *Rust* acknowledged that 'employees' freedom of expression is limited during the time that they actually work for the [Title X-funded] project' but, by a majority, ruled that 'this limitation is the consequence of their decision to accept employment in a project the scope of which is permissibly limited'

---

[85] One Milwaukee judge struck it down but it was otherwise upheld during the first eight challenges.

[86] Case no 95–1065, 1997.

[87] *Pro Choice Network of Western New York v Project Rescue Western New York* 799 F Supp 1417, 1426–1427 (WDNY 1992).

to favour childbirth over abortion. The majority accepted that 'funding by the Government, even when coupled with the freedom of the fund recipients to speak outside the scope of the Government-funded project, is [not] invariably sufficient to justify government control over the content of expression'. But, having referred to a number of cases in which the Supreme Court ruled that government could not restrict speech on government-owned property where that property had been 'traditionally open to the public for expressive ideas' or 'expressly dedicated to speech activity', or where, like in the case of a university, it was a 'traditional sphere of free expression . . . fundamental to the functioning of our society',[88] and having acknowledged that an analogy could be drawn with government subsidy of the doctor–patient relationship, the majority went on to state, without explanation, that 'Title X program regulations do not significantly impinge on [that] . . . relationship' and that, therefore, the question did not need to be resolved.

The characterisation of the gag rule as 'not significant[ly] imping[ing]' on the doctor–patient relationship is mystifying. But it enabled the Supreme Court to treat the gag rule simply as a matter concerning the allocation of government funds, rather than the issue of free speech.[89] Thus the US Constitution permits the Government to regulate the speech of doctors whose wages it contributes to via public subsidy of medical care for the poor, and to do so in a way which is beyond the scrutiny of the courts. The Government may also, according to the decisions in *Maher* and *Harris*, deter women from having lawful abortions by funding pregnancy and childbirth for those in need, while refusing to fund even medically necessary abortions. This kind of government action, falling short as it does of being a legal, as opposed to a practical restriction upon abortion, is subject only to the lowest level of scrutiny: it will be acceptable if it is rationally related to a legitimate government interest.

The Constitution permits the types of abortion restrictions mentioned above, and does so without subjecting them to rigorous scrutiny, if any scrutiny at all. But the Constitution does not permit state courts or the federal government to restrict the activities of anti-abortion protestors, even where those activities put the lives of others at risk, unless the restrictions satisfy an 'intermediate' level of scrutiny. The decision in *Schenck* followed that in *Madsen et al v Women's Health Center*,[90] in which the Supreme Court had ruled that 'content neutral' injunctions that restrict speech, such as exclusion zones around clinics, were constitutionally acceptable only if they 'burden no more speech than necessary to serve a significant government interest'. Thus, in *Madsen*, while a 36-foot exclusion

---

[88] Citing *US v Kokinda* 497 US 720 (1990); *Hague v CIO* 307 US 496 (1939); *Keyishian v Board of Regents* 385 US 589 (1967).
[89] And thus as falling within *Webster, Harris* and *Maher*, see note 17 above.
[90] Note 84 above.

zone outside the clinic and certain noise restrictions on protestors were acceptable as necessary to prevent intimidation, ensure access to the clinic and safeguard the health of the patients using the facility, 300-foot 'no approach' zones around the clinic and its employees' homes were not regarded as acceptable despite the demonstrators' repeated breaches of previous injunctions. The interests of patients and employees in being free from fear, stalking, harassment and intimidation could not overcome the interests of the protestors in being able to exercise their powers of speech at close quarters to those who, for the most part, did not wish to hear.

Comparing constitutions

The US

What does the survey of US law reveal about the potential of entrenched rights? The first point which should be made is the rather obvious one that the effect of entrenchment depends very much on the nature of the rights entrenched: because the US Constitution does not explicitly guarantee women various reproductive freedoms, the protection afforded by it depends entirely upon the interpretation brought by the judiciary to other, more general provisions.

To the extent that woman have been guaranteed any reproductive freedom, the guarantee has depended upon the application of constitutional provisions such as the right to privacy, itself fashioned (arguably in a rather questionable manner) from the 'penumbras' of rights found elsewhere in the US Constitution and applied through the general Equal Protection and Due Process Clauses of the Fifth and Fourteenth Amendments. Even had the Constitution or its Amendments included a clear statement that persons should not be discriminated against on the basis of sex, the right to reproductive freedom might have been carved from this, given that the restrictions discussed in this and the following chapter impact exclusively or predominantly upon women. But there is no such clear guarantee, and the approach taken by the Supreme Court to the Equal Protection Clause and, in particular, to its application to sex (see Chapter 3 above), renders it unsuitable for challenge to anything but the most obvious and unjustifiable sex discrimination.

To the extent that the courts have failed adequately to protect women from sex-based discrimination, to ensure their practical access to abortion or their freedom from punitive pregnancy restrictions or welfare regulations, they may be accused of falling short of the expectations of social liberals. In these respects, however, the courts have not positively made the position of women or minorities worse. They have simply failed to improve on the legislature's approach. The democratic answer to this problem lies with the legislature which is free expressly to protect the interests of women (although it has failed to do so at least as far as the Equal Rights Amendment is concerned). But such a response is not always possible, and it is in these latter situations where the entrenchment of rights can be most harmful to the interests of women.

Germany

Judicial decisions cannot be relied upon to safeguard women's reproductive autonomy any more than those of elected representatives. US examples tend to suggest that the judiciary is more liberal than the legislature on the issue of abortion. In Germany, by contrast, the *Bundesverfassungsgericht* (Supreme Constitutional Court) has twice struck down restrictive abortion legislation on the grounds that it did not do enough to provide the protection to the foetus which was required by the constitutionally protected right to life. This, according to the Supreme Court, required the state to criminalise the procedure.

The first time the *Bundesverfassungsgericht* thus acted was in 1975 in response to legislation which was enacted after the most extensive legislative debates and a huge consultative process. The court, having weighed Article 2, s 2 of the basic law (which stated that 'everyone shall have the right to life and the inviolability of his person') against Article 2, s 1 ('everyone shall have the right to the free development of his personality insofar as he does not violate the rights of others or offend against the constitutional order or the moral code'), and taken into account the 'dignity of man', concluded that the foetus was to be given priority throughout the whole of the pregnancy, and that abortion was a legal wrong though it could be permitted in case of 'grave danger to the pregnant woman's life or serious interference with her health . . . severe ethical, social or psychological distress'. [91]

West German law was reformed in 1976 to restrict access to abortion to cases in which medical personnel deemed abortion 'advisable, considering the current and future living conditions of the pregnant woman, in order to avert a danger to her life or the danger of a grave interference with the physical or mental condition of her health, and which danger cannot be averted by other means reasonably open to her' (the conditions were to be deemed met up to 22 weeks' gestation in cases of rape, incest or severe foetal abnormality, and up to 12 weeks' gestation in cases where the woman found herself in a 'severe predicament') and counselling requirements were tightened up to put the emphasis on physical rather than social reasons for abortion.

[91] M Quaas, Federal Republic of Germany. In D Campbell (ed), *Abortion Law and Public Policy* (Dordrecht: Martinus Nijhoff, 1984). The 'dignity of man' though not, apparently, that of women, is regarded as a keystone of the constitutional value system guaranteed by Art 1, s 1 of Germany's basic law.

In part due to the 1975 decision, a huge disparity in access to abortion existed between East and West German women. While West German border guards were operating under instructions to stop and question women returning from Holland (where a more liberal abortion regime was in place) in order to determine whether they had secured abortions there,[92] women in East Germany were entitled to abortion on request during the first trimester under an equal opportunities law passed in 1972. The disparities were such that the abortion issue threatened at one stage to derail unification, East German women fearing the loss of their reproductive freedom. As a result, the reunification treaty preserved the different laws in the constituent elements of the newly unified Germany and instructed the new, all-German Parliament to devise a new law for the whole country by the end of 1992.

After much debate, the German Parliament passed new abortion legislation in 1992. The legislation provided a slightly more liberal regime than had previously prevailed in West Germany, though it deprived East German women of their previous entitlement to abortion on request to 12 weeks. The *Bundesverfassungsgericht* struck down this legislation, ruling that abortion was permissible only in exceptional circumstances, that criminal penalties should apply, and that abortions could not be carried out in public hospitals or on public health insurance. Women could secure abortions during the first trimester only if they underwent counselling designed to deter them from having the abortion, and only if they could pay for the operation themselves. Under such circumstances the abortion would still be illegal, but neither woman nor doctor would be prosecuted.

Ireland

In Ireland, too, the High Court's reading of the Constitution led it, in 1992, to order that a 14-year-old girl return from England, where she had gone with her parents to secure an abortion, and to forbid her from leaving Ireland for the duration of her pregnancy. The girl had been raped over a period of years by a family friend. The relevant provision of the Constitution stated that: '[t]he state acknowledges the right to life of the unborn, and, *with due regard to the equal right to life of the mother*, guarantees in its laws to respect, and as far as practicable by its laws to defend and vindicate that right' (my emphasis).[93] The medical evidence was that the girl's mental health would be devastated if she was forced to carry the pregnancy to term, and that there was a risk that she would commit suicide. But Mr Justice Costello gave short shrift to the Constitution's 'due

---

[92] J Hadley *Abortion: Between Freedom and Necessity* (London: Virago, 1996), p 43.
[93] Article 40.3.3., 1983 amendment.

respect' to her 'equal right to life' and stated that the risk of her committing suicide was 'much less and of a different order of magnitude than the certainty that the life of the unborn will be terminated' should she be permitted to leave the jurisdiction (internal citations omitted).[94]

It was not until the matter reached the Supreme Court (*Attorney General v X and others*[95]) that the Irish judiciary gave weight to the constitutional provision according equal weight to the life of the woman and permitted the girl to travel abroad in order to secure the abortion which she would otherwise have had a month previously. The abortion issue – in particular the revelation, in the context of the *X* case, of a secret protocol to the Maastricht Treaty to safeguard Ireland's anti-abortion stance – threatened to derail Ireland's accession to Maastricht.[96] But a compromise was reached, Ireland accepted Maastricht and the Irish amended the Constitution to the effect that the right to life of the foetus 'shall not limit freedom to travel between the state and another state . . . [or] to obtain or make available in the state, subject to such conditions as may be laid down by law, information relating to services lawfully available in another state'.

Despite this apparently clear provision, in 1997 another raped child was forced to endure the judicial process in order to be permitted to travel to England in order to have an abortion. The girl was in care and the health authority took the view that its right to take her abroad had to be confirmed by the court, doubt having been raised as to whether the right to travel conferred by the Constitution applied only to individuals. In the event the High Court ruled that, given the risk of suicide, the abortion was medical treatment and the girl could travel independent of the amendment.[97]

Canada

In Canada, by contrast with the position in both Germany and Ireland, the enactment of the Charter of Rights in 1982 resulted, eventually, in the removal of all restrictive legislation on abortion. The Supreme Court had not always been so open to the arguments of the pro-choice movement, in 1975 having declined to find that the same legislation violated the Canadian Bill of Rights 1960, s 1(b) of which recognised 'the right of the individual to equality before the law and the protection of the law'.[98] Such were the concerns of the Canadian Abortion Rights League about the Charter that it argued, in its representations to the Joint Committee

---

[94] Cited by Hadley, note 92 above, p 23.
[95] [1992] IRLM 401, [1992] 1 IR 1.
[96] *Irish Times*, 26 February 1992.
[97] *A and B v Eastern Health Board and others* [1998] 1 ILRM 460.
[98] *Morgentaler v R* [1976] 1 SCR 616.

on the Charter, that the proposed Bill be amended to state that 'nothing in this Charter is intended to extend rights to the embryo or fetus nor to restrict in any manner the rights of women to a medically safe abortion'.[99]

Pro-choice activists feared that the judiciary might interpret the Charter's 'right to life' to include the foetus. But in *Morgentaler* (1988), the Supreme Court ruled that Canada's abortion legislation breached the Charter because it was unduly restrictive of women's access to terminations.[100] Canada's Criminal Code decriminalised abortion only where a hospital committee certified its opinion that the pregnancy was likely to endanger the woman's life or health. Hospitals were not obliged to establish such committees, and committees were not obliged to issue certificates even where the woman's life or health was endangered. All seven judges in the Supreme Court agreed that the State was entitled to impose a degree of hardship on pregnant women in order to protect the foetus, although none suggested what this might consist of. Two of the five majority judges claimed that the law was unconstitutional, not because of the balance it struck between the interests of the woman and those of the foetus, but because it disregarded its own balance (according to the judges, that the woman's life and health were paramount) by denying women abortions even when their lives or health were threatened by the pregnancy. Two others based their decision on the fact that the rules imposed under the Criminal Code were not justified in pursuit of the State's legitimate aim to permit therapeutic abortions, and those only. Michael Mandel pointed out that these approaches required that the actual objectives of the 1969 legislation be overlooked,[101] the intention having been rigorously to restrict access to the procedure and not to guarantee it whenever a woman's life or health was at stake.

Only Madam Justice Wilson, the sole woman on the Supreme Court, approached the question of constitutionality as one involving privacy which she found inherent in the 'liberty' guaranteed by the Charter.[102] Section 7 of the Charter permitting that persons be deprived of this right only 'in accordance with the principles of fundamental justice', Madam Justice Wilson found that legislation which violated another Charter provision (here, freedom of conscience under s 2) offended fundamental justice. Madam Justice Wilson accepted that the interests of the foetus were to be taken into account. But, apart from approving the US approach whereby

---

[99] M Mandel, *The Charter of Rights and the Legalization of Politics in Canada* (Toronto: Wall & Thompson Inc, 1989) p 273.

[100] [1988] 1 SCR 30.

[101] See note 99 above, pp 282–283.

[102] 'Everyone has the right to life, liberty and security of the person and the right not to be deprived thereof except in accordance with the principles of fundamental justice.' The principles of fundamental justice were offended, according to *Big M Drug Mart Ltd* [1985] 1 SCR 295 (*per* Chief Justice Dickson), where any other charter provision was offended which, in this case, Madam Justice Wilson took to be 'freedom of conscience' guaranteed by s 2 – see Mandel for criticism, note 99 above, pp 284–285.

the protection afforded to the foetus increased as time went by, she gave no guidance as to what limits Parliament might be entitled to impose.

Michael Mandel stated in 1989 that: '[f]limsy reasoning aside, the repeal of the abortion law is perhaps the only unqualified good result to come from the Supreme Court of Canada yet'.[103] But the decision should not be regarded as indicative of the wisdom of enacting a Bill of Rights in the UK or elsewhere. For, just as the German judges were unrestricted by law and unanswerable to the public in striking down (albeit limitedly) permissive abortion legislation in 1975 and 1992; so, too, Canadian judges acted on their politics when they struck down Canada's abortion restrictions. Indeed, that the answer to the issue of abortion was not apparent on the face of the Charter was clear from the decision of the provincial Court of Appeal in Quebec in *Tremblay v Daigle*,[104] which was handed down after that of the Supreme Court in *Morgentaler.*

In *Tremblay*, Quebec's Court of Appeal upheld an injunction preventing a woman from having an abortion against the wishes of her estranged lover.[105] The woman had testified that this man was 'dominant, jealous and possessive . . . that he abused her physically . . . [and that on one occasion e]ven though he knew that [she] was pregnant, he pushed her to the floor, threatening to bring her into line once and for all' (internal citations omitted). She testified that she wanted 'to provide for a child in a serene, stable family environment in which there is no violence' and that she believed that Tremblay had 'no reason or interest in the present case except in order to maintain his hold on me'.

The trial judge, in granting the injunction, characterised the conflict in this case as one between the 'right to life' of a 'human being' under the Quebec and Canadian Charters and the 'convenience' of the woman.[106] Put thus, the former was clearly going to prevail. The Court of Appeal, in a 3:2 majority judgment, adopted a variety of reasons. Justice of Appeal LeBel followed the trial judge, declared that *Morgentaler* neither granted an absolute right to abortion nor dealt with the issue of foetal rights, and decided the issue on the balance of convenience. Justice of Appeal Nichols stated that, although in his view neither Charter recognised foetal rights, nevertheless, the right to abortion accepted by the Supreme Court in *Morgentaler* was insufficient to defeat those foetal rights which, he found were 'recognised by custom and implicitly consecrated by our laws'. And Justice of Appeal Bernier concluded, without taking a position on the status of the foetus under either Charter, that the foetus had a 'natural right' to be carried to term, which right could be overriden only by a just cause. All three judges agreed that the woman's reasons for wishing to terminate the pregnancy were 'not serious enough'.

---

[103] See note 99 above, p 287.
[104] [1989] RJQ 1735, 59 DLR (4th) 609.
[105] The original grant of the injunction is at [1989] RJQ 1980.
[106] Cf *Medhurst v Medhurst* (1984) 9 DLR (4th) 252, Ontario High Court of Justice.

The Supreme Court subsequently overruled the lower courts, finding that Quebec's Charter was not intended to confer protection over foetuses as persons and that Quebec's civil laws did not regard the foetus as a person.[107] But, as far as the Charter was concerned, the Supreme Court left the issue open as, state action not being involved here,[108] the Charter had no application and ['t]his Court should generally avoid making any unnecessary constitutional pronouncement'.

The law and politics of abortion

The impact of entrenched rights on women's reproductive freedom turns in part on the nature of the rights entrenched, in part upon judicial attitudes towards them. Whereas, in the US, the judiciary have liberalised abortion, in Germany and, arguably, Ireland, judicial interpretations of the Constitution have increased the restrictions on women. And even where the judicial approach might be regarded as favourable towards women, the survey of abortion regulation points to another difficulty which can arise from the entrenchment of rights. This concerns the clash between law and politics, and the possible repercussions of judicial action. In 1985 the *New Republic* suggested that *Roe v Wade*[109] was the 'worst thing that ever happened to American liberalism. Almost overnight it politicized millions of people and helped create a mass movement of social conservatives that has grown into one of the most potent forces in our democracy'.[110] The decision had, in a sense, taken pro-choice activists by surprise and, although warned by the 'women friendly' *amicus curiae* in the *Roe v Wade* court that 'one of the most dangerous things that could happen now is that women could sit back and think that they had won', *Roe* was in fact followed by a massive garnering of anti-choice sentiment but with relative inactivity on the part of pro-choice activists.[111] *Roe* rendered all existing state laws unenforceable and a deluge of state legislation followed. In the two years subsequent to the Supreme Court's decision, 32 states enacted 62 restrictive statutes on the abortion issue.

One of the difficulties with the way in which abortion law was liberalised in the US was that legislators who wished to placate the anti-abortion lobby could pass laws which were clearly inconsistent with the decision

---

[107] [1989] 2 SCR 530.

[108] This decision turned on the approach taken by the Supreme Court in *RWDSU v Dolphin Delivery Ltd* [1986] 2 SCR 573, see Chapter 3.

[109] Note 1 above.

[110] 25 February 1985, cited by L Epstein and J Kobylka, *The Supreme Court and Legal Change: Abortion and the Death Penalty* (1992: University of North Carolina Press, Chapel Hill), p 207.

[111] *Ibid.* The exception being ACLU which, however, took mainly legal action. There was little grass roots activity.

in *Roe*, thereby gaining public support from the anti-choice groupings, while, secure in the knowledge that the laws would be enjoined, they did not have to attempt any of the usual compromises which are reached in the legislative process.[112] This pattern has been repeated to the present day, and was given encouragement by the Supreme Court in *Webster* in which, in his dissent, Justice Blackmun stated that: 'a plurality of this Court implicitly invites every state legislature to enact more and more restrictive abortion regulations in order to provoke more and more test cases, in the hope that sometime down the line the Court will return the law of procreative freedom to the severe limitations that generally prevailed in this country before January 22, 1973'.

There is no doubt that *Roe v Wade* benefited women to some extent (though largely only those who can fund their own treatment). But its top-down nature coupled with the fact that, in 1973, it represented a much more radical liberalisation of abortion than that generally approved of by public opinion, served to polarise politics around the abortion issue. While women in the US may have had to wait longer for access to abortion in the absence of *Roe v Wade*, and perhaps to have it granted them in more expressly limited terms, things might have progressed further and the right be less vulnerable to any change of personnel in the Supreme Court had the incremental process been allowed to continue in the absence of a ruling by the Supreme Court.[113]

Between 1966 and 1970, 16 US states liberalised their abortion laws, four states repealing their laws entirely in 1970. The legislative approach would probably have been slow, state legislatures waiting for public opinion to force their hands. Nor is it likely that it would have been comprehensive, some of the Bible belt states being unlikely to embrace abortion under any circumstances. But the trend in public opinion was towards liberalisation. In 1972, 83 per cent of Americans supported abortion where women's health was at stake (this was up from 77 per cent in 1962), 75 per cent in cases of foetal abnormality (up from 55 per cent). Only 46 per cent favoured access to abortion for social reasons, but this category had seen by far the largest increase in support in the previous ten years, having stood at only 15 per cent in 1962.[114]

Less resistance might have been generated by the incremental and limited approach, as in the UK, and the US might not now be in the position where politicians point score with abortion, being able to legislate restrictions they could not otherwise get away with politically (the majority of Americans still supporting the right to abortion) in the knowledge

---

[112] *Ibid. Planned Parenthood of Missouri v Danforth*, note 20 above is cited as an example.
[113] This is not to say that the same approach would happen elsewhere – Canada did not react similarly to *Morgentaler v R*, note 100 above. But that might have had much to do with the passage of time (15 years) and the widespread recognition that abortion in Canada was, prior to that decision, far more restricted than in comparable countries.
[114] Epstein and Kobylka, note 110 above, pp 152–153.

that they are just flexing their muscles to appeal to the right wing, while the core right to abortion will be protected by the Supreme Court.

Frank Susman, who represented the plaintiffs in one of the Supreme Court abortion cases, claimed that: 'Many state legislators really don't give a damn whether or not what they pass is constitutional. All they care about is whether or not it will be popular with their constituents, whom they perceive, usually incorrectly, to be conservative on the abortion issue. I think that legislators frequently abdicate their legislative responsibility to the judiciary and, unfortunately, there is no way to prevent it.'[115] And in 1995 the Chicago *Tribune* remarked that 'support for a bill that restricts abortion will protect [politicians] from likely attacks from abortion opponents in upcoming elections'. Even liberal politicians could, according to the *Tribune*, use their support for a restrictive law 'to defend themselves against opposition from the Right' – the very fact that the Supreme Court took the position that there was a constitutional right (however restricted) to abortion meant that politicians could make political capital out of their opposition to it.[116]

By contrast, and given the Irish Constitution's prohibition of abortion, the Irish people were confronted, in the early 1990s, with the full implications of their anti-choice stance. In a country in which opposition to abortion was almost universal, unquestioned and absolute, the plight of a 14-year-old girl raped, impregnated and ordered to remain in Ireland against her will (while her attacker was bailed) horrified many to whom the moral position had hitherto been clear-cut. The *Irish Times* condemned the 'descent into cruelty' demanding to know 'what sort of State' Ireland had become 'that in 1992, its full panoply of authority, its police, its law officers, its courts are mobilised to condemn a 14-year-old child to the ordeal of pregnancy and childbirth after rape at the hands of a "depraved and evil" man? With what are we now to compare ourselves? Ceaucescu's Romania? The Ayatollahs' Iran? Algeria? . . . We have landed in the nightmare'.[117]

Although the constitutional amendments which flowed from the 1992 X case were modest, in 1997, in the wake of another case involving the 'right to travel' (see above), a survey by the *Irish Times* showed that the unthinkable had happened and that 77 per cent of Irish people supported a right (albeit limited) to abortion, 55 per cent a right to terminate pregnancies in Ireland.[118] In December of that year the Irish Government set up a working group to draw up a Green Paper on abortion legislation.

The Irish people were shocked into reconsidering their traditional opposition to abortion by their recognition of the sheer cruelty to which

---

[115] Cited in Epstein and Kobylka, note 110 above, pp 219–220, citing E Rubin, *Abortion, Politics and the Courts: Roe v Wade and its Aftermath* (New York: Greenwood Press, 1987) p 131.
[116] Chicago *Tribune*, 2 February 1995.
[117] *Irish Times*, 18 February 1995.
[118] *Irish Times*, 11 December 1997.

their Constitution had subjected a young girl, a girl in whose shoes many could imagine their daughters standing. The impact on the Irish of being confronted with the product of their democratic voice forced a national reconsideration of moral absolutes. By contrast, Americans never had to consider, as a nation, the human cost of their pre-1973 abortion restrictions. Far from leading the US in a move towards tolerance, the decision in *Roe v Wade* served to underline to those opposed to abortion the rightness of their position, and to stir many of the otherwise apathetic into action. The impact this has had on women seeking abortions has been significant. But the backlash which followed *Roe v Wade* did not confine its effects to the abortion issue alone.

Just as abortion has been the point at which right and left have clashed in the US, the symbol of the struggle between liberals and conservatives, so too, abortion became the touchstone for Bush's appointment of judges, a kind of litmus test of potential judges' politics. President Reagan, whose own election was in part the result of the 'pro-family' *Roe v Wade* backlash, had started this particular ball rolling. According to Dworkin, his Department of Justice imposed 'the most stringent political tests for judicial appointments ever used in this country'.[119] The impact of those appointments has not been confined to the abortion issue. Those who take an anti-choice stance are more likely than their opponents to be socially conservative, and this has had repercussions throughout the spectrum of Supreme Court decision making. Thus, for example, on the issue of affirmative action (discussed in Chapter 7 below) there has been a significant movement to the right: that this might not have happened had the abortion issue not provided a litmus test for judicial appointments is a distinct possibility.

The upshot of *Roe v Wade* has, oddly, been to render the right to abortion vulnerable. Given the effect that it had in whipping up anti-abortion fervour, it set back the cause of legislative liberalisation and left US women in the position in which the right to abortion largely depends upon the personnel of the Supreme Court together with, for the moment, President Clinton's veto power. While the present make-up of the Supreme Court appears to leave the right to abortion intact, if rather more restricted than was previously the case, the appointment of an anti-choice President could, over time, reverse this position. If this were to happen, 16 states and the District of Columbia retain (currently unenforceable) pre-*Roe* abortion bans and ten states still have (again, currently unenforceable) laws requiring husbands' consent to abortion. Many of these will be reimposed if *Roe v Wade* is overruled entirely.

---

[119] R Dworkin, *Freedom's Law* (Cambridge, Mass: Harvard University Press, 1996), p 147.

Chapter 5

Controlling Women

Introduction

Restrictions on abortions have not been the only threat to American women's reproductive freedom. Even more alarming have been moves towards the prohibition of pregnancy for those regarded (whether for reasons of poverty or conduct) as unsuitable to bear children, and increased regulation of pregnant women's behaviour. The first of these threats has come, for the most part, from the judiciary, the second from both state legislatures and judges.

America, in common with many European countries, embraced eugenics during a considerable part of this century. In some states, even as late as the 1970s, many women (most of them black) were tricked or forced into accepting sterilisation as a condition of receiving welfare benefits, abortions or assistance during childbirth.[1] Sterilisation continues to be presented as the contraceptive method of choice to state-dependent American women, to whom it remains the most readily available form of birth control. In 1985, one critic remarked that the 'state makes it easier for a mother on welfare to obtain a sterilisation than to keep warm in the winter, find child care, or provide nourishing meals for her children'.[2]

The spectre of forced, as distinct from merely coerced, sterilisation died away in the US for a couple of decades, but re-emerged in the 1990s with proposals by Ohio's legislature forcibly to sterilise those women who could not overcome drug addictions. The proposal did not become law. But

---

[1] See, for example, *Rolf v Weinberger* 372 F Supp 1196 DDC (1974). See generally D Roberts, 'Punishing Drug Addicts Who Have Babies: Women of Color, Equality and the Right of Privacy' (1991) 104 *Harvard Law Review* 1419, at 1442 ff.

[2] T Shapiro, *Population Control Politics* (Philadelphia: Temple University Press, 1985), p 140. Sterilisation is the most common 'contraceptive choice' for American women, see *Washington Post*, 12 March 1995; K Houppert, 'The Politics of Birth Control: How Prolife Forces Strangle Research', *Village Voice*, 1 October 1996.

'sterilisation', albeit in non-permanent form, resurfaced as a more general issue with the licensing by the US Food and Drug Administration of Norplant, a hormone implant in the upper arm which renders women infertile for up to five years at a time. As soon as the device was approved, it was seized as a method of controlling the reproductive abilities of poor women and those otherwise regarded as unsuitable mothers.[3] In the early 1990s, 13 US states considered moves to induce poor women to have the implant. The inducements were, typically, to consist of payments to those who accepted the device.[4] None of these plans came to fruition. But within two years of Norplant's approval, every US state, together with the District of Columbia, made Norplant available to women reliant on public health care (the morning-after pill remains unavailable to these women[5]). And within two weeks of Norplant's licensing by the FDA in 1991, a Californian judge had ordered a woman convicted of child abuse to accept implantation as a condition of her probation.[6]

This was not the first time that a judge had sought to intervene in a woman's childbearing decisions. Between 1967 and 1989, judges in California, Ohio, Florida, Kansas, Idaho and Arizona had imposed contraceptive (in one case sterilisation) probation conditions on women convicted of child abuse.[7] Judge Boardman, who issued the first Norplant order, had previously imposed a 'no pregnancy' order as a condition of probation for a woman convicted of possession of 0.1 grammes of heroin.[8] According to Judge Boardman in the Norplant case, the defendant's 'current unconceived children have rights, and we as a government have a duty and an obligation to help her and these children'.[9] The judge persisted in making his order in the face of medical argument that the device was unsuitable for the defendant and failed, despite her questions as to its safety, to inform her of the potentially serious side-effects associated with it.[10] And despite the overruling of the 1990 Boardman decision by

[3] *Philadelphia Inquirer*, 12 December 1990, discussed in the *Los Angeles Times*, 13 January 1991. See also *Washington Times*, 24 December 1990 and *St Petersburg Times*, 22 December 1990. The US press still carries headlines such as 'How Norplant can end welfare as we know it' (*New Jersey Law Journal*, 19 August 1996).

[4] *American Lawyer*, October 1996; *Los Angeles Times*, 3 September 1996; *Commercial Appeal*, Memphis, 12 February 1992; J Hand, 'Buying Fertility: The Constitutionality of Welfare Bonuses' (1993) 46 *Vanderbilt Law Review* 715. According to the *Washington Post*, 20 November 1994, Washington's then mayor-elect, Marion Barry, 'called for draconian measures – including, in some cases, a mandatory five-year contraceptive implant (Norplant) for women on welfare'.

[5] 4.1 million women in 1991, according to the *Los Angeles Times*, 13 January 1991. See also J Vance, 'Womb for Rent: Norplant and the Undoing of Poor Women' (1994) 21 *Hastings Constitutional Law Quarterly* 827, at 832; M Henley, 'The Creation and Perpetuation of the Mother/Body Myth' (1993) 41 *Buffalo Law Review* 703.

[6] Darlene Johnson, see note 144 below and accompanying text.

[7] *People v Dominguez* 256 Cal 2d 623 (1967); *People v Pointer* 151 Cal 3d 1128 (1984).

[8] *San Francisco Chronicle*, 27 August 1996.

[9] *Chicago Tribune*, 20 November 1994.

[10] *San Francisco Chronicle*, 27 August 1996. Norplant's side-effects have subsequently been the subject of legal actions and in April 1999 the drug was withdrawn in the UK.

California's Court of Appeal, judges in Illinois and elsewhere followed suit with contraceptive-conditional sentences for women. When the Illinois legislature moved to prohibit forced contraception, a number of state judges ordered women not to become pregnant during probation on child abuse and neglect charges, one going so far as to rule that the woman would have to refrain from 'any activity which has the reasonable potential of causing her to become pregnant'. When this woman became pregnant nine months after the judge's order, she was sentenced to six years' imprisonment. Another Illinois judge extended the maximum sentence on a child abuse charge in order to keep a woman in prison so that she could not become pregnant again.[11] And others have continued to pass such sentences despite rulings from a number of higher courts across the US that contraceptive-conditional probation orders were unlawful (these cases are discussed below).[12]

The threat of legislatively coerced or induced contraception by a particular means (ie Norplant) appears to have retreated, the states having failed to make welfare payments conditional upon, or to offer financial inducements to women to accept, long-term contraception. But many states have chosen to discourage poor women from having children by imposing 'family caps' – policies which deny additional benefits to children conceived and born while their mothers are dependent on welfare. By March 1997, 19 US states operated these caps, the policy having been encouraged by 1996 federal legislation which rewarded states up to $25 million a year in an 'illegitimacy bonus' if they reduced illegitimate birth rates without increasing the rate of abortions.[13] The motivation behind such legislation is considered below and in Chapter 10.

Punishing mothers

The attempts made by judiciary and legislature to discourage reproduction by the 'undeserving' have been coupled with heightened regulation of pregnant women's conduct. Punishments are increasingly being meted out in the US to women who take illegal drugs while pregnant. In 1987, a Californian drug user was charged under a child-neglect statute when her baby died a few days after birth. The charge was dismissed on the ground that the statute was intended to deal with paternal failure to contribute towards the support of the foetus, and was inapt to deal with

---

[11]   *Chicago Tribune*, 20 November 1994 and 14 January 1996.
[12]   See also *Chattanooga Free Press*, 18 April 1996 and *Michigan Lawyers Weekly*, April 1997.
[13]   *Dallas Morning News*, 26 May 1995. Nationally, birth rates dropped 7% between 1990 and 1995, according to the National Center for Health Statistics. Over the same period, rates dropped 17% for black women, who are disproportionately represented in the welfare population.

pre-natal neglect.[14] But in 1988 a New York judge had ruled that a woman's failure to obtain ante-natal care, as well as her use of cocaine, constituted child abuse.[15] Many states amended child abuse laws to include foetuses within their protection in order to target drug-using women, automatically to define drug use during pregnancy as child abuse, to criminalise drug use during pregnancy and/or to require, sometimes under pain of criminal conviction for doctors, drug screening of newborns and the report of positive results.[16] Others passed laws to define pregnant women's drug use or alcoholism as evidence that the child would be abused immediately after birth, or to cast pregnant women as an exception to the general rule that only those substance abusers who pose a threat to themselves or others can be subject to involuntary commitment.[17]

In Michigan, South Carolina, California, New York and South Dakota, women have lost custody of their children, newborn or otherwise, temporarily or permanently, on the basis of positive drug tests during or immediately after pregnancy.[18] Custody, even visiting rights, has not always been renewed after addiction has been successfully treated.[19] And such sanctions have not been reserved for those women whose drug use was illegal. In 1987, a Michigan woman lost custody of her child for a year after taking prescribed valium during her pregnancy and despite being drug free at the time of the custody hearing.[20] In 1991, one commentator remarked on a 'growing trend among legislators to pass laws explicitly criminalizing drug use during pregnancy . . . [and a] growing trend among judges to use the sentencing phase of criminal trials to incarcerate pregnant substance-dependent women, in an attempt to protect fetal health, absent statutes explicitly creating a "fetal abuse" crime'.[21] Some areas were, by this time, testing newborn babies suspected of being in drug-related distress and automatically removing those who tested positive from their mothers.[22]

The first woman to be convicted in the US for drug use during pregnancy was convicted in 1989 of 'drug trafficking' for delivering cocaine, by way of the umbilical cord, to her two children at the moment of their

---

[14] M Burke, 'The Constitutionality of the Use of the Norplant Contraceptive Device as a Condition of Probation' (1992) 20 *Hastings Constitutional Law Quarterly* 207. See also L Paltrow, 'When Becoming Pregnant Is a Crime' (1990) 9 *Criminal Justice Ethics* 41.

[15] See B Steinbock, *Life Before Birth: The Moral and Legal Status of Embryos and Fetuses* (New York: Oxford University Press, 1992).

[16] *Los Angeles Times*, 3 September 1996, *Atlanta Journal and Constitution*, 8 December 1995.

[17] R Sherman, 'Keeping Baby Safe from Mom', *National Law Journal*, 3 October 1988.

[18] See, for example, *Re Valerie D* 233 Conn 492 (1992), Supreme Court of Connecticut; *Re Solomon L* 190 Cal App 3d 1106 (1987). For the position in the UK, see J Fortin, 'Legal Protection for the Unborn Child' (1988) 51 *Modern Law Review* 54.

[19] See, for example, *Re SW* (1987), California Circuit Court.

[20] *Re J Jeffrey* (1987), Michigan Court of Appeal.

[21] B Becker, 'Order in the Court' (1991) 19 *Hastings Constitutional Law Quarterly* 235, at 235. According to the *Futurist*, July 1991, a few have even been threatened with a court-ordered abortion unless they abstain from drugs.

[22] See the *National Law Journal*, 3 October 1988; Sherman, note 17 above.

births.[23] She was sentenced to 15 years' probation by the Florida courts. In the same year Connie Welch gave birth to a baby who was born drug free (save for traces of nicotine and caffeine in his blood), full term, without birth defects, and with size and weight appropriate for gestational age, but who showed some mild signs of 'neonatal abstinence syndrome', the result of her drug use during pregnancy. Welch was found guilty of 'abuse' and sentenced to two years for possession of drugs and five years, to run consecutively, for the abuse.[24] In 1992 a Tennessee woman was sentenced to eight years' probation for aggravated child abuse when, after her cocaine use during pregnancy, her child was born two months prematurely.[25] In the same year, a woman was jailed in North Dakota for recklessly endangering the foetus she carried by her chronic paint sniffing.[26] And a Californian woman who had cocaine and alcohol as she was due to give birth was charged with second degree murder (carrying a minimum 15-year sentence) when her daughter was stillborn.[27] The statute under which she was charged was intended to apply to those who used violence against pregnant women and the foetuses they carried. Also in 1992, Cornelia Whitner was sentenced to eight years' imprisonment on child abuse charges after her baby was born with cocaine in his system.[28]

Where charges of trafficking or abuse were considered inappropriate under state law, women like Georgia's Darla Luster were convicted instead of possession of drugs.[29] Luster's baby tested positive for cocaine at birth, whereupon her probation on a shoplifting conviction was revoked and Luster was thrown into jail, denied bail, prevented even from seeing her baby and charged with distributing drugs to the baby. This charge was thrown out but one of drugs possession was substituted and Luster, having served four months in jail, was sentenced to six years' probation. In 1990, a Massachusetts woman was charged with possession when her baby's urine showed traces of cocaine. By the end of 1992, almost 200 women in 24 states had been prosecuted in connection with drug use during pregnancy. Most pleaded guilty to the charges pressed, or settled for plea bargains. Many other drug-using pregnant women have been punished more severely in respect of drug related and other offences – in particular, for their imprisonment on remand or after conviction in the perceived interests of the foetus.[30] And pregnant Native

---

[23] Jennifer Johnson, discussed at text to note 154 below.

[24] Steinbock, note 15 above; Sherman, note 17 above. This sentence was successfully appealed in *Commonwealth of Kentucky v Welch* 864 SW 2d 280 (1993).

[25] *Gannett News Service*, 4 September 1992.

[26] Sherman, note 17 above.

[27] *Los Angeles Times*, 17 June 1992.

[28] *State of South Carolina v Whitner* (1996) SC LEXIS 120 WL 398164. The US Supreme Court refused to hear Whitner's appeal. 328 US 1 (1997).

[29] *State of Georgia v Luster* 419 SE 2d 32 (1992), Ga Ct App.

[30] Steinbock, note 15 above, p 140; Sherman, note 17 above; *Washington Post*, 13 September 1988; *Los Angeles Times*, 25 April 1989; *Washington Post*, 4 September 1988; *Times Union* (Albany, New York), 28 May 1994; Becker, note 21 above, p 237.

American women are frequently imprisoned for being 'drunk, disorderly and pregnant'.[31]

Significant injuries may be inflicted upon foetuses by maternal drug use. But many of the assumptions about the level of foetal harm associated with illegal drug use during pregnancy have proved to be unfounded, and many of the problems experienced by babies born to drug-using women indistinguishable from those associated with maternal poverty, poor nutrition, ill-health and lack of ante-natal care (this latter being associated with distance from hospital and lack of public transportation, as well as with doctors' reluctance to treat drug-using women and women's fear of criminalisation).[32] No one would suggest that the ingestion of illegal drugs, many prescription drugs, cigarettes, or excess alcohol, is good for pregnant women, or for the foetuses they carry. But the hysteria which has been generated over the issue in the US has served only to demonise women who, for the most part, are desperately underprivileged; are almost invariably addicted to the substances they use; may well be engaged in prostitution, with all the usual accompanying risks of violence; and are frequently denied access to the treatment many of them seek.

The argument typically used to justify the mandatory testing of those suspected of drug use, their criminalisation and, frequently, the loss of custody rights, is that of concern for their offspring, the 'most tragic victims', the 'innocent victims', the 'smallest victims'. But this alleged 'concern' is manifested on occasion by the arrest, handcuffing and shackling of women hours after they gave birth or, worse still, during labour.[33] Babies have been removed from their mothers immediately after birth – this without any assessment of the risk, if any, posed by the mother. All this despite the fact a positive drug test of a woman or newborns may indicate occasional, rather than chronic, drug use – and this perhaps without knowledge of their potential impact on the foetus. A positive result can also be produced by some foodstuffs, or can indicate that a woman has simply been around drug users, where, for example, she has passively inhaled smoke from another person's use of crack cocaine.

The coercive nature of drug-testing programmes is counter-productive, high-profile prosecutions of drug-using pregnant women deterring others

---

[31] Becker, note 21 above, pp 237–238.

[32] D Mathieu, *Preventing Prenatal Harm: Should the State Intervene?* (2nd ed, Washington DC: Georgetown University Press, 1996). See also the Heritage Foundation *Policy Review*, Spring 1995, p 12, citing L Robins *et al*, 'Effects of *in Utero* Exposure to Street Drugs' (1993) 83 *American Journal of Public Health* 3; *Atlanta Journal and Constitution*, 20 December 1992; C Daniels, *At Women's Expense: State Power and the Politics of Fetal Rights* (Cambridge Massachusetts: Harvard University Press, 1993), p 124; *Washington Post*, 13 September 1988, US Department of Health and Human Service's *Public Health Report* (1994), p 647; *Los Angeles Times*, 13 June 1993; L Mayes *et al*, 'The Problem of Prenatal Cocaine Exposure, A Rush to Judgment' (1992) 67 *Journal of the American Medical Association* 406; Roberts, note 1 above, at 1429 ff.

[33] This took place at the Medical University of South Carolina between 1989 and 1994 – see the *Post and Courier* (Charleston), 9 January 1997.

from seeking ante-natal care.[34] Nor, in many cases, is coercion necessary. Women who have been punished for drug use during pregnancy have, in many cases, sought assistance in their attempts to stop using.[35] But such treatment is almost impossible to obtain, many programmes excluding pregnant women and the bulk being targeted primarily or exclusively at men.[36] The failure of states to provide adequate treatment for drug-addicted pregnant women has occurred despite federal requirements that 10 per cent of federal drug abuse, alcohol and mental health services grants be spent on prevention and treatment programmes for alcoholic and drug-dependent women.

Judges are fond of throwing pregnant women into prison to 'protect' their 'unborn children'. But ante-natal care in US prisons is inadequate, pregnant women being denied proper nutrition and exercise.[37] In 1985 a class action was instituted against a Californian women's prison which had denied a pregnant woman medical care for two and a half weeks despite her severe abdominal cramping and bleeding. Her child, born en route to hospital, survived for only two hours.[38] This may have been a particularly severe case, but it was not an isolated one. Perhaps even more alarming, there is 'startling evidence that some prison staff members . . . assign the pregnant women work that requires a great deal of exertion and heavy lifting, even when the women have a history of miscarriage'.[39] And pregnant women do not only suffer inadequate care while in prison. If they are imprisoned for continuing to use illegal drugs while pregnant, imprisonment will not prevent continued use (drugs of all kinds being readily available to prisoners) and may, by removing any support otherwise available to women, actually exacerbate it.

None of this is to suggest that pregnancy or recent childbirth should render women immune from prosecution or imprisonment in cases where

---

[34] Becker, note 21 above, p 241. Fear of the effect of prosecutions on women's willingness to seek ante-natal treatment has caused the American College of Obstetricians and Gynaecologists, the American Medical Association, the American Academy of Pediatricians and the American Public Health Association to oppose policies of criminalisation – see A Dubler, 'Monitoring Motherhood: Note on *Whitner* (1996) 106(3) *Yale Law Journal* 935, citing the Center for Reproductive Law and Policy, *Punishing Women for their Behaviour during Pregnancy* (1996).

[35] *Post and Courier* (Charleston), 9 January 1997; *Chicago Tribune*, 21 May 1989.

[36] W Chenkin, 'Drug Addiction and Pregnancy: Policy Crossroads' (1990) 80 *American Journal of Public Health* 483; Steinbock, note 15 above, p 139; D Roberts, 'Victory for Jennifer Johnson, Lesson for New Jersey', *New Jersey Law Journal*, 26 October 1992; *United Press International*, 6 March 1992; *Arizona Republic*, 9 May 1995; the Hastings Centre *Report*, January 1992.

[37] E Barry, 'Pregnancy Prisoners' (1989) 12 *Harvard Women's Law Journal* 189; P King, 'Helping Women Helping Children: Drug Policy and Future Generations: Confronting Drug Policy: Part 2 (1991) 69(4) *The Milbank Quarterly* 595. See also Becker, note 21 above, p 239, citing S Stefan, 'Whose Egg Is It Anyway? (1989) 13 *Nova Law Review* 405.

[38] Steinbock, note 15 above, p 141.

[39] Stefan, cited by Becker, note 21 above. See also Human Rights Watch, *Global Report on Women's Human Rights* (New York: Human Rights Watch, 1995), Chapter 3, for details of appalling abuse of pregnant women inside US jails.

they commit offences otherwise meriting such punishment. But drug use itself, if it does come to the attention of the authorities, may not even be criminal and, in any event, does not usually result in imprisonment. Women have been punished for behaviour such as valium use and drinking which was not, absent consideration of the foetus, unlawful.[40] Indeed, some supporters of foetal rights go even further than prosecutors and advocate imposing legal duties on pregnant women to take vitamins, calcium and iron supplementation and control their weight as well as to avoid endangering the foetus through exposure to alcohol and nicotine.[41] No advocate of foetal rights has yet to suggest that foetuses be given the right to be nurtured by women free from the effects of poverty. Nor, despite ample evidence that paternal cocaine use affects foetal development, have any men been prosecuted as a result.[42]

Even if drug use was, of itself, illegal, it would not generally be discovered were it not for the fact that pregnant women present themselves to drug-testing hospitals for ante-natal care or for the birth itself. Punitive programmes render women, *because they are women*, vulnerable to prosecution for behaviour which would otherwise go unnoticed. Further, they target only the users of the particular hospitals in which programmes are – generally poor, black women. According to research carried out in Florida in 1989, 15 per cent of all pregnant women used illegal drugs, there being no significant difference between black and white women (the latter being marginally more likely to take drugs during pregnancy). But, of those whose drug use was detected, black women were ten times more likely to be prosecuted than white women.[43] And even if black women are somewhat more likely than whites, Hispanics or native Americans to use illegal drugs when pregnant (other research suggesting that this is the case[44]), the rate at which they are arrested and prosecuted for

[40] See *Re J Jeffrey* (1987), Michigan Court of Appeal; the prosecution of Deborah Zimmerman discussed in the *Dallas Morning News*, 7 December 1997 and the *Guardian*, 7 August 1997; the prosecution of Rosemarie Tourigny discussed in the *Boston Globe*, 16 August 1996; and that of prosecution of Diane Pfannensteil discussed in J Petrow, 'Addicted Mothers: Drug-exposed Babies' (1991) 36 *New York Law School Review* 573. Pfannensteil was charged with endangering her foetus when, on seeking treatment for injuries inflicted by her husband, she was tested for alcohol intake. Statutes in a number of states define alcohol abuse by pregnant women as child abuse – see N Schiff, 'Legislation Punishing Drug Use During Pregnancy' (1991) 19 *Hastings Constitutional Law Quarterly* 197.
[41] See, for example, M Shaw, 'Conditional Prospective Rights of the Fetus' (1984) 5 *Journal of Legal Medicine* 63. See also J Robertson, 'Procreative Liberty and the Control of Conception, Pregnancy and Childbirth' (1983) 69 *Virginia Law Review* 405; *Children of Choice: Freedom and the New Reproductive Technologies* (Princeton New Jersey: Princeton University Press, 1994).
[42] R Yaziki *et al*, 'Demonstration of Specific Binding of Cocaine to Human Spermatazoa' (1991) 26 *Journal of the American Medical Association* 1956.
[43] *New York Times*, 20 July 1990; Roberts, note 1 above and 'Crime Race and Reproduction' (1993) *Tulane Law Review* 1945; D Johnsen, 'Shared Interests: Promoting Healthy Births Without Sacrificing Women's Liberty' (1992) 43 *Hastings Law Journal* 569.
[44] *The Record* (Bergen, New Jersey), 9 December 1994, reporting New Jersey tests.

so doing is completely out of proportion to any greater involvement in drug use.[45] This is suggestive of discrimination in the application of the law.

Punishing pregnant women is unfair, counter-productive and ultimately futile. It may also may represent the top of a very slippery slope. Foetal well-being is maximised when the pregnant woman (otherwise referred to as the 'maternal' or 'prenatal' 'environment') is well nourished, well rested, free from stress and depression. It is clear that cigarette consumption can lead to reduced birth weight and is linked with an increased incidence of miscarriage and sudden infant death syndrome.[46] Inadequate exercise can result in a less than perfect 'maternal environment'. So, too, can excessive exercise, under or over-eating, being too old or too young, taking or not taking various dietary supplements, stress, overwork and, perhaps most significant of all, poverty.

If it is considered appropriate to punish women who use illegal drugs during pregnancy (and to do so, expressly, because of the risk to the foetus), then perhaps it is logical to punish those who put the foetuses they carry at risk by smoking, drinking alcohol, eating too much or too little, exercising too much or not enough, allowing themselves to become stressed or over-worked, feeling unhappy about the fact of their pregnancies.[47] It might even be argued that, prevention being better than cure and foetuses being most vulnerable to damage during the first trimester, all potentially fertile women should be subjected to detailed and enforceable prescriptions relating to smoking, drinking, nutrition, exercise, work and general well-being. This has not, as yet, been suggested. But in 1980, a Californian teenager was ordered to be institutionalised until the birth of her baby because she was considered unable to look after herself properly, a juvenile court ruling that the foetus she carried was a 'child' under the state's welfare code, and that child should be detained until its birth.[48] In 1991, a Californian judge threatened a pregnant probationer that: 'if she got caught smoking, I was going to send her to prison and take away the baby'.[49] And in 1995, a pregnant cocaine user in Wisconsin, was institutionalised for three weeks prior to the birth of her baby. In that case the state appeals court dismissed the argument that her rights were violated by this action, ruling that *only the foetus*, by that stage (the third trimester), according to the court, a 'person' in its own right, was detained.[50]

---

[45] Two or three times as likely, at a stretch and account for around 12% of women, but account for between 75% and 85% of those prosecuted.

[46] ABC *World News Tonight*, 11 April 1995, reporting University of Massachusetts research.

[47] Recent evidence that being unwanted in the womb is associated with increased incidence of schizophrenia.

[48] Kay Smith, discussed in Mathieu, note 32 above, pp 76–77. The case was overturned on appeal on meaning of 'child', but this was after the birth.

[49] *Chicago Tribune*, 11 January 1991.

[50] *State of Wisconsin ex rel Angela MW v Kuuzicki* 561 NW 2d 729 (1997), discussed at text to note 152 below.

Rights of women in pregnancy and childbirth

Women in labour

As if all of this were not sufficiently alarming, the extension of 'foetal rights' also creates the spectre of coercive medical treatment being carried out on or in the woman's body in order to further what doctors perceive to be the interests of the foetus she carries. This has proved a real threat to women in the UK in recent years, forced medical intervention (generally in the form of unwanted caesarean sections) in childbirth being perhaps the most significant threat to British women's reproductive autonomy.

The difficulties in this area arise, in part, because many doctors who treat pregnant women regard themselves as having two patients – 'one . . . inside another'.[51] As soon as women dispute the medical management of pregnancy and childbirth the medical profession tends, despite its frequent protestations to the contrary, to regard them as hostile to the foetuses they carry. Once categorised in this way, it is a small step to treat women as incompetent, mad, wicked, or merely stupid. Given the pressing matter of the health or even survival of the 'second patient', it seems that the pregnant woman's wishes are easily overridden.

The drive to impose unwanted medical treatment on pregnant women, and readily to regard their expressed wishes as, at best, ill-informed, is particularly problematic given the very wide differences of medical opinion which exist as to the necessity for intervention in the childbearing process. A caesarean section is major surgery which, being carried out in the abdominal area, carries a significant risk of post-operative infection, and results in the new mother being much less well after the birth than she would with a normal vaginal delivery.[52] The procedure reduces a woman's chances of having a subsequent vaginal delivery and, causing as it does a weakening of the uterus wall, limits the number of subsequent pregnancies she can safely undertake.[53] While caesarean sections can avert death and injury, they should not be regarded as unproblematic. And, while most caesarean sections are indicated by electronic foetal monitoring (EFM), indications of foetal distress by these monitoring devices are false in up to four out of five cases.[54] Such are the false positive rates

---

[51] Susan Bewley, Director of Obstetrics at Guy's and St Thomas's Hospitals Trust, *Guardian*, 24 April 1997.

[52] Mathieu, note 32 above, p 104, citing E Shearer, 'Caesarean Sections: Medical Benefits and Costs' (1993) 37 *Social Science and Medicine* 1223.

[53] In two of the cases of forced, court-ordered caesareans which came to light in the UK in 1996, women had previously had caesareans and were, according to the doctors, at risk of rupturing their scars. See D Brahams, 'Caesarean Sections by Court Order' (1996) 348(30) *The Lancet* 770. According to E Goodrick and G Salancik, 'Organisational Discretion in Responding to Institutional Practices: Hospitals and Cesarean Births', *Administrative Science Quarterly*, March 1996, until the mid 1980s the general approach was 'once a cesarean, always a cesarean', an attitude dating back to 1916.

[54] Steinbock, note 15 above, p 151.

associated with EFM, and the number of unnecessary caesarean sections performed as a result, that its use does not improve childbirth outcomes.[55] Increased use of caesarean sections is also associated with shortages of midwives – in Mexico City, for example, where there are no midwives, caesarean sections account for 80 per cent of births.[56]

Doctors are very quick to resort to caesarean sections if there is any suggestion of foetal distress. If the slightest risk to the foetus is perceived, caesareans are seen as the course of action least likely to result in litigation. The same appears to be true in relation to induced labour, whether labour is induced early because of concerns about foetal growth or when the due date is past. But while such procedures may be 'safe' in terms of foetal morbidity, it appears that little account is taken by doctors of their effect on women. And this being the case, little appears to be balanced against the avoidance of litigation.

There is much room for debate between pregnant women and the medical profession about the most appropriate management of their pregnancies. This debate might relate to the decision whether or not to attempt a home birth, to whether vaginal delivery should be attempted in the face of complications such as the baby being in the breech position, to how late into the pregnancy the woman can safely work, to the prescription of vitamin supplements and other forms of medication, to the number and timing of ultrasound scans which should be performed.

This is not to suggest that women are as well informed about obstetrics as are the doctors who practise the subject. But recent history of the management of pregnancies gives women every reason to question standard medical procedure. In the 1960s and 1970s, women in labour were frequently given episiotomies, some doctors taking the view that cutting the vaginal opening made deliveries easier to manage. Pregnant women have, in the past, been routinely X-rayed: X-rays are now not administered to pregnant women because of recognised risks to the foetus. The traditional approach to labour was that the appropriate place for a labouring woman was on her back with her feet in stirrups: it is now recognised that, complications aside, this is one of the worst possible positions to adopt. Today, doctors become concerned if women gain too little weight (less than about 21–28 lb or 10–13 kg) over the course of their pregnancies. Yet 20 years ago, many doctors advised women to gain no more than 14 lb (about 7 kg), and routinely administered diuretics (now rarely prescribed) to minimise fluid retention. Until recently, pregnant women were advised to eat liver once or twice a week at least: pregnant women are now advised not to eat this food since it was discovered that massive doses of vitamin A, in which liver is rich, could damage the foetus. It is scarcely necessary to mention the repercussions

[55] Goodrick and Salancik, note 53 above.
[56] Obstetrician Michel Odent, quoted in the *Scotsman*, 11 May 1998.

of the once-routine prescription of thalidomide as a sedative for pregnant women.

Given the unreliability of much medical advice during pregnancy and the questionable practices which have been standard, at various times, in the management of labour, it is scarcely surprising that many women are uneasy about the medical advice they receive during pregnancy and childbirth. Today, for example, some medical practices refuse to refer pregnant women for pregnancy ultrasound scans, issuing dark warnings about the lack of long-term research into their effects on the foetus. Other clinics order such scans at about 12 weeks' gestation for no other reason than to permit more accurate 'dating' of the foetus (which dating is of dubious value). Women who receive ultrasound scans at this stage of the pregnancy will generally also have one at around 20 weeks' gestation to check for foetal abnormalities, and may have any number of scans towards the end of the pregnancy if there are any concerns about foetal development.

Most women, faced with the possibility of improving the lot of the foetuses they carry, will eagerly subject themselves to considerable discomfort in order to do so. Indeed, women who have children imperil their jobs, put at risk their future earning capacity, accept huge restrictions on their freedom. Pregnancy itself imposes significant health risks, risks which are generally shrugged off by women who are more concerned with the health of their babies. And in childbirth women's primary concerns are, almost invariably, with their babies. Most women, if advised to undergo any particular procedure for the sake of the foetus they carry, will do so with alacrity. But women whose primary concern is the well-being of their potential offspring may find themselves in conflict with doctors about how that well-being may best be served. Those who practise obstetrics sometimes appear to favour intervention almost for its own sake,[57] and women frequently experience pregnancy as a struggle between doctors and themselves. And even if, in some cases, the decisions women make about their pregnancies are irrational, ill thought-out or eccentric, coercion can be used on those who do not wish to suffer pain or risk or who, for one reason or another, do not agree with the doctors' views in a particular case, only if their autonomy is sacrificed to the interests of the foetuses they carry.

Legal position in the UK

Below the impact in the US of constitutional rights in this area will be considered. First, however, it is useful to consider the legal position

---

[57] Goodrick and Salancik, note 53 above, found that the use of caesarean sections differed between hospitals in line with the manner of their funding, pointed out the 'costs of waiting for a vaginal delivery' (this being less of a factor in teaching hospitals due to the ready availability of residents).

in the UK prior to the implementation of the Human Rights Act 1998. The general rule, confirmed by the House of Lords in *Sidaway v Governor of Bethlem Royal Hospital*[58] is that adults are free to refuse medical treatment, regardless of the possible consequences and regardless of how irrational the decision, as long as they are 'competent'. 'Competence', in this context, requires that the patient is (1) able to understand and retain information, (2) able to believe it and (3) able to weigh up the pros and cons of an issue to reach a considered decision. This test was set out in *Re C*, in which the High Court supported the right of a paranoid schizophrenic Broadmoor patient to veto the amputation of his gangrenous foot (the operation being necessary, according to his doctors, to save his life) despite the man's delusional belief that he could cure himself (he did, in fact, survive with both legs intact).[59] Specifically in the context of pregnant women, the Court of Appeal ruled, in *Re F*,[60] that because 'an unborn child has . . . no existence independent of its mother', the interests of the foetus cannot be taken into account in determining whether or not pregnant women should be forced to submit to unwanted medical treatment.

The position seems tolerably clear. But in *Re S*[61] the High Court, without considering the issue of competence, issued an order to permit the use of 'reasonable force' to perform a caesarean section on a woman who, on religious grounds, opposed the operation. Relying on a remark made *obiter* by Lord Donaldson MR in a previous case to the effect that 'the only possible qualification' to the right of a competent patient to refuse medical treatment 'is a case in which the choice may lead to the death of a viable foetus', and on his incorrect understanding of the US decision in *Re AC*[62] (see below), Sir Stephen Brown P declared that, in view of the 'desperately serious' situation of the woman and her 'unborn child', whose lives were, according to the doctors' evidence in imminent danger (the woman herself was not represented), the order would be granted.[63]

---

[58] [1985] 1 All ER 643, [1985] AC 871. See also *F v West Berkshire Health Authority (Mental Health Act Commission intervening)* [1989] 2 All ER 545, [1990] 2 AC 1; *Airedale NHS Trust v Bland* [1993] 1 All ER 821, [1993] AC 789.

[59] *Re C (Refusal of Medical Treatment)* [1994] 1 FLR 31. The Court of Appeal in *Re MB* [1997] 2 FCR 541, (1997) 38 BMLR 175, [1997] Fam Law 542 expressed the test in the following terms: 'A person lacks capacity if some impairment or disturbance of mental functioning renders the person unable to make a decision [in the sense that he or she] . . . (a) . . . is unable to comprehend and retain the information which is material to the decision, especially as to the likely consequences of having or not having the treatment in question; (b) . . . is unable to use the information and weigh it in the balance as part of the process of arriving at the decision. If . . . a compulsive disorder or phobia . . . stifles belief in the information presented . . . the decision may not be a true one'.

[60] [1988] 2 All ER 193, [1988] Fam 337, [1988] 2 WLR 1288.

[61] *Re S (Adult: Refusal of Medical Treatment)* [1993] Fam 123, [1992] 3 WLR 806, [1992] 4 All ER 671, [1993] 1 FLR 26.

[62] 533 A 2d 203, 533 A 2d 611 (1988).

[63] *Re S*, note 61 above. Lord Donaldson's opinion was in *Re T (Adult: Refusal of Treatment)* [1993] Fam 95, [1992] 3 WLR 782, [1992] 4 All ER 649, [1992] 2 FLR 458.

The correctness of *Re S* was clearly in doubt. But it remained the working authority on forced caesarean sections for some years during which substantial numbers of women underwent forced, court-ordered caesareans. The orders were generally made at court hearings at which women were unrepresented and about which, in general, they knew nothing until 'presented with a *fait accompli*'.[64] Judges, typically with no experience of this area, generally decided cases 'at a moment's notice' and having been informed that the issue was one of 'life and death . . . unless the doctors intervene quickly'.[65] And even in cases in which orders were not sought, it seems that the threat of court action was used to coerce women into unwanted procedures.[66]

In *Re MB*[67] the Court of Appeal doubted *Re S* and declared Lord Donaldson's *dicta* incorrect, stating that 'every person is presumed to have the capacity to consent to or to refuse medical treatment [and a] competent woman . . . may . . . choose not to have medical intervention, even though the consequence may be the death or serious handicap of the child she bears, or her own death' and that 'the interests of the unborn child should not be taken into account by the courts'.[68]

This decision would appear, at first glance, to stand as a bulwark against the imposition of caesarean sections and other forms of medical intervention upon unwilling women. But despite its restatement of the classic legal position, the Court of Appeal in *Re MB* upheld a High Court order permitting a forced caesarean section. The court order had been issued after a telephone conversation between the judge and the hospital authorities, and approved by the Court of Appeal three hours later after a secret hearing in which MB herself was not represented. The Court of Appeal ordered that the operation be carried out before asking the hospital to file evidence.

The Court of Appeal upheld the order on the grounds that the woman's 'needle phobia' had rendered her incompetent. According to the court, 'panic, indecision and irrationality . . . could be symptoms of' incompetence, and while fear 'might be a rational reason for refusing to undergo' surgery, it 'could also paralyse the will and destroy the capacity to make a decision'.[69] 'It must', the Court of Appeal reasoned, 'be in the best interests of a woman carrying a full-term child who she wants born alive and

---

[64] *Guardian*, 11 March 1997; *The Times*, 23 September 1996 and 23 December 1996 letters page.

[65] *Guardian*, 11 March 1997.

[66] Immediately after the decision, Dr Graham Burt of the Medical Defence Union's medical division suggested that, although '[i]t is not a situation in which legal precedent would apply . . . one could use the case in discussions with patients who were reluctant to agree': *Independent*, 14 October 1992.

[67] Note 59 above.

[68] *Ibid*, applying *Paton v British Pregnancy Advisory Trustees* [1978] 2 All ER 987, [1979] QB 276; *C v S* [1987] 1 All ER 1230, [1988] QB 135 and *Re F (in utero)*, note 60 above.

[69] Press Association *Newsfile*, 26 March 1997.

healthy that such a result should if possible be achieved'. Psychiatric evidence which MB, not being represented in court, was not at liberty to dispute, suggested that she was likely to suffer long-term damage if the baby, which was in breech position, was born handicapped or died (here there was no question of her physical health requiring the procedure).

In this respect the decision in *Re MB* set an alarming precedent. It seems that women will very readily be judged incompetent when their wishes conflict with those of the doctors attending them. If a woman declares that she wants a healthy baby, her refusal to succumb to the dictates of the doctors may be dismissed as the result of 'panic, indecision and irrationality' the 'symptoms' of 'incompetence . . . paralys[is of] the will and destr[uction of] the capacity to make a decision'. Further, if she declares that she does not, both medical profession and judiciary would be very ready to find that this itself rendered her incompetent, if only on the basis that she would be riddled with guilt and suffer psychiatric damage if anything actually did happen to the baby.[70]

For all the lip-service paid by the Court of Appeal in *Re MB* to the right of a woman to determine her own medical treatment, 'competence' leaves the door wide open to forced interventions in the management of pregnancy. The theory is that the interests of the foetus should play no role in determining whether a pregnant woman is entitled to refuse medical treatment. But the approach taken by the courts in this context appears to be very different from that taken in cases, such as *Re C*, in which the interests of a 'third party' are not perceived, whether by the medical profession or the courts, to be at stake. In all of the reported cases which turned on competence, orders for intervention (whether caesarean sections, induced labour and/or 'assisted' (forceps) deliveries) were made by the courts. This being the case it is difficult, despite assertions to the contrary, to believe that the courts are not in fact operating in the interests of the 'unborn'.[71] Indeed, that this is the case has been suggested by a number of judges including Thorpe LJ who, subsequent to the decision in *Re MB*, called for legislation on grounds that no family judge had refused to uphold foetuses' best chances and that 'the obvious risk was restatements of principle by appellate judges which trial judges simply find impossible to follow'.[72] Johnson J, too, in reaching his decisions in *Rochdale Healthcare (NHS) Trust v C*[73] and *Norfolk and Norwich Healthcare (NHS) Trust v W*[74] (discussed below) declared: 'I am afraid the Judge has to do what some may call rough justice. I do not think there is a

---

[70] See *Re S*, 19 December 1996, in which allegations had been made that the woman 'had little interest in her own survival and certainly none in the survival of her baby': *Daily Mail*, 19 February 1997.

[71] See also *Re T*, note 63 above, and cases discussed below.

[72] *Independent*, 5 March 1997.

[73] [1997] 1 FCR 274.

[74] [1996] 2 FLR 613, [1997] Fam Law 17.

possibility of giving attention to the legal niceties. I think the information [sic] of judges is to act on the advice of doctors of proper standing'.

In the *Norfolk and Norwich* case, Johnson J found that a woman who had a history of psychiatric illness and who denied that she was pregnant (she was, in fact, in labour), was not competent to refuse the medical treatment which her doctors thought necessary (a forceps delivery or caesarean section) partly 'because of acute emotional stress and physical pain [suffered] in the ordinary course of labour'. In the particular case, this 'stress and pain' was considered to be aggravated by 'her own particular mental history', and W was declared not competent under the third limb of the test laid down in *Re C*: that is, 'she lacked the mental competence to make a decision about the treatment that was proposed because she was incapable of weighing up the considerations that were involved'. Nevertheless, given that all women in labour could be described as being in a state of 'acute emotional stress and physical pain', the case clearly pointed to an easy option for any judge wishing to declare a woman not competent. Indeed, Johnson J himself took this approach one step further in the *Rochdale* case, which he heard as a matter of extreme urgency in the course of the *Norfolk and Norwich* hearing, the consultant obstetrician being of the view that a caesarean section 'had to be carried out within the hour if the foetus was to survive and risk of damage to the patient's health was to be avoided'.

In contrast with the *Norfolk and Norwich* case, in which a psychiatrist was of the opinion that W was not able to balance the information given to her, the woman in respect of whom the order was sought in the *Rochdale* case was considered by her obstetrician to be 'fully competent'. This did not prevent Johnson J from declaring that C failed the third limb of the competence test laid down in *Re C* on the grounds that she was, at the time: 'in the throes of labour with all that is involved in terms of pain and emotional stress'. According to Johnson J the very fact that the woman, who had suffered so badly after a previous caesarean section that she declared she would rather die than undergo another such procedure, 'could, *in those circumstances* speak in terms which seemed to accept the inevitability of her own death' (my emphasis) meant that she 'was not a patient who was able properly to weigh-up the considerations that arose so as to make any valid decision, about anything of even the most trivial kind, still one which involved her own life'. This approach must be contrasted with that taken by Thorpe J in *Re C*: both the paranoid schizophrenic in *Re C* and the woman in the *Rochdale* case declared themselves ready to die but, whereas the pain of labour was regarded in the latter case as a circumstance rendering that decision invalid, the fact that the patient in the former case suffered from delusions was not regarded as such a circumstance. In *Re L*,[75] too, in which the High Court overrode a

---

[75] Unreported, 5 December 1996.

woman's refusal to allow her labour to be induced, the decision that she was not 'competent' was made partly on the basis of her doctor's assertion that she was 'confused' as a result of the gas and air that she had inhaled as a painkiller. If the use of this painkiller[76] is sufficient to render labouring women incompetent (if, indeed, they are not already incompetent by virtue simply of being in labour), the notion that women have any say in the management of childbirth is a nonsense.

Barbara Hewson, Vice President of the Association of Women Barristers, remarked, in the wake of Johnson J's decisions, that 'women in labour may now expect to be shackled in maternity wards, if they don't do what obstetricians tell them'.[77] That this response was not wholly unwarranted was suggested by the bizarre decision of the solicitors involved in one of the cases to establish a 24-hour legal hotline for hospitals seeking to force medical treatment on unwilling women in labour.[78]

It can only be inferred from the contrast between the approach taken to pregnant women and non-pregnant persons that, despite the rhetoric that the interests of the foetus play no part in determining the right of pregnant women to refuse medical treatment, in fact, the refusal itself is taken as a stamp of incompetence.[79] Far from making any attempt to counter this approach, the Court of Appeal in *Re MB* remarked, of the decision in the *Rochdale* case, only that '[o]ne may question whether there was evidence before the court which enabled the judge to come to a conclusion [on the issue of competence] contrary to the opinion of the obstetrician, and stated that Johnson J 'had very little time and only "the scantiest information" upon which to assess the patient and make a decision'. The problem is that, whenever doctors seek 'emergency' orders to force medical treatment on women in labour, judges will have 'very little time' to make their decisions and the failure on the part of doctors to provide adequate evidence is something which appears to militate in favour of, rather than against, the orders sought.

The Court of Appeal did state, in *Re MB*, that potential problems should be identified as soon as possible so that both parties could take legal advice, that court action should be initiated before an emergency arose, that the woman should be represented in any hearing and that there should be evidence, preferably that of a psychiatrist, as to competence. But there was no suggestion that the grant of orders would turn upon

---

[76] The effects of which, pregnant women are assured, last only for the period during which it is actually being inhaled.
[77] Barbara Hewson 'Litigator's View', *The Lawyer*, 10 September 1996.
[78] *Guardian*, 16 September 1996.
[79] See also *Re L*, 5 December 1996, discussed by the Court of Appeal in *Re MB*, note 59 above. In the aftermath of the *St George's Healthcare NHS Trust* case, note 87 below, Professor Robert Winston was quoted as saying that in some rare cases pre-eclampsia can result in swelling of the brain, 'Some women with this condition become psychotic'. It is presumably only a matter of time until diagnoses of incapacity are routinely based on the fact of pre-eclampsia.

compliance with these guidelines. And, far from being comforted by the decision of the Court of Appeal in *Re MB*, Barbara Hewson wrote of the result that:

> women who reject their doctors' advice could be . . . convicted of 'incompetency', and subjected to house arrest, torture or inhuman and degrading treatment in state hospitals. Forced epidurals, forced episiotomies, forced pubic shaving, forced forceps deliveries, forced general anaesthetic, forced Caesareans, forced medication, forced in utero foetal surgery, forced detention, forced vaginal examinations, forced Aids testing, forced foetal screening, forced abortions.[80]

It should be borne in mind, by anyone inclined to dismiss this warning as absurd, that, until very recently, women were routinely induced, shaved and episiotomied for the sake of administrative convenience, that women have already been forcibly detained and subject to forceps deliveries, general anaesthesia and caesarean sections (indeed, Ms Hewson was subsequently to appear for Ms S who was sectioned as a result of her refusal to undergo a caesarean section on the advice of her GP, see below). So routine is the subordination of pregnant women's wishes to those of their doctors that in 1994 two British midwives were disciplined for their participation in an 'unapproved and unauthorised' birth when they failed to prevent a woman from giving birth in the pool in which her labour was taking place. It was the policy of the health authority for which the women worked not to provide waterbirths, though pools would be made available for the earlier stages of labour. The woman concerned had refused to leave the pool when requested so to do by the midwives.[81] The only apparent failure of the midwives was their failure physically to haul the woman out of the pool against her clearly expressed wishes. This would have been a criminal assault

In the light of this, it is particularly alarming that the Court of Appeal in *Re MB* not only countenanced the use of physical force to overcome women's resistance to unwanted medical intervention, but stated that: '[t]he extent of force or compulsion which may become necessary can only be judged in each individual case *and by the health professionals*' (my emphasis). These professionals, despite the public pronouncements from their organisations, appear to pay scant regard to the physical autonomy of women in labour.

---

[80] *Independent*, 5 March 1997. Also of concern is the fact that the Court of Appeal in *Re MB* and in the *St George's Healthcare NHS Trust* case, see notes 59 and 89, stated that the Official Solicitor, who generally acts for mental patients and coma victims, should be notified of all cases and should 'continue to act as *amicus curiae*' where he was not acting as guardian *ad litem* for the 'mother', should she be unconscious. Barbara Hewson has drawn attention to the fact that the Official Solicitor has, in a number of cases, pressed for forced intervention and that his involvement has, to date, generally (as in *Re S*, 19 December 1996, and in *Norfolk and Norwich Healthcare (NHS) Trust v W*, note 74 above, led to orders for intervention: *The Times*, 8 July 1997.

[81] *Guardian*, 10 February 1994.

Declaring pregnant women incompetent at common law is not the only tool that judges have used in order to override their resistance to medical intervention. A rather novel approach was taken in 1996 (prior to the decisions of Johnson J and those in *Re L* and *Re MB*) by Wall J in *Tameside and Glossop Acute Services Trust v CH*,[82] in which he interpreted forced medical intervention in labour as 'medical treatment given . . . for [a] . . . mental disorder' so as to permit a hospital to act under s 63 of the Mental Health Act 1983 which states that: '[t]he consent of a patient shall not be required for any medical treatment given to him for the mental disorder from which he is suffering . . .'.

It might appear odd that forcing a pregnant woman to undergo induced labour or a caesarean section, on the ground (as it was alleged here) that the foetus was suffering from intra-uterine growth retardation, could be regarded as 'medical treatment given . . . for the mental disorder' of schizophrenia.[83] But Wall J was untroubled by this in the light of recent cases treating the forced feeding of women as 'medical treatment' for anorexia and personality disorders. He defined the induced or surgical delivery sought in the instant case as 'medical treatment' for the patient's mental disorder – this in part because after delivery, medication could resume, also because 'in order for the treatment of her schizophrenia to be effective, it is necessary for her to give birth to a live baby'.[84] On these grounds the judge did not think it 'stretching language unduly to say that achievement of a successful outcome of her pregnancy is a necessary part of the overall treatment of her mental disorder'. (One is tempted to wonder whether it would be have been considered 'stretching language unduly' to regard the successful treatment of Mr C's gangrenous leg, and his resulting survival, as a 'necessary part of the overall treatment' of his mental disorder, any improvement in the mental condition of a patient being hard to effect after his death.)

However dubious the reasoning in the *Tameside* case, it was eclipsed in April 1996 by the order given by Hogg J in *Re S*, in which a woman sectioned under the Mental Health Act 1983 (according to the *Guardian*, 'for the protection of her unborn child'[85]) and detained in hospital against her will, was forced to have a caesarean section. S had had the temerity to disagree with her GP about the severity of the pre-eclampsia with which she had been diagnosed and, as a result, found herself sectioned for assessment under the Mental Health Act (her suspected 'mental disorder' being evidenced, apparently, by her refusal to comply with her doctor's views as to the appropriate management of her pregnancy). S retained a solicitor as soon as she became aware of the strong-arm tactics being deployed

[82] [1996] 1 FLR 762.
[83] For comment see Law Notes in Centre of Medical Law and Ethics, King's College London (1996) 7(1) *Dispatches* 4–5.
[84] Relying, in particular, *B v Croydon Health Authority* [1995] Fam 133, [1995] 1 All ER 683.
[85] 19 December 1996. See also note 70 above.

against her. Her clinical notes indicated that she was fully competent to refuse treatment. Despite this, the doctors sought a court order to perform an emergency caesarean section. She was not permitted to be represented at the court hearing at which authorisation was granted to the doctors to conduct 'any investigations or interventions they deemed necessary, including a caesarean'.[86] Nor, indeed, was she even informed in advance of the hearing.

Hogg J, who issued the order for forcible treatment, heard the matter in her lunchtime break, was incorrectly informed that S had been in labour for 24 hours at the time the order was sought and that she could die at any moment (labour had not commenced).[87] The judge was not told that S was considered medically competent to refuse surgery. She ordered that the procedure go ahead, apparently without considering the issue of competence, on the basis of Sir Stephen Brown P's ruling in 1992 in *Re S*.[88] It may well have been the case that the decision was reached in part because S had been sectioned under the 1983 Act. But, if this was the case, it is hard to imagine how forcible medical intervention could possibly be justified, even on the reasoning in the *Tameside* case, as 'medical treatment' for S's 'mental disorder', given that at the time of the operation S was merely undergoing assessment, only a few hours had elapsed since her forcible detention, and the most that psychiatric evaluation had been able to suggest at that point was that she was suffering from 'moderate depression'.

The section order was lifted from S the day after she gave birth. Her application for judicial review was rejected by Popplewell J on the grounds that it was out of time (S having spent the months after the birth battling with social services to regain custody after her initial rejection of the baby as a result of her experience) and gave rise to no issue of general public importance (the question being whether the Mental Health Act 1983 could be used to detain a pregnant woman against her will and force her to undergo invasive surgery for a physical, rather than mental, disorder). It was not until the Court of Appeal heard the matter in May 1998 that leave for judicial review was granted, together with an appeal against the declaration allowing the caesarean section to be carried out on S (*St George's Healthcare NHS Trust v S, R v Collins and others, ex parte S*[89]).

The Court of Appeal reiterated the clear legal position: that competent patients are entitled to refuse medical treatment regardless of the consequences of such a refusal, and that 'The court does not have the

---

[86] *Ibid.*
[87] *Guardian*, 15 March 1997. It was further noted by the Court of Appeal (in *St George's Healthcare NHS Trust v S, R v Collins and others, ex parte S* [1998] 3 All ER 673, [1998] Fam Law 526) that '[t]he judge had asked how far advanced labour had been. When her question was put to the hospital's legal advisers it was treated as irrelevant . . . the judge did not take up the question again . . .'.
[88] *Re S (Adult: Refusal of Medical Treatment)*, note 61 above.
[89] Note 87 above. See also *Guardian*, 4 July 1997.

jurisdiction to declare that [forced] medical intervention is lawful to protect the interests of the unborn child even at the point of birth.'[90] The Court of Appeal further ruled that the social worker and doctor had not been entitled to take into account the urgent medical need associated with her pregnancy in determining whether her mental disorder had warranted her detention under the 1983 Act and went on to 'repeat and expand' the guidelines established in *Re MB*. In particular, the court stressed that no application should be made to the courts in respect of any competent patient; that medical carers should 'identify as soon as possible whether there is concern about a patient's competence' and carry out the appropriate assessment; that the patient's solicitors be informed immediately of any intended legal action and that any hearing should be *inter partes*.[91] The Court of Appeal accepted, however, that 'Where delay may itself cause serious damage to the patient's health or put her life at risk then formulaic compliance with these guidelines would be inappropriate'.

The decisions discussed above illustrate the dangers faced by pregnant women. For all of the legal rhetoric about women's right to choose their medical treatment, this 'right' is shown to be illusory as soon as the wishes of pregnant woman and medical profession collide. Whether women are sectioned under the Mental Health Act 1983, declared incompetent even in the face of medical evidence to the contrary, or simply operated on regardless of their consent, autonomy in childbirth is very fragile indeed. The problem lies not so much in the letter of the law as in its application (or otherwise) at the front-line.

When doctors, hospitals and the courts are confronted with the prospect of a baby unnecessarily dying in the course of childbirth, their instinct is to act rather than to comply with what are frequently regarded as the irrational decisions of the woman involved.[92] It has been clear since at least 1988 that competent women may not be forced to undergo unwanted medical procedures either for their own sake or for that of their foetuses. But this appears to have little influence on whether, where the interests of woman and foetus are perceived to conflict, her autonomy will be upheld by the doctors or the courts. The reaction to *St George's Healthcare Trust v S* illustrates how little impact decisions in *Re F* and *Re MB* actually had. The 1998 decision was greeted as precedent-setting in its recognition that the woman's right to personal autonomy prevailed even where there was a risk to the life of the foetus. According to the *Mirror* the decision was a 'landmark ruling' and, to the *Scotsman*, it

---

[90] Citing Butler-Sloss LJ in *Re MB*, note 59 above, at 561. See generally note 59 above.
[91] If the patient was not considered able to instruct, the Official Solicitor should be invited to appoint a guardian *ad litem*.
[92] See for example the comment of Dr Peter Terry, a consultant obstetrician and gynaecologist at the Aberdeen Royal Infirmary, in the *Scotsman*, 11 May 1998: the ruling 'won't prevent practitioners making a judgement call. It would be difficult to know what to do, because to allow a patient to die who could be saved [presumably this refers to the foetus] goes against everything I hold dear'.

'effectively overturn[ed] the accepted wisdom that a doctor has a duty to save life'. The BMA 'broadly' welcomed the 'clarification' of the law that the decision was seen to entail, the *Independent* greeted the decision as a 'blow for freedom', and stated that 'mothers' had 'w[o]n the right to refuse Caesareans'.[93]

The US example

Women in the UK have no constitutionally entrenched rights upon which they can rely to resist forced medical intervention. The temptation is to assume that, if we had such rights, we would be in a stronger position. But a glance at the experience of women in the US calls any such assumption into question. In the US, as in the UK, caesarean sections are an increasingly common method of delivery. Indeed the proportion of surgical deliveries is even higher in the US (at around 30 per cent[94]) than in the UK where it currently stands at around 20 per cent, this figure itself representing an increase of about 400 per cent over the last 20 years.[95] In the US, at any rate, this figure has as much to do with doctors' fear of litigation as it has to do with maternal or foetal health. Experts estimate that at least 50 per cent of the million operations performed each year are medically unnecessary.[96] But this has not prevented a trend whereby caesarean sections are forced upon unwilling mothers in the name of foetal well-being. Most caesarean births, however unnecessary, occur with the consent of the woman concerned (whether this consent is fully informed or not). But in 1987, an article in the *New England Journal of Medicine* reported that:

> Pregnant women have been forced to have blood transfusions against their will; they have been sedated, strapped down, and forced to undergo major surgery; they have been physically detained in hospitals when physicians suspected they weren't following medical orders . . . thirty-five of the forty-six states that currently [1993] have living-will laws restrict women's right to die[97] when they are both severely ill and pregnant. In twenty states, pregnant women are disqualified *without exception* from the right to die as soon as they become pregnant . . . Courts now often balance the fetus's claim to life in the last trimester of pregnancy against the civil rights of the woman.[98]

By the late 1980s, there had been 36 attempts to override pregnant women's refusals of medical treatment during the preceding five years,

---

[93] *Mirror*, 8 May 1998; *Scotsman*, 11 May 1998; *Independent*, 8 May 1998.
[94] Up from 5% in the mid 1960s.
[95] *Daily Mail*, 29 August 1996.
[96] *Ibid.*; *The Times*, 18 March 1997.
[97] That is, to refuse life-saving treatment.
[98] Daniels, note 32 above, pp 33–34. See also discussion of *Poole v Santa Clara County Kaiser Hospital* 604575 Sup Ct, Santa Clara, Ely, cited in Sherman, note 17 above; N Rhoden, 'The Judge in the Delivery Room: The Emergence of Court-ordered Cesareans' (1986) 74 *California Law Review* 1951.

court orders having been granted to permit unwanted caesarean sections in 13 of the 15 cases in which they were sought.[99] In many of these cases legal action has been hurried, the woman unrepresented and involved only at the point of being informed of the order.[100] And despite the fact that court orders mandating caesarean sections are sought by doctors claiming that surgical intervention is essential to save the life of the foetus (frequently, the life of the mother too), many of the cases have resulted in babies being delivered vaginally and without complications.[101]

Thirty-six cases of actual or attempted forced medical intervention may not appear to be a large number. But what the recorded figures obscure is the routine subordination of pregnant women's wishes to those of their doctors. And the situation is more likely to deteriorate rather than to improve with time. A 1987 US study of those involved in obstetrics found that almost half supported the involuntary detention of women perceived to pose risks to the foetuses they carry, the same proportion agreeing that precedents set by the courts in relation to forced caesarean sections should be extended to other procedures such as intra-uterine blood transfusions as the procedure became standard.[102] It must be assumed that these doctors shared the views of one retired obstetrician-gynaecologist who wrote to a Florida newspaper, in the wake of a recent judicial decision in this area:

> New sub-specialty areas have emerged in medicine . . . that deal with the needs of the unborn. These doctors are the *advocates for the fetus*, more so than any court-appointed attorney. It *clouds the issue* to involve the legal system when physicians and hospital staffs are well informed and prepared to address the medical, ethical and moral needs of patients and their families.[103] (my emphasis)

Already, surgeons can remove foetuses from women's wombs (leaving intact the umbilical cord) in order to operate directly on the foetus.[104] They can also use micro-surgery to operate within the womb. In 1982, the

---

[99]   V Kolder *et al*, 'Court-ordered Obstetrical Interventions' (1987) 316 *New England Journal of Medicine* 1192, cited by Mathieu, note 32 above. See *Raleigh Fitkin-Paul Morgan Memorial Hospital v Anderson* 42 NJ 421, 201 A 2d 537 (1964); *Jefferson v Griffin Spalding Co Hospital Authority* 247 Ga 86, 274 SE 2d 457 (1981); *Taft v Taft* 388 Mass 331, 446 NE 2d 395 (1983); *Re Jamaica Hospital* 128 Misc 2d 1006, 491 NYS 2d 898 (1985); *Crouse Irving Memorial Hospital, Inc v Paddock* 127 Misc 2d 101, 485 NYS 2d 443 (1985), Sup Ct, all discussed below. See also P King, 'Helping Women Helping Children: Drug Policy and Future Generations' (1991) 69(4) *The Milbank Quarterly* 595.

[100]   Mathieu, note 32 above, p 106, citing Kolder *et al*, note 99 above, p 1193.

[101]   According to Steinbock, note 15 above, four of the first five cases in which orders were issued eventually resulted in normal vaginal deliveries. See also Daniels, note 32 above, p 33, citing J Gallagher, 'Prenatal Invasions and Interventions: What's Wrong with Fetal Rights' (1987) 10 *Harvard Women's Law Journal* 47; Mathieu, note 32 above, p 106.

[102]   Steinbock, note 15 above, p 147, citing a national survey published in 1987 in the *New England Journal of Medicine*.

[103]   This breathtaking piece of arrogance was printed in the *Sun Sentinel* (Fort Lauderdale), 20 March 1997.

[104]   See Daniels, note 32 above, p 19.

first surgery was performed on a 20-week-old foetus and open abdominal surgery has been performed on women in order to access foetuses as young as 15 weeks.[105] As maternal death rates fall and the focus of health carers shifts ever more from the woman to the foetus, foetuses are increasingly being regarded as 'the second patient' in obstetric practice and, it seems, their interests being accorded at least equal weight to those of the women upon whom their survival depends.[106]

The *Guardian* reported, in July 1997, that 'US surgeons have found a way to take tissue from a foetus, grow it in the laboratory, and then implant it in the newborn child'. The technique, which could be used for problems such as improperly developed hearts, intestines or bladders, is expected to be in operation within five years.[107] According to the report, '[t]he ideal is to have "spare" tissue, unique to the baby, ready to repair the defect immediately upon birth'. Presumably this would happen only where defects were recognised during the pregnancy as a result of the usual ante-natal tests. But perhaps all foetuses should be provided with some laboratory-grown tissue just in case of the unforeseen. Tissue would be removed two-thirds of the way through the pregnancy. No mention is made of the fact that this procedure would require that the women, also, would have to undergo an operation.[108]

Constitutional protections

Reproductive freedom

In the face of this catalogue of horrors (restrictions on reproduction, control and punishment of pregnant women, forced medical intervention), what protection has the US Constitution afforded to women? Save for the issues of sterilisation and family cap legislation, none of the practices discussed above has come before the Supreme Court, though lower courts have adjudicated on the merits of forced caesarean sections, the detention of pregnant women and the criminalisation of women for drug use during pregnancy. In some cases these adjudications have served the interests of women. But most of the court decisions which have favoured women in this context have been reached other than on constitutional grounds. And in a number of cases where decisions have been reached on the basis of the Constitution, judicial interpretation of the rights

---

[105] *Newsday*, 24 April 1989.
[106] Goodrick and Salancik, note 53 above.
[107] *Guardian*, 23 July 1997.
[108] The *Today* programme (BBC Radio 4) carried a report on 20 November 1998 of apparently successful *in utero* procedures carried out on foetuses with spina bifida. The procedure has been the subject of a report in *The Lancet*.

protected under it has operated against women's interests. Perhaps ironically, decisions against women's interests have, on occasion, been founded on the very decision, *Roe v Wade*,[109] which established American women's 'right to choose'. That decision was considered in Chapter 4 above.

Taking first the constitutionality of 'procreative' conditions attached to probation cases, and to the broader control of women's fertility by the State. In *Buck v Bell*[110] the Supreme Court upheld the involuntary sterilisation of a girl who, although she had done well at school, was regarded as feeble-minded on account of her 'maritally unworthy . . . shiftless, ignorant and worthless' mother and her illegitimate child, which child had been the result of rape. Displaying scant regard to any arguments about reproductive rights Justice Holmes declared, for the eight strong majority, that it would be 'strange if [the State] could not call upon those who already sap the strength of the State for the lesser sacrifice often not felt to be such by those concerned, in order to prevent our being swamped by incompetence'.

The decision in *Buck* has yet to be overruled, though 15 years later, in *Skinner v State of Oklahoma*,[111] the Supreme Court struck down a law requiring 'habitual' criminals to be sterilised on the grounds that it irrationally distinguished between categories of criminals on grounds which had no 'significance in eugenics'. This was the case in which the court first ruled that strict scrutiny would be applied in respect of 'fundamental rights', which rights it recognised here as including such 'a sensitive and important area of human rights' as procreation, 'a right which is basic to the perpetuation of a race . . . one of the basic civil rights of man'. The Supreme Court did not rule that sterilisation laws would always be regarded as unconstitutional – although such 'conspicuously artificial' distinctions as were drawn here would not withstand scrutiny, states were not 'constrained . . . to ignore experience which marks a class of offenders or a family of offenses for special treatment'. Nor did it depart from its decision in *Buck*, Justice Douglas appearing whole-heartedly to approve of it. And in *Roe v Wade* itself, *Buck* was cited with approval by the Supreme Court for the proposition that the right to privacy recognised by that court in *Griswold v State of Connecticut*[112] and relied upon in *Roe v Wade* did not include 'an unlimited right to do with one's body as one pleases'.

Even if the Supreme Court were today to decide that the interests of the US Government in preventing itself being 'swamped by incompetence'

---

[109] 410 US 113 (1973).

[110] 274 US 200 (1927). As a middle-aged woman, her IQ test showed that she was of average intelligence: Henley, note 5 above, pp 715–716 and 765.

[111] 316 US 535 (1942). The statute was not struck down on the grounds, put to the court, that it relied upon the dubious notion that criminal traits could be inherited, that it (unlike the statute upheld in *Buck v Bell*, *ibid.*) gave the defendant no opportunity to be heard or that it provided a 'cruel and unusual punishment'.

[112] 381 US 479 (1965).

were insufficient to permit compulsory sterilisation of 'defectives', it is not certain that the Supreme Court would disapprove of inducements paid to poor women to use Norplant or the conditioning of access to welfare on the use of contraception, or, indeed, the imposition of a contraception or no-pregnancy order as a condition of probation. As far as 'family cap' legislation is concerned, the decision of the Supreme Court in *Dandridge v Williams*[113] (see Chapter 3 above), and the continuing readiness of the Supreme Court to decide that benefit restrictions do not 'directly and substantially' interfere with the constitutionally protected right to freedom from state interference with living arrangements, makes it most unlikely that any family cap legislation would today be regarded as breaching the Fourteenth Amendment's Equal Protection or Due Process clauses.

What of the constitutionality of inducements or requirements for women on welfare to use Norplant, or any other form of contraception? Dealing first with payments to women on welfare who accept contraceptive implants, it is likely that the Government would be permitted, as in *Maher v Roe*[114] (see Chapter 4 above), to discourage the exercise of a right (here, to reproduce) by refusing to fund it, while choosing to fund its alternative. There would appear to be no reason why, despite the right to procreate (like that to have an abortion) being protected under the Fourteenth Amendment, the State should not choose financially to encourage contraception, rather than procreation, in this context just as, in another, it may choose to favour pregnancy and childbirth over abortion. It could be argued, of course, that such an incentive should be regarded as falling under the 'unconstitutional conditions' rule applied in *Shapiro v Thompson*[115] (see Chapter 4 above), the Government making a payment conditional upon the sacrifice of a constitutionally protected right to freedom of procreative choice. But even if such a right were to be recognised (see below), it is clear from Chapters 3 and 4 that the 'unconstitutional condition' doctrine is not consistently applied.

John Hand's argument that the Supreme Court justices (other than those very supportive of and hostile to the doctrine) reach 'unconstitutional conditions' decisions according to the facts[116] was discussed in Chapters 3 and 4. It was pointed out there that indigent plaintiffs, particularly women seeking abortions, rarely succeeded.[117] And the current trend in the Supreme Court is away from the 'unconstitutional conditions' doctrine. On this basis Hand argues, in relation to the Norplant condition: 'Intuitively, it may be difficult for old, upper class Justices to sympathise

---

[113] 397 US 471 (1970).
[114] 432 US 464 (1977).
[115] 394 US 618 (1969).
[116] J Hand, 'Buying Fertility: The Constitutionality of Welfare Bonuses' (1993) 46 *Vanderbilt Law Review* 715, at 737.
[117] *Ibid.* This subgroup never won, and 69% of indigents lost.

with the plight facing poor, unmarried, pregnant women . . . the Court may adopt the "moral" view that efforts should be made to curb reproduction in the "lower" classes. More often than not, the Court does not overturn conditional laws where the benefit is welfare.'[118]

What of the case where explicit coercion, rather than financial inducement, is used to persuade women on welfare to accept contraceptive implants? The difference, if any, is one of degree rather than substance. Nevertheless, while the former may be viewed as acceptable by a Supreme Court disinclined to apply the 'unconstitutional conditions' approach, it is arguable that the degree of coercion in the latter might impel the court to consider the issue one of 'penalising' a protected right, rather than merely refusing to subsidise it (to adopt the distinction drawn in *Maher*). Equally, if the court were to adopt the analogous approach of distinguishing between those regulations which 'directly and substantially' impinge on protected rights (as in *Lyng v Castillo*, *Bowen v Gilliard* and *Lyng v Automobile Workers*[119]), it is more likely that an explicit threat to existing benefits will amount to such interference than would the threat to withhold additional goods.

The right to privacy in contraceptive decisions has been recognised by the Supreme Court in *Griswold*,[120] in relation to married couples, and in *Eisenstadt v Baird*,[121] in relation to the unmarried. Any ban on the use of contraception by married or unmarried persons will be subject to strict scrutiny by the court: that is, it will be unconstitutional unless the court is convinced that it is necessary to serve a compelling government interest. It is likely also that a requirement to use contraception would be subject to strict scrutiny.[122] But this does not mean that a requirement for women on welfare not to have children, or, indeed, not to engage in sexual intercourse, would necessarily be unconstitutional. Although decisions relating to procreation have been recognised as fundamental in *Skinner* and in *Eisenstadt* and *Carey v Population Services International*[123] (the latter two cases dealing specifically with the right not to procreate), a prohibition upon childbearing by women on welfare might pass scrutiny under the Equal Protection Clause.

The legislation at issue in *Skinner* was not that which prohibited reproduction for a defined period on pain of financial penalty. It was, rather, legislation which required sterilisation, and this was significant in the reasoning of the Supreme Court, Justice Douglas remarking that '[t]here

---

[118] *Ibid*, at 743.

[119] Respectively, 477 US 635 (1986); 483 US 587 (1987) and 485 US 360 (1988). See Chapter 3, note 108 and accompanying text.

[120] Note 112 above.

[121] 405 US 438 (1972).

[122] Justices Brennan and Marshall, dissenting in *Bowen v Gilliard*, note 119, argued that 'no one could contend . . . that a concern for limiting welfare outlays could justify mandatory sterilization of beneficiaries'.

[123] Respectively, note 111 above; note 121 above and 431 US 678 (1977).

is no redemption for the individual whom the law touches . . . He is forever deprived of a basic liberty'. While sterilisation is permanent (or, today, at least presumptively so), an order that a woman not have any children while on welfare is probably not, most welfare receipt (contrary to public perception) being short-term or interrupted.[124] Were the Supreme Court to apply the approach taken in the abortion context in *Planned Parenthood of Southeastern Pennsylvania v Casey*[125] (see Chapter 4 above) and to permit restrictions on (though not complete prohibition of) the constitutionally protected right to reproduce (as it has done in relation to the constitutionally protected right to terminate a pregnancy); it could decide that temporary restrictions on reproduction do not amount to an 'undue burden' on those subject to them, at least where the restrictions serve to further a legitimate government interest (as distinct from being necessary in the pursuit of a compelling one).[126]

The other point to bear in mind is that there is recognised no fundamental right to engage in sexual intercourse outside marriage in the US. It has been suggested that: '*Griswold* and *Eisenstadt* protect the right to have sex free of governmental control and to do so with or without contraceptives'.[127] But in *Bowers v Hardwick*[128] the Supreme Court overturned Georgia's Court of Appeal and upheld a law criminalising sexual intercourse between men. Previously recognised rights to 'family relationships, marriage [and] procreation' bore no 'resemblance to the right asserted in this case', stated Justice White for the majority, and vigilance should be exercised against any further expansion of the Due Process Clause.[129]

While the decision in *Bowers* was concerned with what Justice White categorised as 'acts of consensual sodomy', the grounds upon which it was reached – that only those rights 'implicit in the concept of ordered liberty or deeply rooted in this Nation's history and tradition' would be regarded as fundamental – would equally exclude heterosexual non-marital sex.[130] The Supreme Court expressly refused to extend the asserted right to 'voluntary sexual conduct between consenting adults' to prohibit 'adultery, incest, and other sexual crimes'.

---

[124] Henley, note 5 above, p 753.

[125] Case no 93–150, 1994.

[126] This being the 'rational basis' test, which test 'has become increasingly deferential in recent years': Hand, note 116 above, p 750. See, for example, *Bowen v Roy* 476 US 693 (1986).

[127] *Harvard Law Review* Note 104 (1991) 1660, p 1664.

[128] 478 US 186 (1986).

[129] These cases included *Carey v Population Services International*, note 123 above; *Pierce v Society of Sisters* 268 US 510 (1925) and *Meyer v State of Nebraska* 262 US 390 (1923) (child rearing and education); *Prince v Commonwealth of Massachusetts* 321 US 158 (1944) (family relationships); *Skinner v Oklahoma*, note 111 above; *Loving v State of Virginia* 388 US 1 (1967) (marriage); *Eisenstadt v Baird*, note 121 above; *Griswold Connecticut*, note 109 above, and *Roe v Wade*, note 112 above.

[130] Citing *Palko v State of Connecticut* 302 US 319 (1937) and *Moore v East Cleveland* 431 US 494 (1977), internal citations omitted.

In this, the decision was perfectly consistent with those of the Supreme Court in *Griswold* and in *Eisenstadt* in which, respectively, the court struck down prohibitions on contraceptive use by married and unmarried couples. In *Griswold* the court distinguished between 'the intimacy of husband and wife', which could not be regulated by means of the criminal law, and '[a]dultery, homosexuality and the like' and 'extra-marital sexuality', which could. And even in *Eisenstadt*, in which the court extended the right to privacy to permit the 'individual, married or single, to be free from unwarranted governmental intrusion into matters so fundamentally affecting a person as the decision whether to bear or beget a child', no doubt was expressed as to the constitutionality of legislation criminalising extra-marital sexual intercourse. What was offensive to them was that married persons had access to contraceptives, whether for use with their spouses or otherwise,[131] and that the law had the effect of punishing by pregnancy and childbirth that (fornication) which was punishable under the Massachusetts law by a 90-day prison sentence.

The only remaining question here concerns the differential impact of 'no sex' conditions on men and women welfare recipients (the potential for race discrimination is considered below). In *Michael M v Superior Court*[132] the Supreme Court upheld a statute which criminalised men, but not women, for having sex with minors of the opposite sex on the grounds that it was justified by the State's interest in preventing teenage pregnancies, the impact of which fell only upon young girls. One might argue, by analogy, that the application of 'no sex' conditions to female welfare recipients alone could be the most effective way of preventing welfare pregnancies. Whether or not this argument was acceptable under the intermediate standard of scrutiny applied to sex discrimination, the disparate impact on women of such conditions if applied to all welfare recipients (women being disproportionately exposed to the consequences of its violation) would not be caught under the Equal Protection Clause.[133]

If direct restrictions on procreation were seen as an 'undue burden' on a fundamental right or (in the case of no-sex rules) as intruding too closely into people's bedrooms,[134] they would fail strict scrutiny unless they were 'necessary' to a compelling government interest (here the control of welfare costs). But the very ground on which such rules would fail to pass strict scrutiny itself illustrates the futility of constitutional arguments in this area. For even if legislatures are not permitted to impose procreative or sex conditions on their welfare recipients, they may deny

---

[131] In addition, the statute which forbade the distribution 'of articles intended to be used as contraceptives' did not prohibit the distribution to the same persons of the same articles if the intention was to prevent the spread of disease.

[132] 450 US 464 (1981).

[133] *Washington v Davies* 426 US 229 (1976), discussed in Chapter 4 above.

[134] This was the approach recently taken by Montana's Supreme Court in *Gryczan v State of Montana* to a law criminalising 'deviate' (gay and lesbian) sex: 283 Mont 433, 942 P 2d 112.

them benefit in respect of children born during periods of welfare dependency.[135] The refusal of the Supreme Court consistently to apply the 'unconstitutional conditions' doctrine – in particular, its failure to apply the doctrine in cases concerning welfare and those in which poor women challenge reproductive controls,[136] means that the protection afforded to women in relation to their childbearing choices is far from complete.

Turning, finally, to the constitutionality of reproductive conditions attached to probation orders, Courts of Appeal in California, Ohio, Florida, Kansas and Illinois have struck down such conditions where they have been imposed on women convicted of child abuse. The leading decision is that of California's Court of Appeal in *People v Dominguez*,[137] in which, in respect of a women ordered not to become pregnant before marriage on a robbery conviction, the court ruled that conditions which bore no relationship to the crime of which the defendant was convicted, related to conduct not itself criminal and required or forbade conduct not reasonably related to future criminality fell outside trial judges' wide discretion in setting probation conditions and were invalid.

Neither the Californian nor the Illinois courts considered constitutional issues, while Florida's Court of Appeal expressly stated that 'we have no constitutional difficulty with the conditions imposed, if they are otherwise valid conditions of probation'.[138] But the Courts of Appeal of both Kansas and Ohio did reach their decisions, in part, on constitutional grounds. In *State of Kansas v Mosburg*,[139] the Kansas court stated that 'the probation condition regarding pregnancy unduly intrudes on [the defendant's] right to privacy'. California's Court of Appeals also reached its 1984 decision in *People v Pointer*[140] on constitutional grounds. In that case, which concerned the woman whose rigid macrobiotic diet resulted in her conviction for child endangerment, the Court of Appeals accepted that the procreative condition on probation was valid on the *Dominguez* test,

---

[135] This does not apply to welfare payments in respect of their children. If such a welfare restriction punished children for the 'sins' of their mothers it would conflict with the minority reasoning in *King v Smith* 392 US 309 (1968), in which the Supreme Court struck down a law which, in effect, denied child support payments to lone mothers who were sexually active. Most of the Supreme Court justices rested their decision on a statutory basis, but Justice Douglas argued that the classification of children according to the 'sin' of their mother bore no rational relationship to the purpose of the welfare program in relieving poverty. And in *US Department of Agriculture v Moreno* 413 US 528 (1973), the court ruled unconstitutional a federal provision restricting a particular benefit to households consisting only of relatives, the majority of justices found the classification of 'related' and 'unrelated' households irrational along similar lines.

[136] Hand, note 116 above.

[137] Note 7 above.

[138] The Illinois decision is *People v Ferrell* 277 Ill App 3d 74, 659 NE 2d 992, 1995 Ill App LEXIS 974; that of Florida *Rodriguez v State* 378 So 2d 7 (1979).

[139] *State of Kansas v Mosburg* 13 Kan App 2d 257, 768 P 2d 313, 1989 Kan App LEXIS 54.

[140] Note 7 above. *Dominguez* had, in the interim, been applied by California's Supreme Court in *People v Lent* (1975) 15 Cal 3d 481 and accepted in most US jurisdictions.

since 'in this unusual case the condition is related to child endangerment . . . [and] the harm sought to be prevented by the trial court may
occur before birth'. But the court accepted that probationary conditions
were restricted also by 'constitutional safeguards', notably the right to
privacy found in the Fourth, Fourteenth and Fifth Amendments and
applied in *Roe v Wade* (see Chapter 4 above) and in *Griswold*. These rights
could be circumscribed only 'when circumstances inexorably so require',
and probationers could not 'be denied due process in reliance on the
dictum . . . that probation is an act of grace' (citations omitted).

The interest of the State here lay in the protection of the 'unborn child',
but 'where a condition of probation impinges upon the exercise of a
fundamental right and is challenged upon constitutional grounds', a
determination of whether the condition was overbroad was also required.
Here, the well-being of any future child could be protected by the 'less
onerous' means of requiring that the appellant 'periodically submit to
pregnancy testing; and that upon becoming pregnant she be required to
follow an intensive prenatal and neonatal treatment program monitored
by both the probation officer and by a supervising physician'. This being
the case, the probation order violated the woman's constitutional rights.
More recently, the same Court of Appeal overruled a 'no pregnancy' order
imposed by Judge Boardman, again in part on constitutional grounds.[141]

It is clear that there is some scope in the US Constitution for the restriction of procreative conditions on probation. But it is equally clear
that the impact of probation conditions on fundamental rights will not
necessarily result in a finding of unconstitutionality. In *US v Consuelo-
Gonzalez*,[142] for example, the Court of Appeal of the Ninth Circuit stated
that, while special scrutiny was appropriate in respect of probation conditions which 'unquestionably restrict otherwise inviolable constitutional
rights', there was no 'presumption, however weak, that such limitations
are impermissible' to the extent that they in fact served 'the dual purposes of rehabilitation and public safety'.

None of the cases considered above dealt with women who had already
been found to have used illegal drugs during pregnancy. The application
of procreative conditions to women convicted of child abuse can be challenged under the *Dominguez* test on the basis that the condition would
not be related to the crime in respect of which they were convicted ('[i]t
is not her reproductive capability that the woman wielded badly, but
her power to act as a safe primary caregiver for her children'[143]), that
pregnancy does not amount to criminal conduct and that it is not
reasonably related to future criminality, given the lack of evidence that

---

[141] *People v Zaring* 8 Cal App 4th 362, 1992 Cal App LEXIS 933, 10 Cal Rptr 2d 263, though
here the conditions also fell outwith *Dominguez*.
[142] 521 F 2d 259 (1975).
[143] H Nelson and J Nelson, 'Feminism, Social Policy, and Long-acting Contraception' (1995)
25(1) *The Hastings Center Report* S30.

either pregnancy or the addition of children to families results in increased risk of child abuse. But different arguments might apply in relation to drug-taking women.[144] In the single case (*Pointer*) in which the court regarded the woman's behaviour as posing a substantial risk to any as yet unconceived offspring, California's Court of Appeals was prepared to accept a mandatory pregnancy-testing regime and the imposition of very onerous restrictions should pregnancy occur. And in 1995 a judge in San Jose, California, ordered an alcoholic woman who had been convicted of child neglect to undergo monthly pregnancy tests for five years and, in the event of a positive result, to accept inpatient treatment for the duration of the pregnancy. The woman's husband, who was convicted with her, was sentenced only to one year in prison and six months treatment which she also received.[145]

The US Supreme Court has yet to consider the issue of 'procreative' sentencing. If it were to do so, it is possible that it would follow the approach of the California, Ohio and Kansas courts in finding that such sentencing amounts to an interference with defendant's right to privacy under *Griswold* and *Roe v Wade*. On the other hand, if the procreative condition attached to a probation order made in respect of a woman seen to pose a substantial risk, on account of her drug or alcohol use, to any foetus subsequently conceived, the court might well decide that the interests of the State in protecting the health of future children, and in reducing state expenditure on drug-impaired children, were 'compelling'. As far as the former is concerned, it has been pointed out that: 'this justification depends on the philosophically sticky idea that potential future children can be protected by preventing their very existence'.[146] But in *Skinner*,[147] as approved in *Roe v Wade*, the Supreme Court was prepared to countenance a mandatory sterilisation policy based on eugenics, even one which relied upon the idea that criminal traits were inheritable. Such a policy, it must be presumed, would have been justified on grounds that future potential criminals and society, would benefit from such persons not being born.

Eugenics may be rather less socially acceptable today than it was when *Skinner* was decided. But it is possible that the Supreme Court would accept child welfare and economic arguments in favour of restricting reproduction by women drug addicts. This is particularly true in view of the fact that the legislation at issue in *Skinner* dealt with sterilisation, rather than contraception. Probation orders are, by contrast, made for discrete

---

[144] California's Court of Appeals refused to hear Darlene Johnson's appeal on the grounds that, her probation order having been violated by her use of cocaine, the issue was 'moot': *The Recorder*, 31 July 1995.

[145] San Francisco *Chronicle*, 8 June 1995.

[146] R Dresser, 'Long-term Contraceptives in the Criminal Justice System' (1995) 25(1) *The Hastings Center Report* S15.

[147] *Skinner v Oklahoma*, note 111 above.

periods of time. As to cost-based arguments, while the reduction of state expenditure alone will not, in general, permit the restriction of individuals' constitutionally protected rights (here, the right to procreate under *Skinner* or the right to privacy established in the contraceptive context in *Griswold*),[148] it is by no means certain that the selection of drug-using or, for that matter, child-abusing, women for contraceptive orders would be regarded as invidious. The interest in reproduction is a fundamental one, but it is clear from the decision in *Skinner* that it is not one which the state is absolutely prohibited from restricting.

The only issue which remains is that of overbreadth, which proved fatal to the procreative condition attached in *Pointer*. But even were the Supreme Court to prohibit procreative conditions on this ground, it might accept the kind of onerous conditions suggested by the Californian Court of Appeals in that case. Thus, while it is possible that procreative probation conditions would be struck down comprehensively by the court, the US Constitution might prove compatible with mandatory pregnancy testing and subsequent restrictions on the liberty of women who use drugs, at least where such drug use has been shown to pose a threat to any potential children.

Criminalising motherhood

The utility of the US Constitution in challenging mandatory contraception or non-pregnancy orders applied to women is, at best, unclear. What of the criminalisation of pregnant drug addicts? To the extent that the decisions of the state courts provide any guidance, such prosecutions are generally frowned upon. By January 1997, convictions had been struck down in 19 of 20 appeals by women prosecuted for 'delivering' drugs via the umbilical cord, and for 'child abuse' of a foetus.[149] But these decisions have generally been reached other than on constitutional grounds, turning on the proper interpretation of statutes relating to child abuse or neglect and to the supply of illegal drugs.[150] The same is true in respect of a number of appellate decisions on the sufficiency, on a charge of drug possession against a woman, of evidence that her newborn baby showed traces of drugs,[151] and of at least one case in which the detention

---

[148] *Shapiro v Thompson*, note 115 above having rejected invidious classifications imposed in order to save expenditure.

[149] ACLU press release, 3 January 1997, available on the ACLU's website, http://www.aclu.org.

[150] See, for example, *Reyes v Superior Court* 141 Cal Rptr 912 (1977) California; *Commonwealth v Welch*, note 24 above; *Sherriff v Encoe* 885 P 2d 596 (1994) Nevada; *State v Gray* 584 NE 2d 710, at 713 (1992) (in which the dissenting judge of Ohio relied on *Roe v Wade*); *People of the State of Michigan v Hardy* 188 Mich App 305 (1991) Michigan; *State of Florida v Gethers* 585 So 2d 1140 (1991).

[151] See *Jackson v State of Texas* 833 SW 2d 220 (1992).

of a pregnant woman was ordered for the sake of the foetus within her (*State of Wisconsin ex rel Angela MW v Kuuzicki*[152]).

Where constitutional issues have been aired, they have frequently been unfavourable to the defendants. In *Kuuzicki*, for example, the dissenting judge asserted that *Roe v Wade*, in its recognition of the 'important and legitimate interest in potential life' (see further Chapter 4 above) actually supported the state's right to subordinate the interests of the woman to those of the foetus she carried. And in *Whitner*, in which South Carolina's Supreme Court reinstated an eight-year prison sentence for supplying drugs upon a woman whose babies had tested positive for cocaine at birth, the court took guidance from the recognition, in *Roe v Wade*, of the 'states['] . . . compelling interest in the life of a viable fetus' in defining the viable foetus as a 'child' under the state's child abuse laws. The court rejected Whitner's claim that the conviction violated her right of privacy: 'It strains belief for Whitner to argue that using crack cocaine during pregnancy is encompassed within the constitutionally recognised right of privacy'. According to Whitner's lawyer: 'If the fetus is a person, everything a pregnant women [sic] does is potentially child abuse. Abortion is murder, and women lose the right to make medical decisions on their own behalf during pregnancy'.[153]

The approach taken by South Carolina's Supreme Court has been at odds with that of other state Supreme Courts. But, as pointed out above, the decisions have generally turned on the proper construction of the statute at issue, rather than upon the constitutionally protected rights of the women prosecuted. This approach leaves it open to legislatures to amend their criminal statutes accordingly. In the light of the *Whitner* decision and the tendency, on the part of many judges, to interpret *Roe v Wade* so as to impose positive obligations on women in respect of viable foetuses (as distinct from merely permitting states to regulate abortion at this stage), it is by no means certain that such amended statutes would be regarded as unconstitutional. This is particularly true in the light of the current composition of the Supreme Court which contains a majority of justices who regard the State as having an interest in the foetus throughout the pregnancy. This being the case, it is possible that foetal rights may be protected at the expense of women's autonomy at any stage throughout the pregnancy. Admittedly, such protection would currently be subject to the pre-viability right to terminate (again, see Chapter 4 above) and the Supreme Court might be wary of encouraging terminations by women anxious to avoid criminal liability. But, particularly if legislation was drafted in order to apply whether or not women eventually terminated their pregnancies, it is not beyond

---

[152] Note 50 above. Discussed in the *Chicago Daily Law Bulletin*, 14 July 1997, also the *American Bar Association Journal*, July 1997.
[153] *Morning Star*, Wolmington, 30 October 1997, see also dissent in *State v Gray*, note 150 above.

the bounds of possibility that the Supreme Court might choose to follow
Whitner.

Even if foetal abuse statutes were eventually to be overturned, the willingness of the lower judiciary to convict and sentence in these cases has
resulted in prison sentences, and extraordinarily long periods of probation (which may include, as it did for Jennifer Johnson, random drug
and alcohol testing and prohibitions on going to bars or even restaurants
where alcohol is served[154]) for many women who have not appealed.
Typical among these women was Kim Hoskins, sentenced to up to five
years' imprisonment in July 1997 for child abuse (she had used drugs
while pregnant). Hoskins plea bargained a second degree felony down
to a third degree but said she did not wish to appeal the sentence, hoping instead for an early release. Others have lost custody of their children. And although Kim Hardy's charge of child abuse for using cocaine
during pregnancy was quashed by a Michigan Circuit Court on the
grounds that there was insufficient evidence of physical harm to the baby,
Hardy was denied custody of all three of her children pending the outcome of the appeal.[155] In contrast to the typical approach of the appellate courts towards criminalisation of drug use by pregnant women, they
have generally refused to interfere with lower courts' custody decisions
in this area.

Forcible medical treatment

Turning, finally, to the attitude of the judiciary to forcible medical treatment, to what extent has the US Constitution served to protect women
from treatments carried out, against their wishes, in the perceived interests of the foetuses they carry? The first point which should be made
here is that, to the extent that the courts have refused or overruled orders
for forced medical treatment, they have frequently done so at common
law while eschewing constitutional considerations. Further, in those
judgments in which constitutional issues have been considered, the decision of the Supreme Court in *Roe v Wade* has, on occasion, been interpreted to permit medical treatment to be forced upon unwilling women.

Turning first to the common law; US, in common with English, law
recognises a right to bodily autonomy. In 1891 the US Supreme Court
declared that: 'no right is held more sacred, or is more carefully guarded,
than the right of every individual to the possession and control of his
own person, free from all restraint or interference from others, unless by
clear and unquestioned authority of law'.[156] But this right may be outweighed, in the context of unwanted medical treatment, by the State's

---

[154] Daniels, note 32 above, p 98.
[155] Schiff, note 40 above.
[156] *Union Pacific Railway Co v Botsford* 141 US 250, at 251 (1891).

interest in the preservation of life, the prevention of suicide, the protection of innocent third parties and the maintenance of the ethical integrity of the medical profession.[157] And where the (potential) life of a foetus is at stake, the lower courts have been ready to intervene in the relatively rare event of being requested so to do. Some such orders have been overturned on appeal (although too late to avoid the forced intervention on the women concerned). Others have been upheld, sometimes on constitutional grounds.

In *Jefferson v Griffin Spaulding Co Hospital*,[158] the Supreme Court of Georgia ordered a woman to submit to a caesarean section against her religious convictions and granted the state temporary custody of her 'unborn child' on the basis that the foetus was a 'deprived child without proper parental care necessary for his or her physical health' and that the interest of the state protecting 'a living, unborn human being' outweighed 'the intrusion' into the life of the woman 'and her husband'. The initial order was granted on the basis that '[a] viable unborn child has the right under the US Constitution to the protection of the State through such statutes prohibiting the arbitrary termination of the life of an unborn fetus', citing *Roe v Wade*. The Supreme Court of Georgia upheld the order, declaring that the state had 'an interest in the life of this unborn, living human being', which interest outweighed the right of Jefferson and her husband not to be intruded upon. Two concurring judgments expressly relied on the decision of the Supreme Court in *Roe*, stating, respectively, that '[t]he Supreme Court has recognized that the state has an interest in protecting the lives of unborn, viable children' and that 'the state's compelling interest in preserving the life of this fetus is beyond dispute'.

The first indication of any change in judicial approach appears to have come in 1983, when the Supreme Judicial Court of Massachusetts ruled, in *Taft v Taft*,[159] that the lower court had erred in requiring a 'competent, adult woman to submit to a surgical procedure designed to assist in carrying her pregnancy to term, notwithstanding her religiously based objections to the surgery, where the record revealed no circumstances so compelling as to justify curtailing the woman's constitutional rights to privacy and to the free exercise of her religion'. And in *Re AC*,[160] the District of Columbia's Court of Appeals ruled that a lower court had erred in ordering that a caesarean section be carried out against the wishes of Angela Corder, a 25-week pregnant woman who was suffering from terminal cancer. The Court of Appeals had initially ruled (in *Re AC*) that the general principle against infringement of a woman's right to bodily integrity did not apply where 'she had, at best, two days left of sedated

---

[157] See, for example, *Winston v Lee* 470 US 753 (1985) and *Jacobson v Commonwealth of Massachusetts* 197 US 11 (1905).
[158] Note 99 above.
[159] Note 99 above.
[160] Note 62 above. See Steinbock, note 15 above.

life [this prognosis was in dispute]; the complications arising from the surgery would not significantly alter that progression [and t]he child, on the other hand, had a chance of surviving delivery'.[161] But, on reconsideration, a differently constituted Court of Appeals ruled that the lower court should have considered Corder's competence to decide for herself.[162] Had she had been found incompetent, the lower court should have relied on the substituted judgment procedure whereby all efforts would be made to ascertain what, if competent, she would have decided.

As a practical matter, the decision on competence dealt with the issue before it, but the Court of Appeals went further and considered whether, if the substituted judgment procedure had determined that Corder would not have consented to the caesarean, the procedure could, nevertheless, have been carried out. Reviewing the authorities the court declared that the principle of bodily integrity was of constitutional magnitude. It did, however, point out that the right was not unqualified, and that '[i]n those rare cases in which a patient's right to decide her own course of treatment has been judicially overridden, courts have usually acted to vindicate the state's interest in protecting third parties, even if in fetal state'.[163]

The Court of Appeals expressly did not reach its decision on constitutional grounds, relying instead upon the common law right to bodily autonomy. The decision in *Re AC* appears to have stemmed the tide of court-ordered caesareans which had become increasingly common throughout the 1980s. But it did not prohibit forced caesareans, even on competent women. The court left open the possibility of 'extraordinary or compelling' reasons for forced intervention in the extract above and expressed doubt about the likelihood of such reasons being made out. Nevertheless, the court refused to disapprove of its own decision the previous year in *Re Madyun*,[164] in which it had affirmed the order of a lower court that a caesarean section be carried out on a competent woman whose pregnancy was at full term and whose labour was obstructed. In that decision, the Court of Appeals had considered those cases in which the courts relied upon the 'compelling interests' of the state to override parental objections to the treatment of their children and concluded that, on the facts, 'the state's interest affecting a child already born applies with the same force to an unborn child'.[165] In *Re AC* the Court of Appeals

---

[161] *Ibid.*
[162] 573 A 2d 1235 (1990).
[163] Citing *Jefferson, Raleigh Fitkin-Paul, Re Jamaica Hospital, Crouse*, but noting *Taft v Taft*, all referred to at note 99 above.
[164] 114 Daily Wash L Rptr 2233, DC Sup Ct, 26 July 1986.
[165] Citing *Roe v Wade*, note 109 above, *Jefferson, Raleigh Fitkin-Paul, Re Jamaica Hospital*, see note 99 above and relying on the *dicta* of the Supreme Court in *Prince v Massachusetts* 321 US 158, at 170 (1944) that '[p]arents may be free to become martyrs themselves. But it does not follow that they are free, in identical circumstances, to make martyrs of their children', which *dicta* had been applied by Georgia's Supreme Court in *Jefferson* to the 'unborn infant'.

noted the 'factual differences between *Madyun* and the present case . . .
[in particular, the lack of conflict in the earlier case] between the interests of mother and fetus [and the fact that] . . . the pregnancy was at full
term, and Mrs. Madyun had been in labor for two and a half days. . . . If
another *Madyun*-type case ever comes before this court, its result may well
depend on facts that we cannot now foresee'.[166]

The most recent appellate decision in this area is that in *Re Baby Doe*,[167]
in which the Appellate Court of Illinois ruled that a lower court had erred
in forcing Tabita Bricci to undergo a caesarean section because of fears
that the foetus was seriously underweight. Citing Bricci's common law
right to self-determination, the recognition (not in the context of pregnancy) by the Supreme Court of a 'significant liberty interest in avoiding unwanted medical procedures',[168] the Illinois Constitution's right
to privacy, which right extended to reproductive autonomy, and the
religious liberty protected under state and federal constitutions; the court
ruled that 'a woman's right to refuse invasive medical treatment, derived
from her rights to privacy, bodily integrity, and religious liberty, is not
diminished during pregnancy . . . The potential impact on the fetus
is not relevant'.

The Illinois court concluded that those decisions to the contrary
(*Jefferson* and *re Madyun*) were inconsistent with Illinois law and had failed
to recognise the 'constitutional dimension of the woman's right to refuse
medical treatment, or the magnitude of that right'. Nor would the court
follow the various cases in which women had been forced to undergo
blood transfusions which procedure the court (somewhat controversially)
characterised, by contrast with caesarean sections, as 'relatively non-
invasive and risk-free'.[169] As far as the constitutional arguments were concerned, the Illinois court took the view that the abortion decisons of the
Supreme Court 'further bolster a woman's right to refuse a cesarean section'
by forbidding a 'trade-off between the woman's health and fetal survival
. . . the woman's health is always the paramount consideration [and]
any degree of increased risk to the woman's health is unacceptable'.[170]

The decision in *Re Baby Doe* supports women's right to personal autonomy in the face of foetal protection. But by the time the appellate
decision was reached, Bricci had already proven the doctors wrong by
giving birth vaginally to a normal healthy baby. Under such circumstances,

---

[166] See I Kennedy and A Grubb, *Medical Law: Text with Materials* (London: Butterworths,
1994), pp 358–359 for criticism of this aspect of *Re AC* 533 A 2d 203, 533 A 2d 611
(1988).

[167] 260 Ill App 3d 392 (1994).

[168] *Cruzan v Director of Missouri Department of Health* 497 US 261 (1990) – relying on the Due
Process Clause of the Fourteenth Amendment.

[169] This appears not to take into account the possibilities of transmission of HIV, hepatitis,
etc.

[170] Citing *Roe v Wade*, note 109 above and *Planned Parenthood of Southeastern Pennsylvania v
Casey*, note 125 above.

it must be easier for a court to defend the woman's rights against the perceived interests of the foetus than in a case where the court perceives a real threat to the life of the foetus. Neither the Supreme Court of Illinois nor that of the US agreed to hear further appeals in *re Baby Doe*. This has had the effect that women throughout the US remain vulnerable to court-ordered caesareans, should their doctors seek them and should the judges before whom the cases are heard take a different view from those of the Appellate Court of Illinois and (on second thoughts) of the Court of Appeal of the District of Columbia. The justices of the US Supreme Court, who could have settled the matter once and for all, chose not to make a ruling which would have protected women in the US from the interventionist impulses of a profession under siege from medical malpractice suits and, presumably, from pressures exerted by their insurers.

As recently as March 1997, Dorothy Tolbert was threatened with court action over her refusal to undergo a caesarean section which, in the view of her doctors, was necessary to save the life of the foetus she carried. Again, her doctors promised 'certain death' for the foetus if a vaginal delivery were to be attempted. In this case, as in so many others, the woman eventually succumbed against her religious beliefs and the matter was not litigated.[171] The court had, however, appointed a lawyer for the foetus at the hospital's request despite legal doubts as to whether this was permitted under Florida state law. The foetus's lawyer was to argue that the state's interest in protecting the life of the viable foetus and in preventing the abandonment of Tolbert's other children (see below) trumped her right to privacy, despite the fact that, under Florida law, the foetus is not considered a person and regardless of the explicit right to privacy enshrined in the Florida Constitution. According to an ACLU commentator on the case, lawyers have previously been appointed to represent the foetus in cases where abortions were sought by women under state control.[172]

Discrimination and reproductive control

One very significant point which was raised in the context of women criminalised for drug use during pregnancy concerned the differential impact of the law on white and other women. The same disparity is seen in relation to women forced, in the US, to accept medical treatment during pregnancy. By 1987, 81 per cent of women subject to this type of coercion were African–American or Latina.[173] And, perhaps most shocking of all, even after *Roe v Wade* the courts have not been ready to condemn coercive sterilisation of poor, black women.

---

[171] *The Palm Beach Post*, 5 March 1997.
[172] *Sun Sentinel* (Fort Lauderdale), 5 March 1997.
[173] Kolder *et al*, note 99 above.

In 1977, a Federal Court of Appeals dismissed a civil rights action by a number of black women against a Medicaid doctor who had refused to deliver their third children unless they also agreed to simultaneous sterilisation. The woman alleged *inter alia* that they had been discriminated against on the ground of their race. The Federal Court of Appeals (South Carolina) declared that: 'We perceive no reason why Dr Pierce could not establish and pursue the policy he has publicly and freely announced'.[174] The US Supreme Court refused to hear the appeal.[175] And in 1978, 15 black and Mexican–American women sued a Californian hospital for involuntarily sterilising them. Ten of the Mexican–American women spoke only Spanish, but the consent forms they signed were in English (four of these women did not discover they had been sterilised until much later), and '[t]he women agreed to the procedure either while in labor, under anaesthesia, or while suffering extreme pain and being denied pain killers until giving consent'.[176] The women lost their legal action, the judge deciding that the events resulted from a breakdown in communication for which the hospital was not responsible.

It has been suggested (see further Chapter 10 below) that racism lies behind the drive towards restrictions on reproduction by women dependent on welfare (and, more generally, behind the punitive attitude towards transgressions by pregnant women (black women being particularly targeted because of the perception that most are 'welfare moms' who are, in turn, lazy, promiscuous and irresponsible)). In the face of widespread public antipathy, these 'moms' need the protection of the Supreme Court, just as those selected for sterilisation on the basis of their 'feeble-mindedness' earlier in the century needed that same protection. Then, the court failed the 'feeble-minded', the eugenics movement having 'helped secure a climate in which Congress could set [eugenics-based] quotas for immigrants and the Supreme Court could rule [in *Buck v Bell*[177]] that sterilization was not a violation of constitutional protection'.[178]

The US Constitution, as it has been interpreted by the Supreme Court, contains general restrictions on race and sex discrimination (noted in Chapter 3 above). It might be argued that, the impact of the law on pregnant women not having been even-handed with regard to race, the Equal Protection Clause of the Fourteenth Amendment could be prayed in aid. If it were to be established that black women were being singled out deliberately for drug testing, forced medical intervention, etc, during pregnancy, it must be presumed that such a policy would be regarded as being in conflict with the Fourteenth Amendment. But to

---

[174] *Virgil Walker and Shirley Brown v Clovis Pierce MD et al, etc* 560 F 2d 609 (1977) (Fourth Circuit).
[175] 434 US 1075 (1978).
[176] Shapiro, note 2 above, p 90.
[177] Note 110 above.
[178] *News Tribune*, 7 July 1997.

prove that deliberate discrimination was being practised would be difficult indeed.

In October 1997, a civil action alleging violation of women's constitutional rights by a drug-testing programme carried out at the Medical University of South Carolina, was rejected. Staff initially operated without guidelines as to when women should be tested, and most of the women prosecuted as a result of the Medical University's testing programme were black. The women argued that the programme was carried out only at that hospital, which treated most of Charleston's poor, black population, and that it isolated the use of cocaine, more commonly used by black women (other drugs, used by white women, not being tested for). But Judge Weston Houck ruled that '[n]one of the challenged practices, procedures, or courses of action . . . (had) an adverse discriminatory impact' on the women, any disparate impact resulting from the 'use of cocaine by blacks . . . not the isolation of cocaine by [the hospital] . . . The court concludes that the policy was necessary to help cocaine-dependent babies and their mothers'.[179] Even had Judge Houck accepted the disproportionate impact by race of the Medical University's policy, the decision of the Supreme Court in *Washington v Davis*[180] suggests that no constitutional issue would have been made out.[181]

Conclusion

It is clear from this chapter that US constitutional provisions have not, in general, served to protect women's reproductive freedom. American women have been subject to similar threats, in the context of childbirth, to those under which British women labour. Indeed, the assault which has taken place on pregnant women in the US has extended far further than anything as yet imagined here. Not only have attempts to control pregnant women gone beyond childbirth itself to the duration of pregnancy, but women in the US have also been subject to coercion in respect of their decisions to reproduce (whether in the form of criminal sentences or, more commonly, welfare restrictions), as well as in their attempts to terminate unwanted pregnancies.

Whether or not the use of the criminal law in this area offends the US Constitution, its protection has been, at best, patchy. Further, the threats to women in these areas have, for the most part, come from the judiciary itself. And as far as the most significant threat to reproductive

---

[179] *The Post and Courier*, Charleston, 2 October 1997.
[180] Note 133 above.
[181] In addition, the action of hospitals in testing and reporting women will not necessarily amount to 'state action', in which case no constitutional protection applies: *Blum v Yaretsky* 457 US 991 (1982). See further Chapter 3 above.

decision-making is concerned, it is fairly clear that 'family caps' are consistent with the entrenched rights of US citizens. Women have been afforded some protection from forced medical intervention in the interests of the foetuses they carry. But this protection has been no more extensive than that which, in the view of the courts, is provided by the common law. This, in turn, has rendered American women more, rather than less, vulnerable to coercion than is the case in the UK. In particular, the US courts have countenanced forced medical intervention even in the absence of a threat to the life of a 'third party' (the foetus), in circumstances in which court-ordered intervention would be unthinkable in the UK.

A number of US courts have ordered women to undergo unwanted blood transfusions on the basis that refusal to do so will result in death, the death resulting in the 'abandonment' of the woman's living children. In 1964, for example, Judge Skelly Wright relied upon the State's interest in preventing abandonment of a minor child (in that case, a seven-month-old baby) in ordering a blood transfusion to be carried out against the religion-based objections of a Jehovah's witness.[182] Again in 1985, New York's Supreme Court relied on the interests of a woman's two children in ordering her to receive blood transfusions during kidney stone removal surgery despite her religious objections,[183] and five years later another New York woman was subjected to forced blood transfusion by a court which did not even permit her to be heard.[184] More recently, the higher courts have disfavoured such forced treatment, though generally on common law, rather than on constitutional, grounds.[185] But in *Stamford Hospital v Vega* (1996), which concerned a just post-partum woman, the Supreme Court of Connecticut expressly distinguished the situation from one in which a transfusion was necessary to 'safeguard the health or life of the baby'.[186] And in *Re Dubreuil*,[187] Florida's Supreme Court refused to rule out the possibility that what it recognised as the (state) constitutional right to refuse medical treatment could be overcome by 'a compelling interest to prevent abandonment'.

Constitutional rights cannot be regarded as a panacea. One might argue, of course, that much of the difficulty with the US position lies in the nature of the rights entrenched. In the absence of any express constitutional right to physical autonomy, to control over reproductive decision-making, even to abortion or to be free from discrimination on grounds of sex, US women are forced to fall back on less specific rights to 'due process' and to the less than comprehensive shelter of the Equal Protection

---

[182] *Raleigh Fitkin-Paul Morgan Memorial Hospital v Anderson*, note 99 above.

[183] *Re Winthrop University Hospital* 128 Misc 2d 804, 490 NYS 2d 996 (1985).

[184] This latter case was overruled in *Re Fosmire* 75 NY 2d 218 (1990), although not on constitutional grounds.

[185] See *Stamford Hospital v Vega* 236 Conn 646 (1996) Sup Ct of Connecticut.

[186] *Re Fosmire*, note 184 above.

[187] 629 So 2d 819 (1993).

Clause. In Canada, by contrast, the much more rigorous equality provisions might well do more to protect women from interference in their reproductive decision-making. This issue is considered further in Chapter 10 below. As for the provisions incorporated into UK law from the European Convention on Human Rights, their scope and their likely impact are, too, dealt with in Chapter 10.

Chapter 6

Securing Equality for Women at Work?

Introduction

The next area in which the impact of entrenched rights upon women will be considered is that of work. Women workers in the UK are disadvantaged in a number of respects. Those who work full-time earn only 80 per cent of full-time male workers' average hourly wage, while part-timers earn only 60 per cent. Women are segregated by sex into lower paying occupations and workplaces, and are invariably found at lower levels than men in those occupations which they share. Even within occupations, women earn less than men. This is particularly true of part-time workers, who tend to be most segregated in terms of sex and who are denied the wage rates and other benefits available to men and, to a lesser extent, to women who work full-time.[1]

While part of the gender wage gap which persists in the UK may be the result of other factors, the available evidence suggests that a great deal of discrimination operates.[2] This, and the shortcomings of the UK legislation, are considered elsewhere, but it is clear that the market operates against women. It does so both by virtue of intentional discrimination, generally based on employers' stereotypical views of women as secondary earners; and because of indirect discrimination, whereby requirements placed upon workers are such that women find it more difficult to comply. Far from eradicating discrimination, as traditional economists would suggest, the marketplace has permitted it to flourish, and the amelioration of women's labour market disadvantage requires government action.

Any real commitment to equality in work for male and female workers would require change on a number of fronts. In the first place, steps would have to be taken to combat the tendency in the labour market

---

[1] See A McColgan, *Just Wages for Women* (Oxford: Clarendon Press, 1997), Chapter 2.
[2] *Ibid*, Chapters 3–6.

towards the segregation of female workers into a narrow category (relative to men) of occupations and industries. Secondly, action would be required to ensure that women were not subject to the 'glass ceiling' which currently prevents many from progressing up the hierarchy of jobs. Important in this sphere would be steps to counter the difficulties typically experienced by women when they have children. Finally, real progress would have to be achieved to eliminate the pay differentials which currently result from women's workplace, occupational and industrial segregation, and, in particular, from the under-valuation of typically female work.

Both legal systems considered in this chapter and the next provide protection against workplace discrimination. The manner in which they do so, of course, varies. But the question with which the following discussion is concerned relates not to the level of protection afforded, rather to the impact in this area of overriding constitutional rights. There is no question that the creation of statutory rights – the rights not to be subject to sex discrimination in appointment, promotion, or dismissal, for example; the right to equal pay for work of equal value – have benefited women in the UK.[3] Related statutory rights have assisted women in Canada, the US, and in many countries across the world. But the focus of this book is on constitutional rights which are, by their nature, broad and general – rights, in Canada, to equality 'before and under the law' and to the 'equal protection and equal benefit of the law'; rights in the US not to be deprived of 'life, liberty, or property, without due process of law' and to 'the equal protection of the laws'. All 'rights' must be interpreted by the judiciary. But such is the level of breadth and generality normally associated with constitutional rights, such is their power to trump mere statutory provisions and the potential for conflict between different constitutional rights (this in turn requiring their balancing by the judiciary), that it is crucial to assess the extent to which such constitutional rights have impacted on women at work.

The potential of these 'constitutional', 'overarching' or 'entrenched' rights here is somewhat different from their possible role in the area of reproductive freedom, considered in Chapters 4 and 5 above. In the latter context, in which much of the threat to women comes from the State,[4] entrenched rights can operate as a shield. This is not to say that such rights are adequate to ensure practical access to abortion or to contraceptive services – this and other shortcomings are considered in Chapter 4. But in the context of the workplace, where women's disadvantage

---

[3] Indeed, the final report of the Labour Party's policy review for the 1990s, *Meet the Challenge, Make the Change*, dismissed the idea of a Bill of Rights as insufficiently protective of individual rights and proposed, in its place, a package of specific statutory rights 'to provide a massive extension of individual rights and to extend democracy in Great Britain' – see, generally, K Ewing, 'The Human Rights Act and Parliamentary Democracy' (1999) 62 *Modern Law Review*, forthcoming.

[4] The most significant exception to this is the anti-abortion violence discussed in Chapter 3 above.

emanates almost entirely from the market (legislative discrimination having largely disappeared), the potential of constitutional rights to operate in women's interests is reduced, while their potential to operate against women is very significant. Constitutional rights are binding, in general, only upon the State. This being the case, constitutional protection from discrimination is of little value where, as in the context of work, discrimination flows largely from the private sector. This is further discussed below. On the other hand, as will be seen in Chapter 7 below, such constitutional provisions can be used by employers and others to challenge efforts by government to eradicate discrimination, where these efforts rely on a more radical approach to discrimination than that adopted by the judiciary.

Cross-country comparisons – the problem

There are many similarities in the labour market position of women in the UK, Canada and the US. Although women are more likely to work part-time in the UK than elsewhere,[5] women in all three countries experience segregation at occupational and industrial, vertical and horizontal, levels, and receive considerably lower wages than those which men enjoy. In Canada for example, 'the continuing under-representation of women in senior ranks' was described in 1997 by the Human Rights Commission as 'one of the most persistent' consequences of workplace discrimination.[6] The Commission's *Annual Report* cited the International Labour Organisation's, *Breaking through the Glass Ceiling: Women in Management*, which 'found that most women are still barred from the top levels of organizations, whether in the private or public sector', and another study of women in management which found that 'stereotyping and preconceptions regarding [women's] roles and abilities were the biggest barriers to advancement. In order to succeed, [women] felt the need to consistently exceed performance expectations and to develop a style with which male managers were comfortable.'[7]

The Commission reported that 'women . . . remain concentrated in a narrow range of occupations, particularly the clerical field where one-third are employed, and . . . are still not being compensated equitably for work

---

[5] Canada Bureau of Statistics, *Canada Yearbook* 1997 (Ottawa: Bureau of Statistics).

[6] See also W List, 'Employers Find Rewards in Employment Equity' (1989) 16(1) *Canadian Business Review* 35, cited in L Falkenberg and L Boland, 'Eliminating the Barriers to Employment Equity in the Canadian Workplace' (1997) 16(9) *Journal of Business Ethics* 963; and M2 *Newswire*, 29 January 1997, 'Committee on Elimination of Discrimination Against Women takes up Report by Canada'.

[7] The report also cited *Closing the Gap: Women's Advancement in Corporate and Professional Canada*, sponsored by Catalyst (a US research organisation), and the Conference Board of Canada.

of comparable value . . . women, and in particular pregnant women and women in male-dominated workplaces, are still vulnerable to discrimination [and] . . . even overt harassment remains a feature in the working lives of too many women'. According to the 1997 report, '[n]owhere is the lack of equality for women more obvious than in the area of wages', women earning 70 per cent of men's wages.[8] While part of this gap could, according to the report, be attributed to factors other than discrimination, 'studies of relative job values and wages have repeatedly revealed that work done primarily by women is not compensated equitably in comparison to work done predominantly by men [and] . . . evidence . . . suggest[s] that wage patterns continue to be influenced by traditional views of the worth of so-called "women's work" . . . patterns indicate that attitudes about the relative worth of different jobs do, in fact, influence wages'.

The 70 per cent figure has remained relatively stable since 1994, having fallen from about 72 per cent in 1992.[9] Just as is the case in the UK, the pay gap is not explained by relative educational achievement (women accounted for over half of Canada's university graduates in the 1980s and 1990s but in 1994 earned, as graduates, 72 per cent of male graduates' wages).[10] In Canada, as in the UK, the wage gap persists at the occupational level – in 1990, full-time women professionals and managers earned 64 per cent of their male colleagues' wages, women in clerical, sales and services occupations respectively 75 per cent, 64 per cent and 57 per cent.

Women in the US fare little better. In 1995, between 95 per cent and 97 per cent of the senior managers of the Fortune 1000 industrial and the Fortune 500 companies were male, as were 95 per cent of those in the Fortune 2000 industrial and service companies.[11] Women are under-represented in the executive, administrative, and managerial occupations in every industry.[12] And while women, in common with ethnic minority workers, fare much better in the public than in the private sector, the federal civil service in particular being representative of the US population;[13] even here, women and minorities are found predominantly in the lower echelons. American women own 34 per cent of all US businesses but, together with minority-owned businesses (9 per cent), receive only about 8.8 per cent of the more than $200 billion awarded annually in federal contract awards.[14]

The pattern of occupational and industrial segregation is very broadly similar in the US to that in Canada and the UK. And women in the US,

---

[8] This is a weekly figure.

[9] Note 5 above.

[10] *Ibid.*

[11] US Secretary of Labor Robert Reich, quoted on the ACLU world wide web page, http://www.aclu.org. See also the US Department of Labor, *The Glass Ceiling Report*, March 1995.

[12] A Ewoh and E Elliott, 'End of An Era?: Affirmative Action and Reaction in the 1990s' (1997) 17(4) *Review of Public Personnel Administration* 38.

[13] *Ibid.*

[14] ACLU Press Release, 1 April 1998, see http://www.aclu.org.

too, earn considerably less than their male colleagues. In 1996, full-time women earned 78.8 per cent of men's median wages, hours held constant. Again, the pay gap persists at the level of the occupation. Women managers, for example, earned 77 per cent of male managers' wages in 1996 (again, hours held constant), women professionals 82 per cent, women precision workers 71 per cent and women service workers 83 per cent.[15]

The impact of constitutional rights

In assessing the importance of entrenched rights to women in the labour market, it is useful to focus on the issues of maternity, access to employment and pay. The reason that these areas are of particular interest lies in the relationship between women's subordinated labour market position and their childbearing role; the persistent segmentation by sex of the labour market, and the enduring inequalities in pay between men and women. If these three issues could be tackled effectively, women would see a huge improvement in their working lives and prospects and, consequently, in their existence outside the workplace.

Maternity

The issue of maternity and child care-related rights deserves consideration because it is when women become pregnant or, at any rate, when they give birth, that many first experience the full impact of labour market discrimination. Although women in the UK are entitled to maternity leave (the period of which depends on their length of service with their current employer), the maternity provisions are complex and statutory maternity pay ungenerous. Most women suffer real economic loss as a result of even the shortest maternity leave, and the careers of those who are absent for longer, or who work part-time for a period, almost invariably suffer irreparable damage. Women who return to work at once after maternity leave, and who continue in their previous jobs full-time, frequently experience profound difficulty in reconciling the demands of motherhood with the increasing workplace demand for 'flexibility'. Many jobs are simply not structured around workers who require a degree of predictability in their working hours. And not until adequate provision is made for properly protected and financed maternity leave, until good child care is available at reasonable cost and, most fundamentally, until men and their employers are forced to recognise that parenting is a dual responsibility, will women have a reasonable chance of equality in the workplace.

---

[15] US Bureau of Labor Statistics, *Employment and Earnings*, figures for the last quarter of 1996.

Employment

As far as access to employment is concerned, the most significant issue in this area is that of the extent to which entrenched rights have been interpreted so as to support, or indeed to prohibit, government action designed to integrate the workforce by means of affirmative action, legislative requirements for restrictions in access having largely ceased to exist. Two decades of UK experience with the Sex Discrimination Acts 1975 and 1986 have shown that the requirement of formal equality of access, even coupled as it is with the prohibition of 'indirect discrimination', has not served substantially to undo the ghettoisation of women in women's jobs, women's workplaces. Because no positive obligations have been imposed on employers, the stereotyping of 'male' and 'female' jobs has changed relatively little, and the obstacles facing women who would otherwise attempt to break into male-dominated positions remain almost insuperable. The recognition of indirect discrimination can go some way towards challenging job segregation by demanding that a degree of accommodation be made to women's workplace needs (for example, by permitting part-time working). But the onus remains firmly upon women to challenge existing patterns of work, and the justification by employers of disparately impacting workplace practices is more likely to be successful in those very areas which are most male-dominated, given that the accommodation of female needs by such workplaces will be most at odds with their prevailing norms. It is for this reason that real progress may require that some forms of affirmative action be embraced. The difficulties which may be posed for such schemes by constitutional anti-discrimination provisions are discussed in Chapter 7 below.

Turning, finally, to the issue of discrimination in pay, this matter requires particular consideration because it forms the 'bottom line' of the work relation and lies at the heart of women's workplace disadvantage. Women account for a disproportionate number of the 'working poor' and the low wages available in typically female jobs reduce many single mothers to dependence on the State (again, the issue of affordable child care is of enormous importance here), others to dependence upon their male partners. The latter, in particular, renders women vulnerable to abuse (see Chapters 8 and 9 below). In addition, because of women's lower wages and their reduced access to employment-related benefits such as pensions and long-term sick pay,[16] poverty amongst older women is endemic. Finally, for as long as women remain relatively (to men) underpaid, women will continue to bear the greater share of child care responsibility and thus to have their jobs compromised and their wages held down relative to those of men, men's parental responsibilities will continue to be ignored in the workplace. If, on the other hand, women's wages were

---

[16] *Guardian*, 26 October 1996.

comparable with those of men, the burden of child care responsibility would not inevitably fall upon women, men would have to balance their jobs with their child care responsibilities, employers would have to begin to recognise that *workers*, as distinct from *women*, have to balance work with life, and much of the underpinning of women's workplace disadvantage would begin to disappear. This, in turn, would have significant effects on the poverty experienced by so many women in old age.

The question of pay brings into consideration not only individual issues but also the area of collective rights, in particular, how entrenched rights have impacted on collective bargaining and minimum wage provision. The gender-pay gap and, more generally, the degree of wage dispersion in any particular country, are affected by the degree of collective agreement coverage within that country (as well as by the existence or otherwise of minimum wage regulation).[17] One of the reasons why the UK has the worst gender-pay ratios in the EU is the fact that the gap between the best and the worst-paid workers in the UK is much wider than that in most other Member States,[18] a factor which results both from the low level of collective agreement coverage in the UK and from the lack, at present, of any minimum wage provision. Equally, both Canada and, more particularly, the US, are noteworthy in having very low degrees of union coverage and correspondingly high levels of wage dispersion and of gender wage gap. The US does have a national minimum wage, but it is set at such a low level ($5.15 an hour, more than $1 an hour below its real value in the 1970s[19]) that it provides little more than a safety net against the most extreme type of wage exploitation. And the level of wage disparities are such in the US that, whereas in the early to mid 1980s US women earned 67 per cent of men's pay, had the overall level of wage inequality in the US mirrored that in Australia, women's relative earnings would have been of the order of 80 per cent.[20]

Constitutions and employment equality

Introduction – the US and Canada

From the UK perspective it is tempting to assume that constitutionally entrenched rights would be of benefit to women at work. This assumption

---

[17] McColgan, note 1 above, Chapters 8–10.
[18] *Ibid.* A survey by Eurostat (no 1698/ 7 July 1998, available at http://europa.eu.int/en/comm/eurostat/compres/en/6698/6306698a.htm suggests Britain has a relatively low wage gap but this is countered by another survey by Eurostat (no 6998/ 14 September 1998), available at http://europa.eu.int/en/comm/eurostat/compres/en/8898/6308898a.htm.
[19] *Fresno Bee*, 23 June 1998.
[20] F Blau and L Kahn, The Gender Earnings Gap: Some International Evidence (National Bureau of Economic Research, 1992) Working Paper No 4224.

arises, in large part, because of the role of Europe in the development of anti-discrimination law. Over the last two decades the pattern has been, in the UK, of inadequate national legislation coupled with better provision at the European level. Given our experience of employment equality issues in the UK it is very tempting to assume that, by fixing prohibitions on discrimination, or demands for equality, at a higher level, lackadaisical or indifferent legislatures can be pressurised into providing adequate legislation, or overridden in the event of their failure so to do. In order to explore the issue more fully, it is useful at this point to consider the impact of the US Constitution and the Canadian Charter of Rights.

The US Constitution, as it was originally drafted, contained no prohibition on discrimination, and the Equal Protection Clause of the Fourteenth Amendment was at first interpreted to prohibit only race-based discrimination (see Chapter 3 above). In the employment field, initial challenges to sex-specific 'protective' legislation were not mounted under the Equal Protection Clause.[21] In 1905 the Supreme Court struck down, as an abuse of due process, a New York statute which restricted the hours of those working in the baking trade.[22] But three years later, in *Muller v State of Oregon*,[23] the same court rejected an Equal Protection challenge to state law which restricted the hours lawfully worked by women laundry workers. Upholding the legislation Justice Brewer, for a unanimous court, declared that 'healthy mothers are essential to vigorous offspring, [so] the physical well-being of woman becomes an object of public interest and care in order to preserve the strength and vigor of the race . . . legislation designed for her protection may be sustained, even when like legislation is not necessary for men, and could not be sustained'.[24]

It seemed that the Supreme Court was prepared to take into account the context in which 'discrimination' was challenged where the impugned provisions served to disadvantage women by comparison with men (by rendering them less attractive as employees). In the wake of the *Muller* decision many states enacted protective legislation, which legislation the Supreme Court continued to uphold until the 1970s.[25] In 1923, in *Adkins*,[26] the Supreme Court struck down minimum wage legislation applicable to women as indistinguishable from that declared invalid in *Lochner v State of New York*.[27] But in 1937 the Supreme Court accepted legislation which imposed

---

[21] See, generally, E Cary and K Peratis, *Woman and the Law* (Stokie, Illinois: National Textbook Company, 1978).

[22] In particular, of freedom of contract which was, during the 'substantive due process' era, regarded as a fundamental component of due process.

[23] 208 US 412 (1908).

[24] *Ibid*, at 422–423.

[25] See also *Quong Wing v Kirkendall* 223 US 59 (1912); *Miller v Wilson* 236 US 373 (1915); *Bosley v Mclaughlin* 236 US 385 (1915) in which the Supreme Court read the Equal Protection Clause argument as referring to the different treatment of different classes of women, rather than the different treatment of men and women.

[26] 261 US 525 (1923).

[27] 198 US 45 (1905).

a minimum wage in respect of women workers, declaring that the liberty guaranteed by the Fourteenth Amendment could be qualified by the State's interest in protecting women.[28] In 1948 the Supreme Court accepted regulations forbidding women to be licensed as bartenders, except where they were the wives or daughters of male bar owners.[29]

By 1976, the Supreme Court had recognised that the Equal Protection Clause applied to sex-based discrimination and had adopted an intermediate standard of scrutiny in this context. The clause was subsequently relied upon to challenge discrimination in access to jobs and in pay-related matters. The advances achieved are discussed below, having been felt primarily in the context of pay and benefits. But the Equal Protection Clause prohibits only *direct* discrimination, recognising equality only at the most formal level and requiring only that like is treated alike. This formal approach has permitted that court to find that protective legislation and employer-led exclusions of women from the workforce are violative of the Equal Protection Clause and of Title VII. But, to the extent that state action has attempted to ameliorate the position of women by tackling the effects of past discrimination, it has served to undermine the drive towards substantive equality. Whereas, in earlier years, the Supreme Court was willing to recognise the particular constraints facing women at work (albeit that this recognition was applied to uphold 'protective' legislation the effect of which was to place women at a disadvantage in the workplace), the approach more recently taken by the Supreme Court to affirmative action programmes has been determinedly blind to the broad historical and social context in which such programmes operate. When coupled with the formal approach to equality, US constitutional guarantees of non-discrimination have permitted those already in an advantaged position to thwart efforts to improve the position of the disadvantaged. This is further discussed in Chapter 7 below.

A number of the failings of the US system could be ascribed to the nature of the rights entrenched in that system. The constitutional amendments which together comprise the Bill of Rights, together with the subsequent amendments thereto, are relatively elderly and are concerned more with the quartering of soldiers and the abolition of slavery than with questions of equality. By contrast, Canada's Charter is a modern document, implemented only in 1982, and drawn up specifically to favour a substantive model of equality. Such was Canada's experience of judicial application of its 1960 Bill of Rights that all efforts were made to shape the Charter so as to address the problems associated with the existing 'rights' jurisprudence. Thus, the Charter contains a clear commitment to sex equality 'before and under the law', and affords 'the right to the equal protection and equal benefit of the law without discrimination'. In

---

[28] *West Coast Hotel Co v Parrish* 300 US 379 (1937).
[29] *Goesaert v Cleary* 335 US 464 (1948).

addition, the Charter specifically permits some forms of affirmative action, s 15(2) providing that the equality guarantee 'does not preclude any law, program or activity that has as its object the amelioration of conditions of disadvantaged individuals or groups including those that are disadvantaged because of . . . sex'. The equality rights entrenched in s 15 are such that, if any constitutional rights were to benefit women in the workplace context, these surely would.

The affirmative action provision of Canada's Charter is further discussed in Chapter 7. The reasons behind it, and behind the careful drafting of the equality provisions have been discussed in Chapter 3, as has the approach of Canada's judiciary both to the Charter in general and to ss 15 and 28 in particular. Here the application of the Charter to the situations of specific female workplace disadvantage will be considered.

Pregnancy – the US

In *Cleveland Board of Education v LaFluer*[30] the US Supreme Court struck down, on due process grounds, school rules which required pregnant school teachers to leave work (without pay) four and five months respectively before the expected dates for the birth of their babies. Given that the rules were based only upon (disputable) administrative convenience and the possibility of some 'embarrassment' to the school boards, the boards were found to have acted arbitrarily and irrationally. But this small victory comprised the beginning and the end of the protection afforded to pregnant women by the Supreme Court under the Fourteenth Amendment. In *Geduldig v Aiello*,[31] the court ruled that the exclusion from California's employment insurance programme of normal pregnancy did not violate the Equal Protection Clause of the Fourteenth Amendment.[32] The court did not accept that pregnancy-based discrimination amounted to sex-based discrimination:

> [t]here is no risk from which men are protected and women are not. Likewise, there is no risk from which women are protected and men are not . . . The program divides potential recipients into two groups – pregnant women and nonpregnant persons. While the first group is exclusively female, the second includes members of both sexes.[33]

Justice Brennan dissented, protesting that, whereas all medical conditions specific to men were covered by the insurance scheme, that (pregnancy) unique to women was not.[34] Nevertheless, the court's conclusion that pregnancy-based discrimination did not amount to sex-based discrimination

---

[30] 414 US 632 (1974). Justice Powell concurred on equal protection grounds.
[31] 417 US 484 (1974).
[33] *Ibid*, pp 496–497.
[34] *Ibid*, pp 500–501.

permitted it to apply the rational standard of review (see Chapter 3 above) and uphold the exclusion of pregnancy from insurance coverage on the grounds of cost.

One of the reasons why the Supreme Court found it was able to reach its conclusion in *Geduldig* rested on the fact that the Equal Protection Clause of the Fourteenth Amendment was not interpreted by that court so as to apply to indirect discrimination. This permitted Justice Stewart, for the majority, to declare that '[a]bsent a showing that distinctions involving pregnancy are *mere pretexts* designed to effect an invidious discrimination against the members of one sex or the other, lawmakers are constitutionally free to include or exclude pregnancy from the coverage of legislation such as this' (my emphasis).[35]

The impact of *Geduldig* on pregnancy discrimination has been reduced by the inclusion of pregnancy within Title VII of the Civil Rights Act 1964's prohibition on discrimination. But the decision remains indicative of the general approach of the Supreme Court to discrimination under the Equal Protection Clause of the Fourteenth Amendment. Just as, in *Geduldig*, the Supreme Court adopted a rigorously formalistic approach to discrimination and focused entirely on the question whether the same rule was applied to both men and women, so the court has consistently refused to accept that indirect discrimination is a denial of equal protection under the Fourteenth Amendment.[36] In the employment field this has been partly alleviated by Title VII's application to indirect discrimination. But as far as constitutional rights are concerned, its effect has been to curtail significantly the reach of the Equal Protection guarantee.

Pregnancy – Canada

The approach taken to pregnancy discrimination by the Supreme Court of Canada under the 1960 Bill of Rights was discussed in Chapter 3 above. In *Bliss v Attorney General of Canada*,[37] that court had rejected a challenge to pregnancy-based discrimination both on the grounds that no recognised discrimination had taken place (the detriment suffered consisting of the denial of a benefit, rather than the imposition of a penalty) and that pregnancy discrimination did not amount to sex

---

[35] *Ibid*, pp 496–497. This approach was applied under Title VII in *General Electric Co* 429 US 125 (1976), despite recognition in *Griggs v Duke Power Co* 401 US 424 (1971) that indirect discrimination breached Title VII. The immediate impact of the decisions was negated by the Pregnancy Discrimination Act 1978 which amended Title VII to prohibit discrimination on the basis of pregnancy – see *Newport News Shipbuilding & Dry Dock v EEOC* 462 US 669 (1983). But there is no general right to paid maternity leave in the US – the Family Medical Leave Act 1993 (which permits parents up to 12 weeks' leave in connection with the birth or adoption of a baby) applying only to those whose employers have at least 50 staff.

[36] See Chapter 3 above.

[37] [1979] 1 SCR 183.

discrimination. In *Brooks v Canada Safeway*,[38] the Supreme Court ruled that the exclusion of pregnancy from a health insurance plan amounted to sex discrimination. The court dismissed the argument that 'the decision to exclude pregnancy from the scope of its plan was not a question of discrimination, but a question of deciding to compensate some risks and to exclude others' on the basis that '[u]nderinclusion may be simply a backhanded way of permitting discrimination. Once an employer decides to provide an employee benefit package, exclusions from such schemes may not be made, like in this case, in a discriminatory fashion.' Nor could it be argued that discrimination on the basis of pregnancy did not, itself, amount to discrimination on the basis of sex: 'pregnancy cannot be separated from gender. The fact, therefore, that the plan did not discriminate against all women, but only against pregnant women, did not make the impugned distinction any less discriminating.'

Women are protected under the Charter against discrimination directed at pregnancy. The point which should be made, however, relates to the scope for complaints under that legislation. The Charter does not apply to discrimination in the 'market' unless that discrimination is practised either by the 'government', narrowly defined or, in relation to the specific policies or programmes concerned, by non-government entities appointed to carry out government policies or programmes. Thus, when it comes to an analysis of how the Charter itself has benefited women in the context of pregnancy, the answer is much narrower than that suggested by *Brooks*. Section 15 would certainly be violated by legislation which discriminated on the basis of pregnancy, unless it was saved by s 1 (or, to the extent that it served to benefit women, was regarded as 'affirmative action' within s 15(2)). But the Charter does not prohibit employers from discriminating on grounds of pregnancy. Nor does it require federal or provincial governments to pass legislation prohibiting discrimination on grounds of pregnancy. The Charter would, as in *Brooks* itself, require that prohibited 'sex discrimination' be interpreted to include pregnancy. But neither federal nor provincial government could be required under the Charter to pass legislation prohibiting sex discrimination. This limitation on Charter rights is discussed in Chapter 3 above.

Women, as mothers, are not only disadvantaged in the workplace by pregnancy-related discrimination. More broadly, much of women's employment-related disadvantage stems from the practical demands associated with child care. Any real challenge to women's workplace inequality must come not merely at the level of the workplace, but requires government action to ensure access to affordable and reliable child care provision, as well as to encourage a more even sharing of child care responsibilities, preferably by the provision of non-transferable parental leave both for childbirth/adoption, and in respect of ill children.

---

[38] [1989] 1 SCR 1219.

The approach taken by Canada's Supreme Court in this area has not been to the advantage of women. In *Symes v Canada*,[39] the court considered a challenge to the application of income tax legislation. Revenue Canada treated child care expenses as (non-deductible) 'personal or living expenses', rather than as 'outlays or expenses incurred for the purpose of gaining or producing income from business'. Had such expenses been treated as falling into the latter category they would have been completely tax deductible. Since they were not, Elizabeth Symes received only a limited allowance (between 10 per cent and 30 per cent of actual expenditure in various years) under a separate provision of the Income Tax Act 1952.

The Supreme Court ruled that, the child care allowance provision having been intended as 'a complete legislative response to the child care expense issue', the Charter had no role in interpreting the other provisions of the Act in order to determine whether such expenses should be regarded as 'outlays or expenses incurred for the purpose of gaining or producing income from business'. The majority rejected the appellant's argument that the income tax provisions breached s 15 of the Charter. Insisting that they would have regard only to the provision dealing specifically with child care expenses, the Supreme Court ruled that '[t]he appellant has not . . . proved that [the Act] draws a distinction based upon the personal characteristic of sex . . . it is clear that women disproportionately bear the burden of child care in society [but]. . . . proof that women incur social costs is not sufficient proof that they incur child care expenses.' By contrast, Madam Justice L'Heureux-Dubé found the inference from 'proof that women pay social costs' related to child care to 'proof that women pay child care expenses . . . inescapable'.

The refusal of the majority in *Symes* to see that child care expenses operate, in practice, as obstacles to women's, but not generally to men's, participation in the workforce, is to be regretted. Both women on the court dissented, Madam Justice L'Heureux-Dubé arguing that 'the traditional interpretation of "business expense" was shaped to reflect the experience of businessmen and the ways in which they engaged in business [but] . . . the meaning of "business expense" must account for the experiences of all participants in the field'.

One factor which appeared central to the decision of the majority was its comparison with Elizabeth Symes, not with the self-employed businessmen against who she alleged disadvantage but, rather, against all the employed women who were not permitted to deduct child care expenses from their tax assessments. But, as Madam Justice L'Heureux-Dubé remarked: 'discrimination cannot be justified by pointing to other discrimination . . . This is not a case about the advantageous position in society some women garner as opposed to other women, but, rather, an examination of the advantaged position that businessmen hold

---

[39] [1993] 4 SCR 695.

in relation to businesswomen . . . The gist of [the Court of Appeal's decision] . . . it is preferable that all women be equally disadvantaged relative to men if the alternative is to improve the position of the best-off women'.[40]

Many of those who have supported the decision in *Symes* overlook the position of the minority. Joel Bakan remarks, for example, that poorer women would have ended up footing the bill had Elizabeth Symes been permitted to deduct the totality of her child care expenses from her tax bill.[41] This, as Madam Justice L'Heureux-Dubé suggested, may well be a reason to revise the tax treatment of employed and self-employed people. But it is no reason to prevent even rich women from deducting child care expenses when their male colleagues are entitled to deduct the cost of 'club dues and initiation fees [which] . . . result . . . in business', 'expenses . . . incurred for [a] Rolls Royce and BMW, to the extent that these automobiles were used for business' and 'salaries paid to employees'.[42]

The notion that distinctions between women are not acceptable, while distinctions between men are, serves to infantilise women to an outrageous degree and legitimates the practice highlighted by Craig *et al* in the UK in 1982 whereby 'firms would often recognise differences in skill between the women workers . . . but nevertheless pay all of them at the same rate, justifying the practice on the basis that any differentiation would cause resentment amongst the other women workers'.[43] But the bizarre approach to s 15 comparisons resurfaced once again in *Thibaudeau v Canada*,[44] in which the court upheld tax legislation which taxed child maintenance payments in the hands of (overwhelmingly female) custodial parents, while making these payments tax deductible for (correspondingly male) non-custodial parents. The majority insisted that the legislation 'does not impose a burden or withhold a benefit so as to attract the application of s 15(1) of the Charter', Justices Cory and Iacobucci taking the view that, because the tax regime tended to confer a benefit on the 'post divorce "family unit" ' taken as a whole: '[t]he fact that one member of the unit might derive a greater benefit from the legislation than the other does not, in and of itself, trigger a s 15(1) violation, nor does it lead to a finding that the distinction in any way amounts to a denial of equal benefit or protection of the law'.

Justice Gonthier concurred on the grounds that no discrimination had occurred (this conclusion being made possible by his application

---

[40] She went on to point out that self-employed women averaged a salary of under $30,000 for a 50–70-hour week.

[41] *Just Words: Constitutional Rights and Social Wrongs* (Toronto: University of Toronto Press, 1997), pp 59–60.

[42] Cases cited by Madam Justice L'Heureux-Dubé.

[43] C Craig, J Rubery, R Tarling and F Wilkinson, *Labour Market Structure, Industrial Organisation and Low Pay* (Cambridge: Cambridge University Press, 1982), p 84.

[44] [1995] 2 SCR 627.

of the 'irrelevant personal characteristics' approach to s 15 (see
Chapter 3 above)). He agreed with Justices Cory and Iacobucci that
the appropriate comparision was between, rather than within, 'family
units': 'the group of divorced or separated parents cannot as a whole
claim to suffer prejudice associated with the very existence of the system in question'. In addition, because the regime was 'for the ultimate
benefit of the child . . . [a] fundamental value of our society . . . the distribution of the fiscal impact is therefore not open to challenge under
the *Charter*.'[45]

The majority's acceptance that a 'post divorce "family unit"' had common financial interests, and its lack of concern as to the distribution
of benefits within that unit, beggars credibility. In addition, Justice
Gonthier's approach suggests that all the legislature has to do to exclude
Charter scrutiny is to satisfy the court that legislation is motivated towards
a fundamental good, regardless of whether the means used to achieve
that end are effective, and regardless of what other interests they conflict with. It was left to Justices McLachlin and L'Heureux-Dubé, both of
whom dissented, to identify the distinction drawn by the legislation as that
between custodial and non-custodial parents; to point out that, even
where the legislation did confer a benefit on the couple overall, it did not
require the equitable distribution of that benefit between them; and
to highlight the fact that custodial parents alone were liable to pay tax
on child support payments – *per* Justice McLachlin: 'child support is not
included in the taxable income of other persons in situations similar to
that of the custodial parent'.

Discrimination in access to employment – the US

In the US, Title VII of the Civil Rights Act 1964 prohibits sex discrimination in employment, subject to an exception where sex 'is a bona fide
occupational qualification reasonably necessary to the normal operation
of that particular business or enterprise'.[46] Title VII covers employees in
the private as well as those in the public sector. Because it has been interpreted to extend to indirect as well as to direct discrimination,[47] it gives
more, rather than less, protection than is available under the Equal
Protection Clause. This, together with the narrow approach taken to the
bona fide occupational qualification defence, and the interpretation of
Title VII to prohibit sexual harassment (*Harris v Forklift Systems*[48]), leaves

---

[45] Justices La Forest and Sopinka concurred on the ground that no burden had been imposed or benefit withheld so as to attract the application of s 15(1) of the Charter.

[46] For the evolving application of this see *Phillips v Martin Marietta Corp* 400 US 542 (1971).
Automobile Workers v Johnson Controls Inc 499 US 187 (1991).

[47] *Griggs v Duke Power Co*, note 35 above; *State of Connecticut v Teal* 457 US 440 (1982). See
Washington v Davis 426 US 229 (1976), referred to in Chapter 3 above, in discussing the
approach to the Equal Protection Clause.

[48] Case no 92–1168, 1993.

little scope for reliance on the Equal Protection Clause and most cases involving employment-related discrimination, whether in the public or private sector, are heard under Title VII.

The limitations of the Equal Protection Clauses's application to sex discrimination became apparent in *Personnel Administrator of Massachusetts v Feeney*,[49] which concerned a woman denied advancement in the civil service by virtue of Massachusetts' extreme preference for returning veterans. The veterans, who were over 98 per cent male and who comprised more than 25 per cent of the state's population, were given an 'absolute lifetime' preference in relation to all state civil service jobs, which preference could be exercised 'at any time and as many times as they wish'. While non-veterans were graded in accordance with civil service examination results, training and experience, veterans merely had to pass the examinations in order to be ranked, in order of their scores, above all non-veterans. The effect of the policy was to relegate female civil servants to these lower ranking jobs for which veterans had not applied.

The District Court of Massachusetts had found that, although the policy was facially neutral, had not been enacted in order to discriminate against women, and had been imposed in the pursuit of worthy goals (to reward veterans for service, help them to reintegrate into civilian life, encourage military service and attract 'loyal and well-disciplined people' [sic] to the civil service); its exclusionary impact upon women was so severe that the Equal Protection Clause required the State to use less draconian means in order to further its aims. The case having been remanded for reconsideration in the light of *Davis*[50] the same court found that, by contrast with the policy at issue in *Davis*, Massachusetts' veteran hiring preference was 'inherently nonneutral because it favours a class from which women have traditionally been excluded', and its consequences for women's employment opportunities 'were too inevitable to have been "unintended"'.

The reasoning of the District Court would accord, on both grounds, with that currently adopted in the UK, discrimination which flows from the adoption of inherently discriminatory classifications being regarded as direct, and indirect discrimination being regarded as 'intentional' if the requirement or condition imposed was known by the employer to impact disproportionately upon a protected class. But the Supreme Court in *Feeney* overruled the District Court and held that the distinction made by the policy was 'quite simply between veterans and nonveterans, not between men and women', that the policy had not been adopted 'for the purpose of discriminating against women', and that 'discriminatory purpose' implies more than intent as volition or intent as awareness of consequences; it implies that the decision-maker selected or reaffirmed a

---

[49] 442 US 256 (1979).
[50] Note 47 above.

particular course of action at least in part 'because of', not merely 'in spite of', its adverse effects upon 'an identifiable group'.

Justices Marshall and Brennan dissented, arguing that a legislative intention to advantage one group 'does not, as a matter of logic or of common sense, exclude the possibility that it also intended to disadvantage another'; that 'it will often be impossible to ascertain the sole or even dominant purpose of a given statute'; and that 'since reliable evidence of subjective intention is seldom obtainable, resort to inference based on objective factors is generally unavoidable'. For the dissenters, '[w]here the forseeable impact of a facially neutral policy is so disproportionate, the burden should rest on the State to establish that sex-based considerations played no part in the choice of the particular legislative scheme'.[51]

Discrimination in access to employment – Canada

The approach of the US Supreme Court to sex discrimination in employment has been such that, at least in the context of access to employment, the most significant impact of the constitutional equality provisions has been in the area of affirmative action. This is discussed in Chapter 7 below. Turning next to consider the position in Canada, the Charter of Rights has not been relied upon positively to secure to women employment rights that they would not otherwise have had. Each Canadian province has human rights legislation which *inter alia* prohibits sex discrimination in employment. This has made it unnecessary to rely on constitutional rights. The provincial human rights legislation is far from perfect, in particular because of its general reliance upon individualistic, complaints-based models (as is the case in the UK). But the same model would apply in relation to any Charter-based challenge which would, in addition, be available only against the State as employer. It is the case that the Charter could be used to challenge the exclusion from anti-discrimination protection of a particular, gender-based or otherwise defined group (see *Haig v Canada Chief Electoral Officer*[52] and *Vriend v Alberta*,[53] discussed in Chapter 3 above). While this may benefit homosexual men and women, transsexuals, and other disapproved-of groups, however, it is unlikely to impact upon the position of women.

Pay – the US

Much of the US constitutional jurisprudence relates to employment-related benefits, and to their differential availability to the spouses of male and female workers. Title VII of the Civil Rights Act 1964 applies to sex

---

[51] The only exception appears in remedying proven discrimination – see, for example, *United States v State of Virginia* (Case no 94–1941, 1996).
[52] [1993] 2 SCR 995.
[53] [1998] 1 SCR 493.

discrimination in 'compensation' as well as, more generally, to discrimination in hiring, firing, conditions and privileges of employment, and the Equal Pay Act of 1963 prohibits sex discrimination in relation to payment for 'equal work'. The legislation is inadequate in permitting equal value claims only where the employee can point to the particular practice which results in the pay disparity and in allowing indirect discrimination where there is a 'legitimate business justification'.[54] Narrow as the approach of the Supreme Court may have been, at least latterly, to pay discrimination under Title VII, its interpretation of the Equal Protection Clause entirely to exclude indirect discrimination is narrower still. There can be no argument, therefore, that any shortcoming in the Equal Pay Act/Title VII approach to pay discrimination will be remediable under the Fourteenth Amendment.

This is not to say that the Equal Protection Clause has had no impact in the pay-related sphere. Where job-related benefits are concerned, legislation has frequently discriminated on the basis of sex. Such legislation has been found to violate the Equal Protection Clause. In *Frontiero v Richardson*,[55] for example, the Supreme Court overruled federal legislation which automatically entitled male service personnel to spousal benefits but required that dependency be shown in respect of the spouses of female personnel. Two years later, in *Weinberger v Weisenfeld*,[56] the Supreme Court ruled that legislation which differentiated between men and women workers in terms of the death benefits available to their spouses was unconstitutional and a similar decision was reached in *Califano v Goldfarb*.[57]

In *Califano v Webster*[58] the Supreme Court applied the now-settled intermediate scrutiny to uphold legislation which favoured women in the calculation of retirement benefits, ruling that the provision permitting women to exclude, for the purposes of calculation, three relatively low-earning years (62–65) which, for men, were taken into account 'was deliberately enacted to redress our society's longstanding disparate treatment of women' (internal citations omitted) and, in contrast to sex-based classifications struck down in *Frontiero*, *Weinberger* and *Goldfarb*, was not 'the accidental byproduct of a traditional way of thinking about females'. In *Califano v Westcott*[59] the Supreme Court struck down discriminatory welfare legislation on the ground that it was part of the baggage of sexual stereotypes that presumed that the father had the primary responsibility to provide a home and its essentials while the mother is the centre of home and family life.

---

[54] *County of Washington v Gunther* 452 US 161 (1981); *Wards Cove Packaging Co v Atonio* 490 US 642 (1989).
[55] 411 US 677 (1973).
[56] 420 US 636 (1975).
[57] 430 US 199 (1977).
[58] 430 US 313 (1977).
[59] 443 US 76 (1979), internal citations omitted. See also *Wengler v Druggists Mutual Insurance Co* 446 US 142 (1980).

Pay – Canada

In Canada, two lower court decisions merit initial attention. Both concern 'pay equity' legislation, widely adopted throughout Canada, which aims proactively to deal with discrimination in pay by requiring employers (usually in conjunction with unions where present) to audit their pay structures for discrimination and to eliminate it where found. Such legislation goes beyond 'equal pay' legislation which does not, in general, impose any obligation upon employers to seek out evidence of discrimination. The latter has been in place throughout Canada, and at the federal level, for decades. 'Pay equity' legislation, on the other hand, is very much the creature of the 1980s and 1990s.

The particular 'pay equity' model chosen by various provinces differ, Ontario's widely being regarded as the most radical in its application to the private as well as to the public sector and Manitoba having taken a fairly generous approach to the definition of 'equality' within its Pay Equity Act. Detailed discussion of pay equity legislation is beyond the scope of this book, but what has been of concern to commentators have been issues such as (in Manitoba) the capping of 'pay equity' adjustments to an overall maximum of 3 per cent of the employer's annual payroll costs and (in Ontario) the plight of women in predominantly female workplaces for whom no comparator existed for the purposes of 'pay equity' adjustments.

In *Manitoba Council of Health Care Unions v Bethesda Hospital*,[60] the province's Queen's Bench Division struck down Manitoba's 3 per cent cap as a violation of s 15. More recently, in September 1997, an Ontario court ruled unconstitutional a Conservative amendment to the Pay Equity Act, which had scrapped a procedure designed to enable otherwise excluded women to benefit from the Act (*Re Service Employees International Union and Attorney General of Ontario*[61]). By denying these women the opportunity to eradicate the effects of systemic discrimination, the amendment had discriminated against them. Nor could financial imperatives justify the Charter violation (the costs of the decision being estimated to exceed $400 million).[62]

These decisions both required government expenditure, something the courts are generally reluctant to do. In addition, both reflect the Supreme Court decision in *Eldridge v British Columbia*,[63] in that they require governments which have provided programmes of benefits to administer those programme in such a way as not themselves to discriminate. The

---

[60] (1992) 88 DLR (4th) 60.

[61] *Re Service Employees International Union, Local 204 et al and Attorney General of Ontario, SEIU, Local 204 v Ontario (Attorney General)* (1997) 151 DLR 4th 273, Ontario Court (General Division). The Government subsequently announced its decision not to appeal: *Toronto Sun*, 8 October 1997.

[62] In October 1998, the Government had yet to provide funding in respect of the women affected: Mary Cornish of the Equal Pay Coalition, in the *Toronto Star*, 22 October 1998.

[63] [1997] 3 SCR 624.

decisions in Ontario and Manitoba were of considerable importance in the context of the pay equity programmes administered in those states. But the limits of these decisions must also be noted. Again, the Charter does not demand positive action by government and, while it may render unconstitutional an arbitrary limit on sex-related pay adjustments, or an arbitrary exclusion from 'pay equity' legislation of a particular group, it would not demand that a government embrace such legislation in the first place. This was stressed by Justice O'Leary in the Ontario case:

> The unfortunate state of women prior to the Pay Equity Act, 1987 as the objects of systemic gender wage inequity was created by the marketplace and stereotypical attitudes, not by government. . . . The Charter does not place a positive obligation on government to eliminate such inequity. Rather, the government must not create inequity.[64]
>
> . . . the government of Ontario was under no obligation to enact the Pay Equity Act, 1987. It could likewise have repealed the entire Pay Equity Act . . . without giving rise to any claims of discrimination.[65]

Pay and collective bargaining – the US and Canada

To the extent that the Equal Protection Clause of the US Constitution's Fourteenth Amendment, and s 15 of Canada's Charter of Rights, have permitted challenge to a number of discriminatory pay practices, this is to be welcomed. But the benefits that women have, until recently, gained from high levels of collective bargaining coverage in the Nordic countries and in Australia go far beyond the relatively small increases secured under Canada's various pay equity laws or the application in the US of the Equal Protection Clause.[66] In order to determine how, if at all, the constitutional guarantees have impacted on women's pay in real and substantial terms, it is useful to consider those factors which were identified above as having significant bearing on the gender-pay gap – in particular, the extent and level of collective bargaining and of minimum wage regulation.

---

[64] Citing Madam Justice L'Heureux-Dubé in *Thibaudeau v Canada*, note 44 above: 'Although s 15 of the Charter does not impose upon governments the obligation to take positive actions to remedy the symptoms of systemic inequality, it does require that the government not be the source of further inequality. Such a scheme, in my view, would constitute a source of further inequality.'

[65] Citing *Ferrel and others v Attorney General of Ontario* (unreported, 29 December 1995), in which the same government's repeal of the Employment Equity Act was upheld, Justice MacPherson stated that: 'The purpose of the Charter is to ensure that governments comply with the Charter when they make laws. The Charter does not go further and require that governments enact laws to remedy societal problems, including problems of inequality and discrimination. One can hope that governments will regard this as part of their mission; however, the Charter does not impose this mission at the high level of constitutional obligation.'

[66] McColgan, note 1 above, Chapters 7–10.

As noted in this chapter and in Chapter 3, the US Constitution has proven hostile to, rather than supportive of, minimum wage regulation. Although the tendency of the Supreme Court to strike down minimum wage and other labour regulation has disappeared with the death of substantive due process in the economic field, it is certainly not the case that the Constitution has been interpreted in any way so as to provide affirmative rights such as the right to access to a decent income. (See discussion of *Dandridge v Williams*,[67] *Harris v McRae*,[68] *Maher v Roe*,[69] etc, in Chapters 3–5.)

A minimum wage is now in place in the US, though the level at which it is set means that it does little to improve the lot of most workers, acting only as a guard against the lowest levels of exploitation wages. But any argument that the Equal Protection Clause actually requires the State to set a minimum wage at a level designed to reduce the gender-pay gap, even if that gap could be proven to result from discrimination, would be doomed to fail. In the first place, the Equal Protection Clause prohibits only direct, as distinct from indirect discrimination, and the bulk of the gender-wage gap is related to the latter rather than the former. Secondly, the right to be free of discrimination does not extend to requiring ameliorative action by the State.

Turning to the issue of collective bargaining, the relationship between collective bargaining coverage, levels of wage dispersion generally and of women's wages relative to those of men was mentioned above. The impact of entrenched rights upon collective bargaining has not been beneficial. From the outset, legislation designed to support collective bargaining, in common with that establishing minimum terms and conditions of employment, has been vulnerable to judicial veto and to interpretations hostile to the interests of workers.

Collective bargaining is organised, in the US, on the basis of exclusive representation within 'collective bargaining units', these units in the final instance being determined by the National Labor Relations Board and representation rights being accorded to a union which demonstrates, by means of a ballot, majority support within that unit. The US system is deeply flawed, and has resulted in almost the lowest levels both of trade union density and collective bargaining coverage in the developed world (both figures stand at around 11 per cent in the private sector, to which the relevant legislation – the National Labor Relations Act 1935 – applies). Many of the problems associated with it are beyond the scope of this book.[70] What is of interest here is the impact upon it of judicial interpretations and, in particular, of judicial applications of entrenched 'rights'.

The first point to make is that US trade unionism shares with its UK counterpart a history of judicial assault under the doctrine of criminal

---

[67] 397 US 471 (1970).
[68] 448 US 297 (1980).
[69] 432 US 464 (1977). See also *Griffin v State of Illinois* 351 US 12 (1956).
[70] See K Ewing (ed), *Need to be Heard at Work* (London: Institute of Employment Rights, 1998).

conspiracy, which doctrine was used in the US in the first half of the 19th century, first to declare the very fact of association between workers unlawful as an interference with the 'natural' determination of wages by supply and demand, subsequently to permit the bare fact of association but only to the extent that it was purely voluntary.[71] This latter approach triumphed in 1842 and, in combination with the relative lack of trade union activity in the succeeding quarter century, served to limit actions for criminal conspiracy for a time.[72] But with the resurgence of trade unions came retrenchment on the part of the courts which, from the 1860s onwards, became increasingly ready to find criminal conspiracies where unions, although voluntary, were seen as 'oppressive' to employers.[73] And from the 1870s onwards, the courts used the tool of the labour injunction, issued *ex parte*, to prohibit and criminalise industrial action (these injunctions also generally prohibited otherwise clearly lawful action such as peaceful persuasion[74]), between then and the early 1900s being increasingly ready to intervene on behalf of employers in conflict with organised labour.

Unions did attempt to argue that the application of the English common law doctrine of restraint of trade, upon which criminal conspiracies rested, was inconsistent with the rights guaranteed by the US Declaration of Independence and Constitution. But the conception of liberty which became paramount in the 50 years following the US Revolution was that which emphasised 'the liberty of individuals to use their property *productively*, free from the constraints of collective regulation'. According to this doctrine, 'Republican guarantees of independence and autonomy meant no more than the provision of means whereby individuals might constitute and regulate their own lives and property through the medium of contract', rather than implying 'the establishment of conditions which would enable free men to contract with one another on a basis of real equality by guaranteeing their economic and social independence'.[75] Typical of the judicial approach was the declaration in *The Twenty Journeymen Tailors* case (1836, New York): 'In this favoured land of law and liberty the road to advancement is open to all, and the journeymen may by their skill and industry, and moral worth, soon become master mechanics . . . Every American knows that . . . he needs no artificial combination for his protection'.[76]

The hostility of the US courts towards trade unions was such that, in 1907, the District of Columbia's Supreme Court granted an injunction, in

---

[71] See C Tomlins, *The State and the Unions: Labor Relations, Law and the Organized Labor Movement in America, 1880–1960* (Cambridge: Cambridge University Press, 1985), pp 36 ff.

[72] *Ibid*, pp 44–45.

[73] *Ibid*, pp 47–48.

[74] R Gorman, *Basic Text on Labor Law* (St Paul, Minnesota: West Publishing Co, 1976), p 2 and, *passim*, Chapter 1.

[75] Tomlins, note 71 above, pp 34–35.

[76] *Ibid*, p 39.

flagrant disregard of the First Amendment's guarantee of free speech, to prohibit the leaders of the American Federation of Labor from encouraging a boycott of a company's goods.[77] The following year the Supreme Court ruled that striking workers were liable for conspiracy in restraint of trade.[78] The American Federation of Labor protested, in 1908, that the judiciary 'is depriving workers of their rights as citizens by forbidding the exercise of *freedom of speech, freedom of the press, freedom of assembly and the right to petition*, if, in the opinion of the judge, the exercise of these rights may work injury to the business of some corporation or trust'.[79] But the protest fell on deaf ears and the courts continued to frustrate union aims.[80]

The history of the Supreme Court's approach to industrial relations between *Adair v US*[81] and *NLRB v Jones & Laughlin*[82] has been considered in Chapter 3. The Supreme Court upheld the constitutionality of the basic approach taken by the National Labor Relations Act 1935 (commonly known as the Wagner Act) to industrial relations in the latter case. But the Constitution has continued to impact adversely in the area of industrial relations (and judicial hostility towards trade unions has, more generally, continued to affect the interpretation of the Wagner Act[83]). Not all constitutional adjudication has worked to the disadvantage of employees and their unions – in *Thornhill v State of Alabama*,[84] for example, the Supreme Court struck down legislation which rendered all picketing criminal, ruling that it violated employees' free speech rights, which were protected under the Due Process Clause of the Fourteenth Amendment from unwarranted interference by employers. A similar decision was reached the following year in *American Federation of Labor v Swing*.[85] But in 1942 the court ceased to treat picketing purely as a matter of political speech and subsequently became increasingly willing to permit the right to be balanced against states' interests.[86] These interests included *inter alia* existing legislation prohibiting restraint of trade (where the picketing was designed to prevent access to supplies by self-employed non-union members) and protection of the business of stevedores and potential disruption to a port and its users where the union sought to picket a foreign

---

[77] *The Buck's Stove and Range Company v AFL et al*, 35 *Washington Law Reporter* 525, discussed by Tomlins, note 71 above, p 65. The same court subsequently found the AFL leaders in breach after a refusal to comply.

[78] *Loewe v Lawlor* 208 US 274 (1908), cited by Tomlins, note 71 above, p 65.

[79] Tomlins, note 71 above, p 66.

[80] *Ibid*, p 83.

[81] 208 US 161 (1908).

[82] 382 US 32 (1965).

[83] See *NLRB v Mackay Radio and Telegraph Company* 304 US 333 (1938); *CG Conn Ltd v NLRB, NLRB v Condenser Corporation of America* 128 F2 67 (1942); *NLRB v Draper Corporation* 145 F2 199 (1944); *NLRB v Fansteel Metallurgic Corporation* 306 US 240 (1939); *NLRB v Sands Manufacturing Company* 306 US 332 (1939); *Fibreboard Paper Products Corporation v NLRB* 379 US 203 (1964).

[84] 310 US 88 (1940).

[85] 312 US 321 (1941).

[86] *Bakery Drivers' Local v Wohl* 315 US 769 (1942).

ship.[87] According to one commentator: 'the disinclination to use the First and Fourteenth Amendments to strike down state control of picketing', which disinclination he described as a 'constitutional evolution away from comprehensive protection for concerted activities . . . continues today [1976], even in situations where it might be argued that the communicational interests of the employees and the public are no less weighty (and the interference with the business of the employer no less severe) than in *Thornhill*'.[88]

Not only have property rights been preferred to those of free expression (the latter being unenforceable against private sector employers)[89] but the Thirteenth Amendment's prohibition on involuntary servitude (frequently put forward by trade unionists in support of a constitutional right to strike) has been interpreted only to apply to the 'right of a single individual employee to withhold his services as a means of pressurising an employer to come to terms' (at least to the extent of precluding the issue of injunctive relief or criminal penalty) and not to any collective right to strike. In *Dorchy v State of Kansas*,[90] for example, the Supreme Court upheld the imprisonment of a union organiser who had, contrary to Kansas criminal law, 'conspire[d] to induce others to quit their employment for the purpose and with the intent to hinder, delay, limit or suspend the operation of mining' (internal citations omitted). Dorchy claimed that the legislation, in prohibiting strikes, was 'a denial of the liberty guaranteed by the Fourteenth Amendment'. The Supreme Court ruled that '[t]he right to carry on business – be it called liberty or property – has value. To interfere with this right without just cause is unlawful . . . Neither the common law, nor the Fourteenth Amendment, confers the absolute right to strike.'

Dorchy concerned a strike in the private sector. In the public sector, absolute prohibitions on strikes have been consistently upheld.[91] In addition, constitutional rights have been of significant assistance to employers wishing to resist union organising drives. Not only do employers' property rights allow them, almost without exception, to deny union officials access for recruitment and election-drive purposes (recognition depending upon a majority vote of relevant employees), but the employers' First Amendment free speech rights have been interpreted to permit anti-union campaigning.[92]

The employer who wishes to avoid certification of a union may do so by informing employees of his or her opposition to unions (which information

---

[87] *Giboney v Empire Storage and Ice Co* 336 US 490 (1949); *American Radio Association v Moble SS Association* 419 US 215 (1974).
[88] Gorman, note 74 above, pp 212–213.
[89] See *Hudgens v NLRB* 424 US 507 (1976), discussed below.
[90] 272 US 306 (1926).
[91] Gorman, note 74 above, p 210.
[92] See *Hudgens v NLRB*, note 89 above and *NLRB v Virginia Electric & Power Company* 314 US 469 (1941). See generally Gorman, note 74 above, pp 149–151.

may be imparted at 'captive audience' meetings during working hours, at which employees' attendance is required, and may take the form of individual meetings between employer and employee during which the latter encourages the former to vote against the union).[93] Coercive speech is not permitted but, as the Secretary-Treasurer of the American Federation of Labor–Confederation of Industrial Organizations (AFL–CIO) put it: 'the employer is perfectly free to "report" about what "could" happen to the employees if they organize or about what other employers have done when their employees formed a union. Lawyers may be beguiled by such distinctions but working people see through them.'[94] Unions can, however, be excluded from company property.[95] The AFL–CIO have declared that 'fear' is the biggest single obstacle to recognition drives – despite the fact that elections depend upon an initial 30 per cent show of interest on the part of employees, only between about 20 per cent and 50 per cent of elections result in union success (this success being inversely proportional to the size of the bargaining unit and therefore, perhaps, to the strength of employer resistance).[96]

Turning to consider the impact of entrenched rights on the position of unions and on collective bargaining in Canada, the picture here, too, is gloomy. In 1991 David Beatty wrote, of the first nine years, that:

> the judgments concerning the application of the *Charter* to the rules of labour and employment vindicate . . . claims about the tendency of the courts to manipulate legal doctrine and cases to the detriment of workers and their dependants . . . [they] read as the latest chapter in an uninterrupted tale, whose beginnings reach back to the Industrial Revolution and even earlier times [and show] . . . precisely the same bias against the interests of workers and their unions that plagued the common law rules of tort and crime employed by the judges to control the behaviour of the working class throughout most of the nineteenth and first half of the twentieth centuries.[97]

Beatty's indictment is based not only upon the Supreme Court's decision in *RWDSU v Dolphin Delivery*[98] (see Chapter 3 above for discussion), the effect of which was to deny protection against common law rules to what all but one of the Supreme Court judges was the constitutionally protected right to picket. In a series of cases decided in 1987 and 1990 the Supreme Court excluded from the reach of the constitutional right to freedom of association the areas of collective bargaining and industrial action. Even where the limits on collective bargaining and industrial

---

[93] This being the interpretation adopted by the NLRB under Reagan: B Feldacker, *Labor Guide to Labor Law* (3rd ed) (New Jersey and Englewood Cliffs: Prentice Hall, 1990), p 79.
[94] Ewing (ed), note 70 above, p 32.
[95] See *Babcock and Wilcox Company v NLRB* 351 US 105 (1956), *Hudgens v NLRB*, note 89 above.
[96] 1991–92 figures.
[97] 'Labouring outside the Charter' (1991) 29(4) *Osgoode Hall Law Journal* 841, at 841–842.
[98] [1986] 2 SCR 573.

action were the result of legislation, rather than action which could be deemed 'private' under the *Dolphin Delivery* test, the Supreme Court exempted such legislative action from Charter scrutiny on the grounds that neither collective bargaining nor industrial action formed part of the protected freedom of association. In the *Labour Trilogy*,[99] the Supreme Court upheld the constitutionality of laws which restricted the freedom of various groups of workers to bargain collectively and to take industrial action, ruling that 2(d) protected only the freedom to associate itself, and not the freedom to pursue any 'particular activity on the ground that the activity is essential to give an association meaningful existence . . . The rights . . . to bargain collectively and to strike . . . are not fundamental rights or freedoms. They are the creation of legislation, involving a balance of competing interests in a field which has been recognized by the courts as requiring a specialized expertise.'

In one of the *Labour Trilogy* cases, Justice Le Dain defended this approach by distinguishing between 'the modern rights to bargain collectively and to strike', which rights were 'the creation of legislation', and 'fundamental rights or freedoms' guaranteed under the Charter.[100] But with all due respect to Justice Le Dain, it is difficult to justify the elevation of judge-made 'fundamental' rights over democratically passed 'creation[s] of legislation'. It is also difficult to ascertain why the rights to strike or to bargain collectively are clearly not included within the right to freedom of association, yet (see Chapter 9 below), the right to a fair trial extends to require the disclosure of personal records relating to rape complainants, even in a case in which those records do not form part of the prosecution's case and their alleged relevance depends on a defendant's unsupported assertion that they might contain material on the basis of which a complainant's credibility could be challenged.[101] The Council of Europe recognises both the right to collective bargaining and the right to strike as central to freedom of association.[102] The ILO recognises the former explicitly in Convention 98 and, while it does not expressly embrace the latter in its Conventions, its Committee of Experts does recognise the right 'as one of the essential means available to workers and their organisations for the promotion and protection of their economic and social interests as guaranteed' under Convention 98.[103] It appears that judicial instinct, rather than any clear principle, is at the root of these distinctions.

The approach taken in the *Labour Trilogy* cases stands in contrast with that more usually adopted by the Supreme Court, whereby Charter rights

---

[99] See *Reference Re Public Service Employee Relations Act* [1987] 1 SCR 313; *Public Service Alliance of Canada v Canada* [1987] 1 SCR 424; *Government of Saskatchewan v Retail Wholesale and Department Store Union* [1987] 1 SCR 460.

[100] *Re Public Service Employee Relations Act ibid.* This distinction was adopted by Madam Justice L'Heureux-Dubé in *Haig v Canada Chief Electoral Officer*, note 52 above.

[101] See *Carosella* [1997] 1 SCR 80, discussed in Chapter 9 below.

[102] European Social Charter, Part I and Article 6.

[103] General Survey 1989, para 226. Cited by K Ewing, *Britain and the ILO* (London: Institute of Employment Rights, 1989), p 34.

are protected generously and the Government is then obliged to justify infringements thereof under s 1 (see further Chapter 3 above). Here the Supreme Court 'collapsed the two stages of the review process by considering, and ultimately being very deferential to the public interest promoted by laws in the first interpretive stage of its analysis'.[104] As David Beatty pointed out, the refusal of the Supreme Court to apply freedom of association to the crucial areas of collective bargaining and industrial action permitted that court to uphold legislation 'drafted much too broadly, with restrictions much wider than required to accomplish the Government's objectives'.[105] Alberta's challenged legislation, for example (a challenge to which formed one of the *Labour Trilogy* cases) prohibited 'strikes by *all* public servants in order to ensure uninterrupted provision of essential services affecting lives, health, and safety of the community'. And in the *PIPSC* case, federal legislation imposed sweeping restrictions on the right of federal employees to bargain collectively.[106] In both cases, the legislation was upheld despite the fact that it went well beyond what was necessary in order to achieve the Government's asserted aims. In Alberta, the protection of the 'lives, health, and safety of the community' did not require restrictions on industrial action by public employees not engaged in the provision of essential services. And in the *PSAC* case,[107] the exercise of control over an inflationary economy did not require the Government to restrict collective bargaining not concerned with pay.

Had the court followed its normal approach to rights by interpreting them generously and then permitting limitations under s 1, it would have read 'freedom of association' to include industrial action, and yet permitted legislation restricting or forbidding industrial action or collective bargaining to the extent that this was necessary to achieve the declared aims of the Government. Its refusal to read 'freedom of association' to include some degree of participation in the furtherance of the ends of the association permitted '[l]aws drafted much too broadly, with restrictions much wider than required to accomplish the Government's objectives . . . to stand'.[108]

Conclusion

It is clear from this chapter that entrenched rights should not be seen as a panacea for the disadvantage that women suffer in the workforce. A fuller conclusion about the efficacy of entrenched rights in this context

---

[104] Beatty, note 97 above, p 852.
[105] *Ibid*, p 849.
[106] *Professional Institute of the Public Service of Canada v North West Territories (Commissioner)* [1990] 2 SCR 367.
[107] *Public Service Alliance of Canada v Canada*, note 99 above.
[108] *Ibid*.

will be drawn in Chapter 7, after consideration of their impact on attempts by government to take remedial action to tackle the effects or results of discrimination. But even at this stage it is clear that, in the US, the equal protection guarantee has served to advance the cause of women very little. The Equal Protection Clause has not operated against pregnancy discrimination, the justices of the Supreme Court having been unable to recognise it as sex discrimination *per se* and accepting the distinction put forward in *Geduldig* between 'pregnant and nonpregnant persons'. More generally, the refusal by the Supreme Court to recognise indirect discrimination as a violation of the Equal Protection Clause (even a *prima facie* violation which could subsequently be defended on the intermediate test) has meant that only the most blatant forms of discrimination offend the equal protection 'guarantee'.

It is true that, in the context of programmes providing benefits on death or retirement, the Supreme Court has operated to equalise the positions of men and women. But, although the Equal Protection Clause would be breached by any provision assuming female dependency but requiring male dependency to be proven, it would be consistent with that clause for death or retirement provisions to permit payments only to dependent spouses. In this context, because women tend to earn less than men, female workers would still find that the contributions paid by them over the years buy them less spousal protection than is the case for men. And any benefits secured to women in this respect have been outweighed many times by the damaging impact of constitutional rights upon collective labour power.

The lessons from Canada are somewhat different, the Canadian Supreme Court having taken a much more generous approach to the equality guarantee which, by contrast with that provided by the Fourteenth Amendment, is clear and unambiguous.[109] Nevertheless, the judges of the Supreme Court, consistent with 'classic liberalism's concern with protecting individuals from the coercive power of the state',[110] have interpreted the Charter so as to narrow the potential scope of its protection. This, coupled with the inherent nature of entrenched rights, ie 'to restrain government, to protect the negative freedoms of citizens – freedom from the long arm of the state',[111] has rendered inevitable the Charter's failure to 'alter power relations, redistribute wealth, or promote social welfare'.[112]

---

[109] One should not, however, forget *Symes v Canada*, note 39 above and *Thibaudeau v Canada*, note 44 above, discussed in Chapter 3 above.

[110] J Bakan, note 41 above, p 48.

[111] P Russell, 'The Political Purposes of the Charter: Have They Been Fulfilled? An Agnostic's Report', in P Bryden *et al* (eds), *Protecting Rights and Freedoms: Essays on the Charter's Place in Canada's Political, Legal and Intellectual Life* (Toronto: University of Toronto Press, 1994), p 40.

[112] *Ibid*, pp 40–41: 'The Supreme Court's interpretation of the Charter has minimized its impact on social and economic relations.' (citing *RWDSU v Dolphin Delivery Ltd*, note 98 above; *Reference Re Public Service Employee Relations Act*, note 99 above, and *Irwin Toy* [1989] 1 SCR 927).

Canada's judiciary has taken significant steps towards developing positive conceptions of the State and of freedom, as distinct from the largely negative view prevalent in the US (freedom as the absence of constraint). This development is potentially important in the s 1 context where they may result in determinations that challenged state action is permissible. But, unless these conceptions are interpreted as mandating positive state action, the application of the Charter only in the narrowest public sphere leaves women vulnerable to all the discrimination which flows from private individuals. Finally, neither in the US nor in Canada have the courts shown themselves willing to ameliorate this disadvantage by permitting workers' collectives to benefit from the rights entrenched in those countries' constitutions. The Charter has not assisted, and the US Constitution has positively damaged the position of women workers to the (very considerable) extent that that position relies upon collective workplace strength.[113]

The worst fears of Judy Fudge, Gwen Brodsky and Shelagh Day[114] (see Chapter 3) have not been realised, Canada's Supreme Court having embraced the substantive model of equality, notably in *Andrews v Law Society of British Columbia*[115] and in *Eldridge v British Columbia*[116] (see further Chapter 3 above). And even before the Charter's equality rights had come into force, a number of provincial governments took steps to eradicate legislative discrimination,[117] although uncertainty as to how the Supreme Court would interpret s 15 meant that some governments 'made very little use of the house-cleaning period, and even those that availed themselves most fully of the opportunity were exceedingly cautious in their legislative responses'.[118]

Women have experienced some benefits from Charter litigation. In the 13 years since the implementation of s 15, women have gained, in employment terms, from the pay equity victories in Manitoba and, very recently, in Ontario. It is, in addition, possible that women may have gained under the Charter on the grounds that discriminatory legislation has not been passed which otherwise might have been. It is, however, equally possible that they may have suffered for the same reason. This latter issue, together with that of 'reverse discrimination' or 'affirmative action', and the impact of constitutional rights, more generally, is considered in Chapter 7 below.

---

[113] The only apparent exception lying in the tolerance of both US and Canadian Supreme Courts for agency and closed shops respectively, see *Lavigne v OPSEU* [1992] 2 SCR 211; *Railway Employees' Dept v Hanson* 351 US 255 (1956); and *Railway Clerks v Allen* 373 US 113 (1963).

[114] G Brodsky and S Day, *Canadian Charter Equality Rights for Women: One Step Forward or Two Steps Back?* (Ontario: Canadian Advisory Council on the Status of Women, 1989).

[115] [1989] 1 SCR 143.

[116] [1997] 3 SCR 624.

[117] L Smith (ed), *Righting the Balance: Canada's New Equality Rights* (Saskatoon: Canadian Human Rights Reporter, 1986), p 70.

[118] D Gibson, *The Law of the Charter: Equality Rights* (Toronto: Carswell, 1990), p 45.

Chapter 7

Constitutional Rights and
the Threat to Workplace Equality

Introduction

It is evident from Chapter 6 above that constitutionally entrenched rights have not done a great deal, in either Canada or the US, to improve the position of women at work. But what has not been made clear are the threats that they can present, save to the extent that the US Supreme Court's protection of employers' property rights served, for decades, to thwart legislative efforts to improve working conditions generally through support for collective bargaining. To this example should be added the defeat of Ireland's first legislative efforts to eradicate disability discrimination by that country's Supreme Court, again on the basis of employers' property rights (*Re Article 26 and the Employment Equality Bill 1996*[1]). The prohibition on discrimination did not prohibit differential payment in a case where a disabled person's capacity to work was less than that of another, and required only that employers make reasonable accommodation to the special needs of disabled persons, employers even then being permitted a defence of 'undue hardship'. Nevertheless, the Irish court found it repugnant to the Constitution's protection of the private property rights of employers.

According to the Supreme Court, it was because of the Constitution's recognition that 'the rights of private property "ought" in civil society to be regulated by "the principles of social justice" that the State may, as occasion requires, delimit their exercise with a view to reconciling it with the "exigencies of the common good". It is because such a delimitation, to be valid, must be not only reconcilable with the exigencies of the common good but also with the principles of social justice that it cannot be an unjust attack on a citizen's private property.'

The Supreme Court regarded as 'totally laudable' the Bill's aim 'of making provision for such of our fellow citizens as are disabled', but ruled that

[1] Case no 118/97, 15 May 1997, Supreme Court. Available on LEXIS.

the imposition of the cost of accommodation on the employer constituted an 'unjust attack' upon them. Nor was the provision saved by the 'undue hardship' defence which, where related to 'the financial circumstances of the employer', 'implies that the employer would have to disclose his financial circumstances and the problems of his business to an outside party'.[2]

Regard should also be paid to the decision of the European Court of Justice (ECJ) in *Kalanke v Freie Hansestadt Bremen*.[3] This decision, which limited the availability of affirmative action under EC law, illustrates the dangers, to women, of anti-discrimination provisions. While such provisions, whether they take the form of ordinary legislative rights, EC law or 'constitutional' rights, frequently operate in women's favour, their impact turns on the interpretation of discrimination adopted by the judges who apply them.

The decision in *Kalenke* stands as the exception to the general rule that women's legal rights (and therefore, to a certain extent, their position in the workplace[4]) have been enhanced as a result of the supremacy of EC law over British national provisions.[5] Whereas, for example, the decisions of the ECJ in *Dekker v Stichting Vormingscentrum voor Jonge Volwassenen (VJV-Centrum) Plus*[6] and in *Webb v EMO Air Cargo (UK) Ltd*[7] have resulted in the domestic courts interpreting the provisions of the Sex Discrimination Act 1975 to prohibit discrimination on grounds of pregnancy,[8] and whereas the decisions in *Marshall* and *Marshall (No 2)*[9] have led, respectively, to the removal of discriminatory retirement ages and the upper limits to compensation for discrimination, *Kalenke* has restricted the ability of the British Government to take positive action to improve women's workplace position. The decision is of limited practical importance given the lack of any serious affirmative action programmes

---

[2] The Supreme Court struck down, in addition, a number of equal-pay related provisions and one which imposed vicarious liability on employers.

[3] Case C-450/93 [1996] All ER (EC) 66, [1995] ECR I-3051.

[4] Whether economic integration has improved the position of women and other workers is moot.

[5] Even it has been softened somewhat by the approach taken by the ECJ in Case C-409/95 *Marschall v Land Nordrhein-Westfalen* [1997] All ER (EC) 865, [1998] 1 CMLR 547, [1998] IRLR 39.

[6] Case C-177/88 [1991] IRLR 27.

[7] Case C-32/93 [1994] QB 718, [1994] ICR 770, [1994] 4 All ER 115, [1994] IRLR 482. The House of Lords' decision *(No 2)* is at [1995] ICR 1021, [1995] IRLR 645.

[8] See also Case 394/96 *Brown v Rentokil Ltd* [1998] IRLR 445 and the apparent change of ECJ approach from that taken in Case C-400/95 *Handels-og Kontorfunktionaerernes Forbund i Danmark (acting for Larsson) v Dansk Arbejdsgiverforening (acting for Fotex Supermarked A/S)* [1997] ECR I-2757, [1997] IRLR 643. For the limits of the ECJ's approach see Case C-179/88 *Handels-og Kontorfunktionaerernes Forbund i Danmark (acting for Hertz) v Dansk Arbejdsgiverforening (acting for Aldi Marked k/s)* [1992] ICR 332, [1991] IRLR 31; Case C-342/93 *Gillespie v Northern Health and Social Services Board*, [1996] ICR 498, [1996] All ER (EC) 284, [1996] IRLR 214.

[9] Case C-152/84 *Marshall v Southampton and South-West Hampshire Area Health Authority* [1986] ICR 335, [1986] QB 401, [1986] 1 CMLR 688, [1986] 2 ECR 723, [1986] IRLR 140 and Case C-271/91 *Marshall v Southampton and South-West Hampshire Area Health Authority (No 2)* [1994] QB 126, [1994] 3 WLR 1054, [1993] ICR 893, [1993] IRLR 445.

in the UK. But *Kalenke* should be seen as a warning that the impact of entrenched rights can hinder radical legislative action and, in particular, can operate against the move towards substantive, as distinct from formal, equality. The reactionary potential of constitutional rights is explored in this chapter's consideration of affirmative action and the US Constitution.

Affirmative action

The shortcomings of traditional anti-discrimination provisions in improving access by women to the workplace was mentioned in Chapter 6 above. Despite decades having passed since formal equality of access was required by legislation in the UK, as well as in Canada and the US, the position of most women at the bottom of the job hierarchy, vertically and horizontally segregated by sex, has altered little. Affirmative action programmes attempt to substitute substantive for formal notions of equality by taking positive steps to increase the proportion of women, ethnic minority or other under-represented group within workplaces, colleges, or other institutions in which such programmes are adopted.

Affirmative action programmes can take one of a number of forms. At their least controversial, affirmative action consists of 'outreach programmes' which seek to attract (and, on occasion, to train) otherwise qualified women or ethnic minority candidates to apply for positions. Such programmes do not give preference to the target group in appointment decisions and are, under certain circumstances, lawful in the UK.[10] At the other end of the scale, programmes may give preferential treatment to women or ethnic minority candidates or employees, by favouring them either over equally or less qualified candidates or employees where it comes to hiring and other employment-related decisions.[11] These programmes, often termed 'quota' schemes, are not permitted in the UK (or, indeed, in the EU).

Affirmative action is contentious, giving rise to allegations of 'reverse discrimination', concern for its 'innocent victims' and, frequently, expressions of anxiety as to its impact on the self-esteem of those who benefit from it (though these latter often appear to be 'crocodile tears'[12]). It does raise difficult issues, in particular, in so far as it can contribute to the denigration, by themselves as well as others, of those perceived as having reached their positions other than on the basis of merit. In some of its

---

[10] Sex Discrimination Act 1975, ss 47–49, Race Relations Act 1976, ss 35 and 37–38.
[11] See further C McCrudden, 'The Constitutionality of Affirmative Action in the United States' (1996) 1 *International Journal of Discrimination and the Law* 369.
[12] See R McKeever, *Raw Judicial Power?* (2nd ed, Manchester: Manchester University Press, 1995), p 147, citing Charles Freid, *International Herald Tribune*, 26 May 1986 on President Reagan's Solicitor-General.

forms it can be accused of favouring only the relatively advantaged portions of the disadvantaged group.[13] Further, the practicalities of its operation in the field of race can require, as Justice Stewart pointed out in *Fullilove v Klutznick*,[14] 'the odious practice of delineating the qualities that make one person a Negro and make another white'.[15] These issues are further discussed below. But the assumption that such action operates against merit is unfounded.

The reality, in the US, Canada and the UK, is one where discrimination, conscious and structural, directed against women and ethnic minority groups, is endemic; power (whether in the context of employment or education) is accumulated in white, male hands; and women are hobbled by family needs and responsibilities and the legacy of sex stereotypes which categorise them as unsuited to many forms of paid work, ethnic minorities by generations of disadvantage and the legacy of racism. In the light of this, bland statements about the 'right' of everyone to be treated 'equally' are meaningful only to those who can compete with white men *on white male terms*. The 'merit' against which affirmative action programmes are seen to operate is 'merit' defined by the white, male yardstick,[16] and affirmative action programmes are a very important tool for the amelioration of disadvantage.

'Quota' schemes are extremely controversial.[17] But one could argue that such schemes do no more than place an onus on employers *not* to discriminate on grounds of race or sex by forcing them to confront and deal with the reasons behind sexual or racial imbalances in the workforce. To the extent that non-discriminating reasons for such imbalances are demonstrated, employers' obligations are generally satisfied even where 'quotas' remain unfilled. In practice, what such schemes amount to is a change in the burden of proof so that, in the absence of evidence to the contrary, a presumption operates that women or ethnic minority candidates should be appointed in proportion to their representation in the category of available workers. Where such appointments do not occur, an explanation will be demanded of the employer.[18]

---

[13] This was one of the reasons for Justice Stevens' dissent in *Fullilove v Klutznick* 448 US 448 (1980), further discussed below.

[14] *Ibid.*

[15] *Ibid*, p 531.

[16] This was recognised by President Lyndon Johnson, who instituted the first mandatory affirmative action programme in the US, '[y]ou do not take a man who for years has been hobbled by chains, liberate him, bring him to the starting line of a race saying, "You are free to compete with all the others," and still justly believe you have been completely fair' – commencement speech to Howard University, June 1965.

[17] See, for example, the approach of Justice Powell in *Regents of the University of California v Bakke* 438 US 265 (1978), further discussed below.

[18] J Kellough *et al*, 'Affirmative Action under Fire: The Current Controversy and the Potential for State Policy Retrenchment' (1997) 17(4) *Review of Public Personnel Administration* 52, citing J Jones, 'The Genesis and Present Status of Affirmative Action in Employment: Economic, Legal, and Political Realities' (1985) 70 *Iowa Law Review* 901.

As far as those affirmative action schemes which impose lower entrance or appointment requirements in respect of disadvantaged candidates, it is tempting to balk, on meritocratic grounds, at preference given to less over more qualified candidates on grounds of race or some other characteristic. But the determination of those qualifications actually *necessary* in relation to a particular job or educational programme, and the provision of access on the basis of those qualifications, where the demand for higher qualifications serves to exclude less advantaged candidates, can be seen as nothing more than evidence of a commitment to end indirect, as well as direct, discrimination.

The demand for additional qualifications from more advantaged persons is defensible as a means of selecting the most able from that group. But, where disadvantaged persons are concerned, true commitment to equal access, even on the grounds of merit, requires a recognition that the application of the normal yardstick excludes those who, although otherwise equally 'meritorious', are unable, by reason of their membership of a disadvantaged group, to compete on equal terms. This is not to say that the disadvantaged should be admitted regardless of ability; rather that, given the discriminatory nature of some measures of ability, coupled with a finding that such measures are not necessary in determining ability to do the particular job, or succeed in the particular educational programme, alternative measures are appropriate in relation to the disadvantaged groups.

This becomes clearer by taking an example of an employer in whose workplace promotion turns on seniority and who, until recently, required that all employees work full-time. In the US, as in the UK, indirect discrimination in employment is unlawful – the relevant US provision being Title VII of the Civil Rights Act 1964.[19] Assuming that the full-time work requirement was found disparately to impact on potential women workers and not to be justifiable (whether on the UK or the US test), merely permitting part-time work will address the sex imbalance in the workforce only over the long term and will have the result that women entering employment will, as new entrants, be concentrated in the lower ranks. In addition, the attitude which may well have underlain the full-time work requirement, ie that 'real' workers are those who work full-time (men) and that part-time workers (women) are not sufficiently committed to be given jobs, much less advancement, may well not disappear with the provision of part-time jobs. The demand for full-time commitment may have served, not as a hurdle which was well-intentioned but whose impact was unfortunate, rather as a 'gate-keeping' mechanism designed, however subconsciously, to ensure that

---

[19] This provision prohibits discrimination by employers on the grounds of 'race, color, religion, sex, or national origin'. The US Supreme Court accepted, in *Griggs v Duke Power Co* 401 US 424 (1971), that it extended to indirect discrimination.

the workforce conformed to the employer's culturally specific views of appropriate workers.[20]

There is ample evidence that employers discriminate in relation to recruitment and promotion. Such discrimination is frequently masked by reference to the worker characteristics such as stability, flexibility and compatibility, these factors being applied to favour male or female candidates in line with the sex stereotyping of the job.[21] Where sex or race-based preferences are endemic, and where decisions are reached on the basis of those unspoken characteristics, the removal of formal requirements which discriminate indirectly against women or ethnic minority candidates is insufficient to eradicate discrimination. In the absence of additional ameliorative action including, where necessary, the setting of sex or race-based quotas, there is a real danger that organisations will replace one (discredited) set of 'gate-keeping' practices with another to the same effect.[22]

The point made by Justice Stewart in *Fullilove*, that affirmative action in the race sphere can require 'the odious practice of delineating the qualities that make one person a Negro and make another white' has no application in the context of sex discrimination. But even where race is the issue, the attempt to implement race-based affirmative action can be distinguished from the apartheid practice of distinguishing people by race on the basis that, whereas in the latter the distinctions on which racial categorisation turned were assumed to correspond to fundamental differences between persons, in the affirmative action context this is simply not the case. Race-based distinctions are drawn, in the latter context, so as to categorise persons of different quality or worth. They are not intended to indicate anything about the nature of the persons distinguished. On the contrary, they are designed simply to reflect (in order subsequently to counter) the distinctions found in the labour market in general and, more particularly, in the particular workplace.

Thus, for example, if a London workplace hires Asian employees in rough proportion to their representation in the local workforce, but fails significantly to hire black workers where a significant proportion of the relevant workforce is black,[23] an appropriate affirmative action programme should be tailored towards redressing this imbalance. This categorisation does not turn on the assumption of any fundamental difference between Asian and black workers, or between these workers and other sectors of

---

[20] The same might be true in respect of the application of (indirectly) racially discriminatory tests (as in *Griggs, ibid*).

[21] See, for example, D Collinson, *Barriers to Fair Selection: A Multi-Sector Study of Recruitment Practices* (London: HMSO, 1988), Equal Opportunities Commission Research Series. In Canada, see L Falkenberg and L Boland, 'Eliminating the Barriers to Employment Equity in the Canadian Workplace' (1997) 16(9) *Journal of Business Ethics* 963.

[22] See Falkenberg and Boland, *ibid*, citing *Calgary Herald*, 27 October 1993.

[23] This assumes that the relevant workforce is local – depending on the job it may be regional or national.

the workforce. Rather, it seeks to echo a distinction apparently drawn already, whether deliberately or in practice, by the employer and to redress the imbalance caused by it. The nature of the categorisation drawn is relevant only to whether it is caught by the anti-discrimination legislation (ie an imbalance in the proportion of left-handed workers would not be caught).

The key to appropriate affirmative action programmes is the identification of that group which is disadvantaged in the particular context. It may be that the more advantages within this relatively disadvantaged group will benefit from affirmative action programmes (this often being used as a ground for criticism of such programmes). But this is not a valid basis for any attack on them. Once it has been established that the relevant group is disadvantaged, to reject ameliorative action on the grounds that it will disproportionately benefit the least disadvantaged of that group is to prefer that all members of that group are subject to uniformly bad treatment. This type of reasoning may be pervasive – Craig *et al*'s finding that UK 'firms would often recognise differences in skill between the women workers . . . but nevertheless pay all of them at the same rate, justifying the practice on the basis that any differentiation would cause resentment amongst the other women workers'[24] was mentioned in Chapter 6 above, as was the decision of Canada's Supreme Court in *Symes v Canada*[25] to disadvantage self-employed women as against self-employed men, rather than to give the former an advantage over employed women. But it can hardly be regarded as progressive, and sits particularly uneasily in the mouths of those who generally regard any moves towards substantive, as distinct from procedural, equality as rank Stalinism.

Affirmative action and the US Constitution

The approach of the US Supreme Court to affirmative action was heralded by its attitude towards indirect discrimination and the Equal Protection Clause. This was discussed in Chapter 6 above, the decision in *Personnel Administrator of Massachusetts v Feeney*,[26] in particular, indicating the formality of approach taken by the Supreme Court. The US affirmative action decisions are considered below.

Affirmative action programmes started in the US in 1961 when President Kennedy issued Executive Order 10925, which encouraged government contractors to take affirmative action to improve the hiring and

---

[24] C Craig, J Rubery, R Tarling and F Wilkinson, *Labour Market Structure, Industrial Organisation and Low Pay* (Cambridge: Cambridge University Press, 1982), p 84.
[25] [1993] 4 SCR 695.
[26] 442 US 256 (1979).

promotion rates of ethnic minority workers.[27] In 1965, President Johnson's Executive Order 11246 prohibited federal agencies from contracting with firms that were not committed to 'conscious and deliberate efforts to bring qualified people of color and women into jobs and educational opportunities from which they had been traditionally excluded'. The Office of Federal Contract Compliance issued 'goals and timetables' guidelines in 1968 and 1971, the latter calling for statistical analysis and action to bring the racial balance of workforces into line with those of locally available workforces.[28]

The focus of affirmative action programmes was initially on integrating ethnic minority workers and on improving the access of ethnic minority students to education but in 1967 Johnson added women to the groups covered by anti-discrimination orders and in 1971, under the Nixon administration, the 'goals and timetables' programmes were expanded to include women.[29] Affirmative action programmes became common not only as a price of federal government contracts but also, in both public and private sector, on a voluntary basis and, where serious discriminatory practices had been proven against particular bodies, at the behest of the courts. The policy of affirmative action remained popular at federal level until 1980 when the Republican Reagan administration came into office on a platform hostile to 'raceconscious remedies'.[30] (Reagan's hostility to 'raceconsciousness' did not, however, prevent him from reversing an 11-year-old federal policy whereby tax exempt status was denied to schools and non-profit bodies which practised race discrimination.[31]) Reagan's key anti-affirmative action appointments included that of Clarence Thomas (now Supreme Court Justice Thomas) to the Equal Employment Opportunities Commission and those of Justices Scalia and Kennedy to the Supreme Court.

Despite the readiness of some lower courts to order that discriminators engage in affirmative action, the Supreme Court was never fully comfortable with the doctrine. Its decision in *Griggs v Duke Power Co*[32] gave tacit support to affirmative action by interpreting Title VII of the Civil Rights Act 1964 to prohibit discrimination beyond that which was intentional and taking into account the impact of employment practices on ethnic minority workers. If employers could be obliged, under Title VII,

---

[27] See McKeever, note 12 above, Chapter 5 and the ACLU world wide web page, http://www.aclu.org.

[28] In the same year the Philadelphia Plan, adopted by President Nixon, required all those bidding for federal contracts to establish numerical goals for integration. As Attorney General, the later Chief Justice Rehnquist assured the President that the plan was in conformity with the Civil Rights Act: see McKeever, note 12 above, pp 125–126.

[29] A Ewoh and E Elliott, 'End of an Era?: Affirmative Action and Reaction in the 1990s' (1997) 17(4) *Review of Public Personnel Administration* 38.

[30] *Ibid.*

[31] *Ibid.*

[32] Note 19 above.

to change those practices which served, albeit unintentionally, to discriminate against women or ethnic minority workers, it could be seen as a relatively small step to permit them intentionally to overcome the effects of past discrimination (whether their own or not) by giving those disadvantaged groups a degree of preference (see above).

In 1975 the Supreme Court upheld the constitutionality of a sex-related affirmative action programme in *Schlesinger v Ballard*,[33] a due process challenge to federal naval regulations which provided for the mandatory discharge after nine years' service of men who had failed to achieve promotion, while women were allowed 13 years before discharge. The Supreme Court held that: '[t]he different treatment of men and women . . . results, not from mere administrative or fiscal convenience, but from the fact that female line officers because of restrictions on their participating in combat and most sea duty do not have opportunities for professional service equal to those of male line officers'. But it was significant that this case was decided prior to the adoption, by the Supreme Court in *Craig v Boren*,[34] of 'intermediate scrutiny' in relation to sex discrimination (see Chapter 3 above). In *Schlesinger* the difference in treatment under the naval programme was upheld on this basis that it was rationally related to 'the goal of providing women officers with "fair and equitable career advancement programs".'

Race-based programmes

The constitutional approach to sex-based affirmative action programmes is considered further below. But the bulk of challenges to affirmative action have involved race-based programmes, and consideration is given next to these. Prior to 1978 the Supreme Court had avoided reaching any decision on the constitutionality of such programmes[35] but in *Regents of the University of California v Bakke*,[36] in a highly divided decision, it struck down the quota-based admissions programme operated by the university's medical faculty. Four of the judges (led by Justice Stevens) took the view that any racial quota-based system would offend the 'strict scrutiny' approach which, they concluded, was required under the Civil Rights Act 1964 and that the decision did not, therefore, have to be reached on constitutional grounds.[37] Four judges (led by Justice Brennan) held that 'racial classifications designed to further remedial purposes' were not

---

[33] 419 US 498 (1975).

[34] 429 US 190 (1976).

[35] In *De Funis v Odegaard* 416 US 312 (1974), the Supreme Court by a majority declared a challenge to the University of Washington's programme moot.

[36] Note 17 above.

[37] Title VI mandates that 'No person in the United States shall, on the ground of race, colour, or national origin, be excluded from participation in, be denied the benefits of, or be subjected to discrimination under any programme or activity receiving Federal financial assistance', which the university did.

subject to strict scrutiny, but would comply both with the Civil Rights Act and with the Fourteenth Amendment where they 'serve important governmental objectives and [are] substantially related to achievement of those objectives'. Justice Powell, who cast the deciding vote, agreed with the Brennan block that the matter must be decided under the Equal Protection Clause and with the Stevens block that strict scrutiny must be applied to remedial race-based legislation. Where remedial action was directed at past discrimination by the particular body, it could pass muster under this test. This was not the case here. In addition, Justice Powell accepted that universities could have a compelling interest in taking steps to secure a diverse student group, but demanded 'narrow tailoring' of means to this end and drew the line at rigid quotas such as those operated by the University of California to achieve this purpose.

As a result of Justice Powell's willingness to accept some forms of race-based affirmative action programme, most affirmative action programmes survived *Bakke*. But the tension between the Supreme Court's commitment to 'formal equality' and the steps required to overcome substantive inequality was clear in that court's decision. Justice Brennan (with Justices White, Blackmun and Marshall) characterised the demand for 'color-blind' law as 'aspiration rather than as description of reality . . . we cannot . . . let color blindness become myopia which masks the reality that many "created equal" have been treated within our lifetimes as inferior both by the law and by their fellow citizens'. On this basis they were prepared to fix the appropriate standard of scrutiny for race-based classifications with regard to the purpose of the classification. Describing as 'cardinal' the principle that 'racial classifications that stigmatize – because they are drawn on the presumption that one race is inferior to another or because they put the weight of government behind racial hatred and separatism – are invalid without more', the minority distinguished the discrimination at issue here on the grounds that 'whites as a class [do not] have any of the "traditional indicia of suspectness: the class is not saddled with such disabilities, or subjected to such a history of purposeful unequal treatment, or relegated to such a position of political powerlessness as to command extraordinary protection from the majoritarian political process"'.[38]

Justice Brennan concluded that strict judicial scrutiny was inappropriate in relation to remedial race-based action and took the view that the intermediate standard would provide protection where such schemes had the effect of 'paternalistic stereotyping' or the promotion of racial separatism, or where they carried the 'hazard of stigma' or placed an undue burden on members of the majority. This test was, in his view, clearly made out, the programme being aimed at 'overcoming substantial, chronic minority underrepresentation in the medical profession'

---

[38] Note 17 above at 357–358, citing *US v Carolene Products Co* 304 US 144 (1939).

(which under-representation reduced the number of doctors willing to serve ethnic minority patients). In addition, because minority applicants to the medical school had been born before or at around the time of the Supreme Court's decision in *Brown v Board of Education*[39] (that decision having demanded an end to segregated schooling), these 'applicants . . . must be few indeed who endured the effects of de jure segregation, the resistance to *Brown* . . . or the equally debilitating pervasive private discrimination fostered by our long history of official discrimination, and yet come to the starting line with an education equal to whites'.[40]

Justice Powell found himself unable to interpret the Fourteenth Amendment's demand for 'equal protection' so as to permit action based at the amelioration of societal discrimination. He was willing to allow affirmative action by particular bodies designed to remedy their own past discrimination, where that past discrimination had been determined by 'a legislative or administrative body charged with the responsibility' or by the courts themselves. But he drew the line at permitting classifications designed to help 'relatively victimized groups at the expense of other innocent individuals in the absence of judicial, legislative, or administrative findings of constitutional or statutory violations', maintaining that the burden imposed on individuals (like Bakke) who were not responsible for the past discrimination could not be justified by the attempt to overcome generalised or 'societal' discrimination and that it was 'far too late to argue that the guarantee of equal protection to all persons permits the recognition of special wards entitled to a degree of protection greater than that accorded others'. Responding to the argument that 'benign' discrimination against the 'white "majority"' should be subject to a lower level of scrutiny than that against minorities, he protested that '[t]he concepts of "majority" and "minority" necessarily reflect temporary arrangements and political judgments' and that the 'white "majority" itself is composed of various minority groups, most of whom can lay claim to a history of prior discrimination'.

The weakness in Justice Powell's approach is that it overlooks the context in which the university's affirmative action operated. Majorities and minorities may change over time but, in the context of an affirmative action programme, are easily recognised – 'minorities' consist of historically disadvantaged groups which are under-represented in the institution in question. To the extent that affirmative action programmes successfully address this under-representation, the 'minorities' involved cease to be defined as such for the purposes of affirmative action programmes. Again, the categorisation of persons for the purposes of affirmative action does not turn on the assertion of fundamental differences between them, rather on the combination of historical

---

[39] 347 US 483 (1954).
[40] Note 17 above at 372, citation and footnote omitted.

disadvantage and under-representation.[41] As to Justice Powell's other points, by permitting affirmative action programmes only where the programme operators had been found themselves to have discriminated, he simply excluded consideration of all the preliminary and extraneous hurdles, recognised by Justice Brennan, which faced ethnic minority applicants to the university. In addition, by requiring the finding of discrimination, he undermined much of the potential of affirmative action programmes.

The major problem associated with anti-discrimination legislation is precisely that of proof: in the absence of an admission of discrimination from an employer, a finding of discrimination turns on inferences from whatever facts are available. The burden of proving discrimination rests with the employee and, according to the Supreme Court in *St Mary's Honour Center v Hicks*,[42] remains there even after a *prima facie* case of discrimination has been made out by the employee and any explanation put forward by the employer has been found to be false.

The Supreme Court has not interpreted Title VII so as to render the proof of discrimination easy (one might argue, indeed, as Justice Souter did for the dissenters in *Hicks*, that such proof is virtually impossible to provide). Ameliorative programmes can side-step this programme by assessing the level of discrimination which operates, whether in a particular organisation or more generally, by reference to statistics and by attempting to remove the obstacles which result in this statistical inequality or, where generalised or 'societal' discrimination is at issue, to ameliorate its effects. One benefit of such programmes is precisely that they can bypass the question whether the employer has engaged in any wilful wrongdoing and, by concentrating on future results rather than present fault, base themselves on statistics even where those statistics would not be regarded as adequate to found a discrimination claim.

Obviously, crude measures are inappropriate and it will not be adequate simply to assume that, discrimination aside, all ethnic groups or both sexes would enter particular occupations or jobs in equal proportions. Nor is it fair to require that employers carry the burden of undoing all societal discrimination. But, to the extent that employers themselves can be seen to contribute to the disadvantage suffered by particular groups (whether by failing consistently to appoint 'qualified' members of those groups in reasonable proportion to their application rate, or by adopting recruitment practices which have the effect of excluding members of these groups for reasons unrelated to specific job capacity), it is fair that action should be required of them even in the absence of proof of discrimination in relation to a specific individual.

---

[41] Old Etonians, for example, would not qualify if they were to be under-represented within an organisation etc.

[42] 509 US 502 (1993).

The constitutionality of 'voluntary' and 'temporary' racial quotas in the private sector was upheld by the Supreme Court in 1979 in *United Steel-workers of America v Weber*,[43] in the context of a Title VII claim. In this decision, Justice Brennan found himself in the majority with Justices Stewart, White, Marshall and Blackmun. Justice Brennan interpreted the prohibition on 'discriminat[ion] because of . . . race' consistent with what he regarded as the purpose of the Civil Rights Act (to open to ethnic minorities positions from which they had previously been excluded) and stressed that the provision of Title VII which dealt with preferential treatment (703 (j)) stated that nothing contained in it 'shall be interpreted to require [as distinct from 'to require *or permit*'] any employer . . . to grant preferential treatment . . . to any group because of the race . . . of such . . . group on account of' a *de facto* racial imbalance in the employer's work force.

Justice Blackmun was somewhat troubled by this interpretation but concurred on the grounds that Congress could amend Title VII if it disagreed with the Supreme Court. In 1985 the Supreme Court went further, deciding, in *Bushey v New York State Civil Service Commission*,[44] that *Weber* applied even in the public sector. This decision was not fully explained, the majority simply refusing to entertain an appeal against a lower court's decision upholding the affirmative action programme and failing to address the issue under the Equal Protection Clause.

Meanwhile, the Supreme Court had upheld the constitutionality of a 10 per cent 'minority business enterprise' set-aside in a federal public works programme in *Fullilove*.[45] Of the plurality who upheld the programme, three (led by Chief Justice Burger) reached their decision on the basis that Congress had wide power under the Due Process Clause of the Fifth Amendment 'to enforce, by appropriate legislation' the equal protection guarantee of that Amendment and that 'in the . . . remedial context, there is no requirement that Congress act in a wholly "color-blind" fashion . . . When effectuating a limited and properly tailored remedy to cure the effects of prior discrimination . . . "a sharing of the burden" by innocent parties is not impermissible'. Justice Marshall, with Justices Brennan and Blackmun, concurred on the wider grounds that race-based affirmative action should be scrutinised in accordance with the intermediate standard, which scrutiny the federal programme survived. Justices Stewart, Rehnquist and Stevens continued to oppose, the latter, in particular, condemning the set-aside as 'a perverse form of reparation'.[46] Again, the minority refused to take into account the fact of substantive inequality. Justice Stewart cited the dissenting opinion in *Plessy*

---

[43] 443 US 193 (1979).
[44] 469 US 1117 (1985).
[45] Note 13 above.
[46] See, however, his change of approach in *Metro Broadcasting v FCC* 497 US 547 (1990), discussed below.

v Ferguson,[47] in which Justice Harlan had protested that 'Our Constitution is color-blind, and neither knows nor tolerates classes among citizens. . . . The law regards man as man, and takes no account of his surroundings or of his color'.

Justice Stewart stated that 'today's decision is wrong for the same reason that *Plessy v Ferguson* was wrong'. Refusing to take into account the record of inequality upon which the majority decision rested (in 1976, less than 1 per cent of all federal procurement was concluded with minority business enterprises, although minorities comprised 15–18 per cent of the population), Justice Stewart claimed that Congress legislators have 'neither the dispassionate objectivity nor the flexibility that are needed to mold a race-conscious remedy around the single objective of eliminating the effects of past or present discrimination' and pointed to the lack of evidence that Congress itself 'has in the past engaged in racial discrimination in its disbursement of federal contracting funds'.

Despite the marked differences of opinion in the Supreme Court, affirmative action programmes were generally upheld between 1978 and 1989, for the most part in the face of strong Presidential resistance. Having said this, in 1984 the Supreme Court permitted (under Title VII) a 'last-in, first-out' redundancy programme which had the effect of undoing the ethnic minority gains achieved in the wake of a court-approved affirmative action programme in the Memphis fire authority (*Firefighters Local v Stotts*[48]) and, in 1986, in *Wygant v Jackson Board of Education,*[49] it found unconstitutional a redundancy programme designed to leave intact an increase in the proportion of ethnic minority teachers. Justice Stevens, uncharacteristically, dissented in this latter case, rejecting the strict scrutiny approach because the Board's policy was 'inclusionary' and distinguishable, therefore, 'from a race-conscious decision that would reinforce assumptions of inequality.' He found the Board's policy constitutional under the Equal Protection Clause because it was 'not based on any lack of respect for the . . . race [of majority teachers], or on blind habit and stereotype', that it 'served a valid public purpose, that it was adopted with fair procedures and given a narrow breadth [in this regard he distinguished *Fullilove*], that it transcends the harm to petitioners, and that it is a step toward that ultimate goal of eliminating entirely from governmental decisionmaking such irrelevant factors as a human being's race'.

Justice Marshall, with whom Justices Brennan and Blackmun concurred, reiterated the view, from *Bakke* that programmes designed to 'eliminat[e] the pernicious vestiges of past discrimination' did not require strict scrutiny because they did not impact on fundamental rights 'and because

[47] 163 US 537 (1896).
[48] 467 US 561 (1984).
[49] 476 US 267 (1986).

whites have none of the immutable characteristics of a suspect class'. On the facts before him: 'the turbulent history of the effort to integrate the Jackson public schools – not even mentioned in the plurality opinion', the fact that the Board of Education did not hire its first black teacher until 1954 and that, 15 years later, less than 4 per cent of its teachers were black, the finding of race discrimination at that point and the continued support of the teachers, 80 per cent of them white, for the protectionist lay-off policy; Justice Marshall concluded that the 'state purpose of preserving the integrity of a valid hiring policy – which in turn sought to achieve diversity and stability for the benefit of all students', and the means by which it was achieved, satisfied the demands of the Equal Protection Clause. But the plurality in *Jackson* insisted that 'the level of scrutiny does not change merely because the challenged classification operates against a group that historically has not been subject to governmental discrimination', that past discrimination by the Board of Education was not proven and that societal discrimination was too 'amorphous' to justify affirmative action. Further, Justices Powell and Rehnquist and Chief Justice Burger stated that, even had the Board of Education been able to show a compelling interest, the 'lay-off' policy would not be regarded, given its impact on the 'rights and expectations surrounding seniority' of majority teachers, as a legally appropriate means to achieve that purpose.

The focus of the plurality on the burden imposed on the non-minority teachers is worthy of note, given that the teachers had no contractual right to seniority-related protection from lay-off. What had, in fact, been agreed by all concerned as an appropriate balance between the seniority-related interests of non-minority teachers and the need for effective protection of the equal protection interests of the minority teachers was characterised by the plurality, apparently, as an illegitimate trumping of a paramount interest (that of the majority teachers) by a less fundamental one.

Firefighters Local and *Wygant* showed that the Supreme Court's unease with affirmative action became more acute as the burdens imposed on non-minorities increased. But in the same year as *Wygant* was decided, the Supreme Court in *Firefighters v Cleveland*[50] upheld the use of specific goals to remedy past discrimination under Title VII, and in 1987 the court ruled for the first time (*United States v Paradise*[51]) that courts may set strict race promotion goals to counteract 'long-term, open and pervasive discrimination'. In this latter case, Justice Powell departed from his resistance to strict goals in *Bakke* on the grounds that, in contrast to the University of California, the employer (Alabama State) 'had engaged in persistent violation of constitutional rights and repeatedly failed to carry out court orders'. Justice Stevens concurred on the grounds that the

---

[50] 478 US 501 (1986).
[51] 480 US 149 (1987).

employers had been guilty of 'an egregious violation of the Equal Protection Clause'. The Reagan administration had thus far been denied what it sought: judicial confirmation of the view that 'the constitutional guarantee of "equality" in the law requires public policy to be color-blind, except when correcting the effects of past acts of discrimination against identified individual victims'.[52]

In 1989 it appeared that race (and, presumably, sex) could form the basis for ameliorative programmes where it was established that the institution involved had itself been guilty of discrimination in the past; that educational establishments could pursue a policy of race-based diversity, at least where this did not consist of rigid quotas for ethnic minority students. Private and public sector employers could adopt voluntary and temporary training quotas or other race-conscious methods in hiring and promotion 'to eliminate conspicuous racial imbalance in traditionally segregated job categories'.[53] Affirmative action programmes could be imposed by the courts as well as being embraced voluntarily by employers, and federal programmes could operate race-based set-asides where severe inequality of access had been shown.

The Supreme Court, albeit never clearly, had fashioned an understanding of 'equality' which, contrary to its approach to indirect discrimination under the Equal Protection Clause, gave some support to the substantive model. These judgments were never unanimous and frequently failed even to rest on clear majorities, the level of scrutiny appropriate to remedial programmes was never settled and the issue set social liberals in the court against each other. But until 1989, remedial race programmes, whether carried out at federal or state level, in the public or private sector, voluntarily or at the behest of the courts, had a reasonable chance of being upheld by the Supreme Court. With the replacement in that year of Justice Powell by Justice Kennedy the tide turned. In *Wards Cove Packaging Co v Atonio*[54] the Supreme Court all but overruled its decision in *Griggs*,[55] demanding that the plaintiff in a Title VII indirect discrimination claim identify the business practices which were alleged to result in the racial or sexual imbalance and, further, establish that these practices were adopted not for reasons of business necessity but, rather, for illegal purposes.

Part of the Supreme Court's decision was reversed by Congress in the 1991 Civil Rights Act (eventually accepted by President Bush after the Anita Hill debacle and the bid by former Ku Klux Klan chief David Dukes to become Governor of Louisiana, having been vetoed by him in 1990 on the grounds that it introduced the 'destructive force of quotas into our

---

[52] McKeever, note 12 above, p 156, citing the *International Herald Tribune*, 26 May 1986.
[53] *United Steelworkers of America v Weber*, note 43 above and *Bushey v New York State Civil Service Commission*, note 44 above.
[54] 490 US 642 (1989).
[55] *Griggs v Duke Power Co*, note 19 above.

nation's employment system'[56]). But the change of approach the decision signalled was felt in the affirmative action almost immediately when,
in *Martin v Wilks*,[57] the Supreme Court ruled that non-minorities who
suffered as a result of court-approved affirmative action programmes without having agreed to the programmes could sue under the Fourteenth
Amendment. These suits could be made without time limit, although on
the same day in a sex discrimination case the Supreme Court required
that women who wished to challenge a seniority system must do so within
300 days of its adoption.[58] The decree which had approved the race-based
programme challenged in *Wilks* had been issued in the wake of a finding
that the fire department involved had discriminated against minority candidates in contravention of Title VII, and in advance of a finding on discrimination in promotion practices, but with the issuing court expressing
the view that the department would probably be found to have discriminated in this area also. The majority decision did not refer to the historical context of the case. On this occasion, Justice Stevens delivered the
opinion of the dissenters.

In the same year, in *Croson v City of Richmond*,[59] the Supreme Court
invalidated Richmond's 30 per cent set-aside of public works funds for
minority-owned businesses and, for the first time, ruled that all state and
local use of racial classifications to benefit minorities must meet strict
scrutiny. Despite the subsequent decision of the Supreme Court in *Metro
Broadcasting v FCC*,[60] in which ethnic minority preferences in the award
of broadcasting licences were upheld, Justice Brennan, for the majority,
declaring that 'benign race conscious measures mandated by congress –
even if those measures are not "remedial" in the sense of being designed
to compensate victims of past governmental or societal discrimination –
are constitutionally permissible', the thrust after 1989 was against affirmative action.

The majority in *Metro Broadcasting* had distinguished *Croson* and followed *Fullilove* on the basis that 'race-conscious classifications adopted by
Congress to address racial and ethnic discrimination are subject to a different standard than such classifications prescribed by state and local governments'. The majority upheld the affirmative action programmes on
the grounds that 'they serve the important governmental objective of
broadcast diversity . . . [and] are substantially related to the achievement

---

[56] Ewoh and Elliott, note 29 above.
[57] 490 US 755 (1989). See also *Wards Cove Packaging Co v Atonio*, note 54 above; *Lorance v
AT&T Technologies Ltd* 490 US 900 (1989) and *Jett v Dallas Independent Schools District* 491
US 701 (1989), cited by H Abraham and B Perry, *Freedom and the Court* (6th ed, Oxford:
Oxford University Press, 1994), p 434.
[58] *Lorance v AT&T Technologies Ltd* 490 US 900 (1989). See N Riccucci, 'The Legal Status of
Affirmative Action: Past Developments, Future Prospects' (1997) 17(4) *Review of Public
Personnel Administration* 22.
[59] 488 US 469 (1989).
[60] Note 46 above.

of that objective'. Again those who decided in favour of affirmative action in *Metro Broadcasting* focused on the substantive inequality at which the affirmative action programme was directed – the grossly dispropor-tionate ownership of radio and television stations by white and minority bodies and the impact thereof on both minority and white audiences.[61]

Justice Stevens concurred on grounds similar to those upon which he based his dissent in *Jackson*, stating that government race-based classifica-tions were permissible not only 'as a remedy for a past wrong' but also for 'future benefit . . . I remain convinced, of course, that racial or ethnic characteristics provide a relevant basis for disparate treatment only in extremely rare situations, and that it is therefore "especially important that the reasons for any such classification be clearly identified and un-questionably legitimate" '.[62] Here, because of 'the recognized interest in broadcast diversity' and the lack of stigma attaching either to the 'the favored nor the disfavored class', he regarded his unspecified standard of review as satisfied.

Again, the minority justices (O'Connor, Rehnquist, Scalia and Kennedy) paid scant regard to the evidence of inequality and found that the pro-gramme did not pass strict scrutiny. In *Adarand Constructors v Pena*[63] the minority became the majority with the addition of Justice Thomas while Justice Stevens, once again in the minority, was joined in his dissent by Justices Ginsburg, Souter and Breyer. Justice Thomas was the controver-sial appointment of George Bush who also appointed Justice Souter, the latter turning out to be considerably more liberal than expected. Justices Ginsburg and Breyer were appointed by President Clinton. The Supreme Court in *Adarand* overruled *Metro Broadcasting* and demanded that fed-eral, as well as state and local, affirmative action programmes meet strict scrutiny where they operated on the basis of racial or ethnic classifications. Once again, those who struck down the affirmative action programme paid no regard to the context of inequality. Justice Thomas castigated what he characterised as the view 'that there is a racial paternalism exception to the principle of equal protection' and stated that 'that there is a "moral [and] constitutional equivalence,"[64] between laws designed to subjugate a race and those that distribute benefits on the basis of race in order to foster some current notion of equality'. Justice Stevens for the dissenters, his conversion since the days of *Fullilove* apparently complete, maintained that:

> [t]here is no moral or constitutional equivalence between a policy that is designed to perpetuate a caste system and one that seeks to eradicate racial

---

[61] *Per* Justice Brennan, with whom Justices White, Marshall, Blackmun, and Stevens concurred.
[62] Citing his dissenting opinion in *Fullilove v Klutznick*, note 13 above.
[63] Case no 93–1841, 1995.
[64] Disagreeing with Justice Stevens, dissenting, who maintained that there was no such equivalence.

subordination. Invidious discrimination is an engine of oppression, subjugating a disfavored group to enhance or maintain the power of the majority. Remedial race-based preferences reflect the opposite impulse: a desire to foster equality in society.

Most recently the Supreme Court has declined, in 1995, 1996 and 1997, to hear affirmative action cases. One of the 1995 refusals concerned the consent decree to which the Supreme Court in *Wilks* had permitted challenge.[65] The decree required one black firefighter to be promoted for every white firefighter advanced. The federal trial court upheld the order against challenge by white firefighters affected by it on the grounds that it was intended to remedy past discrimination and a manifest racial imbalance (there was not one black firefighter amongst 94 lieutenants, 31 captains and 15 battalion chiefs), but the Eleventh Circuit Appeals Court reversed on the grounds that the order 'trammelled' the rights of white firefighters and was intended more to balance the races than to remedy the effects of past discrimination.

The 1996 case concerned a diversity-related affirmative action programme at the University of Texas law school, which had been ruled unconstitutional by the Fifth Circuit Court of Appeals on the grounds that (a) the pursuit of diversity could not be regarded as a compelling interest in higher education and (b) a university could not adopt affirmative action to compensate for discrimination in the school system. The former holding was, despite the Fifth Circuit's protests to the contrary, inconsistent with *Bakke* given that, in that case, four of the justices adopted a generous approach to affirmative action programmes and the fifth, Justice Powell, specifically accepted diversity as a compelling goal.[66] As a result, public universities in Texas, Louisiana and Mississippi are not permitted to operate race-based affirmative action programmes previously deemed acceptable under *Bakke.* And in 1997 the Court refused to hear the ACLU's challenge to California's Civil Rights Initiative (Proposition 209), a constitutional amendment which bans sex and race-based public sector affirmative action even where it is necessary to remedy past discrimination, unless the action is adopted by court order.[67]

California's legislation was upheld by the Ninth Circuit Court of Appeals, which reversed the findings of the US District Court, without a full hearing on the issues and on a motion which had sought only the removal of an injunction on the legislation. As a result of the constitutional amendment, all 'preferential' treatment, including outreach programmes and the targeting of specific race or sex-based needs, is unconstitutional

---

[65] See Riccucci, note 58 above.

[66] *Ibid.*

[67] *Coalition for Economic Equity for Wilson.* A further case docketed for 1997 (*Piscataway Township Board of Education v Taxman*) was settled. Such was the concern about the probable outcome that the black leadership forum agreed to pay 70% of the settlement costs: ACLU *News*, 21 November 1997, available on the website listed at, note 27 above.

in California unless required under federal law. An ACLU paper on the legislation points out that even women's university-based resource centres, which provide workshops on sexual harassment, rape, self-defence, etc, are prohibited under Proposition 209. At the same time, the amendment widened the BFOQ exception by permitting sex-based qualifications 'reasonably necessary to the normal operation of public employment, public education, or public contracting'.[68] Previously, sex was regarded as a suspect classification in California and subjected to strict scrutiny under that state's constitution.

The impact of Proposition 209 was immediately felt: admissions of African American, Chicano, Latino and American Indian students were reduced by more than half in Berkeley and, following a similar ban at the University of Texas law school, admissions of African American students dropped by 88 per cent and those of Hispanic students by 64 per cent. This decimation of minority students numbers did not serve to improve the academic calibre of the former – grade point averages and LSAT scores rising by only 0.02 per cent and one point respectively. [69] The University of California's medical school, too, saw minority applications fall by over 30 per cent from 1996 to 1997 while applications from black and Hispanic students to the University of Texas Law School dropped 42 per cent and 14 per cent respectively. [70] According to the President of the University of Michigan: '[Anti-affirmative action] lawsuits threaten the ability of the University to bring together students from a wide array of backgrounds to create the richest possible environment for education and learning [and to play] a leadership role . . . in building a tolerant and integrated society'.[71]

Proposition 209 was passed in the wake of *Adarand*, and efforts are being made to limit affirmative action in Washington, Florida, Colorado, Michigan, Massachusetts, Arizona, Arkansas, Ohio, North Dakota, Texas, Illinois, Montana, South Carolina and Oregon.[72] In 1995, 18 states introduced legislation to curb affirmative action and in 1997, 15 states did so.[73] Only California has, thus far, been successful, but there is huge hostility from some quarters to the policy which the right-wing *American Spectator* classified, in 1995, as 'the most divisive and dangerous issue in American politics – more important than taxes, crime or abortion'. Moves are afoot at the federal level to eliminate affirmative action. President

---

[68] Not necessarily *occupational* sex-based qualifications. Cf *Automobile Workers v Johnson Controls* 499 US 187 (1991).

[69] ACLU Press Release, 6 May 1998, available on the website address given at, note 27 above.

[70] ACLU, *What would our nation's schools be like without affirmative action?*, citing *New York Times*, 19 March 1998 and *Washington Post*, 19 May 1998, see ACLU website at, note 27 above.

[71] *Ibid*.

[72] ACLU *News*, 13 April 1997, website note 27 above; *Chicago Sun Times*, 16 August 1995; American Bar Association *Journal*, February 1998. See also ACLU, *Legislative Roundup* 1997, available on the website.

[73] Kellough *et al*, note 18 above.

Clinton remains at least superficially committed to the practice, having issued a 'strong and emotional defence' of it in response to *Adarand*, speaking of his 'pride and passion', claiming that Republicans were using it as a 'wedge issue' to attract 'angry, white male' voters and adopting a 'mend it, don't end it' policy.[74] But in March 1996, the Ad Hoc Coalition of Concerned Minority Business and Civil Rights Organizations alleged 'a consistent and disturbing pattern of action on the part of certain elements within the Administration in direct contradiction' of the avowed policy.[75]

By 1994 the Republicans had a majority in Congress, and used this to force President Clinton to undertake a review of all federal affirmative action programmes. The review uncovered little evidence of 'reverse discrimination' against white men, finding that the 'vast majority of discrimination in America' was directed against women and members of ethnic minority groups.[76] For all this Clinton, failed explicitly to criticise Proposition 209 and, in 1996, he suspended all federal set-aside programmes for a minimum of three years (this despite its findings of the 'very real, ongoing impact of discrimination'[77]). In 1997, the Clinton administration took a stand against affirmative action in a case which was settled before it reached the Supreme Court.[78] In July 1997 a House subcommittee approved legislation (dubbed by Democrats the 'Equal Opportunity Repeal Act of 1997') introduced by Republican Representatives Canady (a prominent anti-choice activist) and McConnell and designed to prohibit all federal programmes using affirmative action to remove past discrimination. The House Judiciary Committee voted to postpone legislation on the issue in autumn 1997 and both Congress and the Senate defeated a number of proposals in early 1998.[79] But the Canady–McConnell Bill has yet to be heard and as recently as November 1997 Republicans showed their hostility towards affirmative action when they defeated President Clinton's nomination of Bill Lee for assistant Attorney General because of his opposition to California's Proposition 209.[80]

---

[74] ACLU Press Release, 19 July 1995, available on the ACLU website, note 27 above. See also *Chicago Tribune*, 20 July 1995.
[75] ACLU Press Release, 12 March 1996, available on the ACLU website, note 27 above.
[76] *Chicago Tribune*, 20 July 1995.
[77] ACLU Press Release, 22 May 1996, available on the ACLU website, note 27 above.
[78] *Piscataway*, note 67 above, ACLU *News*, 5 September 1997, available on the ACLU website, note 27 above. The Clinton administration had originally backed the school board but changed its tune after the school lost, and lobbied the Supreme Court not to hear the case: see Ewoh and Elliott, note 29 above.
[79] In May 1998, Congress rejected a federal proposal completely to ban affirmative action in public colleges and universities after educators in California and Texas had warned of the trend towards resegregation in their states in the wake of state bans (legislative and judicial) on affirmative action programmes: ACLU Press Release, 6 May 1998, available on the ACLU website, note 27 above.
[80] Eventually Clinton bypassed normal appointments procedure and appointed him Acting Assistant Attorney General for Civil Rights: *Washington Post*, 1 January 1998; *Toronto Sun*, 22 December 1997.

Sex-based programmes

The recent Supreme Court decisions restricting affirmative action have been made in the context of race discrimination, where, as has been mentioned above, the 'strict scrutiny' approach generally applies. If the same approach were taken to affirmative action programmes based on sex, the intermediate standard should be applied and such programmes should be easier to justify, just as discrimination against women is easier to justify under the Equal Protection Clause than that directed at ethnic minority groups.

In *Schlesinger*,[81] above, the application of the lenient standard of review to sex-based affirmative action resulted in a finding of constitutionality. But with the adoption of the intermediate standard in *Craig v Boren*,[82] and its application to affirmative action in *Mississippi University for Women v Hogan*,[83] the Supreme Court ruled that 'the party seeking to uphold a statute that classifies individuals on the basis of their gender must carry the burden of showing an exceedingly persuasive justification for the classification . . . The burden is met only by showing *at least* that the classification serves important governmental objectives and that the discriminatory means employed are substantially related to the achievement of those objectives' (my emphasis, internal citations omitted).[84] This standard is, arguably, higher than that applied in relation to sex discrimination other than in the context of affirmative action, the Supreme Court in *Craig* and subsequently having confined itself to asking whether gender classifications 'serve important governmental objectives and [are] substantially related to achievement of those objectives'.[85]

The majority of the Supreme Court chose to treat the issue in *Mississippi* as the denial of access of a male student to the university's school of nursing, rather than to the entire single-sex university, and found the school's women-only access policy violative of the Equal Protection Clause on the grounds that women were not disadvantaged in access to nursing studies, and that maintaining an exclusively female nursing school 'tends to perpetuate the stereotyped view of nursing as an exclusively women's job'. The District Court, by contrast, had found that 'the maintenance of Mississippi University for Women as a single-sex school bears a rational relationship to the State's legitimate interest "in providing the greatest practical range of educational opportunities for its female student population"'.

Here, as elsewhere, those supportive of affirmative action gave weight to the context in which the discriminatory practices operated (Justice

---

[81] Note 33 above.
[82] Note 34 above.
[83] 458 US 718 (1982).
[84] Citing *Wengler v Druggists Mutual Insurance Co* 446 US 142 (1980).
[85] Justice O'Connor, for the Supreme Court, expressly reserved decision whether a classification that survived intermediate scrutiny would be subject to strict scrutiny.

Powell pointing out the recognised benefits to women of single-sex education: the provision of an environment in which women 'generally . . . speak
up more in their classes, . . . hold more positions of leadership . . .
and . . . have more role models and mentors among women teachers and
administrators'). Justice Powell asserted that 'the equal protection standard generally applicable to sex discrimination . . . was designed to free
women from "archaic and overbroad generalisations"' and that it had
never previously been applied by the Supreme Court 'to invalidate state
efforts to expand women's choices. Nor are there prior sex discrimination
decisions by this Court in which a male plaintiff [as here] . . . had the
choice of an equal benefit. . . . By applying heightened equal protection
analysis to this case . . . the Court frustrates the liberating spirit of the
Equal Protection Clause'.

   In 1987 the Supreme Court ruled, in *Johnson v Transportation Agency,
Santa Clara County*,[86] that women, as well as ethnic minority groups, could
be given preferential treatment in hiring and promotion, even absent
proof of past discrimination by the employer, where such action was
necessary to bring the workforce into line with the local labour market
or population. The decision was reached under Title VII and in accordance with *Weber*,[87] on the ground that the purpose of the affirmative
action was to eliminate 'the effects of employment discrimination'. It
would appear, however, that, had governmental action been implicated,
the application of *Weber* to the Equal Protection Clause in *Bushey*[88]
would have permitted the same result. *Johnson* was the first case in which
the Supreme Court had clearly recognised women as a group entitled
to benefit from remedial action. But the decision was reached just
two years before the Supreme Court's change of approach and the legality of affirmative action for women is inextricably tied to that based
on race.

   The approach taken by the Supreme Court in the *Mississippi* case,
although that court purported to apply intermediate, rather than strict,
scrutiny, suggests that sex-based affirmative action programmes today
would be judged, in practice, according to a similar yardstick to that
applied to race-based programmes. Indeed, in *Jackson*, Justice O'Connor
accepted that: '[i]n particular, as regards certain state interests commonly
relied upon in formulating affirmative action programs, the distinction
between a "compelling" and an "important" governmental purpose [such
as to satisfy, respectively, strict and intermediate scrutiny] may be a neglig-
ible one'. Further, there is one recent sex discrimination decision in which
the Supreme Court appears to impose a higher than intermediate standard
of scrutiny on sex-based classifications.

---

[86] 480 US 616 (1987).
[87] *United Steelworkers of America v Weber*, note 53 above.
[88] *Bushey v New York State Civil Service Commission*, note 53 above.

In *United States v State of Virginia*,[89] in which the Supreme Court struck down the 'male only' admissions policy of the Virginia Military Institute (a higher education establishment), Justice Scalia and Chief Justice Rehnquist dissented on the basis that Justice Ginsburg, for the majority, had applied a strict scrutiny analysis to a sex-based classification. Whether or not this was the case is uncertain, Justice Ginsberg requiring simply that the 'State must show at least that the [challenged] classification serves important governmental objectives and that the discriminatory means employed are substantially related to the achievement of those objectives' (internal citations omitted), and the single sex policy at issue being justified in part on the basis that 'admission of women would downgrade [the institution's] stature, destroy the adversative system and, with it, even the school'. As Justice Ginsberg pointed out, this idea was 'a prediction hardly different from other self fulfilling prophecies' (internal quotes omitted) such as those which had blocked women's access to law and medical schools and, until recently, to the police force. Further, according to Justice Ginsberg, '[w]omen's successful entry into the federal military academies, and their participation in the Nation's military forces, indicate that Virginia's fears for [the institute's] future may not be solidly grounded'.

Virginia's policy would barely have passed even the relaxed standard of review. Nevertheless, Justice Ginsberg, for the majority, did not dispute the claim of Chief Justice Rehnquist that her demand for an 'exceedingly persuasive justification' by the state of a gender-based classification 'introduces an element of uncertainty' into the intermediate test. (Justice Rehnquist, as he then was, had dissented in *Mississippi*.) Of the nine justices, only the Chief Justice and Justice Scalia dissented, Justice Thomas playing no role in the decision, so it may be that the case marks a new approach to sex discrimination. In many contexts this would, of course, be welcome. But, coupled as it is with an apparent increase in judicial hostility for affirmative action, it suggests that sex-based affirmative action programmes are doomed to the same fate as those which operate on racial criteria. Justices O'Connor and Kennedy sided with Justice Ginsburg in *Virginia* but are both much more likely to vote against rather than in favour of affirmative action programmes.

Future for affirmative action in the US

The change of approach marked by the Supreme Court's post-1989 decisions in the context of race-based affirmative action might well be mirrored, in an appropriate case, in relation to sex-based programmes. But, whether or not this is likely to be the case, the falling from judicial

---

[89] Case no 94–1941, 1996. See C Kovacic-Fleischer, '*United States v Virginia*'s New Gender Equal Protection Analysis with Ramifications for Pregnancy, Parenting, and Title VII' (1997) 50(4) *Vanderbilt Law Review* 845.

favour of race-based affirmative action policies has resulted in a wide-spread reaction against those policies. It is perhaps in this respect that women will suffer most. Where states have chosen to attack affirmative action, the attack has extended beyond race-based programmes to capture also those in which sex is used as a factor. This can be seen in the discussion of California's constitutional amendment, discussed above. It was also true of legislation proposed in Texas in 1997 (the legislation was rejected in a ballot of voters and legislation protecting a measure of affirmative action in higher education was signed into law in that year[90]), and the current federal attempts to ban affirmative action apply equally to women and ethnic minorities.

Women have much to lose. According to ACLU statistics, six million have received employment and education opportunities as a direct result of affirmative action programmes, women professionals and black women, in particular, having experienced major gains. In 1995, the head of the US Civil Rights Commission stated that white women were the major beneficiaries of US affirmative action programmes.[91] And in the same year, economist Barbara Bergmann declared that the loss of affirmative action programmes would result in the deterioration of labour market position of blacks, Hispanics, and women generally.[92]

By contrast with the Supreme Court and the Republican administrations of Reagan and Bush, corporate support for affirmative action remains high (68 per cent of corporate chief executives approving of such programmes in 1992, and only 2 per cent opposing them).[93] Bob Dole's opposition to such programmes was particularly surprising given his support for affirmative action during the Reagan era[94] and his sponsorship of the Glass Ceiling Commission whose 1995 report testified to the presence of insurmountable recruitment barriers for women and ethnic minorities, many of these barriers being ascribed to 'the perception of many white males that as a group they are losing the corporate game, losing control and losing opportunity'. Just as this perception underlies much discriminatory action, so, too, it accounts for the hostility of many to affirmative action programmes. Capitulation to it in the latter context is tantamount to giving up the battle against discrimination.

---

[90] As a reaction to the judicial decision – it provided automatic entry for the top 10% in each class and embraced wider than purely academic factors as entry criteria.

[91] *USA Today*, 23 February 1995.

[92] The Costs of Abolishing Affirmative Action to the State and Local Governments of California, manuscript, at 3 (1995). Cited by ACLU affirmative action material on the ACLU website, note 27 above.

[93] 1992 survey by *Fortune* magazine, cited by the ACLU, see website given at note 27 above.

[94] Ewoh and Elliott, note 29 above.

Affirmative action and the Canadian Charter

Turning next to consider the fate of affirmative action at the hands of Canada's courts, even in the absence of s 15(2) of the Charter of Rights the Supreme Court has shown itself rather more open to the benefits of such action than has its sister court in the US. In *Action Travail des Femmes v CNR*,[95] for example, that court upheld an order of Canada's Human Rights Commission that at least one-quarter of those hired for tradition-ally male, blue-collar jobs be women until the proportion of women in that sector of the workforce reached a minimum of 13 per cent (this being the average level of participation of women in such jobs nationwide). Far from following the US path of permitting 'affirmative action' orders only on evidence of the most outrageous discrimination by employers, the Supreme Court accepted that 'systematic discrimination' (defined as 'dis-crimination that results from the simple operation of established proced-ures of recruitment, hiring and promotion, none of which is necessarily designed to promote discrimination') had occurred and that the pro-gramme ordered was 'essential to combat [its] effects'. According to the Supreme Court, the Commission had to be given generous scope to remedy such systemic discrimination 'to render future discrimination pointless, to destroy discriminatory stereotyping and to create the required "crit-ical mass" of target group participation in the workforce, it is essential to combat the effects of past systemic discrimination . . . specific hiring goals . . . are a rational attempt to impose a systemic remedy on a sys-temic problem'.[96]

The decision in *Action Trevail* was reached absent any specific pro-vision permitting affirmative action. It was pointed out, above, that Canada's Charter actually contains such a provision, s 15(2) stating that the prohibition on discrimination does not apply to 'any law, program or activity that has as its object the amelioration of conditions of dis-advantaged individuals or groups including those that are disadvantaged because of . . . sex'. Nevertheless, in the Charter's early days it became apparent that the lower courts were inclined to take an ungenerous approach to s 15(2).[97] Whereas, in *Weatherall v Canada (Attorney General)*,[98] the judge accepted that s 15(2) permitted women guards to search male prisoners in emergency situations, in *Conway v Canada (Attorney General)* (see Chapter 3 above),[99] the Federal Court of Appeals ruled that the employment of women guards on surveillance and frisking duties in the

---

[95] [1987] 1 SCR 1114.
[96] *Ibid*, at 1145, *per* Chief Justice Dickson.
[97] *Apsit et al v Manitoba Human Rights Commission (No 2)* [1988] 1 WWR 629, Manitoba QB; appeal allowed on other grounds (1988) 55 Man R (2d) 263, Manitoba CA.
[98] (1987) 59 CR (3d) 247.
[99] [1993] 2 SCR 872.

attempt to integrate women into prison service employment (there being few women prisoners to guard) went beyond what was permitted by s 15(2). The Supreme Court declared that s 15(2) would protect 'such . . . discriminatory infringements on male privacy as are reasonably necessary to the operation of the affirmative action programme', which did not include, in that court's view, 'non-emergency strip searches . . . or . . . unscheduled, unannounced surveillance of cells'.[100]

The likely attitude of the Supreme Court to affirmative action programmes is significant, given the existence in Canada of 'employment equity' programmes including that adopted by federal government in 1980 and extended in 1996, which applies only to employees in federal public service, federally regulated companies having at least 100 employees and companies which do business with federal government, and those more recently embraced in Prince Edward Island, New Brunswick, Saskatchewan, British Columbia and the Northwest Territories, Nova Scotia and Quebec. It appears, given the substantive approach taken to equality by the Supreme Court, that such programmes are likely to withstand constitutional scrutiny. Light should be thrown on the matter by the forthcoming decision in *Lovelace v Ontario*, an appeal against a decision in which Ontario's Court of Appeal ruled that 'because special programs for the disadvantaged further the guarantee of equality, government action under s 15(2) should be generously and liberally assessed' to the extent that, once it had been found that the purpose of a programme was to ameliorate the conditions of a disadvantaged group, judicial scrutiny should generally cease.[101] But, even if the Supreme Court does take as generous approach to the scope of s 15(2) as it has to s 15(1), this will not of itself do anything to improve women's position at work. Section 15(2) does not mandate affirmative action programmes, any more than s 15(1) requires governments to take any other steps to eradicate discrimination.

Conclusion

What can be said about the impact of constitutional rights on women in the workplace? It is clear from Chapter 6 above that the benefits, for women both in the US and in Canada, have been modest at best. While entrenchment might spur a government into removing legislative discrimination (discriminatory retirement ages, for example, or the exclusion of women from particular categories or hours of work); such discrimination is relatively rare. It is possible, as in Canada, that constitutional equality provisions may be interpreted so as to require that legislative prohibitions

[100] Note 98 above.
[101] 44 CRR (2d) 285, 148 DLR (4th) 126 (1997) Cf *Apsit*, note 97 above.

of discrimination be extended to more categories of workers than might otherwise be the case.[102] But, as was pointed out in *Re Service Employees International Union and Attorney General of Ontario*:[103]

> [constitutional rights do] not place a positive obligation on government to eliminate . . . inequity. Rather, the government must not create inequity . . . the government of Ontario was under no obligation to enact [anti-discrimination legislation] . . . It could likewise have repealed [such legislation] . . . without giving rise to any claims of discrimination.[104]

In addition, it has been seen in Chapter 6 that the non-recognition of indirect discrimination by the US Supreme Court has limited the impact of constitutional equality provisions even against the State (as in *Feeney*[105]). And even in Canada, where the approach taken to equality issues by the Supreme Court has been much more radical, even its judges have balked at finding against the Government in respect of such significant areas of expenditure as taxation, where significant improvements could be made.

The limited nature of the gains possible in this context is the result, in large part, of the source of inequality – the private, market sphere (and, in turn, the private 'private' sphere itself[106]). Entrenched rights do not, in general, operate against private sector wrongdoers. On the other hand, it is clear from the discussion in this chapter that entrenched rights pose very considerable dangers to legislative efforts to ameliorate that private sector discrimination. This has been evident in the discussion of affirmative action in the US and, in the context of Ireland, in the *Re Article 26 and the Employment Equality Bill 1996* decision.[107]

Even in Canada, where a substantive approach to equality has been entrenched in the Charter and, by and large, embraced by the judiciary, the rights entrenched therein have posed significant dangers for women

---

[102] *Haig v Canada Chief Electoral Officer* [1993] 2 SCR 995; *Vriend v Alberta* [1998] 1 SCR 493, discussed in Chapter 6 above.

[103] *Re Service Employees International Union, Local 204 et al and Attorney General of Ontario, SEIU, Local 204 v Ontario (Attorney General)* (1997) 151 DLR 4th 273, Ontario Court (General Division). The Government subsequently announced its decision not to appeal: *Toronto Sun*, 8 October 1997.

[104] Citing *Ferrel and others v Attorney General of Ontario* 149 DLR (4th) 335, in which the same government's repeal of the Employment Equity Act 1993 was upheld, Justice MacPherson: 'The purpose of the Charter is to ensure that governments comply with the Charter when they make laws. The Charter does not go further and require that governments enact laws to remedy societal problems, including problems of inequality and discrimination. One can hope that governments will regard this as part of their mission; however, the Charter does not impose this mission at the high level of constitutional obligation.' Ontario's Court of Appeal upheld the decision: see 168 DLR (4th) 1.

[105] Note 26 above.

[106] 'Private' is used of the market to distinguish it from the public sphere in respect of which entrenched rights generally operate – this market sphere is, more frequently, contrasted as 'public' with the 'private' sphere of the home.

[107] Case no 118/97, 15 May 1997, Supreme Court. Available on Lexis.

at work. One such threat was seen in *Conway*, discussed in Chapter 3 above. Perhaps of even greater concern were the Charter challenges which formed the basis of the decisions in *Schachter v Canada* (1988)[108] and in *Schafer v Canada* (1997).[109] The first of these cases was brought by a man who challenged Canada's Unemployment Insurance Act 1971, which provided parental benefits for adoptive parents and maternity leave for biological mothers, but did not provide paternal leave for biological fathers. On the one hand, such a claim might appear reasonable, and, as Brodsky and Day report, Schachter justified his actions on the ground that 'I see fathers taking a greater share of household responsibilities as being an assist to women'.[110] But, as the authors went on to remark: '[t]he problem with the *Schachter* case is ... the means of pursuing the goal ... There is every reason to think that litigation of this sort ... seriously endangers the minimal and fragile recognition that women's interests have received in the legislative arena.'

Neither Schachter himself, nor the intervening Attorney General, were concerned with the threat to women's interests. Indeed, Schachter suggested that biological fathers be given a share of biological mothers' (15-week) maternity benefits, and Canada's Attorney General argued that, to the extent that any of the provisions were regarded as inconsistent with s 15, they be struck down altogether rather than extended to cover biological fathers.[111] Fortunately, the *Schachter* court chose to respond to the intervention of the Women's Legal Education and Action Fund and to extend, rather than to strike down the provisions when they were found to violate s 15.[112]

Just as the threat to maternity benefits was resisted in *Schachter*, so it was threatened once again in *Schafer*, in which the plaintiff (an adoptive parent) challenged the provision of 15 weeks' maternity leave to women in addition to the 10 weeks' transferable leave applicable to both biological and adoptive parents. The lower court agreed that the provision of maternity leave in these circumstances violated s 15 although, unusually, it decided to extend the leave to adoptive parents. Ontario's Court of Appeal overruled the lower court, ruling that maternity leave was designed specifically to allow for pregnancy and childbirth.

The decisions in *Schachter*, *Schafer* and *Conway* were victories for women. But they should not be seen as evidence that the Charter has been beneficial to women. In each of these cases the threat to women came from the Charter itself, and victory left them no better off than they

---

[108] Discussed in G Brodsky and S Day, *Canadian Charter Equality Rights For Women: One Step Forward or Two Steps Back?* (Ontario: Canadian Advisory Council on the Status of Women, 1989), pp 59–60. The decision of the Supreme Court is at [1992] 2 SCR 679 but deals solely with remedy.

[109] (1998) 18 FTR 199, Ontario Court of Appeal, 8 August 1997.

[110] See Brodsky and Day, note 108 above, p 60.

[111] *Ibid.*

[112] See, subsequently, the decision of the Supreme Court at note 108 above.

would have been in the absence of entrenched rights. Perhaps most fundamental of all the problems highlighted by Canada's experience with the Charter of Rights, in the context of the workplace, is the exclusive focus of that document and, in particular, its interpretation by the courts, on 'government' action. In the context of equality rights this focus results, as was pointed out above, in the inability of those rights to challenge discrimination which arises, as the bulk of that which affects women in the workplace does, in the market.

Chapter 8

Women as Subjects of Criminal Law

Introduction

The final area to be considered is that of criminal justice. Entrenched rights can operate to protect defendants against abuses by the State – whether these abuses consist of undue delays, unacceptable police conduct, or the suppression of evidence useful to the defence. This is not, of course, to say that such protections can take the place of enlightened legislative action. In the US, where commitment to the death penalty appears a matter of national pride, the Supreme Court has refused to rule this penalty unconstitutional as a 'cruel and unusual punishment' (prohibited by the Eighth Amendment) – and this despite its grossly disproportionate application to minority defendants in respect of the killings of white victims.[1] But both the US Constitution and Canada's Charter of Rights have effected some improvements in the criminal justice sphere.[2]

Such protection as entrenched rights can afford against wrongful conviction and unduly harsh sentencing is to be welcomed. But to the extent that such rights operate to reduce the likelihood of conviction of the guilty, it is important not to lose sight of their impact on women in their role as victims of violence.

Contrary to common perceptions, men are more likely than women to fall victim to reported crimes of violence. But the extremely low reporting rates of much 'private' and sexual violence against women makes it difficult to ascertain the relative levels of actual, as distinct from reported, male and female victimisation. In the US, Congressional findings suggest that '4 million American women are battered each year by their husbands

---

[1] *Furman v State of Georgia* 408 US 238 (1972); *Gregg v State of Georgia* 428 US 153 (1976).
[2] In the US, for example, see *Miranda v State of Arizona* 384 US 436 (1966) on the right to remain silent; in Canada, *Reference Re Section 94(2) Motor Vehicle Act* [1985] 2 SCR 486 and *Vaillancourt v R* [1987] 2 SCR 636 (discussed below) on absolute liability offences.

or partners', that '95% of all domestic violence victims are women', that domestic violence accounts for over one-third of hospital emergency room visits by women, and that '[v]iolence is the leading cause of injury to women ages 15–44, more common than automobile accidents, muggings, and cancer deaths combined'.[3] It is estimated that one in six pregnant women in the US is battered, the results of this abuse including miscarriages and stillbirths.[4]

The true level of women's victimisation is probably considerably higher than that suggested by government statistics – others put the number of annual assaults by present or ex-partners at 16 million while estimates of the number of marriages in which violence features vary in the US from one-in-six (3.8 per cent annually) to 50 per cent, with the woman the victim in 90 per cent of cases.[5] Recent figures published by the British Medical Association estimate that one in four women in the UK has been the victim of domestic violence.[6] Every week in the US, around 2,500 women are raped by current or former male partners and a further 90 are murdered, nine out of ten of the latter by men.[7] The bulk of violent assaults on women are carried out by men known to them. In the US, for example, 75 per cent of single-offender violence against women fits this category and, although women are only two-thirds as likely as men to suffer violent attack, six to ten times as many women as men are attacked by someone known to them (non-stranger attacks accounting for two-thirds of all attacks on women and 80 per cent of sex attacks).[8] In 1994, more than 50 per cent of homeless women and children were fleeing violence and, according to FBI statistics, five women were beaten up by men every minute of every day and over 1,400 murdered by male intimates that year.[9] And in the same year, 'between 50 and 85 per cent of the over 4 million women receiving AFDC [Assistance for Families with Dependent Children] have recently experienced or are currently victims of physical and emotional violence at the hands of the adult men in their lives'.[10]

The fear of violence cripples many women. A 1991 US Senate report recorded that '50% of women do not use public transit after dark and

---

[3] Senate Report 138, pp 37–38 and House of Representatives Report 95, 103rd Congress, 1st Session, Violence Against Women Act of 1993, 26 (20 November 1993). About one-third of the assaults involve a weapon, *Chicago Tribune*, 20 March 1994.

[4] National Organisation for Women (NOW) statistics, available on the NOW website at http://www.now.org.

[5] See generally M Carty (1997) 71 *St John's Law Review* 465; C Nego, 'Stopping the Violence', *Modern Healthcare*, 4 April 1998.

[6] *Guardian*, 7 July 1998.

[7] NOW statistics, note 4 above.

[8] *Pheonix Gazette*, 15 February 1996; NOW Press Release, 30 January 1994, available on the NOW website, note 4 above; Bureau of Justice Statistics Press Release, 16 August 1995. These can be accessed from http://www.ojp.usdoj.gov/bjs/pubalp2.htm; the Department of Justice website is at http://www.usdoj.gov/02organizations/index.html.

[9] US *Cosmopolitan*, September 1994.

[10] J Raphael, *Prisoners of Abuse: Domestic Violence and Welfare Receipt* (Chicago: Taylor Institute, 1994).

75% of women do not go to the movies alone after dark due to fear of rape'.[11] And in enacting the 1994 Violence Against Women Act, the US Government recognised that 'women's fear of gender-based violence had resulted in [their] limited participation in the workplace and marketplace'.[12] The annual cost to the US of domestic violence (medical, employment and social) has been calculated as being between $5 and $10 billion, that of violence against women in Canada between $3.15 and $4.2 billion.[13]

The issue of specifically sexual violence is dealt with largely in Chapter 9 below, although there is some discussion of marital rape in this chapter. Such violence is perpetrated overwhelmingly by men and its victims, far more often than not, are female. But even without taking this particular type of violence into account, and whatever the precise rate at which women are victim to violence, one thing is clear. By contrast with men, women are disproportionately more likely to be the victims, rather than the perpetrators, of violence. It follows that women disproportionately bear the cost, rather than the benefit, of additional protections afforded to defendants. While changes to the criminal justice system which have the effect of minimizing the likelihood of unjust convictions must be welcomed, those changes which diminish the chance that perpetrators of violence are convicted serve further to reduce the protection afforded to women by that system.

The private nature of most violence experienced by women (that is, the fact that it is carried out by men known to them) renders it particularly invisible. Not only is such violence less likely to be reported than that which happens in public, at the hands of strangers, but the absence of witnesses to private violence makes it much more difficult to prosecute. In addition, and despite changes over time, private violence is still perceived differently from that which occurs in public. In the US, for example, while the official attitude of the police to private violence has changed from that typical in the 1970s: '. . . "(t)he worst thing you can do is take sides, even if one party is dead wrong . . . You just try to calm them down" . . .'; to a policy of arrest rather than mediation, the official approach is not necessarily reflected in practice, in part because intervening police officers are at a very high level of risk in incidents of private violence.[14]

People often appear to have trouble recognising as violence that which occurs between intimates. But not only are non-stranger attacks far more common for women than those carried out by strangers, they are far more

[11] Senate Report 102–197, p 38.
[12] Carty, note 5 above.
[13] See references at, note 3 above; US Department of State, *Country Reports: Canada*, February 1997.
[14] Carty, note 5 above, citing *New York Times*, 26 January 1973, Buzawa and Buzawa, *Domestic Violence: the Criminal Justice Perspective* (2nd ed, 1996), p 8 and Ford and Regoli, 'The Criminal Prosecution of Wife Assaulters', in N Hilton (ed), *Legal Responses to Wife Assault* (1993).

dangerous for women: injuries are more than twice as likely to be in-flicted in violent offences perpetrated by victims' husbands or boyfriends than by others, and around one-third of female homicide victims in the US (as against under 3 per cent of men) are killed by spouses or other intimates.[15] But domestic violence is trivialised to a staggering extent. Every week in the UK, two women die at the hands of violent partners (the figure for the US is about 27).[16] Yet a recent study carried out for the *Dispatches* programme found that 'domestic violence is still not being treated as a serious crime'. Domestic violence units, where they exist, are not empowered to investigate abuse or to decide whether charges should be brought, and the police rarely follow up even repeat domestic victim-isation. That part of the study which examined 512 cases attended by officers at one London police station found that only 20 per cent led to arrests (the low rate being ascribed either to lack of evidence or victims' unwillingness to press charges); 6 per cent to charges and under 3 per cent (13 cases) to conviction and two cases (less than 0.5 per cent) to a prison sentence. Police forces around the country failed adequately to respond to domestic violence, treated these incidents less seriously than others involving similar degrees of injury (typically charging perpetrators only with 'breach of the peace' or, at best, assault rather than inflicting/ causing GBH or ABH) and detaining them, if at all, only overnight.[17]

In the US, federal legislation was eventually passed in 1995/96 which prohibited anyone convicted of a domestic violence offence (and/or sub-ject to a domestic violence restraining order) from owning or possessing a gun. 150,000 incidents of domestic violence in the US each year involve a firearm, and these incidents are three times more likely to result in death than those in which a blade is used, almost 25 times as likely as those involving other or no weapons.[18] Despite this, attempts were made both during the passage of the Domestic Violence Gun Ban (1996) and subsequently to exempt from its provisions law enforcement officers (this in the face of the particular tendency of police officers to be the per-petrators of domestic violence) and, subsequent to its passage, those con-victed only of domestic violence 'misdemeanours' (rather than felonies) prior to its implementation. (Regardless of the level of injuries sustained by the victims of domestic violence, the few convictions which are achieved are generally in respect of misdemeanours.)[19]

---

[15] *Ibid.* 18% of former but only 3% of latter did not report due to fear of reprisals. See also Bureau of Justice Statistics Press Release, note 8 above and 1991 Senate Report, note 11 above.

[16] S Lees, 'Women: A Fistful of Promises', *Guardian*, 16 April 1998; NOW statistics, note 4 above.

[17] *Dispatches* broadcast, 16 April 1998.

[18] US *Newswire*, 5 December 1996; *Sacremento Bee*, 15 June 1996; testimony of Donna Edwards, Executive Director of the Network to End Domestic Violence, to the Subcommittee on Crime Judiciary Committee, 5 March 1997.

[19] Edwards, *ibid.*

According to some commentators, the highlighting in the US of domestic violence by the 1994 OJ Simpson trial has resulted, increasingly, in the implementation of preventative programmes by health care insurers and providers. But in some US states, victims of domestic violence are denied health insurance coverage on the grounds of what is regarded as a 'pre-existing condition'.[20] And the response of the criminal justice system is as inadequate in relation to this type of offence as it is, in general, to rape. Nor is it only the criminal justice system which fails the victims of domestic violence. In addition, the alternatives available to women who wish to escape abuse fall far short of what is required. These shortcomings have been recognised by the courts in a number of jurisdictions. Frequently, however, this recognition appears to have taken the form of lip-service alone, the courts condemning the inadequacy of provision for battered women while denying any defence to those who finally take the law into their own hands.[21]

Indicative of the generally casual attitude towards intimate violence is the fact that rape within marriage has not, until recent years, been regarded as an offence (as late as 1981, this was not the case in 44 of 52 US states, and marriage remained a defence to rape in England and Wales until 1991, when the House of Lords decided *R v R*[22]). Even now, rapes by husbands and other intimates are overwhelmingly less likely to result in conviction than are rapes by strangers.[23] This may result in part from increased difficulties of proof. But other factors also operate. Numerous studies of the police have shown that officers are incredibly sceptical about rape complaints, in particular, of those in which alleged perpetrator and victim knew each other and which did not otherwise fit the stereotypical picture of 'real' rape (innocent virgin attacked by crazed stranger carrying weapon and resists to the point of serious injury).[24] In addition, the relatively few women whose rape complaints against non-strangers get to trial have a much lower rate of conviction than those assaulted by strangers. Not only will jurors in general be more ready to infer consent to sex between non-strangers (however non-sexual the relationship or slight the previous acquaintance) but, where there is a pre-existing sexual relationship, jurors may be invited to infer consent (or at least belief on the part of the man in consent) the alleged rape can be assimilated to any intercourse which the couple had had prior to it. This assimilation can extend to the point where a jury is invited to infer consent to a violent assault because the

---

[20] NOW statistics, note 4 above.

[21] *People of the State of Colorado v Yaklich* 833 P 2d 758 (1991), *People v Aris* 215 Cal APPl 3d 1178 (1989).

[22] *R v R (Rape: Marital Exemption)* [1992] 1 AC 599, [1991] 3 WLR 767, [1991] 4 All ER 481.

[23] Between 1980 and 1985 at least 12 states followed the Model Penal Code 1980 version and extended husbands' immunity to cohabiting boyfriends.

[24] See, for example, G Chambers and A Millar, *Investigating Sexual Assault* (Edinburgh, Scottish Office Central Research Unit, 1983); J Gregory and S Lees, *Rape and Sexual Assault: A Study of Attrition* (London, Islington Council, 1993).

woman previously endured violence at the hands of the husband or other intimate.[25] Finally, there is a strong sense in many that rape by a partner is simply not as bad a thing as rape by a stranger, that it isn't 'real rape'.

Glanville Williams articulated a common approach to marital rape when he declared, in the wake of *R v R* above: '[t]he fearsome stigma of rape is too great a punishment for husbands who use their strength [to coerce their wives into sex] . . . If a husband is convicted of rape . . . the marriage is likely to be dealt a fatal blow'. He went on to query whether it was 'wise to arm [the wife] with such a powerful weapon as a charge of rape, when its use may greatly impair the happiness of both parties?'[26] Williams' comments betray an absolute blindness to the violence inherent in rape itself, as well as to all the extraneous abuse which accompanies the rape of wives and girlfriends, as well as strangers. Sue Lees' research for a 1994 *Dispatches* programme found just as much violence by present and ex-partners, husbands, friends and work colleagues, as by strangers. Among the rapes reported was one of a 17-year-old whose boyfriend hit her with a plank of wood before raping and buggering her, another of a woman whose former partner threatened to kill her, tore off her clothes and held scissors at her throat as he raped her.

The violence which women suffer in their 'private' relationships and elsewhere accounts for the most significant aspect of their potential inter-action with the criminal justice system. Much of that potential interaction does not reach the courtroom, most incidents of violence against women going unreported or, even if reported, unprosecuted (see above). When women do go to court, they are more likely to be there as victims rather than as defendants. In this they differ from men who are much more likely to experience the system as defendants. This difference has a pro-found impact on the experience that women have of entrenched rights in the criminal justice field, an area further explored in Chapter 9 below.

Women are, of course, charged with many offences similarly to, though in far smaller numbers than are, men. Inasmuch as women are defendants, they will benefit from such procedural and other safeguards as accrue to defendants generally. But one area of criminal liability which is relatively unique to women is their prosecution for using force, whether deadly or otherwise, against intimate abusers. The impact of constitutional rights on these women is considered below.

---

[25] See, for example, *State of North Carolina v Alston* 312 SE 2d 470 (1984).

[26] G Williams, 'The Problem of Domestic Rape', (1991) *New Law Journal* 205. See also *Berry* (1988) 10 Cr App R (S) 13, [1988] Crim LR 325, in which a senior judge declared of a case in which a man had kicked down the door of a former lover's home and raped her: 'this case is far from those in which, for example, a woman walking home has been set upon by a total stranger and violated . . . in some cases the violation of the person and defilement that are inevitable features where a stranger rapes a woman are not always present to the same degree when the offender and the victim had previously had a long-standing sexual relationship'. See also *Cox* (1985) 7 Cr App R (S) 422; *Stockwell* (1984) 6 Cr App R (S) 84.

The law and the battered woman killer

The first point to make about the impact of entrenched rights upon women as victims of violence is that such rights do not bind women's abusers. Women have no constitutionally protected rights not to be beaten and raped by their husbands. And, as indicated in Chapter 3, the State has, in general, no enforceable duty to prevent such abuse. In the US, as in the UK, abusive men can get out on bail after being charged with 'domestic violence' offence, and can return to their victims whether or not injunctions have been granted to forbid them from so doing. Further, the US Eighth Amendment's right to reasonable bail has the effect, save in respect of those charged with murder, that accused persons be denied bail only on the ground that they are likely to flee the jurisdiction if released.[27] In many of the cases considered below, women used fatal force against their abusers only after repeatedly seeking the protection of the police and, in a number of cases, at a time when the defendant was breaching the terms of an injunction by being in their vicinity. Recent research in the UK, too, suggests that violent men regard such injunctions with contempt even where they carry the power of arrest and subsequent imprisonment, this attitude being due at least in part, no doubt, to the willingness of the police and courts to tolerate repeated violations of such orders.[28]

Many women are subject to outrageous violence at the hands of their intimates. A small number of these women eventually kill in order to protect themselves or their children. These women have often found themselves harshly treated by the criminal justice system. Angela Browne, who conducted a large-scale study of battered women, contrasted the behaviour of police in 'immediately arrest[ing] and prosecut[ing]' those women who did eventually kill their abusers with the failure of police forces to respond to the repeated appeals which had invariably preceded such actions.[29] And, while those defendants (typically men) who kill in the heat of anger are frequently successful in pleading provocation or diminished responsibility in the UK (being convicted of manslaughter which, typically carries a term of around four years' imprisonment), women who kill abusive partners have frequently found themselves convicted of murder, this carrying a mandatory life sentence.[30]

The issue of 'battered women killers' has been very much in the public eye in the UK in recent years, the murder convictions of women such as

[27] ACLU Briefing Paper on Crime and Civil Liberties, available on the ACLU website, http://www.aclu.org.
[28] *Dispatches*, note 17 above.
[29] A Browne, *When Battered Women Kill* (New York: Free Press; London: Collier Macmillan, 1987).
[30] See A McColgan, 'In Defence of Battered Women Who Kill' (1993) 13 *Oxford Journal of Legal Studies* 508–529.

Sara Thornton and Kiranjit Ahluwalia sparking widespread dissent, high-profile campaigns and subsequent changes in the application, if not the letter, of the criminal law. The Court of Appeal has, more recently, begun to recognise as relevant to the determination both of provocation and (more usually) diminished responsibility pleas, psychiatric evidence relating to these defendants, including evidence that women might suffer from 'battered woman [wife or spouse] syndrome' (hereinafter referred to as BWS).[31]

To be convicted of voluntary manslaughter and face a likely maximum of a few years' imprisonment is, of course, far preferable to a murder conviction and a mandatory life sentence. But what the UK courts have failed, thus far, to recognise is the fact that many abused women who kill do so in circumstances where they fear, with good reason, for their lives or the lives of their children.[32] And even those strides made by the Court of Appeal under Lord Taylor CJ to fit battered women killers more comfortably within the strictures of provocation appear to be slipping since his retirement. The most recent case to reach the Court of Appeal (*Shah*, unreported, 1998) was dismissed on the grounds that the defendant's evidence of abuse at the hands of the man she killed was 'not capable of belief', this largely because she had not shown any physical signs of that abuse save for one black eye (the defendant wore traditional clothes which, in any event, covered everything but her face) and had never, nor had her doctor or any of her friends, reported the abuse to the police.[33] What the Court of Appeal failed to take into account was the intense social pressure on Shah, an illiterate and friendless immigrant, who was shunned as immoral by her own community and who killed her abuser after he turned his abusive sexual attentions to her daughters.[34]

Self-defence and the battered woman

English law affords a complete defence (self-defence or justifiable force[35]), to a defendant who uses such force as is reasonable to defend herself or another. In such circumstances the defendant must be judged on the

---

[31] See *Thornton (No 2)* [1996] 2 All ER 1023; *Hobson* [1998] 1 Cr App Rep 31; *Grainger* [1997] 1 Cr App R (S) 369. See also *Ahluwalia* [1992] 4 All ER 889, (1993) 96 Cr App R 133 and *Humphreys* [1995] 4 All ER 1008. BWS has been included in the British Classification of Mental Diseases since 1994.

[32] See McColgan, note 30 above.

[33] The appeal was not on BWS but on the grounds that evidence that the defendant suffered from a depressive illness and, accordingly, diminished responsibility, had not been heard at trial: *Independent* 1 May 1998.

[34] *Independent*, 22 February 1998.

[35] Both under common law and s 3 of the Criminal Law Act 1967, see further McColgan, note 30 above.

facts as she saw them (whether her perception of the threat was reasonable or otherwise). The question whether force was 'reasonable' is judged by reference both to whether it was 'necessary', which in turn requires consideration of the perceived imminence of the threat and the possibility of alternative action, and to whether the force used by the defendant was proportionate to the threat perceived by her. While this is an objective test, the leading case of *Palmer*[36] established that defendant's views are 'the most potent evidence' of the reasonableness of such force. Finally, although the use of force will not generally be necessary unless the threat is 'imminent', Lord Morris, in *Palmer*, stated no more than that '[i]f the moment is one of crisis for someone in imminent danger he may have to avert the danger by some instant reaction. If the attack is all over and no sort of peril remains then the employment of force may be by way of revenge or punishment or by way of paying off an old score or may be pure aggression. There may no longer be any link with a necessity of defence.'

If one is subject to an isolated threat of force, then, unless the anticipated assault is imminent in the sense of being expected almost immediately, escape will be possible and can generally be expected to be effective in the long term if accomplished in the short term. Thus, the use of force will not be necessary until the person threatened is almost pinned into a corner. Where, by contrast, the threat comes from a continuing relationship from which escape is seen to be, and may have been demonstrated to be, either impossible or highly dangerous, escape may not be an option even in the absence of an immediately expected assault. Where a woman is attacked by her partner in her home, to require her to flee from that attack is, in many cases, to require her to leave those children with her attacker. Yet frequently, it is precisely at the point when abusive men begin to pose a direct threat to their children that women feel obliged to take defensive action.

Not only may the victim of ongoing violence be unable effectively to escape, rather than to fight, an ongoing or immediately threatened attack, but this inability to escape may extend also to where the threat (express or implied) is less than immediate. The victim of ongoing violence may have to strike when the chance arises, rather than waiting until it is too late. The typical pattern of violent relationships is one in which the abuse escalates through 'cycles of violence' in which a period of mounting tension is followed by an acute battering stage after which there is a period of respite which in turn gives way to mounting tension. Women who live in these relationships often become adept at anticipating violent action, and such women may have to take steps to avert such action before it occurs. These steps might involve attacking an abuser who is asleep or drunk, but who has threatened violence on his awakening.

---

[36] [1971] AC 814, [1971] 2 WLR 831. See also *Owino* [1996] 2 Cr App R 128, [1995] Crim LR 743.

One might claim that, in the absence of an immediate threat, the woman should be obliged to leave. But such action will frequently not suffice to ensure her safety. Escape is rendered very difficult by practical issues such as the lack of adequate social welfare and low-cost housing.[37] This is increasingly the case in the US where punitive welfare cuts have, in most states, been made without regard to the needs of abused women.[38] It was mentioned, above, that up to 80 per cent of women on welfare either are presently, or have been subject to domestic violence. For those currently suffering such abuse, according to the President of the National Organization for Women, 'public assistance is an absolute lifeline', its removal 'a death sentence for tens of thousands of women and children'.[39]

Not only is escape made very difficult by the practicalities of living, but many women experience the most serious levels of violence when they leave or attempt to do so. One large German study, for example, found that in '[n]inety-nine out of 100 cases in which men beat, shot, choked, stabbed or burned their mates to death, the woman was attempting to break out of the relationship'. [40] Even without considering the possible relevance of BWS (below) it is clear that, viewed from the woman's perspective, the use of force might be the only way to escape an escalating spiral of violence which she believes will end with her death.[41]

Women who kill abusive partners frequently do so because they fear that, unless they take action, they will themselves be killed. Sometimes there appears to be a lack of 'fit' between the circumstances of these killings and those traditionally recognised as self-defence. This is particularly the case where the threat to which a battered woman claims to have responded does not appear to have been 'imminent' in the traditional sense of the word. But even where women kill when they are actually under attack, their self-defence pleas are frequently rejected, and more frequently still the defence not even attempted. Examples of such cases include that of Janet Gardner, who seized a knife from the wall behind her and fatally stabbed the man who was throttling her and beating her head against the kitchen door frame. He had regularly beaten, kicked and punched her over a period of five years, and had on one occasion attempted to slit her throat. She had tried to escape him on many

---

[37] See further McColgan, note 30 above.

[38] Welfare repeal ban replaced guaranteed federal assistance to poor parents and children with block grants to states. There is an optional amendment which permits, but does not require, states to protect domestic violence victims – of the first 26 states to implement the legislation only six included any such provision: NOW Press Release, Welfare Bill Endangers Domestic Violence Survivors, available on the NOW website at http://www.now.org.

[39] NOW Press Release, see note 39 above.

[40] *Bis der Tod Euch Scheide* EMMA, 22 January 1980, cited by S Graffe, 'Battered Women, Dead Husbands', 10 *Loyola of LA International and Comparative Law Journal* 1, note 53. See also Browne, note 29 above. In New Zealand, too, women are four times more likely to be killed when they attempt to leave abusers: *Sunday Star* (Auckland), 2 February 1997.

[41] See McColgan, note 30 above.

occasions, but each time he tracked her down and renewed his attacks upon her. The Court of Appeal, in replacing her five-year sentence for manslaughter on the ground of provocation with a two-year probation order on the basis of psychiatric evidence that she was suffering from severe depressive illness triggered by years of abuse, warned that there were 'exceptional circumstances' in the case and opined that the year she had already spent in jail was sufficient to 'expiate in some measure the guilt she must feel for the rest of her life'.[42] The question which springs to mind concerns why Janet Gardner should be expected to feel any guilt about killing in these circumstances.

The UK law of self-defence (justifiable force) appears capable of taking into account the circumstances of battered women. But what is notable is the spectacular failure of the legal system to afford self-defence even to those women who kill in the most apparently reasonable circumstances. The perceived non-application of self-defence to a battered woman who kills may result from the fact that 'reasonableness', in the context of the defence, is an unquantifiable standard. Where such standards are involved, lawyers, like triers of fact, focus on an idealised model of what is reasonable and assess the defendant's conduct against this standard. The relative scarcity of female killers has resulted in a paradigmatically male ideal model and this, together with the incompatibility of aggressive force with stereotypical femininity, means that the apparently gender-neutral concept of reasonableness is actually weighted against the female defendant.[43] This was recognised by the Supreme Court of Canada in *R v Lavallee*,[44] in which Chief Justice Dickson accepted that expert evidence would be admissible to counter the commonly held beliefs that: 'battered women are not really beaten as badly as they claim, otherwise they would have left the relationship [and] . . . that women enjoy being beaten, that they have a masochistic strain in them'.

'Self-defence' and constitutional rights: an introduction to the US

In order to consider whether constitutionally entrenched rights (such as, for example, a right to equal treatment, or a right not to be discriminated against) might assist the cause of women prosecuted for killing violent partners it is useful to look to the position in the US. The Supreme Court of Canada has considered two such cases since the implementation of Canada's Charter of Rights, and these decisions are considered

---

[42] *Gardner (Janet Susan)* (1993) 14 Cr App R (S) 364, *Independent*, 30 October 1992.
[43] See McColgan, note 30 above.
[44] [1990] 1 SCR 852.

below. But they were reached other than on constitutional grounds, and are far outnumbered by the case law from the US.

Turning to the US, first impressions are not promising. Not only are women who take action against extremely violent partners regularly convicted of murder, some such women are subject to, and convicted under, capital murder charges (although executions of women remain very rare). During the 1980s and early 1990s, a third or more of the women under death sentence were guilty of killing men who had 'victimised them with years of violent abuse'[45]. And the blindness which apparently pervades the English legal system and prevents its actors from perceiving self-defence where women kill to protect their own lives and/or those of their children extends also to the US. In *Bonner v State of Alabama*,[46] for example, a jury convicted of manslaughter a woman who, having been abused for years by her husband, shot at by him and attacked on the night she killed him, 'started blocking his assault and then grabbed a knife and stabbed' him (internal citations omitted). And in *People v Humphrey*[47] the defendant was convicted of manslaughter when she shot her husband after an episode during which he beat her, threatened to kill her, shot at her and missed, and beat her again.

Both men in these cases had already shown that they were prepared to kill their partners. Both women were under physical attack at the point at which they killed. It is hard to imagine what alternative they had to the use of force. And if it were the case that jurors felt that the level of force employed by them was disproportionate to the threat confronting them, such a perception of proportionality appears to miss the point that even an unarmed attack on a woman can easily result in her death, particularly where that attack consists of throttling or beating her head against a wall.[48]

The difficulties experienced by women in these circumstances were recognised by Canada's Supreme Court in *Lavallee*[49] and, to some extent, by Washington's Supreme Court in *State of Washington v Wanrow*.[50] In *Lavallee* the Supreme Court allowed the admission of expert evidence to counter the myths associated with battered women and to explain 'the ability of an accused to perceive danger from her partner', which ability could impact on 'whether she "reasonably apprehended" death or grievous bodily harm on a particular occasion'. In *Wanrow*, Washington's State Supreme Court accepted that any instruction limiting self-defence to the use of equal force denied women defendants the equal protection of the law. The trial judge had rejected the defendant's self-defence plea because

---

[45] ACLU Press Release, 3 February 1998, available on the ACLU website, note 27 above.
[46] (1998) Ala Crim App LEXIS 42.
[47] 13 Cal 4th 1073, 921 P 2d 1 (1996).
[48] *Gardner (Janet Susan)*, note 42 above, and *Bonner v State of Alabama*, note 46 above, respectively.
[49] Note 44 above.
[50] 88 Wash 2d 221 (1977).

she had used a gun against an unarmed man. She was five foot four inches tall and had one leg in plaster. The man she killed was over six foot tall. According to the court, the trial judge's demand that the defendant should have repelled her attacker 'without employing weapons in her defence, unless the jury finds her determination of the degree of danger to be objectively reasonable – constitutes a separate and distinct misstatement of the law and, in the context of this case, violates the respondent's right to equal protection of the law'.[51]

The decision in *Wanrow* was significant in the US in its application of the Equal Protection Clause to women who kill their abusers. But the decision did not mark the beginning of any comprehensive application of the principle of self-defence to battered women who kill, much less to any accepted view that the Equal Protection Clause of the Fourteenth Amendment mandated such a practice.

In the US, criminal law is dealt with at the level of the state rather than federally, but many states share similar approaches to self-defence as to other areas of the criminal law. Generally, defendants can only succeed in pleading self-defence if their use of force was reasonable in response to an imminent danger which either existed or which the defendant reasonably perceived to exist. Where the perception of imminent danger is unreasonable, some states allow a plea of imperfect self-defence which has the effect of reducing homicide liability from murder to manslaughter.[52] What is notable about the approach typically adopted in the US is its insistence on imminence and its tendency to impose on defendants a duty to retreat. This latter is frequently waived where a defendant uses force in his or her own home, but the waiver generally only applies where the force is used against an intruder, as distinct from a cohabitee.[53] As far as the imminence requirement is concerned, self-defence is typically rejected in the US unless the threat against which force was used was (or was reasonably perceived to be) 'almost immediately forthcoming'.[54] Typical of the US courts' approach is the decision of Alaska's Court of Appeals in *Xi Van Ha v State of Alaska*,[55] in which the court was at pains to distinguish ' "inevitable" harm from "imminent" harm'. Although the case did not concern a battered woman, the court expressly declared that the same approach would apply to killings by battered women:

---

[51] *Ibid*, at 240.

[52] Evidence of BWS is also used to establish a subjective (albeit not reasonable) belief in the existence of imminent danger where such a belief suffices to establish imperfect self-defence for the purposes of mitigating a murder conviction to one of manslaughter: see *People v Aris*, note 21 above.

[53] See *State of Ohio v Thomas* (1995) Ohio App LEXIS 3244, Ohio CA.

[54] *Xi Van Ha v State of Alaska* 892 P 2d 184 (1995) Court of Appeals of Alaska, discussed below.

[55] *Ibid*. The denial of the defence in cases in which the court accepted that 'killing was motivated by fear and that the fear was as real and as urgent at the time of the killing as it was when the husband was awake and actually capable of immediate physical abuse' can only be regarded as bizarre.

[t]ypically, these cases involve a battered wife who kills her husband in his sleep. Although in such instances there is commonly ample evidence to support a finding that the killing was motivated by fear and that the fear was as real and as urgent at the time of the killing as it was when the husband was awake and actually capable of immediate physical abuse, cases have uniformly refused to apply self-defence to this category of crime. The basis of the refusal has been lack of an immediate threat of harm.[56]

US courts appear to accept that the requirement for imminence could be relaxed in a situation, such as that described by LaFave and Scott where a kidnapping victim 'is informed that he will be killed at the end of the week and whose best opportunity to escape this fate is to kill his kidnapper early in the week. Under such circumstances, "the proper inquiry is not the immediacy of the threat but the immediacy of the response necessary in defence. If a threatened harm is such that it cannot be avoided if the intended victim waits until the last moment, the principle of self-defence must permit him to act earlier – as early as is required to defend himself effectively" '.[57] But they have not been prepared to apply this reasoning by analogy in cases where battered women are threatened with death if they attempt to leave, demanding instead that the woman acted under 'a threat of great bodily injury or death contemporaneously with the killing', 'a demonstration of immediate intention' to injure or kill on the part of the abuser.[58] A number of US jurisdictions have accepted that a self-defence instruction might be given where a person kills a sleeping abuser.[59] But more common is the approach of Alaska's Court of Appeals in *Xi*, applied by the Court of Appeal of California in *Aris*,[60] North Carolina in *State v Norman*[61] and Kansas in *State v Stewart*.[62]

Finally, the US approach to self-defence is harder to satisfy than that in the UK in its assessment of reasonableness. Whereas, in the UK, the objective test is modified to the extent that the defendant's honest and instinctive perception that force was reasonable (ie both necessary and proportionate) is the 'most potent evidence' that it was (objectively) reasonable (see discussion of *Palmer* above), the most generous approach which the US applies is that adopted by Washington's Supreme Court in *Wanrow*, ie whether the use of force was (objectively) reasonable for a person *in the defendant's circumstances*, rather than for another 'reasonable'

[56] W LaFave and A Scott, *Criminal Law* (St Paul, Minnesota: West Publishing Co, 1986) at 5.7(d), vol 1, p 656.

[57] *State of Arizona v Buggs* 167 Ariz 333, 806 P 2d 1381 (1991).

[58] *People v Yaklich* and *People v Aris*, both note 21 above.

[59] *State of New Mexico v Gallegos* 719 P 2d 1268 (1986); *State of Washington v Allery* 682 P 2d 312 (1984); *State of North Dakota v Leidholm* 334 NW 2d 811 (1983), *State of Minnesota v Hennum* 441 NW 2d 793 (1989) (Minnesota).

[60] *People v Aris*, note 21 above.

[61] 324 NC 253, 378 SE 2d 8 (1989).

[62] 243 Kan 639, 763 P 2d 572, 378 SE 2d 8 (1988). See also *Hernandez v State of Kansas* 253 Kan 705, 861 P 2d 814 (1993); *Brooks v State of Alabama* 630 So 2d 160 (1993); *People v Scoggins* 37 Cal 676 (1869).

person faced with a similar threat (real or perceived). In many US states the law on self-defence is less favourable to the defendant, a complete acquittal turning on whether his or her use of force was (objectively) reasonable (ie necessary and proportionate) on the facts as she or he reasonably perceived them to be.[63] Even where the subjective–objective approach to reasonableness is adopted, women's self-defence claims may founder on the imminence requirement which in many US states stands as a separate element of 'self-defence' and is consistently interpreted very narrowly indeed.[64]

Battered woman syndrome: the way forward?

Early US theorists such as Elizabeth Schneider argued that evidence of the psychological effects of repeated assaults could be utilised, together with lay evidence about the history of defendant and deceased, in order to combat the prejudice inherent in the traditionally male model of self-defence, to 'equalise the positions of male and female defendants by recognising their differences' and to allow the question of reasonableness to be assessed in the light of all the circumstances relevant to the defendant.[65]

The impact upon women of repeated domestic violence has been well documented, and generally goes under the title of BWS. It is generally accepted that the 'cycle of violence', mentioned above, commonly induces in women subject to it a state of 'learned helplessness' whereby, partly as a result of the violence itself, partly due to the practical or other constraints upon leaving (fear of reprisals, the perception that her children need a father, or that she is responsible for the abuse and could, by behaving differently, prevent it), 'the battered woman lives with constant fear, coupled with a perceived inability to escape. Eventually, she comes to believe that her only options are enduring the abuse, striking back, or committing suicide'.[66]

The approach advocated by Schneider has, in the main, been followed in the US and defence lawyers typically attempt to introduce evidence that battered women who kill were suffering from BWS. Such evidence can be used to 'explain how a battered woman reacts to the batterer [and] to explain the reasonableness of the battered woman's perception that danger or great bodily harm is imminent'. Evidence of the 'hypervigilance . . .

---

[63] See also *Foreshaw v Commissioner of Correction* 48 Conn App 122 (1998), *State of Kansas v Stewart ibid.*

[64] See, for example, *State v Leidholm* 334 NW 2d 811 (1983).

[65] E Schneider, 'Equal Rights to Trial for Women: Sex Bias in the Law of Self-defense (1980) 15 *Harvard Civil Rights–Civil Liberties Law Review* 623.

[66] *Tourlakis v Morris* 738 F Supp 1128 (1990), US District Court for the Southern district of Ohio.

generated by the cycles of abuse'[67] which mark violent relationships can help to explain why a woman perceived a threat as 'imminent' 'in spite of the fact that her battering partner was passive at the time of the offence[68] "the battered woman's familiarity with her husband's violence may enable her to recognize the subtle signs that usually precede a severe beating"'.[69]

Far from going merely to establish an honest belief in the imminence of an attack, evidence of BWS could help to establish that such a belief was reasonable to the extent that, in the US, it should found a complete defence: 'a battered woman may . . . be "better able to predict the likely degree of violence in any particular battering incident" and in turn may more precisely assess the measure and speed of force necessary to resist'.[70] This has been accepted also by Canada's Supreme Court in *Lavallee*[71] and in *Malott*,[72] although in the latter case the defence was rejected by the court.

Evidence of BWS can be used, in addition, 'to rebut the prosecution's inference that the defendant could have left rather than kill the spouse'.[73] The characteristic of 'learned helplessness', mentioned above, is sometimes used to draw an analogy between the battered woman and 'a hostage or a prisoner of war'.[74] Such evidence may also be used to bolster a woman's credibility in a situation where the prosecution claims that her failure to leave 'the allegedly abusive relationship' should be taken to infer that she did not fear her husband or where she has recanted previous inculpatory statements about an abusive spouse.[75] It may also be used to refute prosecution claims that the 'defendant masochistically enjoyed the beatings her ex-husband had given her'.[76]

By 1990, the appellate courts of 20 states and the District of Columbia had ruled evidence of BWS admissible on a plea of self-defence. And within two years, more than half as many states again had accepted it as relevant (either on the facts before them or in principle).[77] The general approach and growing trend is towards greater admissibility of BWS evidence across the US. But the approach taken by US courts tends to exclude it in those cases where it is most necessary to establish the elements

---

[67] *People v Humphrey*, note 47 above.
[68] *Tourlakis v Morris*, note 66 above.
[69] *People v Humphrey*, note 47 above. See also *US v Marenghi* 893 F Supp 85 (1995) for an extensive discussion of BWS.
[70] *People v Aris*, note 21 above.
[71] Note 44 above.
[72] [1998] 1 SCR 123.
[73] *People of the State of Michigan v Wilson* 487 NW 2d 822, at 824, cited in *Marenghi*, note 69 above. See also *United States v Johnson* 956 F 2d 894, *Bonner v State of Alabama*, note 46 above. Cf *United States v Willis* 38 F 3d 170.
[74] *United States v Brown* 891 F Supp 1501 (1995); *State of Kansas v Hundley* 693 P 2d 475, at 479 (1985), Kansas.
[75] *Bonner v State*, note 46 above; *Arcoren v US* 929 F 2d 1235 (1991), 8th Ct; *People of the State of New York v Ellis* 650 NYS 2d 503, at 509 (1996).
[76] *People of the State of New York v Powell* 102 Mich 2d 775 (1980). Cf *State of Ohio v Thomas*, note 53 above.
[77] *Bechtel v State of Oklahoma* 840 P 2d 1 (1992).

of self-defence. Courts are generally ready to accept evidence of BWS where it appears that a woman reasonably perceived a threat of almost immediate harm even independent of that evidence.[78] But where the threat to which the woman reacted is imperceptible without consideration of the history of abuse, evidence of BWS or even of that history is often excluded on the ground that the defendant has not established the threshold conditions of self-defence.

The particular problem which many battered women experience in pleading self-defence relates to the rigid legal requirements commonly imposed in relation to the defence (see above). Far from functioning as a stepping stone towards establishing the requirements properly interpreted – for example, by helping to establish a subjective belief (whether reasonable or unreasonable) in an imminent (in the sense of·being practically inescapable) threat – many courts exclude evidence of BWS on the basis that the woman has failed to bring herself within those requirements.[79] Other courts permit the introduction of BWS evidence but refuse jury instructions on self-defence where the facts do not fit within the traditional pattern.[80] And in a number of cases the US courts have gone further than excluding evidence of BWS or refusing to direct juries on self-defence, and have actually refused even to admit evidence of the violence directed by the deceased against the defendant on the grounds that, no objective immediate threat having existed, the evidence was not relevant to the defendant's guilt.[81]

The limitations imposed in the US upon admitting evidence of BWS and, more generally, on pleading self-defence, are such that BWS evidence may not serve to assist defendants in those cases in which it is introduced. The courts are quick to point out that BWS does not itself stand as a defence. The question is, rather, whether the defendant qualifies for self-defence or some other complete or partial defence. Evidence of BWS may be helpful in encouraging jurors to overcome their stereotypical notions about battered women – why they do not leave, the extent of violence they suffer, etc. But the very real danger is that the introduction of BWS may serve mainly to provide another hurdle between the battered woman and acquittal: not only does she have to establish the elements of self-defence in the ordinary way, but she then has to show, in addition, that she is properly regarded as a victim of BWS.

Madams Justice L'Heureux-Dubé and McLachlin, of Canada's Supreme Court, warned of the dangers of this approach in *Malott*:[82]

---

[78] Examples of the type of case in which the courts regard BWS evidence as admissible include *State of Ohio v Koss* 49 Ohio St 3d 213 (1990); *People v Humphrey*, note 47 above; *State of Missouri v Williams* 787 SW 2d 308 (1990); *People v Gams* 52 Cal App 4th 147 (1997).
[79] See also *Anderson v Goeke* 44 F 3d 675 (1995).
[80] See also *US v Greyeyes ibid*; *US v Homick* 964 F 2d 899 (1992).
[81] *US v Greyeyes ibid*; *Lumpkin v Ray* 977 F 2d 508 (1992).
[82] Note 72 above.

It is possible that those women who are unable to fit themselves within the stereotype of a victimized, passive, helpless, dependent, battered woman will not have their claims to self-defence fairly decided. For instance, women who have demonstrated too much strength or initiative, women of colour, women who are professionals, or women who might have fought back against their abusers on previous occasions, should not be penalized for failing to accord with the stereotypical image of the archetypal battered woman . . . women with these characteristics are still entitled . . . to have their experiences as battered women inform the analysis.

But the US courts have been less sensitive to the dangers of stereotyping. In *People v Erickson*,[83] for example, the defendant killed a partner who raped her repeatedly, had threatened to kill her 'a good two dozen times' over an eight-month period prior to the killing and, on the night of the killing, had threatened that 'he would kill her if she tried to move out . . . grabbed [her] by the hair and forced her to orally copulate him . . . pushed [her] into her bedroom [and] . . . told her that he would find and kill her if she tried leaving that night'. Her expert witnesses testified that she suffered from BWS, but were not permitted to give evidence about her perception of danger on the night of the killing. The prosecution expert testified that 'that appellant displayed many aspects of [BWS], while she did not display other important aspects of it' and concluded from this that 'there would be nothing to cause a battered woman [who displayed such inconsistencies with the classic symptoms of BWS] to believe that they were [sic] in imminent danger of loss of life had they [sic] stayed in that batter-ing relationship.' Erickson was convicted of first degree murder and sentenced to 26 years to life imprisonment. In *Rice v State of Nevada*,[84] too, the court appeared dubious about the defendant's status as a 'victim' of 'BWS' on the grounds that she, rather than her abuser, was the primary earner.

The result of the typical approach to BWS and, more broadly, to self-defence is that '[i]n 1991, approximately 75% of cases using expert testi-mony on battered spouse syndrome involved situations where the killing occurred during a confrontation'.[85] In such cases, as was discussed above, the evidence can help to dispel popular myths about battered women and to establish the honesty of their perception of threat and, in some jurisdictions, the reasonableness of their response to it. One might ask why it is necessary for psychiatric evidence to be introduced in cases where any adequate consideration of the facts and background would establish the probability that a woman reasonably believed her life to be in real danger. But the apparent hostility of jurors to battered women who kill,

---

[83] 57 Cal App 4th 1391 (1997).
[84] 113 Nev 1300; 949 P 2d 262 (1997), Supreme Court of Nevada. See also *US v Whitetail* 92 Md App 422 (1992); *State of Maine v Anaya* 456 A 2d 1255, Me LEXIS 605 (1983), Supreme Judicial Court of Maine.
[85] H Maguigan, 'Battered Women and Self-defense' (1991) 140 *University of Pennsylvania Law Review* 379, at 396–397.

the difficulty which jurors appear to have in understanding the violence to which such women have been repeatedly subject, appears to render such evidence necessary in many cases.[86]

Another significant danger, which can arise when evidence of BWS is admitted, is that the defendant who is permitted to introduce such evidence may be subjected to a court-ordered psychological or psychiatric evaluation in order that the prosecution can attempt to rebut her claim to suffer from this syndrome. This not only has the potential to distract jurors away from the threat perceived by the woman and the reasonableness, in context, of her response to it, but it also subjects the defendant to examination by the state in the absence of her lawyer, something generally regarded as inconsistent with the defendant's rights against self-incrimination.[87]

Finally, reliance upon BWS seems to invite the courts to declare 'open day' upon the defendant and to permit the introduction of any and all evidence of bad character relating to her. One example of this was seen in *Anderson v Goeke*,[88] in which case all manner of evidence of the defendant's sexual activities was introduced, and its admission defended by the Eighth Circuit Court of Appeals, on the dubious grounds that it went to motive to kill her husband. In *US v July*,[89] too, evidence was introduced of a number of incidents, three years before the killing, in which violence had occurred between the defendant and the deceased. The court accepted these incidents as relevant on the basis that they tended to prove that 'planning, criminal intent and [the defendant's] lack of fear of her husband, all of which were relevant to the issues of premeditation and lack of self-defense' – this despite 'the highly disputed aspect of the testimony [as to] who was the aggressor in the incidents.' Nor was the court concerned by the three-year lapse between the alleged incidents and the killing at issue: because 'the prior acts are disputes between defendant and her husband, some of which involved defendant's use of a knife [this being the weapon with which she killed her husband] . . . the incidents were not too remote'. This decision must be contrasted with that in *US v Shepard*,[90] in which the Eighth Circuit Court of Appeals refused to accept the relevance, on a plea of self-defence, of evidence that the defendant's husband had been abusive some three years prior to the killing.

[86] See also *Burton v Johnson* 948 F 2d 1150 (1991) and case of Kay Weekly discussed in E Gleick, 'No Way Out', *Time*, 23 December 1996.

[87] *Hess v Macaskill* (1995) US App LEXIS 27699; *State of New Jersey v Myers* 570 A 2d 1260, 604 A 2d 598 (1990); *State of Florida v Hickson* 630 So 2d 172, at 176 (1993); *State of New Hampshire v Briand* 547 A 2d 235 (1988); *People of the State of New York v Rossakis* 159 Misc 2d 611, 605 NYS 2d 825 (1993); and *US v July* (1992) US App LEXIS 6394. Cf *US v Williams* 163 FRD 249 (1995); *People v Powell*, note 76 above.

[88] Note 79 above.

[89] (1992) US App LEXIS 6394.

[90] (1995) US App LEXIS 35931. See also *US v Agurs* 127 US 97 (1976) – contrast with *US v Whitetail*, note 84 above.

Self-defence and the Constitution

The extent to which entrenched rights have been of assistance to women who have killed in order to defend themselves from further, possibly life-threatening, violence at the hands of abusive spouses requires considera-tion. A number of constitutional issues might arise. First and foremost, perhaps, any commitment to sex equality would require that women who kill in circumstances in which their use of force is reasonably necessary are given access to the same defence as men who kill in similar circum-stances. It has been pointed out, above, that the situations in which women find themselves the victims of physical (including sexual) violence typic-ally involve intimates, frequently cohabitees. By contrast, men tend to be attacked by strangers or acquaintances. The violence that men suffer tends to be unexpected, whereas that experienced by women is frequently anticipated by its victims in circumstances under which they perceive, whether correctly or not, that they cannot effectively escape it. To the extent that rigid adherence to the 'imminence' requirement, or a formal approach to 'proportionality' prevents such access, an equality-based approach would require the revision of those tests. The former was achieved by Canada's Supreme Court in *Lavallee*,[91] though on the basis of common law, rather than Charter, principles. The latter was accepted by Washington's Supreme Court in *Wanrow*.[92]

Equal treatment or 'protection' is not the only constitutionally relevant argument which could arise in this area. A defendant who is denied access to the evidence necessary to build her defence could resort to a claim under the Due Process Clauses of the Fifth and Fourteenth Amendments (applicable to the federal and state governments respectively) or under the fair trial rights guaranteed by the Sixth Amendment ('the right to a speedy and public trial, by an impartial jury . . . to be confronted with the witnesses against him . . . and to have the Assistance of Counsel for his defence). Sometimes the challenge is based on court rulings. On other occasions, as in *State of Ohio v Fink*,[93] the appellant claims that failure of the defence lawyer to raise a defence deprived the defendant of the ef-fective assistance of counsel guaranteed under the Due Process and Com-pulsory Process Clauses of the Fifth, Sixth and Fourteenth Amendments.

Constitutional claims have not, in general, been of much assistance to battered women who have killed abusive partners. Taking first the Equal Protection Clause of the Fourteenth Amendment, the real problem which arises here is the non-application of that clause to indirect discrimina-tion. Despite the decision of Washington's Supreme Court in *Wanrow* that

---

[91] Note 44 above.
[92] Note 50 above. Not until 1994 did the Supreme Court, in *JEB v State of Alabama* (Case no 92–1239, 1994), recognise that gender-based peremptory challenges to jurors breached the Due Process Clause of the Fourteenth Amendment.
[93] (1995) Ohio App LEXIS 3169.

to demand unarmed resistance alone against a much larger assailant 'constitutes a separate and distinct misstatement of the law and . . . violates the respondent's right to equal protection of the law', the more common approach to Equal Protection Clause arguments was that taken by the Ninth Circuit Court of Appeals in *United States v Wilson*.[94]

The defendant had stabbed her husband in the context of a physical fight and was convicted of involuntary manslaughter and assault with a dangerous weapon (it is common practice in the US automatically to increase the penalty for use of a weapon). She argued that the increase to her sentence which automatically followed from her use of a weapon offended the Equal Protection Clause of the Fourteenth Amendment because 'women need to resort to the use of a weapon to defend themselves against men, but men can inflict the same deadly force against women without resort to a weapon'. The Court of Appeals rejected this argument because, '[t]o demonstrate that a gender-neutral statute unconstitutionally discriminates against women, the challenger must show both adverse impact and invidious intent'.[95] This approach to 'discrimination' under the Fourteenth Amendment is precisely that set out by the Supreme Court and discussed in Chapter 3 above.

The repercussions of the narrow approach to 'discrimination' taken under the Equal Protection Clause can be seen in the decision of North Dakota's Supreme Court in *State of North Dakota Leidholm*.[96] There the defendant argued that North Dakota's imposition of a 'duty to retreat' upon those attacked in their own homes by cohabitants but not by others violated *inter alia* the Equal Protection Clause of the Fourteenth Amendment. The defendant's argument was interpreted by the court to be that 'making an individual's duty to retreat from his dwelling dependent upon the status of the assailant unduly discriminates against the accused if the attacker is a cohabitant', an argument which the court baldly dismissed as having 'no merit'. To a UK lawyer, the argument which should have been made is that the uneven application of the 'duty to retreat' rule impacted disproportionately upon women, who are more likely to be subject to life-threatening force by a cohabitant. Such a claim would have no chance of success, however, as an Equal Protection Claim must rest on an allegation of direct or deliberate discrimination.

Another failed Equal Protection Clause argument can be seen in *Lumpkin v Ray*,[97] in which the defendant claimed that Oklahoma's denial of her ability to argue self-defence, by virtue of its rigid imminence requirement, breached that clause. The defendant argued that she was part of a discrete group of individuals (those affected by BWS) who were disadvantaged by the imminence requirement which, she argued, should

[94]   (1993) US App LEXIS 4584.
[95]   *Personnel Admin v Feeney* 442 US 256, at 273–274 (1979).
[96]   334 NW 2d 811 (1983).
[97]   Note 82 above.

rather be understood to 'limit self defense to circumstances in which the defendant has no alternative to prevent the threatened harm but to use violence'. The defendant argued that the 'cyclical trap of the "battered woman syndrome" sets the battered woman apart from others who have the financial and other resources and support, including reasonable access to police and courts, to supplement their smaller physical size and lack of ability to defend themselves [and that] the "battered woman" should have an opportunity to show the jury that her actions were based on a subjectively reasonable apprehension of imminent bodily harm and therefore at least excusable if not justifiable'. Her claim failed because 'she did not offer at trial evidence on the existence or characteristics of the discrete group of women suffering from "battered woman syndrome". In addition, her arguments on post-conviction appeal were inconsistent as to whether the basis of her equal protection claim was that the Oklahoma self defense statute discriminated against her because she was a woman or because she was a battered woman'.

Given the constraints of the Equal Protection Clause, it is small wonder that the majority of constitutional claims made by battered women have employed different arguments. It should be pointed out here that the vast majority of cases in which the courts have accepted that BWS evidence should have been admitted by the trial judge have turned, not on constitutional arguments, but on the evidential laws of the states concerned. In *Tourlakis v Morris*,[98] for example, Ohio's District Court was able to trace only two cases in which constitutional arguments had been dealt with by the courts at all. In neither of these were such arguments successful. The court rejected the argument that exclusion of BWS evidence was inconsistent with the due process rights under the Fifth, Sixth and Fourteenth Amendments. Despite the State Supreme Court's acceptance of such evidence as admissible between the date of the defendant's trial and that of her appeal, the District Court noted that 'courts are generally granted far more discretion in determining the admissibility of expert testimony than of fact testimony'[99] and ruled that Ohio's previous exclusionary rule was not unconstitutionally arbitrary.[100]

In *Dunn v Roberts*,[101] the defendant did succeed in a due process challenge to the trial court's exclusion of expert evidence. The woman, who was convicted of being an accessory to a number of murders on the basis of nothing more than her presence at the time of the killings, had pleaded a lack of *mens rea* (here, an intention to encourage) on the grounds that she was unwillingly in the company of the killer. Although she had initially voluntarily accompanied the man, her attempts to leave him after

---

[98] Note 66 above.
[99] *Fennell v Goolsby* 630 F Supp 460 (1985).
[100] *State of Ohio v Thomas* 66 Ohio St 2d, at 521–522, 423 NE 2d at 140 (1981), reversed in *State v Koss*, note 79 above.
[101] 963 F 2d 308 (1992).

she learned of his character were thwarted by his threats 'to which he testified' to her and her family if she left. The defendant's initial appeal was rejected by the Supreme Court of Kansas on the grounds that her plea amounted in law to one of compulsion (duress), which defence could not be established 'unless she made a threshold showing that the compulsion was continuous and that there was no reasonable opportunity to escape the compulsion without committing the crime', there having been, in that court's view, numerous opportunities for her escape. The result of this was that the expert evidence was deemed irrelevant to the very issue which it could have gone to prove. The Circuit Court did not decide the case on the issue of compulsion, although it did disagree with the Supreme Court's findings of fact on that issue. Instead, it took the view that, the defendant having made a threshold showing that her mental condition at the time of the offence was likely to be a 'significant factor' at the trial, the court's refusal to appoint a psychiatric expert amounted to a denial of due process.

What was perhaps odd in this case is that a jury would need to be instructed on BWS in order, as the Circuit Court put it: 'why [she] remained with [the killer] despite repeated abuse'. The defendant had been convicted on the basis that an intention to assist the killer could be inferred from the defendant's mere presence, and the nature of the threats to the defendant and her family, should she have attempted to leave the killer, were undisputed. The reason she remained with the killer was because, with good reason, she was too frightened to leave. Yet such, apparently, is the level of hostility towards abused women that, in the view of the appellate court (and this view was presumably accurate, as a jury had convicted her and a judge, initially, sentenced her to 60 years' imprisonment), psychiatric evidence was necessary in order to explain 'why a battered woman is psychologically unable to leave the battering relationship and why she lives in high anxiety of fear of the batterer'.

Dunn does stand as a case in which constitutional guarantees assisted the defendant. But the Due Process Clause does not guarantee that a woman will be afforded justice any more than do the ordinary evidential rules. In *State of Arizona v Mott*,[102] for example, the defendant's due process argument that evidence of BWS should have been admitted to disprove her capacity to form the intent required on a charge of child murder was rejected by the state's Supreme Court (she had failed to protect the child from her abusive partner). The dissenting judge took the view that the defendant's due process rights were infringed by the refusal to admit evidence of BWS.

With regard to the constitutionality of court-ordered psychiatric evaluations, the courts have not been ready, in general, to accept that such evaluations, even in the absence of defendants' lawyers, breach defendants'

---

[102] 931 P 2d 1046 (1997).

Fifth and Sixth Amendment rights against self-incrimination and to counsel. In *Hess v Macaskill*,[103] for example, the US Ninth Circuit Court of Appeals rejected an application for *habeas corpus* based on such an evaluation on the ground that the defendant having put her mental state at issue, no Fifth Amendment breach had occurred despite the fact that she was not advised of her Miranda rights during this evaluation.[104] In addition, because counsel was available to her during breaks from the evaluation, the court did not accept that any Sixth Amendment breach had occurred.[105]

Indeed, the constitutionally guaranteed rights of accused persons do not extend even to requiring that the State disprove self-defence. In a number of states the burden of proving self-defence is on the defence. The Supreme Court refused to scrutinise this rule in *Moran v State of Ohio*[106] a case which, incidentally, involved a battered woman killer. The defendant, who had been 'repeatedly beaten and brutalized' by her husband, choked, hit with a gun, kicked and knocked onto the floor; eventually killed him after an episode during which he had threatened to 'blow [her] damn brains out' when he woke up from having a nap if she did not at that point give him money which he mistakenly thought she possessed. Not having the money, she unsuccessfully sought help and then, 'realizing that she had no way of raising the necessary funds', shot her husband with his own gun. She was convicted of murder in the face of her claim that she had acted in self-defence and suffered from BWS. The jury had been instructed that she had to prove the elements of self-defence 'by a preponderance of the evidence'.

The defendant in *Moran* claimed that the Due Process Clause prohibited her conviction for murder in a case in which 'the jury that convicted her may well have thought it as likely as not that she acted in self-defense'. The majority of the Supreme Court evidently disagreed, Justices Brennan and Marshall dissenting on the grounds that the petition raised a 'substantial constitutional issue . . . a question that this Court has labeled as "colorable" and "plausible" in previous decisions and that has for years divided state courts and lower federal courts'. The dissenters noted that, '[a]lthough traditional self-defense theory may seem to fit the situation only imperfectly, the battered woman's syndrome as a self-defense theory has gained increasing support over recent years' (citations omitted). The dissenting judges noted that the Supreme Court had interpreted the Due Process Clause to require that a defendant be convicted only 'upon proof beyond a reasonable doubt of every fact necessary to constitute the crime with which he is charged'[107] and that the court had, in particular, ruled

---

[103] Note 87 above.
[104] *Hendricks v Vasquez* 974 F 2d 1099 (1992).
[105] Citing *Buchanan v State of Kentucky* 483 US 424 (1987).
[106] 469 US 948 (1984).
[107] *Re Winship* 397 US 358, at 364 (1970).

that the imposition of the burden of proof upon a defendant to establish provocation was 'constitutionally infirm under the Due Process Clause'.[108]

Conclusion: entrenched rights and women as victims of violence

Women who have been the victims of domestic violence have gained little from the rights entrenched in the US Constitution. In the first place, as was pointed out above and in Chapter 3, such rights do not bind the private abusers of women. Nor do they require that the State take action against those abusers. Finally, when women who have themselves taken action have been subject to criminal prosecution, neither the Fourteenth and Fifth Amendment rights to equal protection and to due process, nor the various fair trial rights guaranteed by the Sixth Amendment, have addressed the shortcomings of the criminal law. Not only have such rights failed to alter the stereotypes in order that cases where women kill to protect their lives are recognised as potential cases of self-defence, but even where discriminatory aspects of the law (such as the rigid imminence requirement, or automatically increased penalties for use of a weapon) have been directly challenged, these challenges have for the most part failed.

Some of the shortcomings evident in the US could be addressed by constitutional rights drawn along different lines. It is apparent from the preceding pages, for example, that one of the main reasons for the defeat of constitutional claims lies in the narrow approach taken to discrimination under the Equal Protection Clause. Were the US Constitution to embrace a more expansive equality requirement, that Supreme Court might, like its Canadian counterpart (see the discussion of *Lavallee* above), demand that self-defence be interpreted so as to capture the particular situations in which women, as distinct from men, kill to save their own lives. More generally, however, the difficulties faced by women in the US, as in the UK, are rooted in the attitudes of lawyers, judges and jurors to women who kill. The English Court of Appeal in *Shah* simply did not believe that a woman beaten and raped over a period of years would remain silent about her treatment. The US jury in *Dunn* chose to believe that a woman who was unwillingly in the company of a murderer, whose life and the lives of her family were under threat if she left him, nevertheless intended by her mere presence to encourage him to kill. It is difficult to see what 'rights', however framed and however safeguarded, can achieve against this hostility.

The efficacy of entrenched rights for women subject to violence is considered further in Chapter 9 below, which deals with the potential of those

---

[108] *Mullaney v Wilbur* 421 US 684 (1975). Cf *Patterson v State of New York* 432 US 197 (1977).

rights to improve the position of victims of violence. This chapter has concentrated mainly on the position in the US. Chapter 9 looks, for the most part, at Canada where the implementation of the Charter of Rights has unleashed a torrent of attacks on legislative efforts made over the years to ameliorate the appalling manner in which women who complained of sexual assault were treated at common law. That chapter, read together with this, gives a fuller account of how entrenched rights can impact on women who are victims of violence.

Chapter 9

Victimising Victims

Introduction: women and rape

The prevalence of violence against women was considered in Chapter 8. In this chapter the issue of sexual violence and the potential impact of constitutional rights on the victims of such violence is specifically addressed.

Sexual violence is part and parcel of many women's lives. Diane Russell's 1978 survey indicated that one in four women in the US had been raped, and that three in ten had suffered an attempted rape.[1] Dean Kilpatrick's survey, carried out a few years later, also showed a one-in-four rape rate.[2] And in London in 1982, Women Against Rape found that one woman in every six had been raped, and that a further one in five had suffered an attempt.[3] One in seven married women had been raped by their husbands (at the time this was not a crime and none of these rapes was reported). In Canada, too, between 20 per cent and 50 per cent of women and children are estimated to fall victim to sexual offences in their lifetimes' and 'prosecution and conviction rates for sexual assault are among the lowest for all violent crimes'.[4] According to Justice Cory in *R v Osolin*[5] (discussed below), '99 per cent of the offenders in sexual assault cases are men and 90 per cent of the victims are women' and, as Madam Justice L'Heureux-Dubé declared in *R v Seaboyer*[6] (discussed below), '[p]erhaps more than any other crime, the fear and constant reality of sexual assault affects how women conduct their lives and how they define their relationship with the larger society'.

Accurate statistics are elusive, most rapes and other episodes of private violence going unreported and crime surveys frequently failing to show

---

[1] D Russell, *Sexual Exploitation: Rape, Child Sexual Abuse and Workplace Harassment* (Beverly Hills: Sage, 1984).

[2] D Kilpatrick *et al*, 'Criminal Victimisation: Lifetime Prevalence, Reporting to Police, and Psychological Impact' (1987) 33 *Crime and Delinquency* 479.

[3] R Hall, *Ask Any Woman: London Inquiry into Rape and Sexual Assault* (Bristol, Falling Down Press, 1985).

[4] Madam Justice L'Heureux-Dubé in *Seaboyer* [1991] 2 SCR 577.

[5] [1993] 4 SCR 595.

[6] Note 4 above.

the true picture. Probably only around 10 per cent of women who are raped in the UK, the US, and Canada report the crime to the police (some estimate as low as 3 per cent[7]), and those which are least likely to be reported are those committed by men known to their victims. Many surveys fail to ensure that the respondent is alone and comfortably out of earshot of a possible abuser or of children, or do not adequately define the offences in respect of which questions are asked (with the effect, for example, that women raped by their husbands may not know that any offence was committed).[8] One 'reverse check' study of women who had already reported rape to the police found that half of those raped by men they knew failed to mention this in a later survey even when asked specifically about rape.[9]

Few women report rape. Fewer still see their attackers prosecuted, much less convicted. In the UK, studies suggest that almost half of all complaints of rape and attempted rape are not recorded by the police as crimes (this despite Home Office guidelines requiring that all complaints be recorded unless the woman withdraws the allegation and accepts that it had been false).[10] Even where alleged rapes are recorded by the police, the majority (more than 60 per cent in 1988–90) are not passed to the Crown Prosecution Service (CPS) for prosecution. And of those cases which are passed on, an increasing proportion are not prosecuted (30 per cent in 1995, up from 10 per cent in 1985).[11] CPS practice explains in part the decline in the conviction rate for reported rapes – down from 24 per cent in 1985 to 10 per cent by 1995, with the effect that the number of men convicted of rape has remained constant despite a tripling of reported offences in that period.[12]

Rape and constitutional rights

It was pointed out in Chapter 8 above that entrenched rights give women neither the right not to be abused by their husbands nor the right to be

---

[7] M Torrey, 'When Will We Be Believed? Rape Myths and the Idea of a Fair Trial in Rape Prosecutions' (1991) 24 *University of California, Davis Law Review* 1013, p 1019.

[8] M Koss *et al*, 'The Underdetection of Rape: Methodological Choices Influence Incidence Estimates' (1992) 48(1) *Journal of Social Issues* 61, p 65; testimony of K Rodgers, Executive Director of NOW, to the Senate Judiciary Committee on the Violence Against Women Act 1994, *Federal News Service*, 15 May 1996.

[9] L Curtis, 'Past and Present Measures of Victimization in Forcible Rape', in M Walker and S Brodsky (eds), *Sexual Assault: the Victim and the Rapist* (Lexington DC, Heath, 1976).

[10] G Gregory and S Lees, *Rape and Sexual Assault: A Study of Attrition* (London, Islington Council, 1993); L Smith, *Concerns About Rape* (London HMSO, 1989), Home Office Research Study Series 106.

[11] *Guardian*, 9 March 1995. For the US see T McCahill *et al*, *The Aftermath of Rape* (Lexington Massachusetts, Lexington Books, 1979).

[12] Natasha Walter, *Observer*, 18 January 1998; *Guardian*, 11 November 1997; *Daily Telegraph*, 18 July 1997.

protected by the State from such abuse. The same is true in respect of rape. In this context, the main impact of constitutional rights consists in their role in the criminal prosecution of women's abusers.

Canada's Charter of Rights – the early cases

The most significant developments in this area have arisen in Canada under the Charter of Rights. The Charter's impact has been felt both in terms of the substantive law and also in the regulation of sexual assault trials. The legislature has, since 1983, taken considerable steps to improve the position of sexual assault complainants, encourage reporting and eradicate discrimination from the law[13] (these included an overhaul of the substantive provisions; the enactment of 'rape shield' provisions to restrict the admissibility of complainants' sexual history evidence after judicial misapplication of previous provisions which had left considerable discretion to the judge; and the redefinition of 'consent' to require 'voluntary agreement'[14]). But the implementation of the Charter heralded a sustained assault on these provisions by defendants, the media and the judiciary alike. The only losers, it appears, have been those who would complain of sexual victimisation.

According to an early study on the Charter, men mounted three times as many sex equality-related Charter challenges during the first three years of the operation of s 15. Half of these challenges were in the criminal law context and most of these consisted of challenges to the Criminal Code's sexual offence provisions.[15] The first of these were directed at those which created offences of sexual intercourse with girls under the age of 14, prohibited the indecent assault of women, protected vulnerable girls against sexual interference by their powerful authority figures and which prevented newspapers from naming sexual assault complainants.[16] On four occasions within the first three years of the Charter these challenges resulted in legislation being struck down by the courts, although in at least two of these cases the original decisions were reversed on appeal on the basis that s 15 had not come into force at the time the charges were laid.[17]

The first sexual assault-related Charter case to reach the Supreme Court concerned a legislative prohibition against naming sexual assault

---

[13] Madam Justice L'Heureux-Dubé in *Seaboyer*, note 4 above, citing Jean Chrétien, then Minister of Justice and Attorney General of Canada.

[14] Canada Criminal Code, ss 271–273 and 276–277. The misapplication of the previous sexual history evidence provisions (in particular, *Forsythe v The Queen* [1980] 2 SCR 268) is discussed by Madam Justice L'Heureux-Dubé in *Seaboyer*, note 4 above. The 1982 reform package also included amendments to the corroboration and recent complaint doctrines and to wife rape and anonymity for complainants.

[15] See also G Brodsky and S Day, *Canadian Charter Equality Rights For Women: One Step Forward or Two Steps Back?* (Ontario: Canadian Advisory Council on the Status of Women, 1989), p 58.

[16] Canada Criminal Code, ss 146, 149 and 153. See Brodsky and Day, *ibid*, pp 58–59.

[17] *Lucac and Neely* (1986) 27 CCC (3d) 229; *Ferguson* (1987) 16 BCLR (2d) 273; and *Poirier* (1985) 69 NBR (2d) 1. See generally Brodsky and Day, note 15 above.

complainants. In *Canadian Newspapers Co v Canada (Attorney General)*,[18] newspaper proprietors argued that the ban infringed press freedom and violated s 2(b) of the Charter. Ontario's Court of Appeal agreed and struck down the mandatory aspect of the publication ban while permitting judges to impose a discretionary ban. But the Supreme Court reversed the decision and held that, although the mandatory ban did infringe s 2(b), the interests it served (encouraging reporting by preventing widespread publication, embarrassment and humiliation) rendered it a reasonable limit on press freedom. In particular, these interests would be subverted rather than served by a discretionary ban, so the mandatory ban went no further than was necessary to encourage the reporting of rape. As to the newspaper's arguments that the ban infringed the rights of falsely accused defendants by preventing others also falsely accused from coming forward to give evidence against lying complainants, the Supreme Court ruled that the issue did not arise in this case where the Charter challenge was not made by or on behalf of a defendant.

The outcome in *Canadian Newspapers* was favourable to sexual assault complainants. But the threat posed by the Charter, that it could be used to attack legislative provisions designed to ameliorate the appalling difficulties experienced by women who complain of rape, was evident from that case. The Supreme Court in that case left open the possibility that defendants might successfully challenge the publication ban at issue there. And the first successful Supreme Court challenge to Canada's sexual assault provisions came two years later in *R v Hess and Nguyen*,[19] which involved Canada's 'statutory rape' provisions.

In *Hess*, the defendants relied upon ss 7 and 15 of the Charter to challenge their convictions on charges of having sexual intercourse with a girl under the age of 14 in breach of s 146(1) of Canada's Criminal Code. The Supreme Court, by a majority, ruled that the Criminal Code breached s 7 of the Charter by denying a defence to those who mistook the age of the girl concerned, although Madam Justice McLachlin, dissenting as to the result, took the view that the breach was saved under s 1 (see Chapter 3 above) because girls alone were vulnerable to pregnancy, and the infringement went no farther than was reasonably necessary to achieve the State's objectives: 'one must . . . remember that all that a person need do to avoid the risk of [conviction] . . . is to refrain from having sex with girls of less than adult age unless he knows for certain that they are over fourteen'.

Sexual history evidence and the Charter of Rights

The next significant decision relating to Canada's sexual offences laws came in 1991 in *Seaboyer*,[20] in which the Supreme Court struck down one

---

[18] [1988] 2 SCR 122.
[19] [1990] 2 SCR 906.
[20] Note 4 above.

of the 'rape shield' provisions mentioned above. That provision (s 276 of the Criminal Code) prohibited the introduction of evidence relating to the sexual activity of complainants with persons other than the accused save where it rebutted sexual history evidence introduced by the prosecution, related to specific instances of sexual activity which tended to establish the identity of the person whose sexual activity with the complainant formed the subject matter of the charge or related to sexual activity which took place on the same occasion as that forming the subject matter of the charge, 'where that evidence relates to the consent that the accused alleges he believed was given by the complainant'. Section 277, which provided that 'evidence of sexual reputation, whether general or specific, is not admissible for the purpose of challenging or supporting the credibility of the complainant', was upheld.

The majority decision, which was written by Justice McLachlin, was greeted with 'an almost visceral revulsion' by many women's organisations.[21] The Supreme Court struck down s 276 on the ground that it breached the defendants' rights under ss 7 and 11(d) of the Charter to a fair trial.[22] While s 277 was accepted as excluding only a pattern of reasoning that was 'today universally discredited' (ie that 'a complainant's credibility might be affected by whether she has had other sexual experience'), s 276 had 'the potential to exclude evidence which is relevant to the defence and whose probative value is not substantially outweighed by the potential prejudices to the trial process'.

The majority was concerned by s 276's failure to distinguish between 'the different purposes for which evidence may be tendered' and took the view that its blanket exclusion of sexual history evidence, subject to the narrow exceptions, went further than was required to prevent what the majority saw as the evil against which that section was directed: 'the misuse of evidence of sexual activity for irrelevant and misleading purposes – the inference that the complainant consented to the act or that she is an unreliable witness'. The majority took the view that '[i]n exchange for the elimination of the possibility that the judge and jury may draw illegitimate inferences from the evidence [the section] exacts as a price the real risk that an innocent person may be convicted'.

Having found that s 276 breached ss 7 and 11(d) of the Charter, Justice McLachlin rejected the argument that it was saved under s 1 of the Charter. Although the legislation addressed a 'pressing and substantial objective' by helping 'to exclude unhelpful and potentially misleading

---

[21] S Fine, 'The Most Important Woman in Canada: Supreme Court Judge Beverley McLachlin' (1995) 110 (10) *Saturday Night* 46. See also E Fulton, 'Rape and the Court', *Maclean's*, 2 September 1991.

[22] These provide, respectively, that '[e]veryone has the right to life, liberty and security of the person and the right not to be deprived thereof except in accordance with the principles of fundamental justice', and that '[a]ny person charged with an offence has the right . . . to be presumed innocent until proven guilty according to law in a fair and public hearing by an independent and impartial tribunal'.

evidence of the complainant's prior sexual conduct . . . the rights infringed are not proportionate to the pressing objective' because s 276: 'excludes relevant defence evidence whose value is not clearly outweighed by the danger it presents' and failed to 'balance . . . the objective and the injurious effect of the legislation. [The] provision . . . strikes the wrong balance between the rights of complainants and the rights of the accused'.

The Supreme Court struck down s 276, replacing it with guidelines which stated *inter alia* that evidence of the complainant's sexual history was not admissible 'solely to support the inference that the complainant is by reason of such conduct . . . more likely to have consented to the sexual conduct at issue on the trial; or . . . less worthy of belief', but that such evidence 'may be admissible for purposes other than an inference relating to the consent or credibility of the complainant where it possesses probative value on an issue in the trial and where that probative value is not substantially outweighed by the danger of unfair prejudice flowing from the evidence'. Where such evidence was admitted, 'the judge should warn the jury against inferring from the evidence of the conduct itself, either that the complainant might have consented to the act alleged, or that the complainant is less worthy of credit'.

The reasoning of the majority in *Seaboyer* has been considered in depth elsewhere.[23] Here it is sufficient to point out that, despite Madam Justice McLachlin's repeated assertions that the sexual conduct of complainants was relevant neither to their credibility nor, in general terms, to the likelihood of their consent, a number of the situations in which the majority regarded sexual history evidence as potentially relevant relied in part upon these very 'outmoded and illegitimate notions' concerning credibility and consent. It was its acceptance of such evidence as relevant that resulted in the majority's conclusion that s 276 breached ss 7 and 11(d) of the Charter. Further, by characterising the balance to be struck under s 1 in this case as one 'between the state and the accused', rather than one between the interests of sexual assault complainants (themselves historically and to the present day a disadvantaged group) and those of their alleged assailants, the majority failed to pay much more than lip-service to what Madam Justice L'Heureux-Dubé, dissenting, acknowledged as the appalling difficulties faced by the victims of sexual assault, many of whom do not report the offences committed against them because of 'their perception that the institutions with which they would have to become involved will view their victimization in a stereotypical and biased fashion'.

Madam Justice McLachlin, for the majority, characterised the purpose behind ss 276 and 277 of the Criminal Code as 'the avoidance of unprobative and misleading evidence, the encouraging of reporting and

---

[23] A McColgan, 'The Relevance of Sexual History Evidence' (1996) 16 *Oxford Journal of Legal Studies* 275.

the protection of the security and privacy of the witnesses'. Significantly, she omitted reference to the declared intention of the legislature, by means of a larger reform package which included ss 276 and 277, to eliminate sex discrimination in criminal law. By confining her concern to the blatant misuse of sexual history evidence (which misuse she asserted could be prevented by appropriate judicial screenings and warnings); by concentrating on the latter two perceived purposes of the legislation (which could readily be sacrificed to the greater interest in avoiding wrongful convictions); and by using the past tense when describing the use of sexual history evidence by defence lawyers to discredit complainants and to characterise them as unworthy of protection against sexual assault, Madam Justice McLachlin could readily find s 276 inconsistent with the defendant's Charter rights. By contrast, Madam Justice L'Heureux-Dubé concluded that 'rape mythology' (including the notions that 'women . . . are good or they are bad . . . madonnas or . . . whores', that they are 'fickle and full of spite', that a woman's 'sexual behavior . . . is under the surveillance . . . [so] if a woman says she was raped it must be because she consented to sex that she was not supposed to have', and that 'females fantasize rape') was still operative in the criminal justice system with the effect that women who allege rape are denied a fair opportunity to see their attackers convicted.

Madam Justice L'Heureux-Dubé disputed the assertion of the majority that s 276 was directed primarily at 'encouraging . . . reporting and the protection of the security and privacy of the witnesses' of sexual assault. Rather, the provisions were in part an attempt to 'to eliminate sexual discrimination in the trials of sexual offences through the elimination of irrelevant and/or prejudicial sexual history evidence', one objective of which was to increase the reporting of sexual assaults. According to Madam Justice L'Heureux-Dubé, the very notions of relevance upon which the challenge to s 276 relied were 'informed by stereotype and myth' and that 'any semblance of relevance "play[s] upon internalized assumptions about what women really want and male desires for specific sexual scenarios"'.[24] '[S]exual history evidence preempts considered decision making. . . . The guilt or innocence determination is transformed into an assessment of whether or not the complainant should be protected by the law of sexual assault'. On this reasoning, 'sections [276 and 277] ensure that the ordinary rules of evidence are applied'.

The majority were apparently satisfied with the enlightened nature of Canada's criminal justice system in the 1990s. But as recently as 1985, the Supreme Court of the NorthWest Territories had declared that 'unchastity' was 'logically probative of consent . . . not conclusive, of course, but logically probative', the judge simultaneously accepting that 'our test for

---

[24] Citing E Sheehy, 'Canadian Judges and the Law of Rape: Should the Charter Insulate Bias?' (1989) 21 *Ottowa Law Review* 151.

judicial truth . . . may . . . show . . . rank prejudice; but we use it'.[25] Madam Justice L'Heureux-Dubé pointed out the 'perversity' of the suggestion that 'an objective application of the law of evidence mandates the admission of evidence which exhibits "rank prejudice"'.

In *Seaboyer* Madam Justice McLachlin, for the majority, expressed the view that cases in which the complainant's sexual history evidence would carry sufficient probative value to be properly admissible would be 'exceptional' and that '[t]he fishing expeditions which unfortunately did occur in the past should not be permitted'. Yet in *Osolin* (below), she found herself in the minority and protesting that the cross-examination which the majority in the latter case ruled should have been permitted was excluded by the earlier decision. (The majority chose to interpret *Seaboyer* to the effect that it precluded *only* that sexual history evidence which relied *solely* upon 'groundless myths and fantasized stereotypes'.)

Not only has the admissibility of evidence been stretched beyond that permitted in *Seaboyer* but, since that decision, sexual assault complainants have found themselves under intensifying attack with 'increasingly common attempts to undo publication bans on the complainant's name . . . Defence counsel and accused are revisiting old stories and stereotypes to bolster their challenges both inside courtrooms and to the media . . . the right to full answer and defence is said to necessitate not just making public, but actively publicizing the complainant's identity'.[26]

Charter rights and personal records

The other very damaging issue which has arisen in the wake of *Seaboyer* concerns complainants' medical and counselling records. The first case where this came before the Supreme Court was *Osolin*[27] in which the defence applied to cross-examine a complainant on mental health records which had previously been admitted into evidence on the issue of her competence to testify. The complainant, who had been receiving psychiatric treatment for depression and anxiety, testified that she had been assaulted by a number of men after they had kidnapped her from a trailer where she had had intercourse with another man. The defendant claimed that she had consented to sex with him and appealed his conviction on the grounds that the trial judge had refused cross-examination on the complainant's medical records to show 'what kind of person the complainant is'.

The Supreme Court, by a majority, ordered a retrial on the basis that the judge had erred in refusing cross-examination of the complainant on

---

[25] Citing Justice Marshall in *Oquataq* (1985) 18 CCC (3d) 440, at 450.
[26] J Gilmour, 'Counselling Records: Disclosure in Sexual Assault Cases', in J Cameron (ed), *The Charter's Impact on the Criminal Justice System* (Scarborough, Ontario: Carswell, 1996), p 239, at 240.
[27] Note 5 above.

her medical records. Despite the fact that the defendant's asserted reason for cross-examination on the records was not proper, 'it was the trial judge's duty to ensure that the accused's rights with regard to cross-examination were protected'. Madam Justice McLachlin relied upon her own (majority) judgment in *Seaboyer* to rule that the cross-examination was properly refused.

The dissenters took the view that, where the defence sought to cross-examine on the complainant's sexual history, 'the trial judge must determine whether the defence has demonstrated a potential relevance to the cross-examination capable of outweighing the damage and invasion of privacy it might cause to the complainant'. This, in turn, required that 'the trial judge must ensure that the evidence is tendered for a legitimate purpose, and that it logically supports a defence. Here, the only purpose invoked by the defence for cross-examining the complainant on her medical records was the very sort of improper purpose for which evidence cannot be adduced'. The dissenters did not accept that the trial judge had a duty 'to ensure that all legitimate grounds of cross-examination are explored by counsel', much less to direct cross-examination for purposes which contradicted the arguments relied upon by the defence (as here). Madam Justice McLachlin pointed out that the imposition of any such duty would extend to requiring that, if necessary, the judge either direct counsel to cross-examine or do so her or himself; thereby respectively 'usurp[ing] the right of counsel (and impliedly the accused) to conduct the case as they see fit' and being drawn into the role of counsel. Either course of action was 'inconsistent with the [adversarial] nature of our trial process [and the neutrality of the judge] and would confuse and complicate the prosecution of criminal offences unduly'. Further, 'judicial intervention may harm the case for the defence. Defence counsel may have good reason for leaving untouched an area of cross-examination which may seem to be a fertile ground for exploration to a trial judge who lacks the opportunities available to counsel of exploring and considering the implications of raising the issue'.[28]

In any event, the reasons for which the majority viewed cross-examination on the complainant's medical records as relevant would not, on the facts, have merited this course of action, there being ample other evidence of the difficult relationship between the complainant and her parents (this being put forward as a motive to fabricate) and the defendant's claim of mistaken belief in consent being, as Madam Justice McLachlin pointed out, entirely unsupported by the evidence: '[a]ny man who drags a woman from her home naked and protesting, transports her to a remote place, and there ties her to the bed and has sex with her is at the very least put on notice that she may not be consenting. His failure to inquire is consistent only with . . . an intention to have his way without consent or

---

[28] Citing *Yuill v Yuill* [1945] 1 All ER 183, CA.

wilful blindness as to whether she consented or not'. Madam Justice L'Heureux-Dubé and Justice La Forest joined the dissent on the additional grounds that the medical evidence should not have been admitted in the first place, there being no serious grounds for doubting the complainant's competence to testify.

Access to medical and counselling records is increasingly being sought by defendants in sexual assault trials. This practice is part of what has been described as the 'unprecedented expansion in the scope and sources of what is now claimed to be "necessary" to defend a charge of sexual assault',[29] not least because of the removal of the 'implied consent' defence by the post-*Seaboyer* legislative provisions (see below). According to one Canadian lawyer: 'In terms of past sexual history and credibility, it's all about getting through the back door what they can't get in the front door'.[30]

Much of this expansion has been made possible by the decision in *R v Stinchcombe*,[31] in which the Supreme Court ruled that the Crown was under an obligation to disclose all relevant evidence to the defence in criminal trials, whether or not the Crown relied upon the evidence. This obligation was derived from the accused's right to make full answer and defence under s 7 of the Charter. Post-*Stinchcombe*, defence lawyers have begun increasingly to demand 'access to records from the complainants' past on the basis that they are necessary to enable the accused . . . to exercise his right to make full answer and defence'.[32] The Supreme Court has acknowledged the importance of privacy as an interest protected by the Charter.[33] But where the medical or similar records are those of the complainant in a sexual assault case, this 'broad and independent value' appears to be easily trumped by the rights of the accused.

The first significant decision concerning counselling records was *Ross*,[34] in which Nova Scotia's Court of Appeal allowed an appeal from a man convicted of sexual assault after the complainant's psychiatrist had come forward with evidence which he regarded as relevant to the man's guilt. The psychiatrist had suggested that 'the complainant's testimony could really be wrong even though she believed it to be true'. A disciplinary hearing against him subsequently ruled that the psychiatrist formulated the diagnosis upon which he based his concerns about a possible miscarriage

---

[29] Gilmour, note 26 above. Despite the striking-down of the rape shield provisions in that case, and the horror with which it was greeted by many women's organisations, the wide publicity which surrounded the case and the resulting legislative action served to highlight the discreditable nature of many assumptions which might previously have escaped attention.

[30] Susan Bazilli, quoted in *Chatelaine*, October 1997, p 74.

[31] [1991] 3 SCR 326.

[32] Gilmour, note 26 above.

[33] Madam Justice L'Heureux-Dubé in *Osolin*, note 5 above, citing *Dyment* [1988] 2 SCR 417; *Beare* [1988] 2 SCR 387; *Pohoretsky* [1987] 1 SCR 945 and *Hunter v Southam Inc* [1984] 2 SCR 145.

[34] (1993) 81 CCC 3d 234.

of justice 'without adequate clinical justification'; and that he 'lacked skill and knowledge with respect to the practice of psychiatry'. In the event, no jury heard the medical evidence because, prior to the retrial, Ross pleaded guilty to that and another sexual assault after the Crown was given leave to introduce evidence of very similar offences by him against other women.[35]

The admissibility of counselling records came before the Supreme Court in *R v O'Connor*[36] in which that court, by a majority, ruled that the complainant had no privacy interest in counselling and medical records already disclosed to the prosecution and that *Stinchcombe* applied in full to these records. Further, relevance to the defence 'must be presumed where the records are in the Crown's possession'. And even where records were in third party hands, the Supreme Court was unanimous in holding that disclosure could be ordered. Five of the judges did not address the basis for such disclosure, while Madam Justice L'Heureux-Dubé stated that the right to disclosure existed as an 'adjunct of the right to make full answer and defence'.[37]

A plurality of the Supreme Court held, in *O'Connor*, that the onus in such a case was on the accused to set out the specific grounds upon which production was sought and 'to satisfy a judge that the information is likely to be relevant'.[38] As to the meaning of 'relevance', at the application stage the accused had only to show that 'the information may be useful to the defence'. It should be stressed at this point that this test was to be applied only to records which were not already in the hands of the prosecution, those which the prosecution had regarded as potentially relevant enough to obtain being automatically considered relevant also to the defence. Despite this, the Supreme Court was at pains to emphasise that this 'likely relevance' test 'should not be interpreted as an onerous burden upon the accused' but existed merely 'to prevent the defence from engaging in speculative, fanciful, disruptive, unmeritorious, obstructive and time-consuming requests for production'.

The approach of the Canadian Supreme Court in *O'Connor* can be contrasted with that of a number of US state courts. In both *Commonwealth v Fuller* and in *Commonwealth v Tripolone*,[39] for example, the Supreme Court of Massachusetts ruled that a defendant seeking access to private

---

[35] *MT v Nova Scotia College of Physicians and Surgeons* (1996) 69 CPR (3rd) 340.

[36] [1995] 4 SCR 411.

[37] See also *Carosella* [1997] 1 SCR 80, below. The same five judges ruled that 'although there would appear to be no government action which would trigger the *Charter*'s application [in a case concerning privately held records] . . . the *Charter* is engaged by the fact of the prosecution itself. Where the Crown pursues a prosecution which would result in an unfair trial, this constitutes state action for the purposes of the *Charter*'.

[38] '[I]n the interests of justice' the requirement for a formal application for disclosure should be waived.

[39] *Commonwealth of Massachusetts v Fuller* 423 Mass 216, NE 2d 847 (1996); *Commonwealth of Massachusetts v Tripolone* 425 Mass 487, 681 NE 2d 1216 (1997). See also *People of the State of New York v Elmore*, NY Sup Ct, reported *New York Law Journal*, 1 July 1997.

records in this type of context must demonstrate a 'good faith, specific, and reasonable basis for believing that the records will contain exculpatory evidence which is relevant and material to the issue of the defendant's guilt' (the cases followed contempt orders against a rape crisis and a domestic violence centre respectively for refusal to hand over counselling records for inspection by the court). These cases dealt with records in respect of which respectively, absolute and qualified privilege had been granted by statute, subject to exceptions in criminal cases to the extent that 'information contained therein . . . is exculpatory to the defendant', the existence of such information to be determined by a judge. Without the standard adopted, the Supreme Court of Massachusetts was concerned that there would be 'virtually automatic *in camera* inspection for an entire class of extremely private and sensitive privileged material'.[40] Particularly given the absence, in *O'Connor*, of any statutory provision for disclosure, there is no reason why a similar approach could not have been taken in that case in light of the complainants' acknowledged privacy interests.

According to the Supreme Court in *O'Connor*, if 'likely relevance' was established an order for disclosure should be made and the material examined by the judge who should order production to the defence if 'satisfied that there is a reasonable possibility that the information is logically probative to an issue at trial or the competence of a witness to testify'. The Supreme Court in *O'Connor* stated that the judge should have regard, in deciding whether or not to order disclosure, to 'the extent to which the record is necessary for the accused to make full answer and defence . . . the probative value of the record . . . the nature and extent of the reasonable expectation of privacy vested in the record . . . whether production of the record would be premised upon any discriminatory belief or bias; and . . . the potential prejudice to the complainant's dignity, privacy or security of the person that would be occasioned by production of the record'. But, lest this be thought to suggest any reluctance to permit disclosure, the court went on to remark that '[a]s for society's interest in the reporting of sexual crimes, there are other avenues available to the judge to ensure that production does not frustrate the societal interests that may be implicated by the production of the records to the defence'.

The procedure adopted by the Supreme Court in *O'Connor* renders the production of personal records to the court, if not to the defence itself, virtually automatic.[41] Such an approach simply sweeps aside any claim to protection for sexual assault complainants. Sexual assault is extremely traumatic for its victims and women experience tremendous difficulties in reporting it. The psychological harm done by sexual assault, and

[40] *Tripolone*, note 39 above.
[41] *Chatelaine*, October 1997, reports that 'Before the *O'Connor* case, judges ruled that records should be released in about half the cases where the defence requested them. After *O'Connor*, experts say that rulings shifted even more firmly in favor of the defence'.

the potential for further distress associated with the prosecution of such crimes, means that the provision of adequate counselling and support services for its victims is imperative. As the Massachusetts Supreme Court recognised in *Fuller*: 'the privilege [accorded to counselling records] . . . encourages victims of the brutal and degrading crime of rape to seek professional assistance to alleviate the psychological scarring caused by the crime, which may be more damaging than the physical invasion itself . . . To deal with these problems, the rape victim must have complete confidence and trust in the counsellor who hears the victim's disclosures'.[42]

Canada's Supreme Court itself has recognised, albeit perhaps more in the breach than the observance, that confidentiality is necessary to the provision of such counselling, that records of such counselling may detail '"intensely private aspects" of the complainant's personal life, and describe thoughts and feelings "which have never even been shared with the closest of friends or family"'.[43] Despite all this, confidentiality is almost automatically sacrificed in any sexual assault case in which the defendant chooses to go after the complainant's records.

Disclosure to the defence may well not be ordered by the judge, and even if such disclosure is ordered, the records may not ultimately be accepted as admissible in the trial itself. But as Madam Justice L'Heureux-Dubé recognised in her dissenting judgment in *Osolin*, the damage may already have been done: '[i]t is often imperative that privacy interests be respected at the point of disclosure if they are to be protected at all, as they often cannot be vindicated after the intrusion has already occurred'.[44] And whether or not disclosure is ordered in any particular case, no sexual assault complainant can ever speak in confidence to a counsellor. It is overwhelmingly likely, as a result of this, that less women will come forward for counselling. Less will complain of rape and fewer rapists will be prosecuted. Indeed, early indications show substantial declines in reporting 'once women realized their records could be subpoenaed. Others found themselves forced to choose between counselling or pressing charges'.[45]

By contrast with the very low burden which the majority in *O'Connor* placed on the accused at the initial disclosure stage (see above) Madam Justice L'Heureux-Dubé, who dissented on this issue, demanded that the accused rely on more than 'a bare, unsupported assertion' that the records might impact on 'recent complaint', on 'the kind of person the witness is', on her credibility 'at large', the possibility of a prior inconsistent

---

[42] Note 39 above at 220–222 (1996).
[43] *Per* Chief Justice Lamer in *O'Connor*, note 36 above.
[44] Note 5 above, cited by Gilmour, note 26 above, p 244.
[45] *Chatelaine*, October 1997, reports a survey carried out by the University of Manitoba's Karen Busby at one rape crisis centre at which: 'the number of clients reporting to police dropped from 30 percent to less than 10 percent'.

statement or an allegation of past sexual abuse (internal citations omitted). According to Madam Justice L'Heureux-Dubé, the accused 'must... provide some basis to show that there is likely to be information in the impugned records which would relate to the complainant's credibility on a particular, material issue at trial ... Such requests, without more, are indicative of the very type of fishing expedition that this Court has previously rejected in other contexts'.[46]

The significance of this difference in approach can be seen in the contrasting views of Chief Justice Lamer and Madam Justice L'Heureux-Dubé on the proportion of cases in which 'likely relevance' would be established: whereas the latter stated that records would rarely be relevant: 'the vast majority of information noted during therapy sessions bears no relevance whatsoever or, at its highest, only an attenuated sense of relevance to the issues at trial', Chief Justice Lamer disagreed, basing this conclusion in part on the 'sheer number of decisions in which such evidence has been produced'. (The application of this reasoning to sexual history evidence would, of course, suggest that such evidence must invariably be relevant.)

In *O'Connor*[47] the Supreme Court rejected an application from the defendant that charges against him should be dismissed because of the prosecution's failure fully to disclose all evidence sought by him[48] and in *A (LL) v B (A)*,[49] the Supreme Court's decision which was issued simultaneously with that in *O'Connor*, the court granted an appeal against disclosure on the ground that the proper procedure for ordering such disclosure had not been followed. But the full impact of these decisions and, in particular, of the approach taken by the majority in *O'Connor* to the initial burden on the accused to establish 'likely relevance', was felt in *R v Carosella*,[50] in which the Supreme Court reinstated a stay in proceedings against a man charged with sexual assault.

The defendant had been charged after a complaint by a woman who alleged that he had abused her some 30 years before as a teacher at her school. The complaint had been lodged after the woman visited a sexual assault crisis centre for advice on how to take action against the alleged abuser. She had been interviewed by a social worker for some two hours, and notes taken by the interviewer. Before the defendant's trial an order

---

[46] Note 5 above, at 618, citing Supreme Court and other authorities.
[47] Note 36 above.
[48] Access was refused by the prosecutor who 'couldn't credit what [the defense] was asking for'. No prosecutor had, prior to that trial, 'ever been ordered by the bench to force complainants in a sexual-assault case to authorize release of their lifelong medical records': L Birnie, 'Sins of the Father' (1994) 109(1) *Saturday Night* 32.
[49] [1995] 4 SCR 536.
[50] Note 37 above. See *Chatelaine*, October 1997, for public mischief charges brought against one complainant who, faced with the refusal of Crown Counsel to drop charges, claimed that she had made up her allegation of rape in order to avoid disclosure of counselling records dealing with childhood abuse.

was made, to which both complainant and prosecution consented, for production of those notes. By this point, the notes had been destroyed in accordance with the centre's policy of shredding files relating to cases in which the police became involved.

The trial judge granted the defendant's application for a stay of the proceedings on the ground that the destruction of the notes 'had seriously prejudiced the accused by depriving him of the opportunity to cross-examine the complainant as to her previous statements relating to the allegations she made'. Accordingly, 'the accused's Charter right to make full answer and defence had been breached'. The Supreme Court upheld this order, overruling the decision of British Columbia's Court of Appeal that 'the evidence must disclose something more than a "mere risk" to a Charter right and that in this case no realistic appraisal of the probable effect of the lost notes could support the conclusion that the accused's right to make full answer and defence was compromised' by the destruction of the notes.

According to the Supreme Court: '[a]n accused who alleges a breach of his right to make full answer and defence as a result of non-disclosure or non-production is not required to show that the conduct of his defence was prejudiced'. Even if *O'Connor* rather than *Stinchcombe*[51] was applied (the material never having been in the prosecution's hands), the defendant only had to show a 'reasonable possibility that the information is logically probative to an issue at trial'. The complainant herself had agreed to disclosure of the record, with the result that the second *O'Connor* requirement did not apply, there being no privacy right to balance against the accused's right to disclosure. A stay of proceedings was, in the view of the majority, the only appropriate remedy given that 'irreparable prejudice would be caused to the integrity of the judicial system if the prosecution were continued'.

The decision of the majority in this case was extraordinary. The centre was under no obligation to maintain records. Nor was there anything to suggest that the records contained anything of relevance. The claim for production rested on the bare assertion that the records might contain an inconsistent statement by the complainant: something which Madam Justice L'Heureux-Dubé characterised as the very kind of 'fishing expedition' which her test in *O'Connor* had been designed to exclude.

It was pointed out at the time of the trial judge's order in *Carosella* that the remedy chosen by him was 'startling'. Generally, stays of prosecution are granted only in the 'clearest of cases where the prejudice suffered [by the accused] is irreparable' (internal citations omitted). Further, as Diane Martin pointed out of the original decision: '[t]here was the implicit assumption in the ruling that there is a diminished state interest in cases of sexual assault which results in their treatment by the courts

---

[51] Note 31 above.

as not much more than glorified private tort actions – complainant and Sexual Abuse Centre versus the accused/defendant'.[52] In the event of procedural misconduct by these private actors the State, apparently, loses any interest in the action. Despite this, the majority of the Supreme Court upheld the order for a stay on the ground that '[t]he entitlement of an accused person to production either from the Crown or third parties is a [freestanding] constitutional right . . . [b]reach [of which] . . . entitles the accused person to a remedy under . . . the *Charter*'.

Drawing on cases involving abuse by Crown agents themselves, the majority in *Carosella* cited Supreme Court *dicta* to the effect that 'it is crucial that, at the stage where it is being determined whether an accused's . . . rights were in fact violated, courts not engage in speculation as to whether or not the lack of or lapse in interpretation in a specific instance made any difference to the outcome of the case'. In applying this *dicta*, the majority distanced itself from the statement of Madam Justice L'Heureux-Dubé in *O'Connor* that 'the right of an accused to full disclosure . . . is an adjunct of the right to make full answer and defence [and] . . . not itself a constitutionally protected right' and ruled that the accused had only to bear the 'less than onerous' burden of establishing 'likely relevance' within the plurality test in *O'Connor*. This test having been satisfied by the judge's finding that 'the notes . . . related to alleged sexual incidents in the trial and, therefore, are relevant and material and would more likely than not tend to assist the accused' (a conclusion for which no reason was offered[53]), this discretion had been properly exercised in ordering a stay of proceedings on the basis of his finding that 'the accused had been seriously prejudiced, being deprived of the basic right of the opportunity to cross-examine the complainant on previous statements made by her as to the very incidents of sexual misconduct . . . which are the subject matter of the indictment'.

The majority in *Carosella* took the view that, because the records at issue had been destroyed by 'an agency that not only receives public money but whose activities are scrutinized by the provincial government', '[c]onfidence in the [judicial] system would be undermined' if a stay of proceedings was refused. But the sexual assault centre concerned in the case was not, under any test, an agency bound by the Charter. The centre's funding arrangements did require it to 'develop a close liaison with local health, justice and social service agencies', as was pointed out by the majority. But the centre was under no obligation to make, much less to retain, records of its interviews with sexual assault complainants. Further, as was pointed out at the time of the original stay of prosecution, the effect

---

[52] D Martin, 'Rising Expectations: Slippery Slope or New Horizon?', in J Cameron (ed), note 26 above, p 116. This assumption is not unique to the Supreme Court. Until 1995 in Alabama, rape complainants (alone of all alleged victims) had to pay the cost of their own medical examinations: *Orlando Sentinel*, 28 July 1995.
[53] Cf *La* [1997] 2 SCR 680.

of the order was to 'requir[e] those counselling the victims of sexual abuse to become evidence gatherers – investigators – for the defence . . . Services and relationships that were established to . . . assist survivors of sexual abuse in healing, are being subverted as they are drawn increasingly into the litigation process'.[54]

Not only was the decision in *Carosella* bizarre in its acceptance that the accused's rights under the Charter could be breached by the non-availability of evidence collected by a private third party, which evidence did not form part of the prosecution case, need never have been reduced to written form and had never been viewed, much less accepted as correct, by the complainant herself, but the logic behind that decision could apply in equal measure to a diary allegedly kept but subsequently destroyed or mislaid by the complainant, and to a diary kept by anyone to whom she spoke of the alleged rape. (Indeed, defence lawyers are now subpoenaing journals, as well as 'counseling notes, employment and academic records, medical files and more'.[55])

The only distinction between these situations and that which formed the subject matter of *Carosella* was that the centre received government funding. But, given that the centre did not form part of government and would not have been bound by the Charter in its dealings with the complainant or anyone else, this distinction cannot affect the propriety of a prosecution decision, at least in the absence of a finding that the records could reasonably have contributed to the defendant's case. If this requirement were satisfied it is indeed arguable, as Madam Justice L'Heureux-Dubé accepted, that the Crown decision to persist in a prosecution would breach the defendant's 'right to make full answer and defence . . . as a result of his inability to obtain information that is material to his defence'. But in *Carosella*, the alleged relevance of the destroyed file rested on no more than a bare assertion that it might have contained statements by the complainant (which would, even if they had been made, have been noted in summary form only and not been checked by her) which might have been inconsistent with her subsequent testimony.

The situation is likely to deteriorate further in view of the Supreme Court's imposition, in *R v Dixon*,[56] of a due diligence obligation on defence lawyers in relation to evidence relevant under *Stinchcombe*.[57] This imposition, coupled with the apparently low standard imposed on the police and prosecution in terms of evidence gathering and preservation,[58] may serve to place defendants in sexual assault trials in a better position than that of other defendants. Whereas the prosecution is under no obligation to gather evidence for the defence, *Stinchcombe* having failed to

[54] Gilmour, note 26 above, pp 256–257.
[55] *Chatelaine*, October 1997.
[56] [1998] 1 SCR 244. See also *Burc* [1997] 1 SCR 535.
[57] Note 31 above.
[58] See *La*, note 53 above.

'address the disincentives that the police may have to search for evidence that points away from their theory of a case',[59] sexual assault defendants will generally have a potentially fertile hunting ground in the complainant's personal records, whether these records relate to medical or psychiatric treatment or to counselling. Since failure to pursue such records might well be a failure of due diligence, defence counsel will almost be obliged to press for disclosure. In cases other than those involving sexual assault, by contrast, these records would simply not be considered relevant.

Balancing rights

The potential of counselling records to derail the prosecution of sexual offences is evident from the decision in *Carosella* (above). Seventeen months after the decision in *O'Connor*, Canada's Parliament established a statutory procedure for disclosure of personal records, whether those records are in the hands of the prosecution or not.[60] The procedure owes more to the judgment of Madam Justice L'Heureux-Dubé in *O'Connor* than to that of the majority, and stresses 'society's interest in encouraging the reporting of sexual offences' and the privacy and other interests of the sexual assault complainant. In *R v Mills*,[61] Alberta's Court of Queen's Bench struck down the legislative restrictions on disclosure on the grounds that they were inconsistent with the Supreme Court's decision in *O'Connor*.

In *Dagenais v Canadian Broadcasting Corporation*[62] (discussed below), the Supreme Court had ruled that there was no hierarchy of rights but that, when 'two protected rights come into conflict [freedom of expression and the right to a fair trial], Charter principles require a balance to be achieved that fully respects the importance of both'. The court in *Mills* characterised the balance struck by the provisions at issue in that case as ranking 'privacy rights . . . paramount to the rights of the accused to a fair trial'. It is not clear from the decision why the court in *Mills* regarded the privacy rights as trumping rather than balancing the right to a fair trial in that case unless it considered that, whenever such a balance operated, in its view, so as to restrict the latter right, the right would have been infringed rather than balanced.

It would be difficult to argue that the right to a fair trial could justifiably be infringed.[63] But the question which needs to be addressed relates to the courts' conception of what a 'fair trial' demands. In *Seaboyer*,[64] Madam Justice L'Heureux-Dubé remarked, of ss 276 and 277 of the

---

[59] J Roach, 'Institutional Choice, Co-operation, and Struggle in the Age of the *Charter*', in J Cameron (ed), note 26 above, p 363.
[60] Unless the complainant has expressly waived privacy in records in prosecution hands.
[61] (1997) CRR Lexis 97, Alberta QB. See also *Lee* (1997) CRR LEXIS 100, Ontario, discussed below.
[62] [1994] 3 SCR 835.
[63] This being the position taken in *Lee*, note 61 above.
[64] Note 4 above.

Criminal Code, that '[u]nless one accepts the paradoxical assertion that an accused has the right to a biased verdict, or that the principles of fundamental justice constitutionalize the discriminatory application of the law, the provisions cannot be constitutionally impugned'.[65] And in *O'Connor*,[66] Madam Justice McLachlin stated that the Charter 'guarantees not the fairest of all possible trials, but rather a trial which is fundamentally fair'. The latter required consideration of 'the practical limits of the system of justice and the lawful interests of others involved in the process' as well as the 'perspective of the accused' and, while the former might suggest that the accused be 'shown every scintilla of information which might possibly be useful to his defence' from 'information touching on the events at issue' to 'anything that might conceivably be used in cross-examination to discredit or shake a Crown witness', the latter pointed 'to a more realistic standard of disclosure'.[67] It was on this basis that she dissented from the view of the majority.[68]

The Supreme Court was prepared, in *Dagenais*, to 'balance' the 'right to a fair trial' against 'free expression' interests. But what seems very clear from cases such as *Seaboyer*, *O'Connor* and *Carosella* is that this court, in common with most others, is not prepared to engage in what it perceives as a balance between the 'right to a fair trial' and the complainant's interests in privacy, security of the person or the equal protection of the law. When it comes to such a 'balance', the accused's right to a fair trial trumps all, and any restriction seen to infringe upon this right is bound to be struck down. The constitutional rights of the complainant yield to the defendant's common law rights and can impact upon those rights only to the extent that this impact can be absorbed under common law rubric. But the constitutional rights of the defendant exist over and above those which he enjoys at common law, and so serve further to reduce the protection afforded to complainants.[69]

The only evidential or procedural restrictions which have been upheld in relation to sexual assault are those which do not infringe upon the defendant's fair trial rights *as those rights are understood by the court*. Thus, in *R v L (DO)*,[70] the Supreme Court rejected a s 7 challenge to legislative provisions which permitted the evidence of young sexual assault complainants to be videotaped, subject to conditions, on the ground that they

---

[65] The majority of the Supreme Court did not accept her view that the sexual history evidence was irrelevant, but did not dispute that that which was properly regarded as irrelevant would have no place in a fair trial.

[66] Note 36 above.

[67] Citing *Harrer* [1995] 3 SCR 562.

[68] This accords with Madam Justice McLachlin's approach in *Dagenais v Canadian Broadcasting Corporation*, note 62 above. The majority, with which she concurred, decided it on the grounds that 'When two protected rights come into conflict, Charter principles require a balance to be achieved that fully respects the importance of both rights. A hierarchical approach to rights must be avoided.'

[69] For the approach to disclosure in a non-Charter case see *AM v Ryan* [1997] 1 SCR 157.

[70] [1993] 4 SCR 419.

served to elicit the truth and to preserve evidence, as well as to reduce the trauma to the child, while infringing neither the defendant's right to cross-examine witnesses nor his right to be presumed innocent. And in *R v Levogiannis*[71] the Supreme Court, on similar grounds, upheld legislation which permitted young complainants to testify from behind a screen. But even these small concessions have been rejected in the US, the Supreme Court ruling, in *Coy v State of Iowa*,[72] that the screening of two 13-year-old girls from the man charged with their sexual assault breached the defendant's Sixth Amendment right 'to be confronted with the witnesses against him'. According to the court, the right was breached because the girls 'did not have to see the defendant as they gave evidence against him . . . Even if an exception to this . . . right [to confrontation] can be made, it would have to be based on something more than the type of generalized finding asserted here, unless it were firmly rooted in our jurisprudence' (internal citations omitted). This restriction has the unfortunate effect of insulating the legal system against change with the result that the same categories of victims who have traditionally been ill-served by the criminal justice system will continue to be so, legislative attempts to relieve the burden of newly recognised discrimination being particularly vulnerable to judicial veto.

Constitutions and the common law

The Canadian and US Supreme Courts came to different conclusions in *Levogiannis* and *Coy*, but their general approach in this area is similar. In the US, statutory restrictions on the freedom of defence counsel in rape trials appear to be constitutional to the extent, but only to the extent, that they accord with the judges' common law notions of relevance.[73] A similar approach is taken to legislative measures designed to prevent the admission of complainants' personal records in rape trials. Defendants in the US have been able to demand the disclosure of women's counselling and other personal records on the strength of the Due Process Clauses

---

[71] [1993] 4 SCR 475. See also *Canadian Broadcasting Corporation v Attorney General for New Brunswick* [1996] 3 SCR 480, in which case the Supreme Court upheld provisions permitting exclusion of public – s 1 saved due to interests in encouraging reporting and in protecting privacy.

[72] 487 US 1012 (1988).

[73] See *Shaw v United States* 892 F Supp 1265 (1995); *Hoke v Thompson* 852 F Supp 1310 (1994); *US v Fuller* 589 F Supp 206 (1984), in which the court cited numerous authorities to the effect that the constitutional basis for upholding rape shield provisions rested on its irrelevance and that sexual history evidence would sometimes be relevant (including in cases in which it 'tends to establish bias, prejudice or ulterior motive' or 'a prior pattern of behavior', or the accused's state of mind (citing *United States v Kasto* 584 F 2d 271 (1978); *Doe v United States* 666 F 2d 48 (1981)). See also *Darrow v State of Alabama* 451 So 2d 394 (1984); *People of State of Michigan v Khan* 80 Mich App 605, 264 NW 2d 360 (1978); *Commonwealth of Massachusetts v Elder* 389 Mass 743 (1983); *Hubbard v State of Arkansas* 271 Ark 937 (1973); *Commonwealth of Pennsylvania v Black* 337 Pa Sup Ct 548 (1985); *State of Louisiana v Small* 693 So 2d 180 (1997), CA 2nd Cir, Lou; and *Giles v State of Maryland* (1967) 386 US 66 (1967).

of the Fifth and Fourteenth Amendments, and the Confrontation and Compulsory Process Clauses of the Sixth Amendment.[74]

The importance of the common law to constitutional challenges is such that it is useful to consider why counselling and other records pertaining to sexual assault complainants are considered 'relevant'. Certainly the acceptance by the courts of relevance in this context contrasts with the position in relation to other offences. Generally, where private records have been sought by the accused, applications have typically been rejected on the grounds that they consist of 'no more than a fishing expedition',[75] or that the records involved were 'hearsay . . . potentially based on un-founded allegations, and . . . generally irrelevant'.[76] Another related question concerns why such evidence is actually used, to the extent that this is different. Certainly, attempts by defence counsel in Canada have become ever more common, even before the decisions of the Supreme Court in *O'Connor* and *A (LL) v B (A)* above. And in the US, too, Wendy Murphy (founder of the Crime Victim Advocacy and Research Group, which monitors legal trends in sexual violence cases) stated in 1997 that 'defense attorneys are gaining access to [personal records] with much greater frequency than, I think, we've ever seen before . . . defense attorneys are sending out subpoenas to pharmacies and to hospitals and to psychiatrists, hoping that they come up with something'.[77]

The decisions of Canada's courts in *O'Connor, Carosella, Mills* and *Lee*[78] appear to accept that, in general, counselling and other records will be relevant to the determination of guilt in a sexual assault charge because *inter alia* 'they may contain information concerning the unfolding of events underlying the criminal complaint', 'they may reveal the use of a therapy which influenced the complainant's memory of the alleged events', or 'they may contain information that bears on the complainant's credibility, including testimonial factors such as the quality of their perception of events at the time of the offence, and their memory since' (internal citations omitted).[79] But why is it the case that these perceptions of

---

[74] No Supreme Court decision has yet been reached as to the constitutionality of absolute privilege accorded to the private records of complainants, but that court, too, has generally assessed the constitutionality of statutory privileges by weighing the rights of the accused *as perceived by the judges* against the public interests served by the privilege: *Commonwealth of Pennsylvania v Ritchie* 480 US 39 (1987); *United States v Nixon* 418 US 683 (1974); *Davis v State of Alaska* 415 US 308 (1974) and *Washington v State of Texas* 388 US 14 (1967). See further M Hogan, 'The Constitutionality of An Absolute Privilege for Rape Crisis Counseling' (1989) 30 *Boston College Law Review* 411, at 470–474; W White, 'Evidentiary Privileges and the Defendant's Constitutional Right to Introduce Evidence' (1989) 80 *Journal of Criminal Law and Criminology* 377, at 423–425.

[75] *Gingras* (1992) 71 CCC (3d) 53, discussed by Madam Justice L'Heureux-Dubé in *O'Connor*, note 36 above.

[76] *Gratton* [1987] OJ No 1984, Prov Ct, and *Callaghan* [1993] OJ No 2013, Ont Ct, Prov Div, discussed by Madam Justice L'Heureux-Dubé in *O'Connor*, note 36 above.

[77] S O'Malley, 'The New Reason Rapists Are Going Free' (1997) 189(4) *Redbook*.

[78] Respectively, notes 36, 37, 61 and 61.

[79] Chief Justice Lamer for the plurality in *O'Connor*, note 36 above.

relevance only arise where sexual assault is at issue? In *Osolin*[80] and in *O'Connor*, Madam Justice L'Heureux-Dubé protested that: 'uninhibited disclosure of complainants' private lives indulges the discriminatory suspicion that women and children's reports of sexual victimization are uniquely likely to be fabricated'.[81] And in the US, Wendy Murphy claimed that 'in terms of historical, traditional biases against women, and particularly biases against rape victims, what we're seeing is really the same old song and dance. We're basically seeing defense attorneys taking advantage of the fact that judges and upper courts . . . are of the mind that women are not innately credible, that they have character flaw problems that will probably be revealed in their counseling records . . . there's a tremendous amount of gender bias going on.' As Christine Boyle put it: '[r]elevance' is not a matter of neutral logic in this context but a highly contested concept steeped in sexual politics'.[82]

There is no rational basis for the suggestion that medical, psychiatric or counselling records are relevant to allegations of sexual assault, but not in general to other crimes. The acceptance of such records as potentially, even presumptively relevant relies on the same distrust of sexual assault complainants that has permeated the legal system from its inception and to the present day.[83] But even if it were accepted that such records might contain something which could be considered to some degree logically probative of credibility or of an issue at trial, admissibility at common law turns on the balance between probative value and prejudicial impact as well as on whether the material is logically probative. On this ground, too, personal records, in particular, records relating to sexual assault counselling, should not be regarded even as potentially admissible.

In *O'Connor*, Madam Justice L'Heureux-Dubé argued that 'these records may very well have a greater potential to derail than to advance the truth-seeking process' because (citing her own words in *Osolin*) 'even assuming [the complainant's words] are correctly understood and reliably noted . . . in therapy an entire spectrum of factors such as personal history, thoughts, emotions as well as particular acts may inform the dialogue between therapist and patient. Thus, there is serious risk that such statements could be taken piecemeal out of the context in which they were made to provide a foundation for entirely unwarranted inferences by the trier of fact.'

The danger of out-of-context use of statements made in counselling cannot be over-estimated. In the first place, counsellors rarely take

---

[80] Note 5 above.
[81] It would not reflect, far less promote, 'a society in which all are secure in the knowledge that they are recognized at law as human beings equally deserving of concern, respect and consideration' (citing *Andrews v Law Society of British Columbia* [1989] 1 SCR 143, at 171).
[82] Birnie, note 48 above; S Coughlan, 'Patients' Secrets and Threats to Third Parties' (1995) 15(4) *Health Law in Canada*.
[83] See A McColgan, *The Case for Taking the 'Date' Out of Rape* (London: Pandora, 1996).

contemporaneous notes, they tend to summarise rather than quote counsellees, and misunderstandings on their part will rarely be corrected by the counsellee who is unlikely to read the notes. For this reason, to rely on counselling notes as accurate is to take a very serious risk of being misled. Secondly, defence lawyers are bound to comb records for any admission by the complainant that she feels guilt about the assault, that she was in any way to blame, that she perhaps brought it upon herself by provoking the attack (see for example the allegedly relevant note in *Osolin* about the complainant's concern that she may have misled the defendant in some way). It is inevitable that any such disclosure by the complainant will be taken as tantamount to a confession of false complaint. Yet it is characteristic of rape victims that they suffer guilt – so characteristic that this symptom is one of those recognised as indicative of rape trauma syndrome which has been widely recognised by the courts in the US and has been taken cognisance of in the UK. The fact that a woman who is being counselled for sexual assault states that she was at fault says a great deal more about the injury inflicted upon her than it does about a defendant's guilt.

Sex and credibility

The alleged relevance of counselling and other records is dubious to say the least. But what is equally important is the recognition of why the introduction of such records is actually sought. These records should not be excluded simply because, in general, they have little or no probative value to credibility or to any issue at trial. Nor should they be excluded simply because the threat of their admission is likely to deter women from seeking counselling, and from pressing or persisting with sexual assault complaints. In addition to these issues, a significant danger relating to complainant's personal records is that, if they are admitted into the trial process they will, as Madam Justice L'Heureux-Dubé warned in *Osolin*, be used by defence lawyers to 'invite prejudice against the witness by the trier of fact . . . there is serious risk that such information will be used to draw impermissible inferences and encourage the trier of fact to rely on myths about the credibility of sexual assault victims to the prejudice of both the witness and the trial process'.

In the particular case, Madam Justice L'Heureux-Dubé was forced to conclude that lawyers for the accused 'hoped to use expert testimony on the medical records to invite the jury to draw inferences about the credibility of the complainant based on, among other things, her past sexual history'. These, as she pointed out, were 'precisely the inferences' which Parliament, in adopting the rape shield provisions discussed above, 'has attempted to prevent'. Again, in *O'Connor*, the same judge warned against permitting the 'pernicious' practices of the past 'to reappear under the guise of extensive and unwarranted inquiries into the past histories and private lives of complainants of sexual assault. We must not allow the defence to do indirectly what it cannot do directly under s 276 of the Code. This would close one discriminatory door only to open another.'

Once evidence of a complainant's sexual history reaches the jury, it is clear from the experience in Canada, the UK and the US, that this evidence will be taken to discredit the complainant, to render her in the eyes of the jury less worthy of the protection of the law.[84] It seems that jurors believe that women who are sexually active lie about rape and that they either consent indiscriminately, or that their lack of consent to any particular sexual contact is not a lack of consent which should result in punishment for a man who chooses to ignore it. This notion may not be one to which they consciously subscribe, but the admission of sexual evidence allows the defence to feed into anachronistic cultural assumptions about women and sex. The focus is shifted from the question of whether the complainant has been raped on this occasion, to the question of whether she is a 'rapeable' woman.

The Supreme Court in *Seaboyer*[85] appeared to reject the traditional view that a woman's sexual history was relevant to her credibility and to the likelihood of her having consented to the sexual intercourse at issue in a trial. But, by permitting the introduction of sexual history evidence on whatever ground, the decision allows juries to continue to judge women on the basis of their sexual behaviour. Sexual assault complainants are subject to attack on the grounds of their sexual behaviour, through physical evidence such as the humiliating display of their underwear, or on the basis of private medical and counselling records. Complainants are made to appear cheap, unworthy of protection, not the kind of women sexual assaults upon whom merit the full force of the law. The question is less one concerning exactly what the defendant did, and whether the woman consented; rather, whether she is a woman whose refusal of sexual intercourse is such that the full weight of the criminal law should be visited upon the man who fails to respect that refusal.

This was recognised by the US District Court for South Dakota in *US v Shaw*,[86] in which that court refused to admit a variety of claims about the alleged youthful sexual escapades of the complainant whose foster father was convicted of having 'carnal knowledge' of her when she was 11–12 years old. According to the judge, had the evidence been admitted, 'the jury . . . could have concluded . . . that [the complainant] with her sexual past could not have been raped or assaulted or that she somehow deserved to be raped and/or assaulted after engaging in the sexual activities alleged'.[87] This particular US judge held that the sexual history evidence was properly excluded in order to avoid such a punitive approach

---

[84] See McColgan, note 23 above.
[85] Note 4 above.
[86] Note 73 above.
[87] *Ibid*, at 1274. See McColgan, note 83 above, for analysis of the prevalence of victim-blaming in this context.

to the complainant. Not so one Canadian judge who, having determined that a rape complainant was a prostitute and 'a liar' (the latter apparently on no other ground than that the jury had acquitted her alleged attacker), revoked the ban on publication of her name which he had previously imposed at her request.[88] This judge appeared to regard public humiliation as the appropriate punishment for sexual activities of which he disapproved.

To the extent that the admission of sexual history evidence has been restricted in Canada by s 276 of the Criminal Code (and doubts have been expressed as to the constitutionality of the revised provision), jurors may be deprived of some of the material upon which they would otherwise draw conclusions about a complainant's entitlement to legal protection. But, where defence lawyers succeed in having evidence admitted relating to the counselling records of complainants, it is likely that the complainant can be attacked by means of this evidence. Not only may such records themselves contain details of complainants' sexual activities – recognised symptoms of rape trauma syndrome include sexual difficulties and emotional disorders; but rape victims regularly experience 'fear, depression, guilt . . . substance abuse'.[89] The difficulties which may arise from any discussion of feelings of guilt have been mentioned above. But even leaving this and sex-related material aside, mention that a sexual assault complainant has experienced depression or become involved in substance abuse can be used to indicate that the complainant is psychologically flawed, 'flaky', unworthy of belief.

In addition to using personal records to introduce prohibited sexual history evidence relating to the complainant and otherwise to invite prejudice against her, it appears that defence lawyers use the threat of production to pressurise women into abandoning rape cases. In August 1997 a US programme discussed a report about 'a disturbing new wave of intimidation tactics used against women who report rape'.[90] The 'intimidation tactics' consisted of demands for access to women's counselling and other medical records, which demands one complainant testified had caused her to drop her charge. Not only had the complainant been informed that legal arguments over disclosure would take one to three years (she had already been in pre-trial arguments for over three years) but 'I also chose to walk away because I could not protect the other people

---

[88] See opinion of Justice Sopinka in *Adams* [1995] 4 SCR 707. Women's sexual activity can be used against them also where they are defendants in other trials – see for example *Anderson v Goeke* 44 F 3d 675 (1995), discussed in Chapter 8 above.

[89] K Duncan, 'Lies, Damned Lies, and Statistics? Psychological Syndrome Evidence in the Courtroom After *Daubert*' (1996) 71(3) *Indiana Law Review* (available on the world wide web at http://www.law.indiana.edu/ilj/ilj.html), citing D McCord, 'The Admissibility of Expert Testimony Regarding Rape Trauma Syndrome in Rape Prosecutions' (1985) 26 *British Columbia Law Review* 1143, at 1187–1188. See also discussion of *O'Connor* complainants in *Chatelaine*, October 1997.

[90] CNBC News Transcripts, 6 August 1997, discussing O'Malley article, note 77 above.

whose privacy had been invaded. When they read my counseling records, they also read information about my father, my mother, my ex-husband, my sister, her family and my friends.'

Another rape complainant whose 'personal psychiatric and counselling and medical records' were obtained by the defence stated that '[i]t was an intimidation tactic hoping that I wouldn't bring the case to trial'. Wendy Murphy claimed that the increasingly common defence tactic 'forced [women] to choose' between privacy and prosecution. These tactics, according to Murphy, are designed more 'to wear [complainants] down . . . than provide the defence with information pertinent to the case'.[91]

Substantive rape law

It can be seen from the foregoing that neither Canada's Charter of Rights nor the US Constitution has done a great deal to improve the position of women who complain of sexual assault. Nor has the impact felt under the Charter been confined to the procedural aspects of sexual assault trials. It has also been experienced in the substantive laws relating to sexual assault.

The legislative revision which took place in the wake of *Seaboyer*[92] did reduce the scope of the 'mistaken belief in consent' defence by excluding it where 'the accused did not take reasonable steps, in the circumstances known to the accused at the time, to ascertain that the complainant was consenting' and by incorporating what has been referred to as a ' "yes" means "yes" ' provision: ie the definition of 'consent' to exclude situations where 'the complainant expresses, by words or conduct, a lack of agreement to engage in the activity; or . . . a lack of agreement to continue to engage in the activity'.[93] But this change in the sexual assault laws should not be regarded as a benefit of the Charter, having been no more than a fortuitous consequence of damage inflicted upon those laws by the Supreme Court in *Seaboyer*. And the revision was achieved despite, rather than because of, the Charter.[94] Finally, the approach taken to the

---

[91] O'Malley, note 77 above.

[92] Note 4 above.

[93] See *R v Ewanchuk* 169 DLR (4th) 193, 131 CCC (3d) 481 for the Supreme Court's interpretation of this legislation. The case was an appeal from a decision by Alberta's Court of Appeal in which a judge remarked that the victim of an alleged sexual assault 'did not present herself [to the accused] in a bonnet and crinolines', *Globe and Mail*, 13 October 1998.

[94] P Monahan, 'The Charter Then and Now', in P Bryden *et al* (eds), *Protecting Rights and Freedoms: Essays on the Charter's Place in Canada's Political, Legal and Intellectual Life* (Toronto: University of Toronto Press, 1994); *New York Times*, 21 February 1992; *Maclean's*, 17 February 1992. The 'reasonable belief' clause was retained despite Charter arguments after advice from government lawyers.

mistaken belief defence by the Supreme Court still leaves much to be desired. Madam Justice McLachlin's dissent in *Osolin*[95] has already been mentioned. In *R v Esau*,[96] too, Madam Justice McLachlin protested the Supreme Court's acceptance that a trial judge should have instructed a jury on mistaken belief where the defendant had sex with a woman in circumstances where 'the complainant [was] so drunk that she [was] unable to communicate [and thus was] incapable of giving consent'. Madam Justice McLachlin dissented from the view of the majority on the grounds that 'where the complainant was on any view of the evidence quite drunk, the absence of any evidence of steps taken by the accused to ascertain consent precludes him from raising the defence' of mistaken belief.

The decision of the Supreme Court in *Hess*[97] and its impact on Canada's statutory rape provisions has been referred to at the beginning of this chapter. Of more general significance is the decision in *R v Daviault*,[98] in which the Supreme Court recognised intoxication as a defence to crimes including sexual assault. Alcohol plays a significant role in sexual assaults as it does more generally in crimes against women. Many men who assault women seek to explain and excuse their actions by reference to intoxication, as they also seek to excuse and explain their actions by reference to the behaviour of the women, and, indeed, of the children they attack.[99]

In Canada, as in the UK, intoxication has not traditionally been accepted as a defence to crimes of 'basic' or 'general' intent, which in the UK includes rape and, in Canada, sexual assault. What this means is that a defendant cannot rely on intoxication to deny having the *mens rea* of a crime which can be committed recklessly. In such a case, the state of being intoxicated acts as a substitute *mens rea* for the crime of basic intent and the defendant should be convicted. The substitution of intoxication for an element of the *mens rea* in crimes of basic intent may offend logic, since fault elements such as recklessness cannot generally exist in the abstract but must fulfil the particular requirements for the crime charged (in assault, for example, recklessness is foresight of the possibility that the victim might apprehend the immediate application of unlawful force, or may in fact be unlawfully touched; in rape, awareness that the other party may not be consenting, or a 'couldn't care less' approach to whether she or he is consenting or not). But what it lacks in logic it makes up for in terms of social defence – if intoxication renders someone more likely to behave in a harmful way, that person will not be excused liability for the harmful conduct on the grounds that she or he

---

[95] Note 5 above.
[96] [1997] 2 SCR 777.
[97] *R v Hess and Nguyen*, note 19 above.
[98] [1994] 3 SCR 63.
[99] See D Scully and J Marolla, 'Convicted Rapists' Vocabulary of Motive: Excuses and Justifications' (1984) 31 (5) *Social Problems* 530; D Scully, *Understanding Sexual Violence: A Study of Convicted Rapists* (Boston, Unwin Hyman, 1990).

was voluntarily intoxicated. If, on the other hand, intoxication was not voluntary, or was not a causal factor in any alleged assault, the intoxication will, respectively, result in acquittal (so long as *mens rea* was absent) or will be wholly irrelevant to guilt.

It may be harsh to pin criminal liability on those whose intoxication was such that they truly did not know what they were doing. But it is as simple to avoid such liability by desisting from such a degree of intoxication as it is to avoid other criminal liability by resisting the temptation consciously to commit offences. In *Daviault*, however, the Supreme Court ruled that the substitution of intoxication for the *mens rea* of crimes of general intent breached ss 7 and 11(d) of the Charter: '[t]he mental aspect of an offence has long been recognized as an integral part of crime, and to eliminate it would be to deprive an accused of fundamental justice'.[100] The majority ruled that, while the *mens rea* requirement for crimes of general intent could be 'minimal' (in sexual assault, consisting simply of 'an intention to commit the sexual assault or recklessness as to whether the actions will constitute an assault'): 'the presumption of innocence requires that the Crown bear the burden of establishing all elements of a crime, including the mental element of voluntariness ... To deny that even a very minimal mental element is required for sexual assault offends the Charter in a manner that is so drastic and so contrary to the principles of fundamental justice that it cannot be justified under s 1 of the Charter.'

The decision in *Daviault* may be contrasted with the approach of the Supreme Court to the issue of constructive liability. In the early days of the Charter, the Supreme Court adopted quite a radical approach to the substance of criminal law, interpreting the Charter in *Reference Re Section 94(2) of the Motor Vehicle Act (BC)*[101] so as to require a defence of due diligence even to crimes of strict liability and, in *R v Villiancourt*[102] and *R v Martineau*,[103] striking down Canada's legislative offence of constructive murder on the ground, according to the majority, that '[t]he principles of fundamental justice require that a conviction for murder be based upon proof beyond a reasonable doubt of subjective foresight of death' (the majority). But by 1992 the approach of the Supreme Court had changed, and in this and later years the court upheld offences in which the *mens rea* element did not extend to the consequences of the defendant's actions (*De Sousa*[104]), as well as to those which imposed an objective test of liability (*Hundal,*[105] *Crieghton*[106]). By 1995, commentators were suggesting that the court 'has been retracing its steps along the road to constitutionalizing

[100] Note 98 above.
[101] [1985] 2 SCR 486.
[102] (1987) 39 CCC (3d) 118.
[103] (1990) 58 CCC (3d) 353.
[104] (1992) 76 CCC (3d) 124.
[105] (1993) 79 CCC (3d) 97.
[106] (1993) 83 CCC (3d) 246 and three companion cases.

the general principles of fault'.[107] In *Daviault* the Supreme Court refused to adopt this latter approach in the context of sexual assault.

Justice Cory, for the majority, disputed the argument of the minority that self-induced intoxication could properly be substituted for the *mens rea* in crimes of general intent, referring to studies which characterised intoxication as the facilitator or self-excusing factor, rather than as a cause, of crime. He pointed out that effects such as these do not provide a defence for criminal behaviour, but insisted, nevertheless, that extreme intoxication should be accepted as a complete defence. It is hard to follow the logic of at once denying intoxication as a cause of crime while excusing intoxicated crime (which, if it was not caused by the intoxication, would presumably have occurred in any event) and, as Justice Cory went on to suggest, criminalising extreme intoxication *per se*. Whatever the intentions behind the decision, its effect has been to permit defendants, not merely to mitigate their fault by explaining and excusing violent behaviour (particularly violent and sexually violent assaults against women and children) by reference to intoxication (this being standard practice), but to use alcohol entirely to exonerate themselves.[108] And while Justice Cory suggested that it was 'obvious that it will only be on rare occasions that evidence of such an extreme state of intoxication can be advanced and perhaps only on still rarer occasions is it likely to be successful',[109] within five months the decision had been successfully relied upon by three defendants charged with assaults on women.[110]

Such was the concern generated by *Daviault* that, almost immediately, Canada's Justice Department put forward legislative proposals. The approach initially adopted by the legislature was, as the Supreme Court had suggested, to create a crime of 'criminal intoxication leading to harmful conduct'.[111] This proposal was greeted with hostility by women's groups, relying as it did on the discredited assumption that 'given too many drinks,

---

[107] T Litkowski, 'The Charter and the Principles of Criminal Responsibility', in J Cameron (ed), note 26 above.

[108] The *De Moines Register* (16 November 1994) characterised the decision of the Supreme Court as a warning to women that '[m]en may do treacherous things when they are drunk, but the onus is on you not to cross paths with them when they're doing it' and (18 November 1994) quoted a women's shelter worker to the effect that it had resulted in a 'floodgate of fear'.

[109] Citing an Australian study (G Smith, 'Footnote to *O'Connor's* Case' (1981) 5 *Criminal Law Journal* 270) which suggested that the impact of similar law reform there had been minimal.

[110] *Toronto Sun*, 25 February 1995. Alberta's Court of Queen's Bench acquitted Carl Blair of assaulting his wife after he took large quantities of alcohol and prescription drugs; a Quebec court acquitted Pierre Theriault of spousal assault on the grounds that his consumption of a large quantity of cocaine prior to the assault had rendered him unaware of his actions (*Facts on File World News Digest*, 15 December 1994; *New York Times*, 10 November 1994). And in *Jensen* [1996] Ont CA LEXIS 286, Ontario's Court of Appeal left open the question whether *Daviault* required that a man whose mistaken belief in consent resulted from his intoxication was entitled to an acquittal.

[111] *De Moines Register*, 18 November 1994.

any man is liable to assaulting women sexually'.[112] This was the very assumption, of course, which Justice Cory for the majority in *Daviault* had rejected despite his suggestion for legislation along these lines. In February 1995 the Justice Department put forward fresh proposals which were enacted as Bill-72 in September of that year. Bill-72 introduces a new section to the Criminal Code which states (s 33.1) that absence of voluntariness or of *mens rea* shall not be a defence to offences which include 'as an element an assault or any other interference or threat of interference with the bodily integrity of another person' where *inter alia* a person is in 'a state of self-induced intoxication that renders the person unaware of, or incapable of consciously controlling, their behaviour'.

Bill C-72, which has been described as an 'in your face' response to *Daviault*,[113] is sure to be challenged to the Supreme Court on the grounds of asserted breach of defendants' ss 7 and 11 rights. While it is likely to be found in breach, it may withstand s 1 scrutiny on the basis that, unlike the rule struck down in *Daviault*, it is legislation rather than judge-made law and so merits a degree of judicial deference out of place in relation to the common law. Certainly, the majority of the Supreme Court stressed in *Daviault* that it was dealing with common law rather than with legislation and, as the Information Note to Bill C-72 states: '[t]he public policy considerations underlying the new standard of care [imposed in relation to intoxication] were not presented to the Supreme Court, and therefore could not be factored into the Court's *Charter* analysis'.[114] Having said this, the Court of Queen's Bench in *Mills*,[115] gave little deference to the legislation's enactment of disclosure restrictions or to the preamble to the Bill by which those provisions were enacted.

Conclusion: entrenched rights and women as victims of violence

It can be seen from the discussions of rape in this chapter and of the legal treatment of battered women who kill their abusers in Chapter 8 above that the efficacy of entrenched rights for protecting women as victims of violence is far from clear-cut. Constitutional entitlements to equal protection, due process and a fair trial have not eradicated the deep-rooted discrimination which prejudices women who kill abusive partners. This chapter has considered the positive danger that constitutionally protected rights can pose for the victims of violence in their potential to

---

[112] *Ibid.*
[113] M Schaffer, 'Criminal Responsibility and the Charter', in Cameron (ed), note 26 above, p 321.
[114] *Ibid*, p 323.
[115] Note 61 above.

thwart legislative efforts to ameliorate the position of the (predominantly female) victims of sexual assault. While it would be difficult to argue with measures designed to prevent unjust convictions, judicial perceptions of the injustices wrought by legislative provisions designed to protect sexual assault victims owe more to ingrained attitudes of hostility towards this category of complainants than they do to substantial threats of injustice. The constitutionalisation of defendants' rights serves, in this area, to perpetuate the discrimination suffered by women at the hands of the legal system.

The prevalence of sexual assault in Canada has been mentioned above. Canada's Charter guarantees equality to women 'before and under the law and has the right to the equal protection and equal benefit of the law'. Any meaningful 'equality' requires that women do not live in fear of sexual assault. This was recognised by the Government of Canada in its preamble to the post-*Daviault* Bill (see below), in which it accepted that: 'violence has a particularly disadvantaging impact on the equal participation of women in society and on the rights of women and children to security of the person and to the equal protection and benefit of the law as guaranteed by sections 7, 15 and 28 of the . . . *Charter* . . .'.[116] But for all of this, the Charter has served to exacerbate, rather than to reduce, the difficulties associated with prosecuting sexual assault and the disbenefit which women, as victims of sexual violence, have suffered in Canada as a result of the Charter, has not been balanced by any gains on their part.

In the US, too, the existence of the Federal Bill of Rights has been consistent, over the course of centuries, with the most restrictive and discriminatory rape laws which have included, in particular states and at various points in time, not only the acceptance (exclusive to rape trials) of the relevance of complainants' sexual history both to consent and to credibility; and similar marital exemptions to that which existed in England and Wales until 1991; but, in addition, requirements that the woman resist sexual intercourse 'to the utmost', that every element of rape (that is, force, penetration, and the identity of the offender – these requirements applied to no other crime) be corroborated; and, in many southern states during the 19th century, that the victim be white.[117]

Women's experience of Canada's Charter of Rights has consisted in part of a succession of cases rendering the prosecution and conviction of alleged rapists ever more difficult and providing a defence of intoxication, to men accused *inter alia* of rape and domestic assault. In the US, too, although constitutional guarantees such as those to due process, equal

---

[116] Schaffer, note 113 above, pp 313, 322.

[117] See M Clemens, 'Note: Elimination of the Resistance Requirement and other rape law reforms: the New York experience' (1983) 47 *Albany Law Review* 871, at 879–880; M Block, *An Accusation Easily to be Made: A History of Rape Law in Nineteenth-Century State Appellate Courts 1800–1870* (University of Louisville, 1992), MA Thesis, pp 105–107; J Marsh *et al*, *Rape and the Limits of Law Reform* (Boston Massachusetts, Auburn House Publishing Co, 1982), p 102. See also L Goldstein, *The Constitutional Rights of Women* (Wisconsin, University of Wisconsin Press, 1988).

protection, etc, have not enabled women to challenge the inadequacies of the law relating to rape (its historical non-application to husbands, requirements for 'utmost resistance', etc), they have permitted defendants to have women's sexual history evidence admitted in court in the face of legislative prohibitions on this practice, and to gain access to counselling and other records even where those records have been accorded absolute privilege by statute.

One of the primary reasons for this difficulty is the traditional view of the criminal defendant as a vulnerable individual pitted against the might of the State. This view is frequently accurate. But it is important not to lose sight of the fact that the violence which women, as well as children, tend to suffer is itself institutionalised. Whether they are raped by their husbands or their teachers, the constitutional rights accorded to those few rapists who ever reach court serve further to bolster the power of the oppressors.

The facts behind the *O'Connor*[118] case provide a very powerful example of this. O'Connor, a bishop by the date of his trial, committed the offences in respect of which he was eventually convicted when headmaster of a government funded, church-run residential school for aboriginal children. The school was one of about 80 which existed nationwide between the 1880s and the 1970s and which were designed to assimilate aboriginal children into white Canada, a process which often involved children being 'forced to attend, separated from their families 10 months of the year while Catholic and Protestant instructors tried to steer them away from their native spiritual beliefs . . . Students were punished for speaking their native languages, [and] force-fed white culture'. It has also become increasingly apparent that regimes at these schools included 'rapes, beatings, suicides, suspicious deaths, humiliating punishments, even the use of a homemade, low-voltage electric chair'.[119]

Those girls who were sexually assaulted by O'Connor in his position as headmaster had no recourse against him at the time. Thirty years on, when action was eventually taken against him, they were no more than witnesses in the prosecution run by the State. O'Connor's lawyers sought access to their mental health records in order to present them as 'neurotic, unstable, and not to be believed'. This access was refused by the prosecutor who 'couldn't credit what [the defense] was asking for'. The trial judge then demanded what no trial judge in Canada had ever before ordered: that the prosecution 'force [the] complainants to authorize release of their lifelong medical records', and this in a hearing at which no complainant was present.[120]

The model of criminal cases upon which the constitutional rights of defendants rests is one which sits unhappily with the private violence to

---

[118] Note 36 above.
[119] *Roanoke Times & World News*, 1 December 1996.
[120] Birnie, note 48 above.

which women and children are subjected at the hands of their oppressors. The extent of this violence is only now being realised, and the entrenchment of rights can, as was pointed out above, serve to ossify legal rules in line with perceptions of fairness embedded in the common law. According to one commentator, writing in the US, '[t]he best method to determine whether admission [of any particular evidence] is required by the Constitution is to apply the jurisdiction's standard rules of evidence to the proffered . . . evidence. Because standard rules of evidence are premised on general principles developed over many years, exclusions of evidence under those rules are almost always constitutionally justified.'[121] But these rules may themselves be tainted by discrimination and prejudice (such as, for example, the traditional mistrust of sexual assault complainants), in which case constitutionally protected rights serve merely to perpetuate the discrimination suffered by the traditionally disadvantaged.

Rights do not enable the victims of criminal offences effectively to demand the equal protection of the law, either at the level of theory or in practice. They do enable defendants to attack every legislative provision designed to ameliorate the position of the victims of gender-related crimes such as rape. The problem is not that of balancing the rights of victims against those of defendants in general. Rather, attempts made to place the (usually female) victims of sexual assault in a similar position to that of the victims of unisex violence are thwarted by the tendency of entrenched rights to privilege traditional judicial perceptions of relevance over those which are the result of conscious attempts to eradicate discrimination from the law.

The existence of the Charter in Canada has had the effect that each legislative attempt to ameliorate the position of the victims of sexual assault has been vulnerable to judicial override and, as a result, to doubt. In *Osolin*,[122] for example, Justices Iacobucci and Sopinka reserved judgment as to the constitutionality of s 276 of the Criminal Code after its amendment in the light of *Seaboyer*.[123] Even though this appears to have come to nothing, the legislative provisions having been modelled very closely on the guidelines established by the Supreme Court in *Seaboyer*, the stress experienced by women complaining of rape is multiplied by the uncertainty as to what rules will be applied to them. As for the other recent legislative amendments, it has been seen above that the post-*O'Connor* amendments relating to personal records have already been ruled unconstitutional in Ontario and Alberta and the post-*Daviault* amendments are under significant threat.

Nor are these the only problems raised by the entrenchment of rights in the criminal justice arena. As already noted, the Supreme Court has

---

[121] D Haxton, 'Rape Shield Statutes' (1985) *Wisconsin Law Review* 1219, at 1271–1272, cited by Madam Justice L'Heureux-Dubé in *Seaboyer*, note 4 above.
[122] Note 5 above.
[123] Note 4 above.

given complainants and their counsellors standing to challenge orders for the introduction of private records. The recognition of such parties in *A (LL) v B (A)*[124] followed that court's decision in *Dagenais*[125] in which that court allowed the Canadian Broadcasting Corporation to appeal a publication ban imposed on a fictional television drama about the sexual assault of children in orphanages, at a time when trials based on similar facts were pending. The Criminal Code did not appear to allow the CBC any appeal from the ban which was imposed by the lower court at the behest of the accused. The Supreme Court ruled that the protection of the CBC's Charter right to freedom of expression demanded 'full and effective remedy', which remedy it supplied by granting third party applicants who asserted an infringement of their Charter rights a direct appeal to the Supreme Court.

The decision in *Dagenais* has been criticised on the basis that '[b]y drawing third parties directly into the proceedings, *Dagenais* initiated a major reconfiguration of the criminal trial process, which unquestionably compromises a conception of that process as a contest between the state and the accused . . . rights of equality and privacy do not fit within the traditional scheme of criminal adjudication'.[126] In addition, the provision of appeal for third parties may result in very substantial delays in the criminal process. And, as Madam Justice L'Heureux-Dubé pointed out in her dissenting judgment: 'applying the Charter to court orders could result in endless loops of litigation where even final orders of the Supreme Court of Canada . . . could be challenged at first instance on Charter grounds. This would be a strange and unjustifiable situation which could paralyse our judicial system by removing the certainty from supposedly final judgments'.

The difficulties raised by *Dagenais,* and by its application to complainants and their counsellors, are real. But in the absence of a right to intervene, there is no mechanism by which sexual assault complainants, or others implicated in Charter decisions, can challenge the assault on their constitutional rights which may occur. To the extent that complainant's records are already in the hands of the Crown, the decision in *O'Connor* suggests that no appeal will be permitted by complainants on the grounds of any invasion of privacy. But where records, whether they be medical, counselling or even private documents such as diaries kept by the complainant, have not been gathered by the Crown, the decision in *O'Connor* recognises a right to privacy, albeit not one which will be readily taken to outweigh the defendant's interest in the disclosure of allegedly relevant material. In these circumstances, it is imperative that appeal exists against orders for disclosure. In *O'Connor,* for example, the initial order for

---

[124] Note 49 above.
[125] Note 62 above.
[126] J Cameron, 'Tradition and Change under the Charter', in J Cameron (ed), note 26 above, pp 228–230.

disclosure (the first ever to compel 'complainants in a sexual-assault case to authorize release of their lifelong medical records' was made without the presence in court of a single complainant).[127]

The granting of standing to sexual assault complainants and their counsellors in *A (LL) v B (A)* (above) was essential if women are to have any defence to unrestrained disclosure of their personal records in the context of sexual assault trials. But that decision cannot be regarded as making good the harm done to women by *O'Connor* and in *Carosella*.[128] As Diane Martin pointed out in a comment upon the Supreme Court decisions in *O'Connor* and *A (LL) v B (A)*, although 'the elevation of the legal and constitutional interests of witnesses and other "third" (or non) parties to party status . . . accords to them a startling degrees [sic] of control over the course of criminal proceedings' and adds 'distinct problems of trial delay, complication and expense', '[t]his new status for individual complainants will do little . . . to advance the goal of encouraging more victims of sexual and intimate assault to bring their accusations forward. No individual victim who has received counselling can know whether his or her records will ultimately be protected, and being advised of *Charter* rights to assert is little comfort'.[129]

And even where complainants or their counselling services are accepted as having standing to appeal the orders of trial judges on the basis of their Charter rights, constitutional litigation is very expensive. Legal aid is not always made available to prospective challengers, and federal funding for such challenges[130] and organisations such as the Women's Legal Education and Action Fund, which have played a substantial role in pursuing Charter claims, do not have the resources to intervene in every case where, for example, a complainant's privacy rights are at stake. In such circumstances: '[f]or the ordinary or poor litigant who might want to claim a constitutional remedy but whose case will not make law, or otherwise attract a source of funding or expert legal assistance *pro bono, Charter* remedies remain quite illusory, or something for the rich or criminally accused'.[131]

---

[127] Birnie, note 48 above.
[128] Note 37 above.
[129] Martin, note 52 above, pp 121 and 107.
[130] *Ibid*, p 105.
[131] *Ibid*, pp 105–106.

Chapter 10

Rights for Women?

Introduction

Before turning to consider the application of the UK Human Rights Act 1998, it is useful to recap on a number of general themes which have arisen throughout Chapters 4–9 above in relation to the application of entrenched rights in the particular contexts considered. It is apparent that the approach taken to the meaning of discrimination and/or equality has been crucial to the application of entrenched rights – whereas, in the US, 'equal protection' in the employment sphere has served mainly to place under threat the substantive pursuit of equality through affirmative action, Canada's Supreme Court has embraced a much more purposive approach to the Charter's equality provisions with the effect that, even absent the provision expressly permitting affirmative action, its understanding of discrimination would extend to allow such action. Nor has the significance of the approach to discrimination/equality been confined to the employment sphere – the application of sex discrimination to cover pregnancy discrimination has implications for the constitutional approach to denials of women's reproductive autonomy. Only where pregnancy discrimination is regarded as sex discrimination can intervention in pregnancy and childbirth have equality implications.[1]

Another important issue which arose concerned the tendency of entrenched rights to apply exclusively in respect of 'government', and to 'protect the negative freedoms of citizens', rather than to 'alter power relations, redistribute wealth, or promote social welfare'.[2] Even the positive

---

[1] Having said this, the Canadian Supreme Court's apparent retrenchment towards the formal model of equality has been noted in Chapter 3 above.

[2] P Russell, 'The Political Purposes of the Charter: Have They Been Fulfilled? An Agnostic's Report'. In P Bryden *et al* (eds), *Protecting Rights and Freedoms: Essays on the Charter's Place in Canada's Political, Legal and Intellectual Life* (Toronto: University of Toronto Press, 1994), pp 40–41: 'The Supreme Court's interpretation of the Charter has minimized its impact on social and economic relations' (citing *RWDSU v Dolphin Delivery Ltd* [1986] 2 SCR 573; *Reference Re Public Service Employee Relations Act* [1987] 1 SCR 313 and *Irwin Toy* [1989] 1 SCR 927): see further Chapter 6 above.

conceptions of the State and of freedom developed by Canada's Supreme Court have not impelled that court to require state action, and the application of the Charter only in the narrowest public sphere leaves women vulnerable to all the discrimination which flows from private individuals and powerful corporations. While government intervention designed to eradicate discrimination in the marketplace is likely to be permitted in Canada (as distinct from the US), such intervention cannot be required. According to one critic:

> [t]he Charter creates a metaphorical fence around individuals that is enforced by the courts through nullification of trespasses by the state . . . Positive rights . . . require the state to act by providing some benefit . . . either directly, through a social policy . . . or indirectly, through social legislation that imposes obligations on private actors . . . Such claims do not fit with the state-as-Leviathan conception imbedded within the Court's jurisprudence.[3]

The non-application of entrenched rights to the private sector, coupled with the generally negative, rather than positive, obligations they impose on the State, is of all the more concern in the light of evidence that the existence of such rights may incline politicians to leave things to the judiciary. This tendency was noted in relation to abortion in the US, where politicians frequently gain political points by passing swingeing anti-abortion legislation on the assumption that such legislation will be defeated by the courts, thereby sparing them the social costs of its implementation (see further Chapter 4 above) at the same time as gaining them favour with the religious right. In Canada, too, one-time Minister for Justice, Kim Campbell, stated in 1994 that she had 'begun to note a very disquieting trend among legislators to leave difficult decisions to the courts . . . This is . . . nothing less than an abdication of Parliament's role as the primary agent of social change in Canada'.[4]

Even in those cases in which legislatures do act in order to improve the position of disadvantaged groups (whether by affording women pregnancy rights, embracing affirmative action or restricting the use of sexual history evidence in rape trials), entrenched rights can be used in order to challenge those improvements. Not only the equality rights themselves but also property rights, the right to life of the foetus, etc, can be used to defeat legislation (as in the case of Ireland's disability discrimination legislation and, twice, in respect of Germany's abortion legislation[5]). In such cases entrenched rights can become a tool by which hard-won struggles (whether in respect of employment, reproductive, or criminal justice

---

[3] J Bakan, *Just Words: Constitutional Rights and Social Wrongs* (Toronto: University of Toronto Press, 1997), pp 48–49.
[4] K Campbell, 'Parliament's Role in Protecting the Rights and Freedoms of Canadians', in Bryden *et al* (eds), note 2 above, pp 29–30.
[5] See, respectively, Chapters 7 and 4 above.

rights) can be undone at the whim of an aggrieved individual or a power-ful corporation.[6] This danger is particularly acute where (as in the area of sexual history evidence, discussed in Chapter 9 above) the legislature takes steps to counteract the prejudicial attitudes of the common law itself.

The danger posed by constitutional rights means that women's organisations must seek intervener status whenever women's interests are seen to be at stake, a tactic which requires the use of scarce resources on continual re-inventions of the wheel. Failure to intervene can result, as in *R v Daviault*[7] (see Chapter 8 above), in decisions which are extra-ordinarily inimical to the interests of women – in that case, the accept-ance of extreme intoxication as a defence to rape on the basis solely of disputed scientific evidence from a single witness.[8] The need for intervention is particularly acute where, as has frequently been the case in Canada, Attorneys General are reluctant to uphold women's rights against challenge by men.[9] Appropriate interventions can be successful exercises in damage limitation. But even where they do occur, it is doubt-ful whether the court is a suitable forum for the determination of social issues such as the appropriate period of maternity leave, and of its relationship with leave for the adoption of a child (this being one of the issues in *Schachter v Canada*,[10] see Chapter 7 above). As Kim Campbell pointed out:

> [c]ourt cases are about the interpretation and the application of the law,
> usually to specific fact situations. They are . . . often inappropriate for
> deciding broad policy issues affecting a large number of people . . . The
> adversarial process . . . [w]hile [it] . . . has proved its value in resolving
> differences of fact and in applying the law to those facts, . . . is not designed
> to ensure that all considerations relevant to value-laden policy decisions are
> identified.[11]

There are powerful arguments that the courtroom is simply not the proper forum for dealing with issues such as the approach of the crim-inal justice system to intoxication, or the length and distribution of maternity/paternity leave. Whereas the legislature can take into account

---

[6] See also *Shkwarchuk v Hansen* (1984) 12 CRR 369 in which a Saskatchewan court struck down the common law rule of consortium because it did not apply to women.

[7] [1994] 3 SCR 63.

[8] In J Cameron (ed), *The Charter's Impact on the Criminal Justice System* (Scarborough, Ontario: Carswell, 1996), roundtable III (p 300), Assistant Minister (AG Ontario) Michael Code. There were no intervenors and the court had before it no social science data.

[9] See discussion of *Schachter v Canada* [1992] 2 SCR 679 in Chapter 7 above. See also *Tremblay v Daigle* [1989] 2 SCR 530, [1989] RJQ 1735, 59 DLR (4th) 609, [1989] RJQ 1980, discussed in Chapter 4 above, in which the Attorney General did not take a position on whether, despite the previous decision in *Morgentaler* [1988] 1 SCR 30, an abusive ex-partner should be able to prevent an abortion.

[10] *Ibid.*

[11] Campbell, note 4 above, pp 25–26.

wider issues and, as the Canadian legislature did in the post-*Daviault* debate, seek a representative selection of scientific opinion or such other evidence as may be relevant, courts are generally dependent on the evidence given by the defence and prosecution-appointed 'experts' before it. One could argue, as the Ontario's Assistant Attorney General did (in response to *Daviault*) that the system might be revised to enable 'the courts . . . to find better ways of creating sufficient social science records to find legislative facts'.[12] But even if the problems associated with funding and accommodating intervenors (see above) could be resolved, the question which must be put is whether a court is the right place to determine essentially political issues such as whether a state should permit extreme drunkenness to result in the acquittal of those who rape, assault, maim or even kill.[13]

Much of the damage which might otherwise have been inflicted upon Canadian women as a result of the Charter has failed to materialise, at least at the level of the Supreme Court, because of the approach taken by the senior judiciary to 'equality' within s 15. Indeed, Canada's experience underlies the point made in Chapters 2 and 3 above concerning the importance, to the application of entrenched rights, of the attitude of the judiciary. Again, as underlined in Chapter 2, this renders particularly important the type of people appointed as judges and, accordingly, the procedures by which they are selected.

European Convention on Human Rights

Having considered the impact of entrenched rights in Canada and the US, an assessment of the potential impact in the UK of the implementation of the Human Rights Act 1998 is appropriate. Before turning to the particular areas considered in Chapters 4–9 above, some general remarks will be made in relation to the approach taken under the Convention to discrimination and the issue of state action and, in so far as it concerns standing, to the positive threats posed by entrenched rights. The other general themes outlined above will be considered in the context of employment, abortion, etc.

Discrimination

Considering first the approach to discrimination, the first point which must be made concerns the lack of any general equality provision in the

---

[12] Note 8 above, p 306.
[13] The Government of Canada stressed the political nature of this determination in the preamble to its post-*Daviault* Bill: see M Schaffer, 'Criminal Responsibility and the *Charter*: The Case of *R v Daviault*', in Cameron (ed), note 8 above, p 313.

Convention or, accordingly, in the Human Rights Act 1998.[14] Article 14 provides only that: '[t]he enjoyment of the rights and freedoms set forth in this Convention shall be secured without discrimination on any ground such as sex, race, colour, language, religion, political or other opinion, national or social origin, association with a national minority, property, birth or other status'. The European Court of Human Rights has recognised that Article 14 does not require a violation of other rights under the Convention in order to come into operation: such an interpretation would rob the provision of any effect.[15] Rather, a violation can be found, in combination with (an)other Article(s) of the Convention, where no violation of the other Article(s), taken alone, has occurred.[16] The formula recently applied by the Commission has been to the effect that an Article 14 complaint may be established where the subject matter of the discriminatory treatment 'relate[s] to' or 'falls within the scope of'[17] or is 'covered by'[18] a right or freedom elsewhere guaranteed by the Convention and the European Court of Human Rights has, since 1984, taken the approach that '[a]lthough the application of Article 14 does not necessarily presuppose a breach of [a substantive Article] . . . there can be no room for its application unless the facts at issue fall within the ambit of one or more of the latter'.[19]

The significance of this restricted scope will be returned to below. At this point, however, it is important to note that 'discrimination' within Article 14 is interpreted more restrictively by the European Court of Human Rights than that term is understood in relation to the equality guarantees of the EC Treaty. In the first place, alleged violations of Article 14 generally involve direct and overt discrimination, although 'the "badge" of differentiation relied on in the legislation or decision . . . may be challenged by the applicant as not being the "real" reason for distinguishing him from others'.[20] But the European Court of Human Rights

---

[14] An additional protocol on the prohibition of discrimination is planned, the European Council's Standing Committee for Human Rights having adopted a decision in March 1998 giving it terms of reference 'to elaborate, before 31 December 1999, a draft additional protocol or protocols to the ECHR broadening, in a general fashion, the field of application of Article 14' (see European Council website, http://www.coe.fr/index.asp, at http://www.coe.fr/cm/dec/1998/622/41.htm). The potential significance of this protocol is unclear. The gap in the current provision was highlighted by Kevin McNamara MP, HC Debs 16 February 1998, col 804, see further Chapter 2 above.

[15] *Abdulaziz, Cabales and Balkandali* (1985) A 94, 35. This was recognised also by the Commission in Appl 84105/78, *X v Federal Republic of Germany* DR 18 (1980) 216.

[16] See also Appl 4045/67 *X v Federal Republic of Germany* (1970) 13 *Yearbook* 698, pp 704–706.

[17] Appl 5763/72 *X v Netherlands* (1973) 16 *Yearbook* 274, p 296; Appl 5935/72 *X v Federal Republic of Germany* (1976) 19 *Yearbook* 276, p 288.

[18] Appl 6573/74 *X v Netherlands* DR 1 (1975) p 87, at 89, cited by P van Dijk and G van Hoof, *Theory and Practice of the European Convention on Human Rights* (2nd ed, The Netherlands: Kluwer, 1990), p 535.

[19] *Abdulaziz, Cabales and Balkandali*, note 15 above; *Rasmussen v Denmark* (1984) A 87, 12 7 EHRR 371.

[20] D Harris, M O'Boyle and C Warbrick, *Law of the European Convention on Human Rights* (London: Butterworths, 1995), pp 476–477.

generally gives 'short shrift [to] . . . claims attributing covert and discreditable motives to governments'.[21]

Article 14 permits of little scope for indirect discrimination. The provision may extend to this type of discrimination – in the *Belgian Linguistics*[22] case the European Court of Human Rights referred to the 'aims *and effects*' (my emphasis) of legislation. But, according to Harris *et al*, 'the burden upon the applicant to establish that it exists is severe'. Further, the tendency, discussed below, to elide or merge distinct discrimination issues is evident also in this context.[23] In *Abdulaziz v UK*,[24] for example, a minority of the European Commission of Human Rights took the view that an immigration rule which required that fiancés had previously met, in order that the non-patrial be permitted access to the UK, was 'indirectly racist', tending as it did disproportionately to disadvantage men from the Indian sub-continent, arranged marriages being particularly common in that area. In rejecting this particular claim, however, the Court ignored the impact of the rule and simply examined the purpose behind it (preventing bogus marriages).[25]

Under Article 14, as under Article 119 and the other EC equality provisions, discrimination can be justified. A further significant difference which arises here is that, while in EC law, direct sex discrimination can be justified only in line with particular EC provisions, and not in general terms, direct discrimination may be justified under Article 14 of the Convention. In a sense this is inevitable, Article 14's list of prohibited grounds of discrimination neither short nor exhaustive.[26] But the test for justification which has been adopted by the European Court of Human Rights, even in terms of direct sex discrimination, is considerably more relaxed than that applied by the European Court of Justice to indirect discrimination. In the *Belgian Linguistics*[27] case, the European Court of Human Rights ruled that Article 14 is violated by discrimination having 'no objective and reasonable justification'. Discrimination in pursuit of a 'legitimate aim' would be justified unless it was 'clearly established that there is no reasonable relationship of proportionality between the means employed and the aim sought to be realized'.

This approach is almost the reverse of that which applies under Article 119 and related EC law. Whereas, under the latter, the onus is on the alleged discriminator to satisfy the courts that practices which impact

---

[21] *Ibid*, p 477, citing *Abdulaziz, Cabales and Balkandali*, note 15 above, and *Handyside v UK* (1976) A 24.

[22] (1968) A 6, 1 EHRR 252.

[23] Note 20 above.

[24] *Abdulaziz, Cabales and Balkandali*, note 15 above.

[25] *Ibid*, see also Harris *et al*, note 20 above, pp 477–478. Harris *et al* also discuss *X v Ireland* (1978) A 25, in which the European Court did not examine why no Loyalists were interned beyond the Government's statement that their activities were directed differently.

[26] With such lists, any prohibition on discrimination must generally be understood to mean arbitrary, unfair, etc, discrimination.

[27] Note 22 above.

disproportionately upon men or women 'correspond to a real need, [are] appropriate with a view to achieving the objectives pursued and [are] necessary to that end',[28] discrimination (direct or indirect) will breach Article 14 only if it has 'no objective and reasonable justification having regard to the aim and effects of the measure', or 'there is no reasonable proportionality between ends and means'. In the *National Union of Belgian Police*[29] and *Swedish Engine Drivers' Union*[30] cases the European Court of Human Rights took an even more restricted approach to Article 14, asking only whether the treatment at issue had a justified aim in view or whether the authorities pursued 'other and ill-intentioned designs'.[31] Again, the significance of this approach to discrimination will be considered further below.

Finally, van Dijk and van Hoof point out that, while the well-established approach to discrimination under Article 14 calls for, in the first place, a comparison of the treatment afforded to persons categorised on Article 14 or analogous grounds, followed by consideration of the issue of justification, in practice these steps are generally merged (or the first overlooked) with the effect that discrimination is not subject even to the level of scrutiny provided for in the *Belgian Linguistics* case.[32] This has already been mentioned in connection with *Abdulaziz*. In *Dudgeon v UK*,[33] too, the European Court of Human Rights skipped to considering the justifiability of protecting those under 21 from the perils of homosexual sex without comparing the rules for heterosexual (or lesbian) sex and failed, therefore, to consider whether such arguments justified the differential treatment of homosexuals, as distinct from the restriction of intercourse with young persons generally.[34]

Another shortcoming of Article 14 is that, by contrast with the equality provisions of EC law, it permits the removal of discrimination by levelling-down, rather than up, of the provisions at issue. Thus, for example, Britain's response to the decision of the European Court of Human Rights in *Abdulaziz* (in which Britain's immigration rules were found to violate Article 14 read together with Article 8, in that they provided less favourable treatment to the husbands and fiancés of patrial women than to the wives and fiancées of patrial men) was to withdraw the more favourable treatment from the wives of patrial men.[35]

---

[28] Case C-170/84 *Bilka-Kaufhaus, Bilka-Kaufhaus GmbH v Weber von Hartz* [1986] ECR 1607, [1987] ICR 110, [1986] 2 CMLR 701, [1986] IRLR 317.

[29] (1975) 1 EHRR 578.

[30] (1975) 1 EHRR 617.

[31] According to van Dijk and van Hoof, note 18 above, pp 545–546: 'Article 14 has been deprived of much of its meaning, since only those inequalities for which no objective and reasonable justification can be found are considered to conflict with it.'

[32] *Ibid.*

[33] (1981) A 45, 4 EHRR 149.

[34] See also *Grandrath v Federal Republic of Germany* (1967) 10 *Yearbook* 626.

[35] See P Gardner and C Wickremasinghe, 'England and Wales and the European Convention', in B Dickson (ed), *Human Rights and the European Convention* (London: Sweet & Maxwell, 1997), p 83.

For all of these shortcomings, it can be said, in defence of Article 14 and its interpretation by the European Court of Human Rights, that it is concerned with a substantive rather than with a formal model of equality. In *Gudmundsson v Iceland*,[36] for example, the Commission rejected an Article 14 claim against Iceland's progressive income tax structure on the basis that unequal cases could and should be treated unequally in proportion to their inequality'. According to the Commission, such a system 'is not discriminatory, provided the progressive measure is proportional and consequently results in a fairer distribution of income than would be the case without it'. In this area, as in so many others, a generous 'margin of appreciation' was to be accorded to the Contracting Parties.[37] The benefit of this approach is that, in the unlikely event that significant affirmative action measures were to be adopted in the UK (and to the extent that these were compatible with EC law – see further Chapter 6 above), it is unlikely that these measures would offend Article 14. Further, in this context and given Article 14's parasitic nature, no violation of it can be established except in connection with another Article of the Convention. It is possible (though unlikely) that the jurisprudence of Article 3 may develop to the extent that all discrimination based on race or sex might be regarded as 'inhuman and degrading treatment'. But this is unlikely, given the very narrow approach of the European Court and Commission to that Article (see below).

State action

Turning next to the general application of entrenched rights only against the State, a number of points can be made in connection with the European Convention on Human Rights and its incorporation in the Human Rights Act 1998. Article 1 of the Convention provides that Contracting States 'shall secure to everyone within their jurisdiction the rights and freedoms' guaranteed under Articles 2–18. While only Contracting States can themselves be called to answer before the European Court of Human Rights, the scope of their obligations is not merely themselves to honour the rights and freedoms set out in the text of the Charter, but to 'secure' those rights and freedoms. Important and related questions which arise in this context concern the extent to which

---

[36] Appl 511/59 (1960) 3 *Yearbook* 394.

[37] The 'margin of appreciation' doctrine, discussed in van Dijk and van Hoof, note 18 above; Harris *et al*, note 20 above, pp 12–15, refers to the practice by which the Convention organs allow a measure of discretion to the Contracting Parties in relation to Convention rights in recognition of the fact that (according to the European Court in *Handyside v UK*, note 21 above, paras 48–49) '[b]y reason of their direct and continuous contact with the vital forces of their countries, state authorities are in principle in a better position than an international judge to give an opinion on the exact context of those requirements of [morals] as well as on the "necessity" of a "restriction" or "penalty" intended to meet them'.

the Convention imposes positive obligations (as distinct from mere restrictions) upon Contracting States, and the extent, if any, to which those states can be held responsible for violations by private persons within their jurisdictions.

The European Court of Human Rights has accepted that the Convention imposes some positive obligations upon Contracting States (in *Marckx v Belgium*,[38] to provide equal treatment to the children of unmarried parents; in *Airey v Ireland*,[39] to provide practical access by way of financial assistance to particular litigants). More recently, in *B v France*[40] the European Court of Human Rights accepted that Article 8's right to respect for private and family life might impose positive obligations on the authorities with respect to transsexuals, although any such obligation did not extend to requiring amendment of the birth register. All of these cases concern Article 8, but it is clear on its face that Article 6 imposes positive obligations (for example, to provide interpreters where necessary, and legal aid at least in the criminal law context and 'when the interests of justice so require'). In addition, Article 11 has been interpreted so as to impose some positive obligations upon the state. In *National Union of Belgian Police*,[41] for example, the inclusion of the words 'for the protection of his interests' in the guarantee of freedom to join a trade union was taken by the European Court of Human Rights to imply a right to a union capable of serving those interests – this, in turn, imposed an obligation on the authorities to hear, though not necessarily to consult with, unions. And in *Association A v Federal Republic of Germany*,[42] the Commission ruled that, while trade unions had a freedom, rather than a right, to conclude collective agreements with employers, Article 11 did impose an obligation on the authorities to help to make this possible. Most recently, in *A v UK* the European Court of Human Rights ruled that Article 3 was breached by a failure on the part of the State to protect from inhuman and degrading treatment at the hands of a private individual.[43] This case is further discussed below.

In addition, Article 2 clearly imposes a protective obligation in relation to life. In the context of Article 14, too, some positive obligations have been recognised by the Convention machinery in a manner similar to that adopted by Canada's Supreme Court in *Eldridge v Columbia*[44] (see Chapter 3 above). Thus, according to the Commission in *X v Federal*

---

[38] (1979) A 31, 2 EHRR 330.
[39] (1981) A 41, 13 EHRR 622.
[40] (1994) A 232-C, 16 EHRR 1. Some measure of positive obligation was accepted also in *Abdulaziz, Cabales and Balkandali*, note 15 above; *Rees v UK* (1986) A 106, 9 EHRR 56; and *Cossey v UK* (1990) A 184, 13 EHRR 622.
[41] Note 29 above. See also *Swedish Engine Drivers' Union*, note 30 above, discussed below.
[42] (1983) DR 34.
[43] 23 September 1998, available on the European Court of Human Rights homepage http://www.dhcour.coe.fr/.
[44] [1997] 3 SCR 624.

Republic of Germany,[45] although the Convention for the most part protects 'freedoms', rather than 'rights', the former generally requiring only the non-intervention of the State for their satisfaction, to the extent that state authorities do act in areas covered by the Convention guarantees, they are obliged to do so without discrimination on sex or other protected grounds, unless that discrimination would be justified under Article 14.

Comparing the Convention approach to that in the US and Canada, the former appears on its face to be more generous. But closer comparison shows that this may not be the case. Canada's Charter imposes positive obligations on the State in terms of fair trial rights. And the positive obligations recognised in *B v France* and *Marckx* (above) are similar to (indeed, in the former case do not appear to go as far as) those imposed by Canada's Supreme Court under s 15 of the Charter (see, for example, *Eldridge*). The US Supreme Court, too, has found a constitutional prohibition against discrimination on the basis of illegitimacy which extends to the imposition of some positive obligations on the State.[46] And *Airey* (above) can be explained as a decision that, where the State itself stands between a citizen and her fundamental rights (there the right to a family life legally separated from her husband), the State is obliged not to render that hurdle insurmountable on the grounds of cost. Thus understood, the decision accords with those of the US Supreme Court.[47] The only category of cases which appears to impose positive obligations beyond those imposed in Canada and the US are those under Article 11, and in respect of these it can be argued that they do no more than to pay lip-service to the existence of any positive right to freedom of association, the European Court of Human Rights never actually finding a Contracting Party in breach.

In any event, to the extent that positive obligations are imposed upon Contracting Parties by the Convention, the Contracting Parties enjoy a very wide measure of discretion in determining how those obligations should be implemented. In *Airey*, for example (discussed further below) the European Court of Human Rights was at pains to point out that the right of effective access under Article 6(1) did not require that Ireland provide legal aid in relation to separation proceedings – it could, for example, have simplified the relevant proceedings. Equally, in *Schmidt and Dahlström v Sweden*[48] (discussed below), the European Court of Human Rights affirmed the Contracting Party's 'free choice' with respect to the manner in which trade unions might be permitted to protect the inter-

---

[45] Appl 84105/78 *X v Federal Republic of Germany*, note 15 above.
[46] See L Tribe, *American Constitutional Law* (2nd ed, Mineola, New York: The Foundation Press Inc, 1988), pp 1553–1619; *Mills v Habluetzel* 456 US 91 (1982).
[47] See Tribe, note 46 above, pp 1626 ff; *Griffin v State of Illinois* 351 US 12 (1956); *Douglas v State of California* 372 US 353 (1963); *Boddie v State of Connecticut* 401 US 371 (1971); *MLB v SLJ*, Case no 95–853, 1996, Supreme Court.
[48] (1975) 1 EHRR 637.

ests of their members. Unless it can fairly be said that the State has taken
no steps to secure those rights which it is obliged to give positive effect
to, no violation will be found.[49]

As far as the responsibility of states for violations of guaranteed rights
and freedoms by private persons is concerned, the position is rather less
clear. Some commentators take the view that Article 13's provision of the
right to a remedy '*notwithstanding* that the violation has been committed
by persons acting in an official capacity' (my emphasis) makes it 'clear
. . . that the State must provide for a remedy for any violation, whether
committed by it or by a private individual'.[50] Others dispute this, taking the
view that Article 13 is not conclusive one way or the other as to Contracting States' responsibilities for private violations and that the case law
does no more than to indicate the possibility that, in future, such an
effect might be ascribed to the Convention.

To the extent that the Convention does provide some protection, albeit
in an indirect form, from private violations of guaranteed rights and
freedoms, this appears to be the result of the obligations imposed upon
Contracting States by Article 1 'to secure' these rights and freedoms and
by Article 13 to provide an effective national remedy for violation.[51] In
1967 the Registrar of the European Court of Human Rights stated that
the use of the word 'notwithstanding' in Article 13 'admits implicitly, but
inevitably, that breaches of the Convention may be committed by private
individuals', and in 1980 the Deputy Secretary to the European Commission
on Human Rights declared that 'the States Party are obliged by Article
13 to provide a remedy in domestic law against violations committed by
private persons' as well as those by public authorities.[52] A number of
Contracting States in which the Convention has been incorporated into
domestic law follow this approach but, according to Drzemczewski, '[t]he
extent to which the Convention organs may hold a state party responsible for violations of the Convention's provisions by private persons or
organizations is difficult to determine with any accuracy'.[53]

In its report on the *Belgian Police* case[54] the Commission concluded that
the State could 'under certain circumstances be responsible for' interference by 'other individuals, groups or organizations' with rights and

---

[49] See also *B v France* (1981) A 41, 13 EHRR 622; *Abdulaziz, Cabales and Balkandali*, note 15
above – because 'the notion of "respect" is not clear-cut [a] . . . wide margin of appreciation' was appropriate; *Johnston and others v Ireland* (1987) 9 EHRR 203; *Plattform 'Ärzte
für das Leben' v Austria* (1988) DR 44, European Commission of Human Rights; (1988) A
139, 13 EHRR 204, European Court of Human Rights. See generally A Drzemczewski,
European Human Rights Convention in Domestic Law: A Comparative Study (Oxford: Clarendon
Press, 1983), Chapter 8.

[50] F Jacobs, and R White, *The European Convention on Human Rights* (2nd ed, Clarendon
Press, 1996), p 19.

[51] van Dijk and van Hoof, note 18 above, pp 78 and 526–527.

[52] Drzemczewski, note 49 above, p 205.

[53] *Ibid*, pp 207–214, 221.

[54] Note 29 above.

freedoms guaranteed under the Convention. And in *Young, James and Webster v UK*,[55] the Commission stated that 'there are Articles of the Convention which oblige the State to protect individual rights even against the action of others . . . Art. 11 is such a provision as far as dismissal on the basis of union activity or as a sanction for not joining a specific trade union is concerned . . . the State is responsible under the Convention if its legal system makes such dismissal lawful'.

The European Court of Human Rights accepted the Commission's conclusions in this respect.[56] But Drzemczewski pointed out in 1983 that, in general 'the attitude of the European Court . . . remains more cautious, and it appears from [the *Swedish Engine Drivers* and *Schmidt* cases] . . . that, for the present, it has intentionally refrained from expressing an opinion on this matter'.[57] More recently, and subsequent to Drzemczewski's comments, the European Court of Human Rights accepted in *X & Y v The Netherlands*[58] that the positive obligations inherent in the Convention 'may involve the adoption of measures designed to secure respect for private life even in the sphere of the relations of individuals between themselves'. This case, in which the European Court found a violation of Article 8, related to the State's failure to provide a mechanism whereby sexual assault proceedings could be brought on behalf of a handicapped child who was not competent to bring proceedings on her own account. In *Plattform 'Ärzte für das Leben' v Austria*,[59] too, the European Court agreed with the Commission that '[g]enuine, effective freedom of peaceful assembly [as guaranteed by Article 11] cannot . . . be reduced to a mere duty on the part of the State not to interfere . . . Like Article 8, Article 11 sometimes requires positive measures to be taken, even in the sphere of relations between individuals, if need be'.

In this case, both European Court and Commission agreed that Austria was obliged by Article 11 to provide protection for anti-abortion demonstrators from counter-demonstrators, this being required to permit effective demonstration about controversial issues.[60] But the European Court of Human Rights laid down no general theory in *Plattform*, confining itself to the observation that '[l]ike Article 8, Article 11 sometimes requires positive measures to be taken, even in the sphere of relations between individuals, if need be'. In *Costello-Roberts v UK*[61] the European Court of Human Rights again showed itself reluctant to impose any general obligation on Contracting States in a case concerning a violation of Article 3's prohibition on inhuman and degrading

---

[55] Appl 7601/76 (1977) 20 *Yearbook* 520.
[56] (1982) 4 EHRR 38.
[57] Note 49 above, p 222. Cf van Dijk and van Hoof, note 18 above, p 20.
[58] (1985) A 91.
[59] (1988) A 139, EHRR 204.
[60] No breach was found on the facts however, given the wide discretion permitted to Contracting Parties.
[61] (1993) 19 EHRR 112.

treatment.[62] Deciding in favour of a complaint relating to corporal punishment in private schools, the European Court ruled that Article 3 applied *not* by reason of any general obligation on Contracting Parties to secure the rights guaranteed by Article 3 against private individuals, rather upon the obligation imposed upon the UK by the Convention's First Protocol in respect of education, which responsibility could not entirely be delegated to the private sector.[63]

Subsequent to *Costello-Roberts* the European Court reached a much more radical decision in *A v UK*,[64] which concerned a complaint relating to the caning of a nine-year-old child by his step-father. In that case the European Court ruled that Articles 1 and 3, taken together, required that states:

> take measures designed to ensure that individuals within their jurisdiction are not subjected to torture or inhuman or degrading treatment or punishment, including such ill-treatment administered by private individuals . . .[65] Children and other vulnerable individuals, in particular, are entitled to State protection, in the form of effective deterrence, against such serious breaches of personal integrity.[66]

Here a breach of Article 3 was found because the acquittal of the assailant by a jury on the grounds that he had administered 'reasonable chastisement' signalled a failure of the law to 'provide adequate protection to the applicant against treatment or punishment contrary to Article 3'.[67]

The *A v UK* case marks a significant development since *Costello-Roberts* and adds Article 3 to the others (2, 8, 11 and 14) in respect of which a measure of *'drittwirkung'* has been recognised by the European Court of Human Rights. The exact extent of this indirect effect of Convention Articles is as yet unclear. In 1990, van Dijk and van Hoof suggested that, while 'it may be inferred from the changing social circumstances and opinions that the purport of the Convention *is going to be* to secure a certain minimum guarantee to the individual also in his relations with other persons . . . the exact scope under the Convention of State responsibility for private acts or omissions has not yet been clearly defined'.[68] Jacobs and White were, by contrast, much more confident in this regard

---

[62] *Albeit* by enforcement against the State, rather than the school.

[63] Cf *Soering v UK* (1989) A 161, 11 EHRR 439, in which the European Court of Human Rights accepted that Article 3 might be violated by extradition of a person subsequently likely to be subject to inhuman and degrading treatment.

[64] 23 September 1998, available on the European Court of Human Rights homepage http://www.dhcour.coe.fr/.

[65] Relying on *HLR v France* Reports 1997-III 758.

[66] Relying on *X & Y v The Netherlands*, note 58 above; *Stubbings and others v UK* Reports 1996-IV 1505, and the United Nations Convention on the Rights of the Child, Articles 19 and 37.

[67] Significant in this respect was the fact that the burden was on the prosecution 'to establish beyond reasonable doubt that the assault went beyond the limits of lawful punishment'.

[68] Note 18 above, pp 18, 78 and 213–214.

in 1996, theirs being the statement (above) that 'the State must provide for a remedy for any violation, whether committed by it or by a private individual'.[69] But whatever the position is under the Convention itself, the issue of most concern is the *domestic*, rather than the *international*, legal position.

At first glance the non-inclusion of Article 1 within the Human Rights Act 1998 (inevitable as this was, given its nature as an undertaking between the Contracting Parties) suggests that the 'rights brought home' under that Act might be less likely than those under the Convention to attract protection from violations by individuals, as well as by the State itself. (In *A v UK*, for example, it was specifically the combination of Articles 1 and 3 which was regarded by the European Court of Human Rights as founding the successful claim.) But closer examination of the Act reveals that the matter of private violations, like that of the State's obligation to take positive action to secure the rights and freedoms guaranteed under the Convention, is more, rather than less straightforward under domestic than under international law.

In order further to consider the impact of incorporation it is useful to recap the model adopted by the Human Rights Act 1998. Section 3(1) imposes an obligation upon the courts '[s]o far as it is possible to do so', to 'read and give[] effect to' primary and subordinate legislation 'in a way which is compatible with' the Convention rights listed in Schedule 1 to the Act (Articles 2–12 and 14, together with Articles 1–3 of the First Protocol and Articles 1 and 2 of the Sixth Protocol, all 'as read with Articles 16 to 18'). Section 4 permits declarations of incompatibility by the higher courts (High Court and above) while 6(1) makes it 'unlawful for a public authority to act in a way which is incompatible with' the incorporated rights. 'Act' is defined to include 'a failure to act' and, crucially, 'public authority' is defined to include courts and tribunals.[70] Section 6(1) does not apply if 'as a result of one or more provisions of primary legislation,[71] the authority could not have acted differently'.

State action: obligations under the Human Rights Act 1998

In the context of state action, consideration should be given to the extent to which the rights incorporated by the Human Rights Act 1998 will:

(1) give rise to positive obligations on the part of the State; and
(2) be actionable in respect of violations by private individuals.

---

[69] But this confidence appears to be the result more of interpretative differences than of any intervening decisions by the European Court of Human Rights – certainly the weight of opinion is against Jacobs and White, note 50 above. See, for example Harris *et al*, note 20 above, p 20.

[70] Human Rights Act 1998, ss 1 and 6. The act of a public authority is not unlawful if required by primary legislation and 'failure to act' does not include a failure to introduce, etc, primary legislation or a remedial order.

[71] Or provisions made thereunder, s 6(2).

The answer to (1) turns on the wording of the rights themselves, as listed in Sched 1, and of s 6 of the 1998 Act. The Convention rights do not include any provisos to the effect that they can be violated only by positive action taken by the State: Article 2, for example, states that '[e]veryone's right to life shall be protected by law'; Article 3 that '[n]o one shall be subjected to torture or inhuman or degrading treatment or punishment'; Article 8 that '[e]veryone has the right to respect for his [sic] private and family life, his [sic] home and his [sic] correspondence'. The wording of these Articles suggests that they give rise to positive rights. Further, as was pointed out above, s 6 of the 1998 Act renders unlawful an omission by a public authority, where that omission is incompatible with one or more of the Convention rights.

It would thus appear that, subject to the proviso that a failure to legislate does not amount to a breach of s 6, the failure of a public authority to secure by law the protection of life, protection from torture or degrading or inhuman treatment, respect for private and family life, etc, will breach that section. The right to respect for private and family life is, of course, subject to restriction 'in accordance with the law and [as] necessary in a democratic society in the interests of national security, public safety or the economic well-being of the country, for the prevention of disorder or crime, for the protection of health or morals, or for the protection of the rights and freedoms of others'. The rights accorded by Articles 9 (freedom of thought, conscience and religion), 10 (freedom of expression) and 11 (freedom of assembly and association) are similarly restricted. But subject to these inherent restrictions and those permitted under Articles 16–18, Articles 9–11, like those discussed above, appear to give rise to positive obligations on the part of the State (these obligations, once again, not extending to the obligation to pass primary legislation).

Turning now to (2), consideration of the extent to which the rights incorporated by the Human Rights Act 1998 will be actionable in respect of violations by private individuals. If the Human Rights Act 1998 were interpreted, as is suggested above, so as to require that 'respect for private life' be secured against private employers, or that proper recourse be provided against 'inhuman and degrading treatment' (for example, sustained battering) by private individuals the question which arises, given the lack of any legislative obligation, is how these rights may be secured. Section 6 does not make actions by private individuals unlawful and s 7 permits freestanding actions under the Act only against public authorities.[72] But the obligation on the courts to interpret national legislation, 'so far as it is possible to do so', so as to comply with the Convention rights incorporated, and the s 6 obligation on the courts, as public

---

[72] Or public/private bodies – see further Chapter 2 above and s 6(3)(b) of the Human Rights Act 1998.

authorities, to act compatibly with the Convention rights (unless prevented by primary legislation from so doing), together produce a degree of horizontal effect. The impact of the former is clear, while the latter goes beyond an obligation to act 'compatibly with the Convention . . . in cases involving other public authorities' to impose a duty to 'develop[] the common law in deciding cases between citizens'.[73] Persons (whether natural or legal) will not, under s 7, be permitted to sue private bodies or individuals directly under the Human Rights Act 1998. They will, however, be able to call in aid the Convention rights in relation to statutory or common law suits.

Standing

Before turning to consider the potential of incorporation in the substantive areas considered in Chapters 4–9, it is useful briefly to consider the issue of standing. As was mentioned in Chapter 2 above, the Human Rights Act 1998 may be relied upon only by a person who 'is (or would be) a victim of' an act rendered unlawful by that legislation. The significance of this is apparent when consideration is given to a number of Canadian cases (*Schachter v Canada*,[74] *Schafer v Canada*,[75] *Andrews v Law Society of British Columbia*[76]) in which interventions were made by organisations such as the Women's Legal Action Fund to avert findings inimical to women's interests which might otherwise have been made under the Charter.[77]

The Canadian experience suggests that the restriction of standing may have very serious repercussions for the development of Human Rights Act jurisprudence. It was stressed by UK Government Ministers throughout the Human Rights Bill debates that 'interest groups will still be able to provide assistance to victims who bring cases under the Bill, including the filing of amicus briefs'.[78] It has been suggested, in the context of the European Convention organs, that the willingness of the European Court of Human Rights to permit the filing of amicus briefs by interested

---

[73] The Lord Chancellor (HL Debs 24 November 1998, col 783). Lord Irvine had, however, stated previously that 'full horizontal effect' would be a 'step too far' (HL Debs 18 November 1998, col 798). See generally W Wade, 'The United Kingdom's Bill of Rights', in Beatson *et al* (eds), *Constitutional Reform in the UK: Practice and Principles* (Oxford: Hart, 1998).

[74] [1992] 2 SCR 679.

[75] (1988) 18 FTR 199, Ontario Court of Appeal, 8 August 1997, discussed in Chapter 7 above.

[76] *Andrews v Law Society of British Columbia* [1989] 1 SCR 143, discussed in Chapter 3 above.

[77] Cf *Daviault*, note 7 above, which may have been the result in part of the absence of any intervenors.

[78] Mike O'Brien MP, HC Debs 24 June 1998, col 1082. A similar statement was made by the Lord Chancellor, HL Debs 5 February 1998, col 810. For debate on this matter see HC Debs 24 June 1998, cols 1058–1091 and HL Debs 5 February 1998, cols 805–812 and 24 November 1997, cols 823–833.

parties (a practice common also in the US) has mitigated the effects of this restriction at the European level.[79] How, if at all, this will translate to the UK courts remains to be seen. The matter is one for particular concern, as was pointed out in both the Commons and the Lords, given the Government's exclusion of procedural rules whereby the European Court permits interventions by interested organisations.[80] Lord Lester was particularly scathing of this shortcoming in view of the right of intervention granted to the Crown in any case in which a declaration of incompatibility might be issued.[81] What is tolerably clear is that the Government's failure to establish a human rights commission, together with the restrictions planned in respect of civil legal aid (discussed further below), will have the effect of restricting access to its benefits for those of small and moderate means, while paving the way for its use by the powerful and wealthy.[82] It is also apparently the case that the restriction on interventions would prevent, for example, a sexual assault complainant such as those who intervened in *O'Connor*[83] (see Chapter 9 above) from asserting any right to privacy in a defendant's Human Rights Act claim for access to her medical or other records.

Abortion and reproductive freedom

Turning to the possible impact of the Human Rights Act 1998 on women's access to abortion, the first point which should be made is that the European Convention on Human Rights, in common both with the US

---

[79] B Dickson, 'The Common Law and the Convention', in Dickson (ed), note 35 above, p 215.

[80] Edward Garnier MP, HC Debs 24 June 1998, col 1065; Lord Lester, HL Debs 24 November 1997, cols 825–826.

[81] Lord Lester, note 80 above, 'I do not see any justification for placing the Government in that uniquely privileged position, depriving the courts of the benefit of other third party interventions'. See also Robert Maclennan MP, HC Debs 24 June 1998, col 1069, 'It would be particularly advantageous if it were possible in those first years for interest groups such as Liberty – the National Council for Civil Liberties – and Justice, and organisations such as Victim Support, Amnesty International and the Northern Ireland Standing Advisory Commission on Human Rights to have the right to come forward as interested parties. A peculiarly unhappy result of what is proposed is that they might even be excluded from roles as *amicus curiae*. [The amendment under discussion] . . . would ensure that the provisions of section 31(3) of the Supreme Court Act 1981 were maintained in the new circumstances and reinstate what I understood to be the Labour party's position on these matters before it took office. The consultation paper "Bringing Rights Home" intended that public interest cases should be taken by bodies such as those that I have mentioned.'

[82] See Robert Maclennan, note 81 above: 'The importance of that is, if anything, made greater by the Government's reluctance to acknowledge the case for a human rights commissioner . . . If there is no human rights commissioner and it is necessary for individuals to establish that they are victims – not just that they have a substantial interest – I fear that we may find that, in bringing rights home, we have narrowed the safeguards, rather than widened them.'

[83] [1995] 4 SCR 411.

Constitution and Canada's Charter of Rights, is silent on the matter. Article 2, however, protects the right to life and Article 8 the right to 'respect for private and family life'. The European Court of Human Rights has not ruled directly on abortion, although the matter was at issue in *Open Door Counselling and Dublin Well Woman v Ireland*,[84] an Article 10 (freedom of expression) case which arose from Ireland's restrictions on the provision of information about abortion services in the UK. Both European Commission and Court declined to rule under Article 2 or 8, finding instead a violation of Article 10. But the European Court did accept that 'the right to life' was 'one aspect' of Irish morals, although it was not 'necessary to decide whether "others" [in Article 8] . . . extends to the "unborn" . . . [or] to examine whether the foetus is encompassed by the right to life in Article 2'. While the margin of appreciation accorded to Contracting Parties in the field of morals was wide, it was 'not unfettered and unreviewable' and, in this particular case, a majority of the European Court took the view that Ireland had gone beyond the restrictions which could properly be imposed in its justifiable aim to protect its national morals.[85]

In addition to the European Court's ruling in the *Open Door* case, abortion cases have come before the Commission on a number of occasions. The approach taken by it does not suggest that the Convention would be particularly helpful to women seeking abortions. In *Brüggeman and Scheuten v Federal Republic of Germany*,[86] the first case in which abortion came before the Commission, that body expressly left open the issue whether Article 2 prohibited abortion. The case involved a challenge to Germany's strict criminal prohibition on abortion (see Chapter 4 above) on the grounds that it interfered with the applicants' right to family life (protected under Article 8) because it required them to renounce sexual intercourse, to use methods of contraception of which they disapproved on medical grounds, or to carry unwanted pregnancies to term. The Commission took the view that the German regulations served to protect, within Article 8(2) of the Convention, the rights of 'others' – here of the 'life growing in the womb': '[p]regnancy cannot be said to pertain uniquely to the sphere of private life. Whenever a woman is pregnant, her private life becomes closely connected with that of the developing fetus'.

The Commission therefore concluded that the regulation of abortion did not necessarily interfere with women's private lives. Subsequently, in *Paton v UK*,[87] the Commission stated that Article 2 did not recognise an unqualified right to life for the foetus (this would have prohibited abortion under any circumstances, thereby valuing life of the foetus more

---

[84] (1992) A 246, (1993) 15 EHRR 244.
[85] Five dissenting or partly dissenting judges, having the support of eight judges, were filed.
[86] (1976) 19 *Yearbook* 382, (1978) 10 DR 100.
[87] Appl 8416/79 (1980) 19 DR 244.

highly than that of the pregnant woman). But it refused to decide whether Article 2 applied to any extent to the foetus, stating that such a decision was unnecessary given that the termination at issue was at an early stage (ten weeks) and exclusively on medical advice (in order to avert injury to the woman's mental or physical health). The Commission ruled that the complaint was manifestly unfounded.

The decision in *Paton* has been criticised on the ground that it too widely protected the woman's 'right to life' in a situation where this was not at stake (the case concerning a 'social clause' abortion).[88] Of rather more concern is the room that it leaves open for the restriction of abortion on the basis of the right to life of the foetus. The right to life under Article 2 does not extend to a right to physical integrity save 'in so far as an injury to it constitutes a threat to life'.[89] Article 3 may, as van Dijk and van Hoof point out, protect physical integrity. But 'as long as the question of whether Article 2 is applicable to the unborn life has not been answered in the negative, [the reasonableness of the weighing of the woman's and foetus' interests under] will have to be reviewed in each individual case'.[90]

In *H v Norway*[91] the Commission again refused to exclude the possibility that Article 2 would offer protection to the foetus in certain circumstances, but did not indicate what those circumstances were (in that case the Commission accepted Norway's provision of abortion up to 14 weeks where 'pregnancy, birth or care for the child may place the woman in a difficult situation of life'). Of significance was the wide margin of appreciation accorded by the Commission to the Contracting States on the grounds that the area was a delicate one, and one in which national laws differed considerably. And in the *Open Door* case, the Commission went so far as to rule that the suppression by states of information relating to abortion was within the discretion permitted to them by the Convention.

Particularly alarming is the scope that Article 8 (which commands respect for private and family life) allows a prospective father to challenge an abortion decision reached by the vessel in which his potential offspring resides. Whereas, in *Knudsen v Norway*,[92] the Commission rejected a challenge to abortion regulation by a minister of religion on the grounds that he was not a 'victim' and therefore did not have standing, his position was contrasted by the Commission with that of a putative father who could claim to be differentially affected by a threatened abortion. In *Paton*, the plaintiff was the husband of a woman who had had an abortion. This challenge failed on the facts, but the recognition under Article 8 of the

---

[88] See van Dijk and van Hoof, note 18 above, p 219.
[89] Appl 8278/78 *X v Austria* (1980) 18 DR 154.
[90] Note 18 above, p 220.
[91] Unreported, 1990, cited in *Re MB* [1997] 2 FCR 541, 38 BMLR 175, [1997] Fam Law 542, discussed in Chapter 5 above.
[92] Appl 11045/84 (1985) 42 DR 247.

'interests' of the foetus means that the provision provides little protection for any right to abortion. The same is true of Article 2 which, as has been pointed out above, does not protect a woman's right to personal autonomy.

What of protection from 'discrimination' under the European Convention on Human Rights? According to the current understanding of discrimination in the employment field, action taken on the grounds of pregnancy amounts, in the UK and Europe (though not in the US), to action taken on the ground of sex. An argument could be made that the restriction of abortion discriminates against women in relation to Article 8's right to 'respect for . . . privacy and family life'. The success of such a claim turns on the approach taken by the British courts to 'discrimination' under the Human Rights Act 1998. The first issue which should be considered is whether a difference in treatment had been made out. It was pointed out, above, that the European Court of Human Rights is less than meticulous in determining the appropriate comparison which should be drawn at this step. Whereas, under the European Court of Justice approach, the pregnant woman should be compared to a non-pregnant man, with the effect that abortion restrictions clearly infringe upon the freedom of the former,[93] it is likely that the European Court of Human Rights might, on the basis that pregnancy does not lie solely within the sphere of private life, reject such a comparison on the grounds that the pregnant woman and the man were not in analogous positions as required by that court in *Lithgow and others v UK*.[94] (Alternatively, the European Court might move straight to the justifiability stage (as in *Dudgeon*[95]) without consideration of the differential impact upon men and women of such regulation.) Much will depend upon whether the British courts approach Article 14 'discrimination' in a manner similar to that adopted in the context of EC law, or in keeping with the approach of the Convention organs. Given the failure of those courts adequately to grasp the former, it is likely that the latter will prevail.[96]

In the unlikely event that a court was satisfied that discrimination had occurred, it would consider the issue of justification. Turning to the justification test, the contrast between it and that applied in EC law was noted above, Article 14 being breached only if the discrimination has 'no objective and reasonable justification having regard to the aim and effects of the measure', or 'there is no reasonable proportionality between ends and means'. Given that the purpose of abortion restrictions is not

---

[93] See Case C-32/93 *Webb v EMO Air Cargo (UK) Ltd* [1994] QB 718, [1994] ICR 770, [1994] 4 All ER 115 [1994] IRLR 482 and *No 2* [1995] IRLR 645, HL. For the limits to the ECJ's approach, see Case C-342/93 *Gillespie v Northern Health and Social Services Board* [1996] ICR 498, [1996] All ER (EC) 284, [1996] IRLR 214.
[94] (1986) 8 EHRR 329.
[95] Note 33 above.
[96] See A McColgan, *Just Wages for Women* (Oxford: Clarendon Press, 1997), Chapters 3 and 4.

to discriminate against women, and given also the Commission's position on pregnancy, it is likely that the protection of the 'unborn' would amount to such a justified aim. And even if the British courts were inclined to adopt the more radical, EC law approach to justification, the obligation imposed by Article 2 may well prevent them from so doing in this context.

The foregoing examination of the approach taken under the European Convention on Human Rights suggests that, while the incorporation of the Convention is unlikely to act as a safeguard on the right to abortion in the UK, it could actually operate so as to restrict access to abortion in accordance with the recognition of the, albeit restricted, 'right to life' of the foetus. At present, the 'right' to abortion in the UK, such as it is, turns on the wording of the Abortion Act 1967 which, as shown in Chapter 4 above, permits abortion on the certification of two doctors that the termination is necessary on (very widely defined) health grounds. As far as the right of others to challenge abortions taking place under the 1967 Act is concerned, the relevant law in Great Britain (this does not include Northern Ireland) is set out in the decision of the High Court in *Paton v Trustees of BPAS and Another*,[97] a case in which a man unsuccessfully sought to enjoin his wife from obtaining, and a doctor from performing, an abortion without his consent (he subsequently took his claim to the European Commission). According to Sir George Baker P, the man did not, either in his own right or on behalf of the foetus, have any 'legal right enforceable at law' such as was necessary before any injunction could be issued. In particular, the foetus had no rights 'of its own at least until it is born and has a separate existence from the mother'.

Turning to the impact of incorporation on this area, it was pointed out, above, that 'as long as the question of whether Article 2 is applicable to the unborn life has not been answered in the negative, [the reasonableness of the weighing of the woman's and foetus' interests under that provision] will have to be reviewed in each individual case'.[98] The model of incorporation which the Government proposes to adopt does not oblige the courts to follow the jurisprudence of the European Convention (s 2 of the Human Rights Act 1998 stating that they 'must take into account', rather than that they are bound by, decisions, opinions, etc, of the European Court of Human Rights and the Commission and the Committee of Ministers).[99] But it is likely that the courts will recognise a right to life, albeit limited, for the foetus under Article 2 as incorporated. Further, the British courts will not be constrained by the 'margin of appreciation' accorded to Contracting Parties by the European Court of Human

---

[97] [1978] 2 All ER 987. In Scotland, see *Kelly v Kelly* 1997 SLT 896, 1997 SCLR 749. See also *C v S* [1988] QB 135.
[98] Note 90 above.
[99] See HC Debs 3 June, cols 388–413 for the significance of this.

Rights.[100] British judges would, therefore, be free to adopt a more radical line 'in defence of the foetus' than that thus far taken by their European brethren. The Human Rights Act 1998 does not permit British judges to strike down the Abortion Act 1967 if they were to decide that it was, perhaps in respect of a late-term abortion permitted under the 1967 Act, incompatible with Article 2. On the other hand, were a declaration of incompatibility to be made, the Government might well feel obliged to reform the law even in the fact of widespread British support for the provisions of the 1967 Act.[101]

It is possible, further, that an application such as that which formed the subject matter of the *Paton* cases, albeit at a later stage of pregnancy, could result in an order restraining termination.[102] Certainly, the finding of the Commission in the *Paton* case left room for subsequent determinations that such abortions are incompatible with Article 2. The

---

[100] The doctrine has no role in the national courts, its purpose being to 'give the benefit of the doubt to a domestic jurisdiction' (Jack Straw MP, HC Debs 17 June 1998, col 433). This was recognised by Edward Leigh MP (HC Debs 20 May 1998, col 1049): 'the margin of appreciation can, by its definition, be used only by an international court, not by a national court. A national court will not say to itself, "We believe that international courts are better placed to deal with these issues, so we shall not deal with them", because it is a national court . . .'. Its potential role has, nevertheless, given rise to much discussion in parliamentary debates on the Human Rights Bill. See, for example, the comments of Sir Nicholas Lyell (HC Debs 21 October 1998, col 1295) 'the commission and the court in Strasbourg have also recognised that there must be a "substantial margin of appreciation". That is Strasbourg jargon, which means a substantial discretion and latitude should be given to each member state in respect of the exact method of implementation of the high principles set out in the convention. That margin of appreciation must also apply to domestic judgments based on the convention.' See also Sir Nicholas Lyell, HC Debs 20 May 1998, cols 975–976, 'we should recognise that [the Strasbourg institutions] are usually careful and cautious in their approach to interpreting the convention. In recent years in particular, they have given a great deal of weight to margin of appreciation, which they and our own judiciary should be careful to do' and the comments of Dominic Grieve MP (HC Debs 3 June 1998, col 424).

[101] Though see comments of Jack Straw, Secretary of State for the Home Office, HC Debs 21 October 1998, col 1301, 'it is possible that the Judicial Committee of the House of Lords could make a declaration that, subsequently, Ministers propose, and Parliament accepts, should not be accepted . . . abortion . . . provides a good example . . . it is possible to conceive that . . . a particularly composed Judicial Committee of the House of Lords reaches the view that provision for abortion in either the United Kingdom or part of the United Kingdom is incompatible with one or another article of the convention. Although the Committee would be entitled to say that such provision was incompatible with the convention, such a view would create very great controversy and, in some quarters, considerable social anxiety. We judged that, in that event, it would be wrong simply to accept what the Committee had said and that a right to abortion, albeit quite properly limited and developed in this country over a period of 30 years, should suddenly be cast aside. My guess – it can be no more than that – is that, whichever party was in power would have to say that it was sorry, that it did not and would not accept that and that it was going to continue with the existing abortion legislation.' See also *Plattform 'Ärzte für das Leben' v Austria* and notes 49 and 59 above, for the impact of incorporation on restrictions on anti-abortion activists. This could prove problematic if the anti-abortion movement gains ground.

[102] Abortions are currently permitted under the Act's 'social clause' (see Chapter 4 above) up to the 24 weeks.

courts are obliged to interpret the 1967 Act 'so far as is possible' so as to render it compatible with Article 2 as that, in turn, is interpreted. This might well result in a requirement that medical discretion be exercised in line with a limited foetal right to life, in which case injunctions might be granted on the grounds of failure adequately to take that right into account. It is true that, in *Paton*, Sir George Baker stated 'it would be quite impossible for the courts . . . to supervise the operation of the 1967 Act'.[103] Armed with the right to life of the foetus, however, this approach might change. And even if, in relation to a particular termination, a Human Rights Act 1998 challenge was unsuccessful, the woman involved will be subject to unwanted publicity and will, almost invariably, undergo a later termination than would otherwise have been the case. A few days can make the difference between a relatively simple dilation and extraction procedure and an induced labour.[104]

An uncomfortable question which needs to be raised concerns the motivation of men who try to force ex-partners to continue with unwanted pregnancies. In a number of the cases which have reached the courts, allegations of violence have been made against men seeking to enjoin abortions (discussed in Chapter 4 above, these include *Kelly v Kelly*[105] and the Canadian case of *Tremblay v Daigle*,[106] in both of which women were enjoined from having abortions and the injunctions upheld on first appeal).[107] In these circumstances, permitting challenge to abortion decisions by women serves merely to add to the armoury with which batterers control the victims of their abuse. The *Daily Record* pointed out, during the Scottish *Kelly v Kelly* case, that:

> if James Kelly won his case, we could see a situation where . . . women . . . might . . . be threatened with the law if they refused to comply with whatever health rules the would-be father thought necessary. He could force her to stop smoking, insist she kept every health appointment and perhaps decide that his baby would be better off if she packed in her job. He could have a say in how and where she gave birth . . . whether she had pain relief in labour . . . whether she opted for a caesarean. Perhaps he would have a case for forcing her to breastfeed.[108]

It is ironic, in light of this threat, that the very men most likely to benefit from the incorporation of Article 2's 'right to life' are those who themselves pose a significant risk to the health of both foetus and pregnant

---

[103] Citing Scarman LJ, in *R v Smith (John)* [1974] 1 All ER 376, at 378.
[104] See, for example, discussion of *Kelly v Kelly*, note 97 above; *Herald* (Glasgow), 26 May 1997.
[105] *Ibid.*
[106] Note 9 above, Supreme Court, [1989] RJQ 1735, 59 DLR (4th) 609, Court of Appeal, [1989] RJQ 1980, discussed in Chapter 4 above.
[107] By contrast with the Court of Appeal in *Tremblay*, the Scottish Court issued its injunction despite finding against Mr Kelly: *Independent*, 25 May 1997, *Daily Record*, 27 and 28 May 1997.
[108] 26 May 1997.

women. The desire to control every aspect of his victim's life is characteristic of the batterer who, by assaulting his pregnant partner, increases the
risk of miscarriage and stillbirth.[109]

Female vessels

What of the implications of incorporation for women's vulnerability to
forced medical treatment during pregnancy, or for punitive measures
taken against drug use or other inadvisable behaviour on the part of pregnant women? The latter has yet to appear, at least as a reported matter,
in the UK. But, as revealed in Chapter 5 above, the former has been an
issue of significant importance over recent years. As a matter of law, if
not in practice, the English common law endorses the right of pregnant
women to bodily autonomy.[110] There are difficulties with the determination of competence and the tendency of the courts to order intervention
in the heat of the moment, and examine the legal position later. But,
in theory at least, the decisions of the Court of Appeal in *Re MB*[111] and
St George's Healthcare NHS Trust v S, R v Collins and others, ex parte S[112] are
protective of pregnant women. The question which must be asked is the
extent, if any, to which incorporation of the European Convention on
Human Rights in the 1998 Act will impact on women in their disputes
with doctors over the management of their pregnancies and labours.

In *Re MB*, the Court of Appeal referred to the decisions of the
European Commission in *Brüggeman and Scheuten*,[113] *Paton*,[114] *H v Norway*[115]
and the *Open Door* case,[116] concluding that the Commission had not yet
reached a decision on, or indeed expressed an opinion as to, the application of Article 2 to the foetus at a stage later than ten weeks (this should,
in fact, have been 14 weeks, as a result of *H v Norway*): 'We do not consider that this court can gain any assistance on this issue from the opinions of the Commission'.[117] But whatever the approach taken by the Court
of Appeal in *Re MB*, there are strong grounds to suspect that incorporation of the Convention may change the approach of the higher English

---

[109] See, for example, the facts in *Re A-O (Minors)*, 6 February 1998 LEXIS, CA, for a fairly
typical account of the controlling behaviour of a batterer post-divorce.
[110] See Chapter 5 above.
[111] [1997] 2 FLR 541, (1997) 38 BNLR 175, [1997] Fam Law 542.
[112] [1998] 3 All ER 673, [1998] Fam Law 526.
[113] Note 86 above.
[114] Note 87 above.
[115] Unreported, 1990.
[116] Note 116 above.
[117] The court noted the contradictions, unremarked in *Paton*, within the US authorities
(see Chapter 5 above), but took the view that appellate decisions were moving in the
direction of the English approach (ie towards respect for the woman's autonomy).

courts in this area, while reinforcing the instincts of those confronted with medical declarations of impending doom.

The decisions in *Re MB* and *Ex parte S* turned on the absence of any right to life on the part of the foetus. To the extent that any such right were to be recognised, it could well be the case that the decision in *Ex parte S* would go the other way (the autonomy of the woman in *Re MB* having been overridden in any event by her perceived lack of capacity). Certainly in Ireland, where the right to life of the 'unborn' is accorded precedence over the interests of the pregnant woman, it is most probably the case that forcible caesareans would be permitted, perhaps even required, under the Constitution.[118]

The position under the Convention is less clear than that in Ireland, no express declaration having been made of a right to life for the foetus. But it is at least possible that, given Article 8's limited application to the pregnant woman, '[p]regnancy cannot be said to pertain uniquely to the sphere of private life. Whenever a woman is pregnant, her private life becomes closely connected with that of the developing fetus', together with the scope which remains for recognition of some, albeit limited, right to life of the foetus (whether by the European Convention organs, or the British courts on their behalf), women may find that the personal autonomy held so dear by the common law gives way, if only in extreme cases, to foetal rights. It might be argued that forcible intervention in pregnancy or childbirth amounted to a violation of Article 3 (which protects against 'inhuman and degrading treatment'). But this Article is a very difficult one in respect of which to prove breach, the very seriousness with which its guarantees are taken rendering Convention organs loath to apply it readily.

Most of the cases in which violations of Article 3 are found or alleged concern treatment imposed for the purpose of punishment or, at any rate, in connection with a deprivation of liberty. In 1987, Fawcett described as the 'broader view' of the Article that 'inhuman treatment could be taken to be cruelty in any form, that is, the infliction of pain or suffering *for its own sake*' (my emphasis).[119] The Article has been raised in connection with torture, forced sterilisation,[120] the ill-treatment of prisoners, extradition and deportation and, in *Abdulaziz*,[121] the refusal of entry to the intended spouses of patrials.

In the *East African*[122] cases the Commission had accepted that 'discrimination based on race could, in certain circumstances, of itself amount to

---

[118] See Chapter 4 above. It is still not lawful for a woman to have an abortion in Ireland regardless of medical need.

[119] J Fawcett, *The Application of the European Convention on Human Rights* (Oxford: Clarendon, 1987), p 41. The 'narrower view' was that the treatment had to be 'outside the expected range of human behaviour' or required 'enormity of . . . pain or suffering'.

[120] The sterilisation case related to Nazi practices and was out of time.

[121] *Abdulaziz, Cabales and Balkandali*, note 15 above.

[122] (1970) 13 *Yearbook* 994.

degrading treatment within . . . Article 3'.[123] But more indicative of the general tone of cases under the Article is the statement in *Abdulaziz* that the sex discrimination which was found to have occurred displayed no 'contempt or lack of respect for the personality of the applicants . . . [and was] not designed to, and did not, humiliate or debase, but was intended solely to achieve [other aims and] . . . cannot therefore be regarded as "degrading" '.[124] Nor is the decision in *Herczeg-falvy*,[125] in which the European Court of Human Rights accepted that a violation of Article 3 could occur in the case of forced medical treatment, as distinct from punishment or interrogation techniques, a great deal more helpful in the present context. Although a woman subjected to forced medical intervention might be likened to a detainee (there the applicant was a detained psychiatric patient), a complaint relating to force-feeding was rejected in that case on the basis that necessary medical treatment cannot be regarded as 'inhuman and degrading'.

In *Herczeg-Falvy*, it is true, the incompetence of the patient was crucial in permitting this finding despite his non-consent to the medical treatment. But it might equally be argued, in the case of pregnancy-related medical interventions, that the interests of the foetus must be balanced against the wishes of the mother in determining whether the treatment might properly be regarded as 'inhuman or degrading'. The absence of punitive motivation on the part of the interveners is, it might be thought, likely to militate against a finding that Article 3 had been breached.

The balancing process which, as mentioned above, will become a distinct possibility in cases involving perceived conflict between the rights of the woman to self-determination and those (however limited) of the foetus to life, is likely to be felt, in particular, in the sphere of medical treatment and surgical intervention, given the very late stages of pregnancy at which such procedures are currently carried out. The other issue in this area which renders incorporation particularly problematic is that it involves common law, rather than legislation. The decisions of the Court of Appeal in *Re MB* and *Ex parte S*, insofar as they were of most general application, concerned the scope of the common law right to self-determination – in particular, the status of that right where its exercise had implications for the foetus. It would not be difficult for the courts to determine their answer to this question differently were there to be recognised a right to life for the foetus, particularly in view of the fact that so comparatively little stands between the full-term foetus and independent life. It is true, of course, that a caesarean section or, as the case may

---

[123]   *Ibid.* But there the intention of the legislation was to discriminate.

[124]   *Abdulaziz, Cabales and Balkandali* (1985), note 15 above. In the *Greek* cases, too, the Commission identified as central to Article 3 'such treatment as *deliberately* causes severe suffering, mental or physical, which in the particular case is unjustifiable' (my emphasis): (1969) *Yearbook* XII Part II 186.

[125]   (1993) A 244, 15 EHRR 437.

be, an unwanted suction or forceps delivery, is a far greater invasion of personal autonomy ('private life', under Article 8) than the blood tests previously authorised by the Commission on the grounds of Article 8(2)'s 'rights of others' (the tests being administered to determine paternity and blood-alcohol levels).[126] But the vision of an unborn baby struggling for life against the malevolence or perceived irrationality of the 'maternal environment' in which it is held captive may well be too powerful for the judiciary to overcome, armed as they will be with the tools with which to distinguish such a case from that of the unencumbered applicant in *Re C*[127] (see Chapter 5 above). Incorporation of Article 6's right to 'a fair and public hearing' (further discussed below) might go some way towards discouraging the granting of *ex parte* injunctions enforcing unwanted medical treatment. But these are already frowned upon by the Court of Appeal, save in emergency situations (see Chapter 5), and Article 6 may, too, give way in case of such emergencies. Nor, in any event, is there any guarantee that a court addressed by a pregnant woman's lawyer will decide in her favour. It may well be the case that the incorporation of the Convention rights will suffice to tip the balance in favour of forcible intervention, at least in cases where the pregnancy is close to term.[128]

Women at work

With regard to the position of women in the employment sphere, the very limited scope of Article 14 means that sex discrimination in this area can be challenged under the Human Rights Act 1998, as under the Convention, only to the extent that it relates to a right or freedom protected under Articles 2–12.[129] Of these, only Article 6 ('[i]n the determination

---

[126] Appl 8278/78 *X v Austria* (1980) 18 DR 155 and Appl 8239/78 *X v The Netherlands* (1979) 16 DR 184.

[127] *Re C (Refusal of Medical Treatment)* [1994] 1 FLR 31.

[128] Cf, however, the opinion of Balcombe LJ in *Re MB*, note 11 above. Responding to arguments that the foetus' right to be born was protected by Article 2 of the European Convention he cited the judgment of the Commission in Appl 8416/79 *Paton v UK*, note 87 above: 'The "life" of the foetus is intimately connected with, and cannot be regarded in isolation from, the life of the pregnant woman. If Article 2 were held to cover the foetus and its protection under this Article were, in the absence of any express limitation, seen as absolute, an abortion would have to be considered as prohibited even where the continuance of the pregnancy would involve a serious risk to the life of the pregnant woman. This would mean that the "unborn life" of the foetus would be regarded as being of a higher value than the life of the pregnant woman. The "right to life" of a person already born would thus be considered as subject not only to the express limitations [set out in the Convention] . . . but also to a further, implied limitation.' According to Balcombe LJ, 'far from assisting counsel's submission, art 2 of the Convention, as interpreted by the European Commission, is in my judgment against him'.

[129] For a more general discussion see KD Ewing, 'The Human Rights Act and Labour Law' (1999) 28 *Industrial Law Journal* (forthcoming).

of his [sic] civil rights and obligations . . . everyone is entitled to a fair and public hearing within a reasonable time by an independent and impartial tribunal established by law'); Article 8 ('[e]veryone has the right to respect for his [sic] private and family life'); and Article 11 ('[e]veryone has the right to freedom of peaceful assembly and to freedom of association with others, including the right to form and to join trade unions for the protection of his [sic] interests') are at all likely to be implicated in connection with the issues considered in Chapters 6 and 7 above.

This is not to say that any such claims are likely, still less likely to succeed; only that it is conceivable that, for example, one might argue that a dismissal on the grounds of pregnancy or 'immoral' living arrangements (for example, on the part of a teacher in a non-denominational school[130]) demonstrated a failure to respect 'private and family life' in violation of Article 8 (or Articles 8 and 14 read together), or that discriminatory access to collective bargaining arrangements contravened Articles 8 and 11. Having said this, the Article 8 interference might be regarded as justified under Article 8(2) which permits 'interference . . . for the protection of health or morals' particularly if, given the equal application of an 'immoral behaviour' policy to men and women, no Article 14 issue was raised.[131] As to the issue of pregnancy, discrimination based on this would, in any event, contravene the Sex Discrimination Act 1975 interpreted in accordance with the Equal Treatment Directive.[132]

It is possible that the non-availability of legal aid in industrial tribunals might be regarded as a breach of Article 6, and that the delays associated, in particular, with equal value claims might breach that provision's guarantee of trial 'within a reasonable time'. Taking first the issue of legal aid, the European Court of Human Rights ruled in *Airey*[133] that, although no presumption arose in civil, as distinct from criminal, cases, as to legal aid entitlement, Ireland's provision of legal separation orders only to those who applied to the High Court, Mrs Airey not being in a position so to do, violated Article 6(1).[134] (Mrs Airey alleged physical and mental

---

[130] The position with regard to church schools is somewhat more complex, tireless and well-supported campaigning by the churches resulting in a proviso (s 13) that 'If a court's determination of any question arising under this Act might affect the exercise by a religious organisation (itself or its members collectively) of the Convention right to freedom of thought, conscience and religion, it must have particular regard to the importance of that right'. Attempts had been made – see HC Debs 20 May 1998, cols 1013–1069 and, most recently, 21 October 1998 (HC Debs, cols 1337–1348) to have the churches excluded entirely from the reach of the Act.

[131] See also *Stedman v UK* (1997) 23 EHRR CD 168 and *Ahmad v UK* (1981) 4 EHRR 126 for cases in which the Commission and the European Court of Human Rights respectively gave short shrift to employment-related claims of religious discrimination. In *Stedman*, for example, the Commission stated that a woman's dismissal for a refusal to work on a Sunday was a dismissal 'for failing to agree to work certain hours rather than for her religious beliefs as such'.

[132] See Case C-32/93 *Webb v EMO Air Cargo (UK) Ltd* [1994] QB 718, [1994] ICR 770, [1994] 4 All ER 115.

[133] Note 39 above.

[134] *Ibid.* Article 6 specifically provides right to legal aid in criminal cases.

cruelty by her husband towards her and their children.) According to the European Court, Article 6(1) 'is intended to guarantee not rights that are theoretical or illusory but rights that are practical and effective'. Mrs Airey was entitled to be put in a position 'properly and satisfactorily' to present her case.

This particular issue may turn out to be of more general application in view of the UK Government's current proposals for the removal of legal aid from civil cases (discussed further below). Having said this, the European Court in *Airey* stressed the nature of the case they were dealing with, representation being rendered essential by the need to examine expert witnesses and the high degree of emotional involvement by the parties: 'marital disputes often entail an emotional involvement that is scarcely compatible with the objectivity required by advocacy in court'. In *Munro v UK*,[135] the Commission refused to apply *Airey* so as to provide a right to legal aid in a defamation case, stressing that the case at issue in *Airey* had repercussions for the children to the marriage, distinguishing this from the reputation at stake in *Munro* and pointing to the inherently risky nature of defamation proceedings. Even more salient to the current issue, in *X v UK*[136] the Commission, dealing with a challenge relating to legal aid before industrial tribunals, interpreted *Airey* to the effect that 'only in exceptional circumstances, namely where the withholding of legal aid would make the assertion of a civil claim practically impossible, or where it would lead to an obvious unfairness of the proceedings, can such a right be invoked by Article 6(1)'.

According to the Commission, 'Industrial tribunal proceedings are designed to be conducted in a practical and straightforward manner without too much emphasis on formalities . . . legal representation . . . is by no means a requirement in such proceedings'.[137] It is certainly the case that industrial tribunals were created with the intention that they would provide relatively simple, informal arenas for the determination of employment-related legal disputes. The extent to which this aim has been met is questionable, many commentators decrying the extent to which tribunals have become mired in formalism with the result that, in practice, legal representation may be necessary to success. What is true in general is true a thousand times over in the context of equal value cases, the law relating to which is among the most complex of any and success in which is almost inconceivable without legal representation.

It may be that the approach taken by the Commission in *X v UK* is not absolute and that, particularly were the issue to be considered by the UK

---

[135] Appl 10594/83 (1987) 52 DR 158.
[136] Appl 9444/81 (1984) 6 EHRR 136.
[137] See also *Stedman v UK*, note 131 above, in which the Commission rejected a claim that the UK's two-year qualifying period for unfair dismissal protection breached Article 6. According to the Commission, this 'restricti[on of] access to an industrial tribunal . . . pursued the legitimate aim of offering protection to those in established employment . . . without burdening the employer to the extent that dismissal within a two year probationary period was likely to lead to court proceedings'.

courts without application of the 'margin of appreciation' (this being inappropriate in the national context[138]), a claim under Article 6 might succeed.[139] Having said this, even where positive obligations are imposed upon Contracting States by the European Court of Human Rights, as in *Airey*, the discretion as to how those obligations may be satisfied is particularly wide. In the context of equal value claims the government could well put forward an argument that the role of the Equal Opportunities Commission in supporting suitable cases was sufficient to satisfy its Article 6 obligations (particularly in view of the wide discretion given to the implementation of positive obligations by parties to the Convention[140]). And even if this were not to succeed in practice, much incorporation of Article 6 in this regard does not really advance the position of equal value litigants, since any argument which could be run under Article 6 could equally be made under Article 119 of the Treaty of Rome (which imposes a directly enforceable obligation upon Member States to 'ensure and subsequently maintain the application' of the principle of equal pay).

Turning next to the matter of delays, these have been a matter of much unfavourable comment in equal value cases. While average delays are in the region of a few years, some applicants wait for over a decade before a final determination is reached.[141] But the approach of the Employment Appeal Tribunal has been to speed matters up by dismissing cases on highly dubious grounds and, in the case of at least one industrial tribunal, to reduce the applicant's chances of success by dispensing with the services of an independent expert and assessing the relative value of the relevant jobs itself.[142] Even if the British courts were to regard equal value case delays as giving rise to a breach of Article 6 (and it is not at all clear that they would[143]), their response may impair the position of equal value claimants.

---

[138] See notes 37, 49 and 100 above.

[139] Particularly perhaps where litigation itself involved Convention rights, in which case the duty on the tribunal to have regard to the enormous weight of jurisprudence developed by the Convention organs might be regarded as making self-representation by a layperson inadequate.

[140] See above, at text to note 139.

[141] See McColgan, note 96 above, Chapter 4.

[142] *Ibid*, especially discussions on *Reed Packaging Ltd v Boozer and another* [1988] ICR 391, [1988] IRLR 333, *Bromley and others v H & J Quick Ltd* [1988] ICR 623, [1988] IRLR 249, *Davies v McCartneys* [1989] ICR 705, [1989] IRLR 439.

[143] See *X v UK* (1973–81) 3 EHRR 271. In criminal matters the guarantee is 'designed to avoid that a person charged should remain too long in a state of uncertainty about his fate'. Four years eight months was not considered unreasonable taking into account complexity, appeals, etc. The test is likely to be less rather than more strict in civil matters, though in *R v Secretary of State for the Home Department, ex p Phansokpar* [1976] QB 606 the Court of Appeal took the view that undue delay in performing legal obligations was an abuse and in *EMA v ACAS* [1980] IRLR 164, the House of Lords took the view that this would be the case, though not on the facts. In *Darrell v UK* (1993) A 272 the European Court of Human Rights found a breach in a case where nine years elapsed between the dismissal of an employee and the rejection of his appeal by the Employment Appeal Tribunal. In that case, however, the Commission had found that there was no particular complexity involved – this could not be said in relation to equal value cases.

The possible application of Article 6 to equal value claims is likely to be very limited. It is generally agreed that a complete overhaul of the equal value procedure is required, and the Equal Opportunities Commission (EOC) has recently called for the imposition of positive duties upon employers to examine and eradicate discrimination from their pay structures in accordance with the procedure set out in the EOC's Code of Practice on Equal Pay.[144] But even if Article 6(1) has some application, it is inconceivable that it could be relied upon to construct a new equal value procedure along these or any other lines. It might assist a handful of individual applicants. But the real impact of the Equal Pay Act, and of Article 119 and the Equal Pay Directive, has not been at this individual level. Rather, significant improvements have been achieved where rulings made have been of general application (such as the decision of the House of Lords in *R v Secretary of State for Employment ex p EOC*,[145] which resulted in the equalisation of the qualifying periods for employment protection of part-time and full-time workers[146]), and where trade unions have used the threat of equal value claims as a bargaining tool in the drive to improve women's wages. It is hard to see any potential role for Article 6 in these areas.

The Convention and collective rights

The importance of collective bargaining to women's employment rights, in particular, to their pay, has been emphasised throughout this book. What impact is the incorporation of the Convention likely to have in this area? Article 11 of the Convention provides that '[e]veryone has the right to . . . freedom of association with others, including the right to form and to join trade unions for the protection of his interests'. The right to trade union membership could be regarded as carrying with it the right to collective bargaining – certainly, the ILO Conventions treat the right to free collective bargaining as an essential element of freedom of association,[147] and the European Court of Human Rights has accepted that the words 'for the protection of his interests' are not without meaning as would

---

[144] EOC, *Equality in the 21st Century: A New Sex Equality Law for Britain* (Manchester: EOC, 1998).

[145] [1993] ICR 251, [1993] 1 All ER 1022.

[146] Equally, while the gradual equalisation of retirement provision has not been an unqualified good for women, it, too, followed upon the decisions of the ECJ in *Marshall v Southampton and South-West Hampshire Area Health Authorities (Teaching)* [1986] 2 All ER 584, [1986] QB 401, [1986] IRLR 140 and Case C-262/88 *Barber v Guardian Royal Exchange Assurance Group* [1990] 2 All ER 660, at 700, [1990] ECR 1889.

[147] See Convention 98, though not even the ILO regards compulsory recognition as mandatory. See generally KD Ewing, *Britain and the ILO* (2nd ed, London: Institute of Employment Rights, 1994).

be required, for example, if freedom of association was to be interpreted to extend only to the bare right to be a member of a trade union.[148]

Save for the periods 1971–74, and 1975–80, recognition (the precursor in the UK to collective bargaining) has not been an enforceable right in the UK. Prior to its election in May 1997 the Labour Government had committed itself to a compulsory recognition where a majority of the 'relevant workforce' wanted recognition. Protracted discussions ensued between the Confederation of British Industry and the Trades Union Congress about the detail of the procedures, and in May 1998 the Government finally published the *Fairness at Work* White Paper which, as anticipated, proposed a model based on the US recognition procedures (in that recognition is granted at the enterprise level in respect of 'bargaining units' after a ballot carried out on the recommendation of a third party), although with a number of important modifications.[149]

Implications of incorporation of the Convention

It is far too early to speculate as to the efficacy of the new recognition procedures, not least because they have yet to be given final form. But a number of points can be made even at this stage about the possible implications of incorporation in this area. Despite their recognition of the application beyond mere freedom to hold a union membership card of the guarantee of freedom of association, the approach of the Convention organs to Article 11 has not been generous. On the one hand, the European Commission and European Court of Human Rights have been ready to interpret Article 11 so as to restrict the rights and freedoms of trade unions. In *X v Belgium*,[150] for example, the Commission proposed that 'the very concept of freedom of association with others also implies freedom not to associate with others or not to join unions' (this despite indications in the *travaux préparatoires* of Article 11 that there was no intention to ban closed shops). In *Cheall v UK*,[151] the Commission ruled that admission to and expulsion from a trade union would generally be a matter for trade union rules although, where the dismissal was in breach of the union rules, was in accordance with arbitrary rules or entailed exceptional hardship, the State could be obliged to protect individuals from abuse of a union's dominant position. In *Young, James and Webster*,[152] the European Court of Human Rights ruled that the UK had breached Article 11 by permitting trade union non-members to be dismissed after

---

[148] *National Union of Belgian Police*, note 29 above. Cf House of Lords in *Associated Newspapers v Wilson, Associated British Ports v Palmer* [1995] 2 AC 454, [1995] 2 WLR 354, [1995] 2 All ER 100, [1995] IRLR 258, discussed below.

[149] See, generally, A McColgan, 'Fairness at Work: Some Legal and Practical Issues' (1998) Croner's *Employee Relations Review* 20.

[150] (1970) 4 *Yearbook* 708.

[151] Appl 4125/69 (1971) *Yearbook* XIV 198.

[152] Note 56 above.

a closed shop came into operation in their workplace. And in *Sigurjonnson v Iceland*[153] the European Court confirmed the existence of a full right of non-association under Article 11. By contrast, Article 11 has not in general been invoked by the Convention organs in defence of trade unions – indeed, to this date the European Court of Human Rights has not upheld a single application alleging breach of trade union rights under Article 11, although a number of such complaints have been made.

In *National Union of Belgian Police*[154] the European Court of Human Rights stated that it was 'incumbent on the authorities to allow the unions sufficient scope' to enable them to serve the interests of their members. But even here the European Court ruled that, although trade unions should have a right to be heard by the authorities before a decision regarding their members was taken, this did not amount to a right to recognition. In the *Swedish Engine Drivers' Union*[155] case the European Court ruled that the authorities, as employers, are not obliged to conclude a collective agreement with any particular trade union and, in *Schmidt and Dahlström*,[156] that, even if Article 11 provides a right to strike, it may be restricted by national legislation. Again, while the right to freedom of association included a right to further the interests of their members, taking strike action was only one way in which trade unions could be 'enabled, in conditions not at variance with Article 11, to strive, through the medium of their organizations, for the protection of their occupational interests'. It was for the national authorities to determine the manner in which trade unions could do so.

To the extent that Article 11 imposes obligations, those are very broadly articulated and leave a wide area of discretion to the State to determine the manner in which they might most appropriately be given effect to.[157] Certainly, the European Court of Human Rights has not interpreted Article 11 to extend as far as, much less to exceed, the rights imposed by Article 6(2) of the European Social Charter, which obliges Contracting Parties (including Great Britain) 'to promote, *where necessary and appropriate,* machinery for voluntary negotiations between employers and employers' organizations and workers' organizations, with a view to the regulation of terms and conditions of employment by means of collective agreements' (my emphasis).[158]

---

[153] (1993) 16 EHRR 462.
[154] Note 29 above. See also M Janis, K Kay and A Bradley, *European Human Rights Law* (Oxford: Clarendon Press, 1995), p 223.
[155] Note 30 above.
[156] Note 48 above.
[157] Note 138 above and A Robertson and J Merrills, *Human Rights in Europe: A Study of the European Convention on Human Rights* (3rd ed, Manchester: Manchester University Press, 1993) p 162.
[158] The Charter, unlike the Convention, is enforceable by means of a reporting mechanism alone, which mechanism has proved largely unworkable as a result of differences between the Committee of Experts appointed to oversee its application and the government bodies associated with it.

Harris *et al* point out that, while the *Belgian Police, Swedish Engine Drivers* and *Schmidt and Dahlström* cases: 'create the appearance that Article 11(1) guarantees only the barest minimum of implied rights for trade unions . . . in each application the trade union or its members had extensive rights in the national legislative systems which could be seen cumulatively as allowing for the effective exercise of the positive right to organise'. They suggest that 'a State which conceded only the bare minimum of rights to organised labour could not be confident that it was complying with Article 11'.[159] It is arguable that, in the absence both of any compulsory recognition procedure and (by contrast with the case elsewhere in Europe) of active state support for (and/or participation at the national level in) collective bargaining, a breach of Article 11 might be made out. Certainly, in Great Britain at the present time, trade unions are empowered to take almost no action 'through the medium of their organizations, for the protection of their occupational interests'. Recognition is 'voluntary', ie in the gift of the employer, and no state support is provided through the use of contract compliance (indeed, this has been expressly prohibited in local government since 1988) or otherwise. Trade unions and their officials retain immunity from tortious liability incurred in the course of otherwise lawful action, at least in the periods between judicial creations of new heads of liability. But individuals, whether trade union members or not, are unprotected from dismissal during industrial action, which action invariably amounts to breach of their contracts of employment. Careful as the Commission and European Court of Human Rights have been to avoid specifying the manner in which the Contracting Parties should fulfil their obligation to allow trade unions sufficient scope to serve the interests of their members, it would appear that room must be left for some kind of effective action, which room is lacking in the UK.

It may be that some guidance will be provided by the European Court of Human Rights in *Wilson v Associated Newspapers, Palmer v Associated British Ports*,[160] which is currently awaiting reference by the Commission after a finding favourable to the applicants (assuming that no settlement is reached with the British Government). But whatever the outcome of that case, the implementation of the White Paper, *Fairness at Work*, proposals are likely to go a long way towards remedying any incompatibility which may be found to exist between British labour law and Article 11 requirements. Even, and assuming the existence of such incompatibility, if the proposals did not suffice to bring British law into conformity (for example, because no recognition procedure is available in workplaces with 20 or fewer staff, and while those dismissed while on official *and lawful* industrial action may have their cases heard by a tribunal, they may nevertheless

[159] Note 20 above, p 430, Janis *et al*, note 154 above, p 223.
[160] Appls 30668/96, 30671/96 and 30678/96.

be dismissed in circumstances in which reinstatement will not be ordered), the significance of incorporation is simply (but, quite possibly, very importantly) that it will be the British courts, rather than the European Convention organs, which will determine the Article 11 issue in the first instance. It was pointed out above that, in so doing, the courts will not be bound by European jurisprudence, though they will have to take it into account. It is instructive therefore, at this point, to consider the approach of the British courts to freedom of association in general, and to collective bargaining and industrial action in particular.

Attitude of the UK courts

Since the inception of the trade union movement the attitude of the judiciary in the UK has been hostile. From the early 18th century, in which trade unions (and, subsequently, strikes) were declared criminal conspiracies, through the creation, throughout the late 19th and 20th centuries, of a range of economic torts deployed against industrial action, to *Associated Newspapers v Wilson, Associated British Ports v Palmer*,[161] in which the House of Lords ruled that failure to pay a wage increase to trade union members was an 'omission' rather than an 'action' rendered unlawful by legislation and that, further, the trade union membership on the grounds of which that legislation prohibited action to be taken against employees 'involve[d] no more than the member's right to hold a membership card and to avail him/herself of such services as the union may provide to the member which do not impinge on the member's employer', the courts (certainly those not exclusively involved in labour law) have construed common law and legislation against the interests of trade unions and, to the extent that those interests were coincident, their members.[162]

Particularly instructive, when considering the issue of recognition, are the decisions of the courts in *Powley v ACAS*,[163] *Grunwick Processing v ACAS*,[164] *EMA v ACAS*[165] and *UKAPE v ACAS*,[166] all of which concerned the recognition provisions established by the Employment Protection Act 1975. In *Grunwick* the House of Lords ruled at once that the employer could prevent the Advisory, Conciliation and Arbitration Service (ACAS) from accessing employees whose views they wished to canvass, and that the failure of ACAS to take into account those views rendered void its recognition recommendation. In the *UKAPE* and *EMA* cases the House of Lords eventually vindicated the exercise by ACAS of its discretion.

---

[161] Note 148 above.
[162] See generally S Deakin and G Morris, *Labour Law* (2nd ed, London: Butterworths, 1998) pp 6 ff; J Hendy QC, *Every Worker Shall Have the Right to be Represented at Work by a Trade Union* (London: Institute of Employment Rights, 1998).
[163] [1978] ICR 123.
[164] [1978] ICR 231.
[165] [1980] IRLR 164.
[166] [1979] ICR 303.

But these decisions were reached only after the recognition procedure had been dismantled by the Conservative Government, and did not undo the paralysing effect that the decisions of the lower courts had had on the exercise by ACAS of its powers. Finally, the *Powley* case is instructive, despite having been reached only at the level of the High Court, in encapsulating in a particularly raw form the innate hostility of the judiciary to the abuse of individual rights which that body perceives as inherent in the granting of rights to trade unions. In *Powley*, in which the High Court held that ACAS had failed satisfactorily to discharge its statutory duties, Mr Justice (now Lord) Browne-Wilkinson declared that: 'as a result of this statutory machinery an individual can have a substantial measure of control over his own working life delegated to an agent, or trade union, which he has not selected and may even have his own conditions of service varied without his consent . . . the court should seek to ensure that, *as in the case of compulsory purchase powers*, the conditions for the use of the powers conferred [upon ACAS] . . . are strictly construed'.[167]

What is perhaps most remarkable about this analysis is its opposition of interests, not between employer and employee, but between employee and trade union. Nowhere in the judgment is the recognition that individual employees, save for the fortunate few, cede control over their working lives to their employers, and that the only factor capable of providing a balance to employer power is that of a trade union. And as to the fact that collective agreements can, in the event that they are incorporated into contracts of employment (and only then[168]), result in changes to employees' terms and conditions of employment, this is no different in law, and far more likely to benefit employees in practice, than a contract which permits a measure of power to the employer unilaterally to change conditions of employment. Yet the courts have proved far less concerned about the potential for abuse of these such terms (and, indeed, extended their reach by imposing implied obligations relating to flexibility and co-operation upon employees) than Mr Justice Browne-Wilkinson was about the impact of collective agreements.

Impact on collective bargaining in the UK

What does the experience of the European Court of Human Rights and British jurisprudence indicate about the likely impact of incorporation on collective bargaining? On the one hand it is probable that such incorporation will not afford to trade unions any rights that they do not already have (or, at any rate, will not possess on legislative implementation of the broad proposals set out in *Fairness at Work*). Even if some

---

[167] See also Douglas Hogg MP, HC Debs 21 May 1998, col 1109 '[the recognition] proposals are a serious infringement of the rights of employees who do not want union recognition in their businesses'.
[168] See *Singh v British Steel Corporation* [1974] IRLR 131.

incompatibility between UK law and the Convention could be postulated, the hostility with which the British courts regard trade unions renders it most unlikely that any suit on the part of a trade union or trade union member would succeed, in which case the only appeal would be by way of reference to Strasbourg. The wide margin of appreciation afforded by both the Commission and the European Court of Human Rights to Contracting States, particularly where (as here), positive obligations rather than negative restrictions are at stake, together with the 'opaque language of the Court' may make it difficult for the applicant to demonstrate' a violation of Article 11.[169] It is at least possible that such a demonstration might be even more of a challenge in a case where the British courts had already considered that there was no violation of the incorporated Article.[170]

Without recognition in the workplace, British employees (unlike many of their Continental counterparts) are denied the protection and benefit of collective agreements. Such are the shortcomings of Article 11 and British jurisprudence, pointed out above, that incorporation is extremely unlikely to improve access to and coverage of collective bargaining. It is entirely possible, on the other hand, that such incorporation will permit employers and anti-union employees to thwart the procedures proposed in the recent White Paper, and in other respects to set back the position of women in the workplace.

The major issue which arises concerns the potential for judicial intervention to derail the recognition provisions proposed in *Fairness at Work*. A great deal of discretion is afforded by the proposals to the Central Arbitration Committee (CAC) whose role it will be to order a ballot of employees in the relevant bargaining unit after an initial show by the trade union applying for recognition of 'reasonable support' among those employees 'such as to make it likely that there could be a majority in favour of union recognition' and assuming that the trade union has not achieved majority membership within that unit (in which case recognition will generally be awarded). Since the late 1970s the scope of judicial review has expanded beyond measure, with the result that more, rather than less, intervention, can be all but guaranteed in relation to the role of the CAC as we enter the 21st century.

The incorporation of the European Convention on Human Rights will only strengthen the hand of the judges in this respect. In addition to the bread-and-butter rights already recognised in actions for judicial review, judges will have at their disposal employers' Article 6 rights to a fair and public hearing of their civil obligations (prior, for example, to the imposition of a procedure agreement), their Article 10 rights to campaign

---

[169] Harris *et al*, note 20 above, p 430.
[170] This may be what is meant by the frequent references (see Chapter 2 above) to the benefits of the British courts having a role in the development of Convention jurisprudence.

against a recognition vote (and, possibly, an Article 11 right not to be forced to associate with a trade union and First Protocol Article 1 rights to the peaceful enjoyment of possessions including prior contractual rights against employees[171]). Even if such challenges eventually come to nothing, they have the power to entangle the CAC in the paralysis of litigation which ACAS experienced in connection with the 1975 provisions. Finally, even if the Convention's incorporation results in no such difficulties, it will not address the real nexus between collective bargaining and reductions in the wage gap – however it is interpreted, Article 11 will never realistically require the degree of centralisation which accounts for the relationship between high levels of collective bargaining coverage and significant reductions in the gender-wage gap.

Women as victims of violence

What changes can be expected as a result of incorporation as regards the issue of women and violence? Throughout this book it has been apparent that the area of defendants' rights is one in which entrenched rights can be of great significance. Not only do such rights tend to provide defendants with remedies against due process violations such as those associated with undue delays and the admission or exclusion of various types of evidence, but they may also impact on the substance of the criminal law, in cases where criminal offences are by their nature drawn in discriminatory terms or where they fail to accord with fundamental principles of the criminal law (as in *Daviault*[172]).

The potential of entrenched rights to improve the quality of justice afforded to criminal defendants is, of course, a benefit. But what became clear in Chapter 9 above was the downside of incorporation. To the extent that the judiciary is permitted to apply a 'substantive due process' approach, ie to pass judgment upon the substance of the criminal law (whether the *mens rea* requirements for murder, or the role of voluntary intoxication as a defence), entrenchment serves to insulate the common law from democratic reform. The same is true even in those cases where judges confine their attention to procedural matters such as those relating to the admissibility of evidence.

---

[171] Jacobs and White, note 50 above, state that 'Goodwill in a business constitutes possessions [citing *Van Marle v The Netherlands* (1986) 8 EHRR 483, para 41] . . . Ownership of a debt will constitute a possession where it has crystallized [citing Appl 12164/86; *Agneessens v Belgium* (1988) 58 DR 63; *Stran Greek Refineries* 19 EHRR 293, paras 58–62]. Similarly a contractual right to fee adjustments for general practitioners is a possession', citing Appl 12947/87 *Association of GPs v Denmark* (1989) 62 DR 226.

[172] Note 7 above.

The 'fundamental principles' which judges apply, through entrenched rights, are the principles which, at best, they distil from the common law background. The difficulty which arises here is that the flaws underlying the common law may be precisely why an impugned piece of legislation was passed. For that legislation to be overruled on the basis of common law 'principles' simply marks a triumph for the common law over that established by the legislature on the basis, at least in theory, of a democratic mandate. On other occasions these 'principles' appear to be pulled from judicial wigs, ie 'found' despite being in direct contradiction to the common law previously applied.[173] It is hard to escape the conclusion, at least where such 'principles' are found to contradict legislation, that entrenchment serves to elevate at best the position-specific shared views, and at worst the personal whims, of the judiciary above democratically created legislative rules.

From a practical perspective these problems could perhaps be overlooked if the substance of judicial lawmaking was preferable, in relation to a particular area of concern, to that of legislation. It should be clear from Chapters 8 and 9 and above that this is not the case in relation to women as victims of violence either in Canada or in the US. But what might be expected in the UK from the implementation of the Human Rights Act 1998?

The provisions of the European Convention Articles which would govern this area are contained in Article 6, read in conjunction with Article 14. Article 6 provides for a 'fair and public hearing within a reasonable time by an independent and impartial tribunal established by law' in the determination of criminal charges. It also enshrines the presumption of innocence and affords certain 'minimum rights' which include the right for a defendant (Article 6(3)(c)) 'to defend himself in person or through legal assistance' and (Article 6(3)(d)) 'to examine or have examined witnesses against him'.

How is Article 6 likely to be applied in the British courts, and to what areas highlighted in Chapters 8 and 9 is it likely to have application? Taking first the matter of rape trials, at present in England and Wales the matter of sexual history evidence is governed by the Sexual Offences (Amendment) Act 1976, s 2 of which provides that: 'except with the leave of the judge, no evidence and no question in cross-examination shall be adduced or asked at the trial, by or on behalf of any defendant at the trial, about any sexual experience of a [rape] complainant with a person other than the defendant'. Section 2(2) goes on to provide that any application for leave must be made in the absence of the jury, and shall be granted 'if and only if [the judge] is satisfied that it would be unfair

---

[173] See for example the decision of the Supreme Court of Canada in *Thompson Newspapers v Canada* [1990] 1 SCR 425 and commentary by P Hogg, *Constitutional Law of Canada* (2nd ed, Ontario: Carswell, 1992), pp 1035–1037.

to the defendant to refuse', and s 2(4) states that the section does not authorise the admission of any evidence or the asking of any question 'which cannot be adduced or asked apart from this section'.

The judicial application of s 2 of the 1976 Act has been the subject of extended criticism elsewhere.[174] Such detail is beyond the scope of this chapter but, notwithstanding s 2(4), the judges have applied s 2 so as actually to extend, rather than to reduce, the scope for the introduction of sexual history evidence. In particular, whereas the traditional common law position was that sexual history was generally irrelevant to consent, unless it went to show that the complainant was a prostitute, or of 'notoriously immoral character', or if it related to intercourse with the defendant himself, post-1976 the Court of Appeal took the view that, because it was 'clear that [Act] . . . was aimed primarily at protecting complainants from cross-examination as to credit . . . if questions are relevant to an issue in the trial . . . for instance relevant to the issue of consent . . . they are likely to be admitted'.[175] This approach has been followed by the courts since, and has entailed a general acceptance by those courts that sexual history evidence may, in circumstances outside the traditional common law categories of prostitution or 'notoriously immoral character', be relevant to the issue of consent.

Given the approach of the judiciary to s 2 of the 1976 Act, it is hard to imagine that any Human Rights Act 1998 challenge to the legislation could found a declaration of incompatibility: s 2 does not require the exclusion of any evidence which is regarded as being relevant to an issue at trial – anything which, in the words of Lord Lane CJ, 'if [a jury] did hear it, might cause them to change their minds about the evidence given by the complainant'.[176] Even where sexual history evidence is put forward as relevant to credibility, it will not be excluded by s 2 unless it seeks to suggest that the complainant ought not to be believed *by reason only that* she 'has had sexual experience with other men to whom she was not married'.[177] And even then, the exclusion was only a general one to which 'there will always be exceptions'.

It would appear that s 2 of the 1976 Act ought to be insulated from judicial review under the Human Rights Act 1998 by virtue of its very weakness, not least as will have to be interpreted 'as far as possible' to comply with Article 6. Indeed, having already been interpreted so as to allow in all evidence that judges regard as relevant (save only for that which depends for its relevance solely upon the notion that 'unchaste' women lie), it is difficult to conceive how the general right to a 'fair . . . hearing', or the particular right in Article 6(3)(d) 'to examine

---

[174] A McColgan, 'Common Law and the Relevance of Sexual History Evidence' (1996) 16 *Oxford Journal of Legal Studies* 275.

[175] *Viola* [1982] 1 WLR 1138 discussed in McColgan, note 174 above.

[176] *Viola, ibid,* at 1042–1043.

[177] *Ibid.*

or have examined witnesses against him', could impose any further interpretative obligations upon the courts.[178]

Restricting the right to personal cross-examination

The real dangers in this context consist in the potential impact of the
incorporated rights on law reform. There has been considerable pressure
in recent years for reform of British law to reduce the circumstances under
which evidence of complainants' sexual history may be introduced in
evidence. This pressure has increased with the dramatic reduction in
conviction rates in rape trials since 1990 (11 per cent in 1995, the last
year for which figures are available, down from 37 per cent in 1990) –
despite there being a steep rise in the number of reported assaults (which
have quadrupled to 5,000 in the same period) – and with a recent spate of
cases in which men accused of rape have insisted on conducting personally
the cross-examination of complainants.[179] This latter, in particular, has
drawn public attention to the appalling treatment that complainants
suffer in rape trials.

In May 1998 the Home Secretary, Jack Straw, reported plans to ban defendants from cross-examining alleged victims of rape and sexual assault,
and indicated changes in respect of sexual history evidence more generally, which evidence he suggested was often introduced to 'break [com-
plainant's] overall credibility' and the 'unnecessary' use of which had, in
his view, generated 'widespread concern'.[180] According to a Home Office
source quoted in a press report, cross-examination as to women's sexual
history was taking place 'in "virtually every single case" . . . and was seen
as a tactic by the defence to try to persuade the victim to drop her case'.[181]

Mr Straw indicated that a report would be published and amendments
included in a Criminal Justice Bill to prohibit 'unrepresented defendants . . . from personally cross-examining victims in rape and other serious
sexual assault cases and 'to outline clearly when evidence on previous
sexual history may be admitted'[182]. It is expected that a legislative ban
will be imposed upon defendants engaging in personal cross-examination
of their alleged victims in cases of rape and serious sexual assault, legal
aid always to be available in these cases: 'it is thought defendants who
dispense with their barristers in order to question their victims in person
would either have to hire new counsel, or lose the right to cross-examine
the woman'.[183] In addition, guidelines dealing with the use of sexual
history evidence are expected.

[178] Certainly this particular exclusion has withstood muster in Canada – see *Seaboyer* [1991]
2 SCR 577, discussed in Chapter 9 above.
[179] *Independent*, 21 May 1998.
[180] *Ibid*, M2 *Presswire*, 21 May 1998.
[181] Press Association *Newsfile*, 19 May 1998 and M2 *Presswire*, 21 May 1998.
[182] Press Association *Newsfile*, *ibid*.
[183] *Ibid*.

It is too early to say with any confidence how these proposals might be affected by the Human Rights Act 1998 when it is implemented. Taking first the proposed ban on personal cross-examination, Articles 6(3)(c) and (d) provide *as a minimum* that a defendant has the right '*to defend himself in person* or through legal assistance . . . and *to examine* or have examined *witnesses against him*' (my emphasis). These provisions are not subject to any exception, but the choice is not necessarily one for the defendant to make and Contracting Parties may insist that defendants are legally represented where the interests of justice so require.[184] The European Court of Human Rights has even accepted that Contracting States may appoint additional defence lawyers, again in the interests of justice, against the defendant's wishes and, depending on the circumstances, in a case in which the defendant might have to bear the cost.[185] The circumstances in which a violation of this Article has been found tend to concern cases in which the defendant has been denied the chance to be present *at all* – and even this does not necessarily amount to a breach.[186] In fact, the right 'to defend himself in person' appears to provide, at best, a right to be involved in the trial process. In *Kremzow*, for example, the European Court found a breach of Article 6 where the defendant had been subject to criminal proceedings *in abstentia* which resulted in the imposition of a life sentence. According to the European Court, given the importance of the issues at stake it was 'essential to the fairness of the proceedings that he be present . . . and afforded the opportunity to participate in it together with his counsel'.

It would appear, from this brief consideration, that the restriction of the right to personal cross-examination should be consistent with Articles 6(2) and (3)(c) and (d) of the Convention and, in the absence of any other interference with the right to a 'fair trial', consistent also with the general right provided under Article 6(1). Having said this, the fact of incorporation will throw this issue open for decision by the British courts, in particular, for consideration by them of whether 'the interests of justice' require such restriction. Unconstrained as these courts will be by the margin of appreciation applied by the Convention organs, and unbound as they will be by the jurisprudence of those bodies, they might reach a different conclusion. Whereas the courts may well be inclined towards deference in some areas, it is likely that they will regard this sphere as one in which they are particularly competent.

It is possible that the courts will determine that the intervention of the legislature in this matter goes beyond what is required 'in the interests of justice', not least in view of the guidelines laid down by the Court of Appeal in *Brown*.[187] In that case, the court refused the defendant leave to appeal

[184] *Croissant v Germany* (1992) A 237-B; Appl 8923/72 3 DR 43, Appl 7592/76 14 DR 64; Appl 722/60 5 *Yearbook* 104, Appl 2676/65 CD 23.
[185] *Croissant v Germany*, *ibid*, para 27.
[186] *FCB v Italy* (1991) A 208-B, *T v Italy* (1992) A 245-C, *Kremzow* (1993) A 268-B.
[187] (1998) 148 *New Law Journal* 694; *The Times*, 7 May 1998; *Independent*, 8 May 1998.

against a sixteen-year sentence imposed for rape and indecent assault. He had cross-examined his victims personally, 'pausing between questions for up to ten minutes and making repulsive suggestions to them'.[188] Lord Bingham CJ stated that judges could and should prevent defendants from deliberately prolonging cross-examination, and from humiliating the complainant, if necessary by taking over the process him or herself. In addition: 'If the defendant seeks by his dress, bearing, manner or questions to dominate, intimidate or humiliate the complainant, or if it is reasonably apprehended that he will seek to do so, the judge should not hesitate to order the erection of a screen in addition to controlling the questioning'.[189]

Lord Bingham CJ stated that Parliament could remove the right not to be represented, but remarked that this would be regarded by some as an infringement of their 'customary rights'. The Lord Chief Justice appeared to prefer that a trial judge restrain the defendant from abusing his freedom to cross-examine witnesses personally which restraint was, in his view, well within the judge's powers: 'The trial judge is the master of proceedings in his court . . . He is not obliged to give an unrepresented defendant his head to ask whatever questions, at whatever length, the defendant wishes.' In a case in which a defendant chose to represent himself, the trial judge should notify him in advance of the restraints which would be imposed upon him and, if he did not comply, the judge could intervene: 'The exercise of these powers will always call for the exercise of a very careful judgment', but the Court of Appeal would support interventions which did not cause injustice.

It is not possible, of course, to extrapolate from a single case such as *Brown*. But, if the Canadian experience is anything to go by, the courts have proved jealous of legislative intervention in what they regard as their area of expertise, and ready to wield the Charter to decisive effect (see Chapter 9 for discussion of *R v Seaboyer*,[190] *R v Mills*,[191] and *R v Lee*[192]). In Britain, too, in the application of the Sexual Offences (Amendment) Act 1976, the courts appear to have preferred judicial notions of relevance to legislative rules and further comments by Lord Bingham CJ about the proposals to restrict the rights of rape defendants add to the suspicion that, armed with the Human Rights Act 1998, the courts might well seek to subvert such legislation.[193] It is, of course, the case that amendments to the right to personal cross-examination will be made by primary legislation and will, therefore, not be susceptible to removal by the courts. But,

---

[188] Press Association *Newsfile*, 6 May 1998.
[189] *Ibid.*
[190] Note 178.
[191] (1997) CRR LEXIS 97, Alberta QB.
[192] (1997) CRR LEXIS 100, Ontario.
[193] Roy Amlot QC, Chairman of the Criminal Bar Association, stated that the restriction of the right of personal examination 'went too far', regarding it as he did as 'such a fundamental right' and preferring additional powers for judges to control cross-examination: *Daily Telegraph*, 7 March 1998.

to the extent that they could not be dealt with by interpretative methods, a declaration of incompatibility may well result in a legislative U-turn as, indeed, may judicial pronouncements about the compatibility of any such change with defendants' rights even before it is made.

Sexual history evidence

Turning next to the broader issue of sexual history evidence, any exclusion of this could be challenged both under the general fair trial right (on the argument that its exclusion prejudiced the defendant's right to same) or, more particularly, as a violation of the Article 6(3)(d) right to the examination of witnesses. What is the likely result of any such challenge? Again, the right to cross-examine witnesses, though not subject to any exceptions on the face of Article 6, is not absolute but is intended, rather, to ensure equality of arms between defendant and prosecution.[194] It is clear, for example, and has been reiterated by the European Court of Human Rights on countless occasions, that Contracting Parties have the right to establish their own rules of evidence, though these must be within reasonable parameters.[195]

The cases in which the European Court of Human Rights has found a violation of Article 6(3)(d) have not been concerned with national rules restricting the scope of cross-examination, rather with very obvious inequalities between the parties. Again, the European Court has reiterated on every occasion that rules of evidence are a matter for national law, subject to the obligation to provide a fair trial and the wide discretion afforded thereto. Violations were found in *Bönisch v Austria*,[196] in which the defendant was allowed no challenge to the evidence which convicted him (that evidence having been given by someone who initiated the prosecution as well as acting as the court's expert witness); *Brozicek v Italy*,[197] in which a defendant was convicted *in absentia* after manifestly insufficient efforts had been made to notify him of the proceedings; and *Barberà, Messegué and Jabardo v Spain*,[198] in which three defendants accused of terrorist offences were denied any opportunity to examine a key prosecution witness. In *X v UK*,[199] by contrast, the Commission rejected a claim by former MP Bernadette Devlin that her Article 6(3)(d) rights had been breached by her conviction, in respect of indulging in and inciting riotous behaviour, after a magistrate's refusal to permit her to call a

---

[194] See *Unterpertinger v Austria* (1986) A 110; *Kostovski v Netherlands* (1989) A 166, 12 EHRR 434.

[195] *Kostovi v Netherlands ibid*; *Schenk v Switzerland* (1988) A 140, 13 EHRR 242; *Barberà, Messegué and Jabardo v Spain* (1989) A 146, 11 EHRR 360; *Windisch v Austria* (1990) A 86, 13 EHRR 281; *Lüdi v Switzerland* (1992) A 238, 15 EHRR 173.

[196] (1985) A 92, 9 EHRR 191.

[197] (1989) A 167, 12 EHRR 371.

[198] (1989) A 146, 11 EHRR 360.

[199] (1993) 12 EHRR CD 113.

large number of witnesses. Again, according to the Commission, the national authorities had wide latitude to determine what evidence was relevant.

The issue in respect of which restrictions on sexual history evidence might come to grief is, precisely, the determination of relevance. Whereas the British courts have interpreted s 2 of the Sexual Offences (Amendment) Act 1976 so as to permit the introduction of everything considered relevant, this being precisely the reason why that Act has failed to protect rape complainants; any more rigorous restrictions would conflict with judicial perceptions of relevance. It is at this stage that the British courts, again unconstrained by the margin of error accorded national authorities by the European Court of Human Rights, might well take the view that such restrictions operated so as to deprive the defendant either of his Article 6(3)(d) right to 'examine or have examined witnesses against him and to obtain the attendance and examination of witnesses on his behalf under the same conditions as witnesses against him' (his sexual history, save generally where it involves commission of criminal offences, being unrestricted save in accordance with the normal rules of relevance).[200] If the promised guidelines did not take the form of primary legislation the court could strike them down. And even if they did, judicious interpretation might rob any restrictions of much of their effect and, if this was not possible, a declaration of incompatibility would be likely to result in legislative change.[201]

Access to personal records

The other areas in which questions might arise under the Convention concern the provision of access for the defence to the personal records of complainants. This has become an important issue in Canada, particularly as access to sexual history evidence has become more restricted. In England, too, applications for disclosure of such records have become increasingly common. In 1994 the *Guardian* reported an increasing trend in rape and sexual assault cases for defence lawyers to seek disclosure of confidential files from doctors and social workers in the course of 'fishing expeditions', about which trend the BMA had expressed serious concern in terms of its threat to medical confidentiality.[202] And in *R v H(L)*,[203] Mr Justice Sedley stated that 'It has become standard practice for defence lawyers in rape and indecency cases to seek to compel the

---

[200] This could be a breach either of Article 9(3)(d) or it read in conjunction with Article 14.
[201] Even if no breach of Article 6(3)(d) were found, a court might take the view that, taken into account with any other matters, the sexual history restrictions were such as to deprive the defendant of his right to a fair trial under Article 6(1). See, for example, Appl 343/57 *Nielsen v Denmark* 2 *Yearbook* 412.
[202] AAP *Newsfeed*, 18 March 1998 reports a similar increasing trend also in Australia.
[203] [1997] 1 Cr App R 176.

production of any social services, education, psychiatric, medical or similar records concerning the complainant in the hope that these will furnish material for cross-examination'.[204]

As far as English law is concerned, the prosecution is under an obligation to disclose to the defence all evidence 'which in the prosecutor's opinion might undermine the case for the prosecution against the accused'.[205] Disclosure generally includes the report of the police surgeon, which report often contains information about the complainant's sexual, medical and psychiatric history.[206] As for medical and other records in the hands of third parties, orders for disclosure should be made only in relation to a document 'likely itself to be admissible in evidence' and 'not merely documents likely to afford or assist a relevant line of enquiry or challenge'. In particular, according to the Crown Court in *R v H(L)*, the duty to disclose did not extend to 'material which might simply be useful in cross-examination'.[207]

Incorporation might pose some problems in relation to the restriction of disclosure by the prosecution, the European Court of Human Rights having ruled in *Edwards v UK*[208] that Article 6 imposes an obligation on prosecution lawyers to disclose to the defence all material evidence whether favourable to the accused or otherwise. This would certainly appear to extend beyond that which is currently required to be disclosed, though the European Court did rule in *Bendenoun v France*[209] that, while 'the conclusion of a fair trial may . . . entail an obligation' to supply evidence within the possession of the prosecution upon which it did not propose to rely in court, this obligation required that the defendant had requested such evidence and given 'if only briefly, specific reasons for his request'. In *Bendenoun* the European Court found that no violation of Article 6(1) had occurred because the defendant had failed to 'put forward any precise argument to support his contention that . . . he could not counter the charge' without being provided with the evidence sought.

---

[204] *Ibid* – By issuing and then challenging refusals to comply with witness summons, this being the only way of obtaining third party disclosure.

[205] Criminal Procedure and Investigations Act 1996, s 3(1)(a), abolishing previous common law rules.

[206] It being regarded as 'good clinical practice [to] obtain from the victim a full medical history', presumably because they are questioned on these subjects, 'victim[s] often also give details of previous sexual experience and possibly of past psychiatric problems [which] . . . information will . . . be recorded in his [sic] notes': B Hill and K Fletcher-Rogers, *Sexually Related Offences* (London: Sweet & Maxwell, 1997). According to *Keane* [1994] 2 All ER 478 'all information must be recorded and revealed to the investigating officer'.

[207] [1997] 1 Cr App R 176, citing *Reading Justices, ex parte Berkshire Council* [1996] 1 Cr App R 239 on the application of the Criminal Procedure (Attendance of Witnesses) Act 1965, s 2. See also *Azmy* [1996] 7 Med LR 415, (1997) 34 BMLR 45. Where materiality is disputed see *Whittle* [1996] Crim LR 904 and see *D v NSPCC* [1978] AC 171 for public interest immunity.

[208] (1992) A 247-B, 15 EHRR 417.

[209] (1994) A 284.

Justice for battered women killers?

As regards women who kill their abusive partners, to what extent will the incorporation into British law of the right to a 'fair trial' shape that law so as to take account of the experiences of women, as well as those of the men who have traditionally been its subjects? Here it is appropriate to consider the interrelationship of Articles 6 and 14. Even if a breach of Article 6, standing alone, could not be made out, Article 14 permits a finding of breach to the extent that women are discriminated against in the provision of those rights safeguarded under Article 6.

The issues which have arisen in Canada and the US in connection with battered women killers include whether evidence concerning 'battered woman syndrome' (BWS) should be admissible in court and the extent, if any, to which the normal rules of self-defence can and should be shaped to fit the battered woman. Evidence of BWS has been admissible for a number of years in the British courts (see Chapter 8 above).[210] It is possible that such a condition could be introduced on a plea of self-defence to support the defendant's alleged belief in the existence of an imminent threat. But such a combination has yet to be reported in any appellate decision and, given the lack of success battered women have in pleading self-defence,[211] it is questionable whether such evidence would make any substantial difference. The US experience is illustrative of the fact that merely admitting such evidence can create as many difficulties as it resolves.

Returning to the question of self-defence, the legal position in the UK is more favourable to the defendant than is the case either in Canada or the US. The defendant is judged on the facts as she honestly (rather than reasonably) believed them to be; the test of reasonableness is, though objective, extremely favourable to the defendant; and 'imminence' is not the hard-and-fast requirement that it is in many US states.[212]

The failure of the English legal system to afford a defence to battered women killers was criticised in Chapter 8 above. The problem appears to lie not in the admissibility of BWS (the admissibility of evidence being, in any event, 'primarily a matter for regulation under national law'),[213] but in the attitude of the courts to women who kill. Article 14, read with Article 6, guarantees the right to a fair trial without discrimination based upon sex. If it were the case, for example, that a female defendant was subject to different and less favourable rules of evidence than those applied to men, Article 14 would be violated (indeed, given that this would

---

[210] See *Thornton (No 2)* [1996] 2 All ER 1023; *Hobson* [1998] 1 Cr App Rep 31; *Grainger* [1997] 1 Cr App R(S) 369. See also *Ahluwalia* [1992] 4 All ER 889, (1993) 96 Cr App R 133 and *Humphreys* [1995] 4 All ER 1008.

[211] Even, see discussion of *Shah*, *Independent*, 1 May 1998 in Chapter 8 above, of succeeding in BWS-related diminished responsibility/provocation pleas.

[212] See also *Hudson and Taylor* [1971] 2 QB 202.

[213] See text to notes 195–199 above.

surely contravene the right to a 'fair trial' under Article 6, a breach of that Article would surely be made out). But the discrimination to which women are subject as defendants is far more subtle – there is no suggestion that they are denied self-defence *because* they are women (whether overtly or covertly). Rather, the problem is that the circumstances in which women typically kill under a threat (whether real or perceived) of unavoidable and great harm do not generally correspond to the common perception of circumstances requiring the use of force in self-defence, this perception in turn being shaped by the fact that most self-defence cases, like most criminal cases generally, have involved male defendants.

It is hard to see, in the face of this problem, how the incorporation of the Convention rights will make any significant difference to battered women who kill. The application of Article 14 to indirect discrimination is less than clear, the test of justifiability easy to satisfy (in this case, on the basis that 'extension' of self-defence would serve to acquit revenge killers[214]) and the area one in which a very wide measure of discretion is given to Contracting Parties (not least because of the variety of legal systems which operate within them). It is possible that the British courts would, faced with an Article 6/8 argument, remind themselves that the test for self-defence/ justifiable force/ s 3 of the Criminal Law Act 1967 relates to the necessity and proportionality of the defendant's use of force, imminence being a factor to be taken into account in considering the question of necessity, rather than a free-standing and conclusive requirement. But the obligation upon the judiciary to provide defendants with fair trials exists regardless of incorporation, the Article 6/14 argument is, on the existing European Court of Human Rights jurisprudence, tenuous, and these are the very courts which have, in general, been blind to the experiences of battered women. It is unlikely, to say the least, that incorporation will result in radical change in this respect.

Indeed, the decision of the European Court of Human Rights in *McCann, Farrell and Savage v UK*[215] suggests that incorporation might operate against the interests of women who kill to save their own lives. In that case the European Court ruled that Article 2 of the Convention permitted the use of 'no more force than absolutely necessary'. If, in the wake of a challenge on grounds similar to those in *A v UK*[216] (ie an argument that UK law fails to protect the right to life by permitting the acquittal of a woman who killed because she believed, whether mistakenly or not, that her use of force was necessary because she feared that an abusive partner would kill her rather than permit her to escape), the UK courts tightened up the rules relating to self-defence,

---

[214] Particularly given the tendency to justification against purpose, as distinct from impact, as noted in the discussion of the *Abdulaziz* case, note 15 above.

[215] (1996) A 324, 21 EHRR 97.

[216] 23 September 1998, available on the European Court of Human Rights home page http://www.dhcour.coe.fr/.

any potential development of the law in favour of these women would be thwarted.

Perhaps in anticipation of the likely judicial attitude, self-defence is rarely even argued in Britain in cases where battered women have killed their abusers. Leaving aside the difficulties potentially generated by the *McCann* case, could it be argued that the failure of defence lawyers to argue self-defence in suitable cases or, where appropriate, to seek to introduce evidence of the psychiatric effects of continued abuse on their clients, breached those clients' human rights? In the US, as shown in Chapter 8, many of the constitutional arguments that are made in relation to battered women rest on the alleged violation of the Sixth Amendment's right to 'effective counsel'. By contrast, Article 6's right to a 'fair trial' requires minimal protection from the State in this regard. While, in *Tripodi v Italy*,[217] the European Court of Human Rights found a violation of Article 6 in a case in which the appointed lawyer did not attend his client's hearing *at all*, having failed to seek an adjournment on the grounds of his inability to attend; the European Court in that case stressed, as it has done on many occasions, that Article 6's guarantees are breached only where the failings of the lawyer are 'manifest', or 'sufficiently brought to the attention of' the authorities. It is inconceivable that failure of counsel to argue justifiable force/self-defence, particularly in a case in which the use of that defence would be considered innovative or controversial, would amount to such a breach.

The only way in which incorporation might benefit battered women, together with the victims of rape, is the possibility that Article 8's 'right to respect for . . . private and family life' might extend to requiring 'the adoption of measures designed to secure respect for private life even in the sphere of the relations of individuals between themselves', 'respect for private life' being interpreted, in turn, to include legal redress in the case of sexual assault and domestic violence.[218] This approach was taken by the Court in *X & Y v The Netherlands*,[219] discussed above. Equally, in the wake of *A v UK* (1998),[220] it could be argued that the failure of the legal system adequately to protect women from violence at the hands of their partners breaches Article 3. But the obstacle in the former case was legal and absolute, and the violation in *A v UK* lay in the law, rather than in practice.

The difficulties experienced by rape complainants are, in large part, inherent in the private nature of the crime, the widespread distrust of women who complain of it and the prevailing view that 'consent' in the

---

[217] (1994) A 281-B, 18 EHRR 295. See also Appl 22083/93 *Stanford v UK* 18 EHRR CD 18, Commission, and 19 EHRR 32.
[218] Perhaps also Article 3 – Julia Mason who was cross-examined for days by her rapist in person, has made a complaint to the Commission – *Observer* 18 January 1998.
[219] Note 58 above.
[220] 23 September 1998, see http://www.dhcour.coe.fr/.

context of sexual intercourse is a 'fuzzy' concept, and it is hard to imagine that any positive obligations imposed on the State by Articles 8 (or, less likely, Article 3) extend to ensuring the conviction of the guilty, as distinct from the possibility of criminal prosecution. As far as the victims of domestic violence are concerned also, many factors can be pointed to which militate against high prosecution rates not least, and particularly where intimate abusers are concerned, the frequent reluctance of victims to persevere with charges. Much could be done to reduce the difficulties caused by factors such as the grant of access orders to violent ex-partners (with the effect that they are often able to continue abusing the children's mother).[221] But incorporation might well result in increased respect for the father's right to family life, which is likely only to compound the present view that, almost regardless of the father's behaviour, contact is in the best interests of the child.[222]

Conclusion

The survey which has been attempted over the course of this book suggests that women will have little to gain, in the sphere of reproduction and employment, or in their roles as victims of violence, from the incorporation of the European Convention on Human Rights. This is not to say that there are no benefits to be had – no attempt has been made to survey the incorporated rights in general, nor even to consider their impact on women and girls in their many other roles (as pupils, mothers, wives and cohabitees, property holders, deportees, to name but a few). My purpose is not to argue that incorporation or any other form (weak or strong) of entrenching rights is without any advantages, either to women or to people in general; rather to point to some of the pitfalls associated with such rights. I have chosen to focus on women, and then only in particular spheres, but a number of the general conclusions drawn can be extrapolated.

The first point which can be made is a broad one concerning the relative importance of rights and the wider political context in which they operate. The issue is best illustrated by considering the US. That system couples the constitutional protection of 'human rights' with commitment to the death penalty, which penalty is imposed on the poor, the black, the young and the mentally retarded. It combines a commitment to 'Equal Protection' and a prohibition of 'cruel and unusual punishment' with a prison regime which, by coupling the presence of male guards in women's prisons with inadequate control of strip-searching, surveillance

---

[221] See *A v N (Committal: Refusal of Contact)* [1997] 1 FLR 533.
[222] See, for example, *Re H (Minors)* 23 January 1998 LEXIS, CA.

and sexual contact, renders rape, sexual harassment and victimisation absolutely endemic throughout that regime.[223] It provides a constitutionally
protected right to privacy which simply does not apply to those who are
financially dependent on the State.[224] This group is forced by lack of funds
to cede control over living arrangements and, in effect, reproductive
decision-making, to the State – and this in a system in which maintenance
is extremely difficult to obtain and in which, in many states, women can
be obliged to sell their family homes to meet legal fees for divorce, this
in turn forcing many onto welfare.[225]

The US Constitution, in particular the character of its Bill of Rights
and successive amendments as 'limitation[s] on the State's power to act,
not as . . . guarantee[s] of certain minimal levels of safety and security',[226]
serves to protect the fortunate while denying the needy any right to access
to most of those benefits enjoyed by others. Federal and state governments are targeting welfare recipients, in particular, single mothers (who
account for 80 per cent of all recipients) for increasingly punitive measures. Conservatives like Charles Murray call for the abolition of welfare
payments, even of food stamps and Medicaid for the poor, and for the
re-introduction of orphanages.[227] And by 1994, according to the *Nation*,
'an 'emerging bipartisan consensus' between figures from Murray to Bill
Clinton and the *New York Times*:

> that unwed mothers, particularly teenagers and, to a lesser extent, divorced
> moms, are the driving force behind poverty, crime and a host of other ills
> [and] . . . a competition over how to prevent the poor and 'Illegitimate' from
> being born in the first place. And since this is America, land of family values
> and pro-life, this end must be achieved in a way that combines the minimum
> of money and the maximum of social control. Forcing welfare recipients to
> use Norplant . . . has an appeal that, say, simply making all birth control free
> and accessible does not. As for abortion, forget it. We are moving toward a
> system that will force poor pregnant women to give birth and will then take
> their babies away.'[228]

The punitive attitude towards 'welfare moms' is at one level mystifying.
Eighty per cent of women in receipt of welfare have experienced domestic
violence, and the availability of welfare has been characterised by NOW

---

[223] Human Rights Watch, *The Human Rights Watch Global Report on Women's Human Rights* (New York: Human Rights Watch, 1995), Chapter 3.

[224] See, generally, Chapter 2.

[225] See L Tanenbaum, 'Divorced from Justice', 264 *The Nation*, 6 January 1997, p 31. Most states have eliminated alimony despite the fact that only 60% of married women work (30% of them part-time) and women's median contribution is only 36% family income – further in contested cases working mothers generally lose custody to working fathers – 70% even if father was abusive or an absentee.

[226] *DeShaney v Winnebago County* 489 US 189 (1989).

[227] C Jencks and K Edin, 'Do Poor Women Have a Right to Bear Children?', *American Prospect*, Winter 1995.

[228] 30 May 1994.

as absolutely crucial in enabling women to escape such violence. But in 1994 it was remarked that '[t]he "welfare question" has become the race question and the woman question in disguise . . . Welfare has become a code word . . . that enables white Americans to mask their sometimes malignant, sometimes benign racism behind false concerns about the suffering ghetto poor and their negative impact on the rest of us'.[229] The 'welfare question' has united much of white America in collective hysteria over the 'spectre of the mythical black welfare mother, complete with a prodigious reproductive capacity and a galling laziness, accompanied by the uncaring and equally lazy black man in her life who will not work, will not marry her and will not support his family'.[230] (The typical recipient of welfare is, in fact, a white woman with small children.[231])

The current welfare-bashing is particularly to be condemned in view of the fact that most of those receiving welfare simply cannot earn enough to support their families without it. In 1989, less than 50 per cent of working women aged between 25 and 34 in the US earned enough to support two children.[232] Unless these women are able to rely on a partner they have no choice but to depend, at least in part, on the State. Nor is it an answer to declare, as the Clinton administration did in 1995, that 'people should not have children until they are ready to support them' – almost half of those children who are dependent on welfare at any given time were born to parents married at the time of their birth, most of whom could, while married, manage to support themselves and their children.[233] But forcing women to remain with the fathers of their children, even if the choice was theirs, is likely only to expose them to violence and their children to harm. Much of the 'welfare problem' is not the fault of its recipients, but the result of constitutionally permissible government choices of 'competitive labor markets, open borders, and weak labor unions', which choices have had the result that 'most marginally employable adults will need some kind of public assistance if they have children'.[234]

These last remarks are not intended to suggest that the incorporation of the European Convention will set the UK down the road to American-style approaches to sentencing or welfare, simply to underline the fact that entrenched rights must not be regarded as a panacea against the ills of government. These rights, in particular, those adopted by the UK, are limited in their scope and their impact. They do not substitute for political action and, in addition to the dangers they pose, for example, to legislative action designed to safeguard women's autonomy or to secure substantive equality in the workplace, they can lull those who would

---

[229] *Ibid.*
[230] *Observer* Magazine, 2 January 1994.
[231] *Ibid.*
[232] *Ibid.*
[233] *Ibid.*
[234] *Ibid.*

otherwise engage in political action into taking their 'eye off the ball' and allowing reactionary politics to triumph.

The dangers posed by constitutional rights are particularly acute where, as will be the case in the UK, the rights themselves leave much to be desired. Emphasis has been placed at various points throughout this book on the differences between the US Bill of Rights and associated amendments (which restrict the quartering of troops yet do not include any equal rights provision save for the very limited Equal Treatment Clause), and Canada's Charter of Rights, with its modern concern for equality, including the legitimation of affirmative action, and its deliberate failure to protect property. Even if the US and Canadian judiciary were similarly minded, the content of their respective rights provisions would result in substantially different outcomes.

If real efforts were to be made in the UK to provide rights which would provide its subjects with fair and equal chances of participation (these and other rights being reflected in the current rhetoric about the evils of social exclusion[235]), if not fair and equal outcomes, entrenchment would certainly not stop with the rights and freedoms provided by the 1951 Convention. These provisions were adopted in the aftermath of the Second World War by a Europe scarred by the effects of Nazism and under perceived siege from Communism. According to its Preamble, the Convention was only the 'first step' towards the implementation of the 1948 Universal Declaration of Human Rights, silent as it is about freedom of movement and residence, rights to asylum, to nationality and to take part in government and, as has been mentioned above, equality before the law.[236]

According to its first drafter, the scope of the Convention was limited because 'for the moment, it is preferable to limit the collective guarantee to those rights and essential freedoms which are practised, after long usage and experience, in all the democratic countries. While they are the first triumph of democratic regimes, they are also the necessary conditions under which they operate'.[237] In addition, many were of the view at

---

[235] That the agenda is rather different was suggested by Beatrix Campbell (plenary session, Charter 88 conference on the Human Rights Act, 30 May 1998). She pointed out, in relation to the first report of the social exclusion unit, that it was more concerned with how to enforce school attendance and avert the perceived threat posed by the socially excluded to others than to address the reasons behind that exclusion.

[236] Jack Straw MP stated (HC Debs 17 June 1998, col 406) that 'the convention had its origins in a desire to protect the individual against the abuse of power by the state, rather than to protect one individual against the actions of another. The history of the establishment of the Council of Europe and the great desire at the end of the war that states in Europe should never again be able to oppress their citizens as Nazi Germany and the axis powers had done, explain why the convention places on the state responsibilities in respect of its treatment of residents and citizens.'

[237] Teitgen, *rapporteur* of the Legal Committee of the Consultative Assembly of the Council of Europe, who drew up first draft, cited in van Dijk and van Hoof, note 18 above, pp 213–214.

the time that different supervisory mechanisms were suitable for these rights and for 'social rights' such as those subsequently embodied in the Social Charter (the supervisory mechanisms of which have proved largely ineffective).[238]

Whatever the reason for the differential treatment of these 'essential' and what are commonly termed 'social' rights (rights to work, to housing, to social security and to the protection of health, to minimum working conditions, to fair remuneration, to organise and to bargain freely[239]) by the Convention, it is appropriate to question whether this same approach to rights is acceptable in the UK in the late 20th century. One might argue that any rights are better than none at all – certainly, it is hard to quibble with the provision of a legal right not to be tortured, or to be interned without trial.[240] But the danger of legitimation, whether as a result of judicial interpretation, or because of gaps in the content of human rights codes, has been referred to above.[241] And of even more concern, the failure of the Human Rights Act 1998 to balance the Convention rights against those provided for (and accepted by Britain) in the European Social Charter[242] creates the danger that the latter will be further marginalised. Where, for example, an employer wishes to challenge an order relating to collective bargaining on the basis of his rights under Article 6, 10, or 11 of the Convention (or Article 1 of the First Protocol thereto), the absence of any clear enforceable 'right' of employees and their unions to engage in collective bargaining (such as could, for example, be incorporated from Article 6 of the Council of Europe's Social Charter) not only renders judgment in the employer's favour more likely than would otherwise be the case, but also accords 'human rights' justification to that outcome.

Even if the UK were to adopt a different or an additional 'Bill of Rights', it is impossible ever to guarantee protection against the threats to civil liberties which might arise in the future. Even if, for example, the right to abortion (or, more generally, to decision-making in the area of reproduction) were to be expressly provided for in a UK Bill of Rights, other rights would not be. The nature of the rights which require protection from assault differ over time – the spectre of pregnant women being forced to undergo surgery to correct defects on foetuses *in utero*, for example (see Chapter 5 above), could not have been thought of 50 years ago when the technology which makes this possible now did not exist.

---

[238] van Dijk and van Hoof, note 18 above, pp 214–215 challenge the assumption that the two are clearly distinguished: 'The classic distinction therefore, certainly for some rights, is better explained by history than by essential differences in character'.

[239] All of which are contained in Council of Europe's Social Charter.

[240] European Convention on Human Rights, Articles 3 and 5.

[241] See *Ireland v UK* (1977–80) 2 EHRR 25.

[242] This must be distinguished from that adopted by the European Community and subsequently incorporated into the Social Chapter appended to the Treaty of European Union by the Maastricht Treaty, and subsequently into the TEU itself by the Amsterdam Treaty.

It is simply not possible specifically to detail all the 'rights' upon which future citizens may need to rely upon against the instruments of the State. This brings us to the next major problem with constitutionally entrenched rights.

The approach of the judiciary remains absolutely fundamental in terms of developing rights, as it is fundamental in the balancing of rights where they conflict. At root, the incorporation of rights renders the judiciary, rather than the legislature, responsible for their defence. By contrast with our current system of judicial review, this protective role is not confined to ensuring that the executive and other wielders of power act within the authority delegated to them. Nor is it restricted (as it is, in theory, at present) to gap-filling and interpretation. Instead, in any system of entrenched rights, the final arbiter of those rights (whether *de jure*, as in the US or *de facto*, as in Canada) is the judiciary. Certainly, a judicial decision that no breach has occurred (whether in primary or secondary legislation, by the police, the courts or any other public authority) will provide to the official action in question a veneer of respectability. And even in the UK, where no power will be given to the judiciary to overrule primary legislation, the determination by a higher court that the Government has breached the incorporated rights will create enormous pressure for legislative amendment.[243]

Rights do not exist in a vacuum, but have to be balanced against other rights. Where no entrenched rights exist, the balance is one for the legislature to strike (or to delegate to the executive). The outcome of this balancing will not, of course, appeal to all. To the extent that freedom of speech includes the right to protest and that this protest is, for example, directed against abortion clinics, a legislative balancing of the free speech against (for the sake of argument) the right to terminate a pregnancy without fear of violent attack, intimidation, or loss of privacy will either, or both, curb the rights of protestors or (and) those of women who seek abortions. Equally, to the extent that some form of recognition procedure is provided in order effectively to permit trade unions, in accordance with Article 11 of the Convention, to protect the interests of their members, this Article 11 right will have to be balanced against the employer's Article 10 right to campaign against recognition (this, in the US, amounting to virtual *carte blanche* for intimidation of individual employees) and, perhaps, further rights accorded by Article 11 and Article 1 of the First Protocol.

In the final analysis, the question which must be asked is whether the legislature or the judiciary has shown itself best suited to perform the necessary balancing act. To a very large extent, the answer depends upon the particular interests of the person to whom the question is

---

[243] See, for example, the discussion in Chapter 1 above of Lord Borrie's remarks in the House of Lords, HL Debs 3 November 1997, col 1275.

posed. Whereas a tobacco company operating in Canada, or an anti-union employer in the US, would resoundingly give its support to the judiciary, women seeking abortions would incline towards the judiciary in Canada and the US, but towards Parliament in Germany.

What of the UK? In the areas which have formed the substantive subject matter of this book, the best that can be said of the judiciary is that its attitude has been highly questionable. The great strides which have been made by women in the workplace are owed entirely to the legislature, whether at UK or at EC level. But if one considers the British approach to pregnancy discrimination (prior to the decision of the European Court of Justice in *Webb v EMO*[244] – see Chapter 7 above), the apparent ineptitude of the courts in applying the genuine material factor defence under the Equal Pay Act 1970,[245] and the outright hostility which emasculated the enforcement powers of the CRE (and hence of the EOC);[246] one would have to question the extent to which this same judiciary is a satisfactory champion of women's 'rights'. In relation to the last of these issues, as in relation to judicial control of ACAS during the 1975–80 recognition procedure, judges acted precisely because of what they regarded as unwarranted interference with rights. The problem was, of course, that the rights protected were those of employers, this in turn because of judicial myopia as to the impact of those rights on workers.[247]

Similar points could be made about the judicial approach to rape complainants. Whereas Parliament has attempted to regulate the introduction of sexual history evidence, judicial shortcomings in this matter having become evident prior to the passage of the Sexual Offences (Amendment) Act 1976, judges have reacted by preferring their common

---

[244] Note 93 above.

[245] See McColgan, note 96 above, Chapters 3 and 4. This ineptitude has, regrettably, reached the House of Lords, see *Strathclyde Regional Council and others v Wallace and others* [1998] 1 All ER 394, [1998] 1 WLR 259, [1998] ICR 205, [1998] IRLR 146, in which Lord Browne-Wilkinson suggested that: 'The correct position under s 1(3) of the Equal Pay Act 1970 is that even where the variation is genuinely due to a factor which involves the difference of sex, the employer can still establish a valid defence under sub-s (3) if he can justify such differentiation on the grounds of sex, whether the differentiation is direct or indirect.' This is not only contrary to the clear meaning of s 1(3) of the 1970 Act; it is also without authority in EC law (see, for example, the comments of Advocate General Elmer in Case C-249/96 *Grant v South-West Trains Ltd* [1998] All ER (EC) 193, [1998] 1 FCR 377, [1998] 1 FLR 839, [1998] IRLR 206, [1998] ICR 449 'according to the court's case law . . . direct discrimination cannot be justified [under Art 119] by reference to objective circumstances').

[246] See Lord Denning in *Science Research Council v Nasse* [1979] QB 144, CA, condemning the fact that the CRE's investigative powers enabled it to 'interrogate employers . . . up to the hilt and compel disclosure on a massive scale . . . You might think that we were back in the days of the inquisition'. Lord Hailsham, too, speaking in the House of Lords debates on the Race Relations Bill (373 HL Debs 20 July 1976, col 745) likened the powers of the CRE to those of the Star Chamber.

[247] Whether, as in *Powley*, note 163 above, Browne-Wilkinson J's failure to recognise the employer, rather than the union, as the real threat to the individual employee's rights or, as in the CRE cases, judicial failure to grasp the endemic nature of workplace discrimination.

law (and at times highly questionable) notions of relevance over the expressed will of Parliament, and in doing so have rendered the 1976 provisions largely ineffective.[248] To the extent that the Human Rights Act 1998 will give judges the power to intervene in the face of attempted amendments in this and other areas, the outcomes are unlikely to benefit women.

As far as the issues of abortion and the control of pregnant women are concerned, one could argue that the judiciary first carved an exception to criminal liability for abortion in *Bourne*,[249] in which a defence of medical necessity was recognised in a case where a young girl posed a suicide risk had she been forced to continue with the pregnancy. What is perhaps interesting in this respect, as in the context of battered women killers, is the potential for beneficial judicial development in the absence of legislative action. Where Parliament has not been able or willing to deal with problems as they become apparent, the courts have at times been willing to ameliorate difficulties whether, as in the case of abortion, they were posed by statute or, as in provocation, largely by the common law (the abolition by the House of Lords of the marital exemption for rape in *R v R*[250] is a further example). Lest this be taken as a vindication of the judiciary over Parliament, it is important to bear in mind that, on entrenchment, the judiciary will be empowered and obliged to interpret and apply the particular rights guaranteed – in the abortion context it is at least possible that this will operate so as to restrict, rather than facilitate, access to abortion. In addition, it is highly possible that entrenchment may contribute to legislative inactivity by encouraging Parliament to abdicate difficult or controversial issues to the courts.

A further very significant problem which arises concerns access to the rights entrenched. It is likely that legal aid will be all but unavailable in connection with Human Rights Act cases, civil legal aid being due for almost complete abolition subject to provision for a very small number of 'public interest' cases likely to include single numbers of Human Rights Act cases annually. Litigants are advised to turn to contingency fee arrangements, a suggestion Lord Ackner condemned as 'absurd [in] litigation which will be uncertain and which will not in many cases ask for damages, but if they are obtained, they are so small that with the cap applied to them they will attract no solicitor'.[251] This problem is, of course, aggravated by the restriction of standing under the Act. But while private litigants will find themselves confined to raising human rights issues in the

---

[248] The current crisis relating to personal cross-examination by defendants is also, in part, the result of inadequate exercise by judges of their power to regulate proceedings in the courtroom, this in turn because of concern as to the likely approach of the Court of Appeal.
[249] [1939] 1 KB 687.
[250] [1992] 1 AC 599, [1991] 2 All ER 257, [1991] 2 WLR 1065, [1992] Crim LR 207.
[251] HL Debs 18 November 1997, col 473.

context of legally aided criminal and other cases, corporations will be subject to no such restrictions.

In the final analysis, entrenched rights are not the most effective mechanism for those who wish to pursue substantive equality. As Peter Russell pointed out in 1994, of Canada's *Charter* rights:

> a constitutional charter of rights is an ill-conceived instrument for promoting equality in civil society . . . The Charter is used to attack legislation and government programmes for what they do – not for what they fail to do. But those who seek equality of social and economic condition need a strong state that can and will intervene in civil society to redistribute power and wealth and enhance the welfare of those most vulnerable to the free play of market forces.[252]

---

[252] Russell, note 2 above, p 40; L Falkenberg and L Boland, 'Eliminating the Barriers to Employment Equity in the Canadian Workplace' (1997) 16(9) *Journal of Business Ethics* 963, citing B Marotte, 'Equality Between the Sexes Sounds very 90s But Reality Reflects 50s', *Montreal Gazette*, 4 March 1992.

Index